BUSINESS and PROFESSIONAL Communication in a Digital Age

Jennifer H. Waldeck
Chapman University

Patricia Kearney
California State University, Long Beach

Timothy G. Plax
California State University, Long Beach

P9-DEF-323

WADSWORTH
CENGAGE Learning

Australia • Brazil • Japan • Korea • Mexico • Singapore • Spain • United Kingdom • United States

WADSWORTH
CENGAGE Learning

Business and Professional Communication in a Digital Age
Jennifer H. Waldeck, Patricia Kearney, and Timothy G. Plax

Senior Publisher: Lyn Uhl

Publisher: Monica Eckman

Senior Development Editor: Greer Lleuad

Development Editor: Barbara Armentrout

Senior Assistant Editor: Rebekah Matthews

Editorial Assistant: Colin Solan

Media Editor: Jessica Badiner

Marketing Program Manager:
Gurpreet S. Saran

Marketing Communications Manager:
Courtney Morris

Senior Content Project Manager:
Michael Lepera

Art Director: Linda Helcher

Print Buyer: Doug Bertke

Rights Acquisition Specialist:
Mandy Groszko

Production Service/Compositor:
MPS Limited, a Macmillan Company

Text Designer: Ke Design

Cover Designer: Riezebos Holzbaur/
Christopher Harris

Cover Image: ©Shutterstock/Altay Kaya

For product information and technology assistance, contact us at
Cengage Learning Customer & Sales Support, 1-800-354-9706
For permission to use material from this text or product,
submit all requests online at **www.cengage.com/permissions**.
Further permissions questions can be emailed to
permissionrequest@cengage.com.

Library of Congress Control Number: 2011937660

ISBN-13: 978-0-495-80798-8

ISBN-10: 0-495-80798-2

Wadsworth
20 Channel Center Street
Boston, MA 02210
USA

Cengage Learning is a leading provider of customized learning solutions with office locations around the globe, including Singapore, the United Kingdom, Australia, Mexico, Brazil and Japan. Locate your local office at **international.cengage.com/region**

Cengage Learning products are represented in Canada by Nelson Education, Ltd.

For your course and learning solutions, visit **www.cengage.com.**

Purchase any of our products at your local college store or at our preferred online store **www.cengagebrain.com.**

Instructors: Please visit **login.cengage.com** and log in to access instructor-specific resources.

Printed in Canada
1 2 3 4 5 6 7 15 14 13 12 11

Jennifer dedicates this book to her parents, Polly and Henry Waldeck.

Pat and Tim dedicate this book to Charles Tucker, Jack Kirby, and Harry James Callahan and to the memory of Mary Elizabeth and Truman Ross.

Contents

Modules

MOD 1

How Do I "Get In and Fit In" to My Organization's Unique Culture?

- What Is Organizational Culture?
- Life at an Organization
- Getting In: Determining Whether a Job is a Good Fit
- Interview Tips
- Evaluate Messages You Receive During the Interview
- Fitting In: Assimilating Into Your Company's Culture

MOD 2

How Can I Practice Ethical Communication Behavior at Work?

- Scenarios in Ethics
- What Are the Most Common Ethical Problems in Business Settings?
- What Are Some Other Ethical Issues to Consider When Communicating at Work?
- Strategies and Solutions: How Do We Make Ethical Decisions?

MOD 3

How Do I Give Specialized Presentations?

- Introducing a Speaker
- Presenting an Award
- Accepting an Award
- Tributes
- Toasts
- Eulogies

MOD 4

What Do I Need to Know about Business Etiquette?

- Strategies and Solutions
- Make Sure Your Dining's Fine
- Keep the Cubicle Courteous
- Practice Phone Politesse
- Be Mindful of Your Netiquette
- International Business Etiquette

Acknowledgments

Many people helped to make this book possible, and we thank everyone who, in both small and large ways, made this happen. We begin by thanking our Wadsworth Cengage Learning editorial team, including Monica Eckman, executive editor and cheerleader extraordinaire; Greer Lleuad, senior developmental editor; Rebekah Matthews, assistant editor; Jessica Badiner, media editor, Michael Lepera, senior content project manager; Ed Dionne, project manager at MPS Content Services; Barbara Armentrout, developmental editor and copyeditor; Elisa Adams, copyeditor; and Linda Helcher, art director.

A special acknowledgment goes to Dr. J. Christopher Jolly, academic specialist at the Bickerstaff Center for Student-Athlete Services at California State University, Long Beach. Chris authored seven of the modules and prepared the Instructors' Manual, student tutorial quizzes, and Join In classroom quizzing content.

We appreciate the advice of reviewers who helped us develop the content of this book. We listened and we learned. Thank you to Scott McLean, Arizona Western College; John Parrish, Tarrant County College; Christa Brown, Minneapolis Community & Technical College; Kenneth Harris, Palo Alto College; Chad Edwards, Western Michigan University; Alan Heisel, University of Missouri at St. Louis; Terre Allen, California State University at Long Beach; Charles Roberts, East Tennessee State University; Heather Allman, University of West Florida; Marianna Larsen, Utah State University; Tracey Holley, Tarleton State University; Martha Macdonald, York Technical College; Steve Mortenson, University of Delaware; Julie Gowin, University of Maryland; Allison Searle, University of North Florida; Marisa Garcia Rodriguez, California Lutheran University; Frank Kelley, Drexel University; Deric Greene, Stevenson University; Jessica Ebert, Northern Illinois University; Fiona Barnes, University of Florida; Jacqueline Reece, University of South Florida Polytechnic, Lisa Houle, Globe University, Stephanie Webster, University of Florida; Lisa Johnson, Centura College; Kathleen Norris, Loyola Marymount University; Suzanne Buck, University of Houston; Jennifer Karchmer, Western Washington University; Elaine Gale, California State University at Sacramento; Katherine Castle, University of Nebraska at Lincoln; Scott Wilson, Central Ohio Technical College; Robert Milstein, Northwestern College; Melissa DeLucia, Albertus Magnus College; Diane Matuschka, University of North Florida; Astrid Proboll, Holy Names University; Bassey Eyo, St. Cloud State University; Juliann Scholl, Texas Tech University; Erik Timmerman, University of Wisconsin at Milwaukee; Judith Collins, Kansas State University Salina; Alex Yousefi, ECPI College of Technology; and Cynthia Vessel, Northwestern College.

Perhaps our biggest supporters were those students in COM 310 at Chapman University and COMM 334 at California State University at Long Beach who pilot-tested our book; gave us invaluable feedback throughout the development of the chapters, modules, and activities; and encouraged us to publish this book so that other students might learn from it, too.

Many others contributed to this endeavor by testing out some of our ideas in their own instruction, allowing us to opt out of other work assignments, sharing with us ample examples of communication issues at work, affirming our interest to pursue this undertaking, and giving us lots and lots of emotional or collegial support to complete this project. The list is long: Dr. Fran Dickson, Dr. Patrick Quinn, Dr. Jennifer Bevan, Jennifer McMurray, Robert Scher, Craig Leets, Jake McIntyre, Dr. Kerry J. Ritter, Ted Ross, Shawn Campbell, Dr. Melvin L. DeFleur, Dr. Margaret (Peggy) H. DeFleur, and Dr. Gerry Riposa, among others. Thank you all.

Dear Students

The critical predictors of becoming a successful professional are probably not what you might think or what you might have been told. It's not the prestige of your degree. Neither is it the amount of your highly technical training nor the power of your attitude. It may not even be your college major or the area of your expertise. What will make all the difference in your success at work is your ability to communicate well. That's what this book is all about: how to communicate effectively in your professional life.

We wrote this book for you and about you. After teaching courses in business and organizational communication over the years, we've learned a lot about what students want and need as they struggle with, explore, and manage their professional lives. As we conceived, wrote, developed, and revised this book, we relied extensively on feedback from students like you. We listened to what they had to say, and we have a pretty good idea of what they want to know.

If you are like most of our students, you may be eager to learn how to get a job, prepare for interviews, and negotiate a fair and competitive salary and compensation. If you are like them, you will want to know how to find just the right job, how to better manage your time, and how to create a "balance" between your work and personal lives.

In this book, you will discover ways to manage challenging or difficult relationships at work, such as a bad boss, an irritating co-worker, or a romantic hookup gone bad. You will learn how to give all kinds of professional presentations, including briefings and sales pitches. And you'll discover rules for writing memos, responding to email messages, and using social media for professional networking. Facilitating meetings and working in teams are all integral to the modern-day workplace, requiring you to use specialized communication skills. For those who are considering a career in consulting or training, we've included information on how you can make that happen.

Our book is one of the first business and professional communication texts developed specifically and uniquely for the online environment. Although a number of electronic communication texts exist, they are simply an electronic file of a traditional book. Not so with this book. Think of this as your business communication app. Whether you purchased the traditional print book or the more modern e-version, you will notice a number of important web-based links to online examples, video, flash animation, surveys, graphics, and other materials that will make your learning experience a richer, more interactive, and exciting one. Sixteen separate online modules are also available to you, designed as virtual and digital educational opportunities. These self-paced, student-centered modules are designed as short, 10- to 15-minute learning experiences that supplement your book.

If you want a short module to help you outline a presentation, we have one for you. If you want a brief module to help you prepare for a phone or video interview, we have one for you. If you haven't yet written a professional résumé, we have a module to help you write one. If you need to use APA or MLA, we have a module to help you do that. If you are concerned about getting a job that's the right fit for you, we have a module to help you make a good decision. And if you're suffering from job-search rejection as you're looking for work, we have a module designed specifically with you in mind.

As you navigate your way through the book, the online modules, and all the other companion resources (such as sample online exam questions and PPT slides), feel free to email* us and let us know what you think. Keep in mind these questions: What chapters and modules did you find especially useful? What other chapters or modules would you like to see us include for future consumers of the book? What additional videos or online resources have you come across that you think students might like or need?

With this course and text, you will learn how to be a more effective communicator in whatever profession you choose. And when you become a more skillful communicator at work, you will also be more successful. We are eager to help you make that happen.

Sincerely,

Jennifer, Pat, and Tim
Jennifer Waldeck, Chapman University
Pat Kearney, California State University at Long Beach
Tim Plax, California State University at Long Beach

*Please email your comments to the first author, Jennifer Waldeck at waldeck@chapman.edu.

About the Authors

Jennifer Waldeck (Ph.D., University of California, Santa Barbara) is an assistant professor of Communication at Chapman University, in Orange, California, where she teaches undergraduates and is on the core faculty of the M.S. program in Health and Strategic Communication. She specializes in instructional and organizational communication research, with an emphasis on the effective use of new and emerging technologies for learning purposes. Her research has appeared in such journals as *Communication Monographs, Communication Education, The Journal of Applied Communication Research, Communication Research Reports,* and *The Journal of Business Communication*. She is the author of more than one hundred research articles, chapters, instructional texts, professional reports, and proprietary instructional packages. Before joining the faculty of Chapman, Waldeck was the director of curriculum development for Scher Group, a Cleveland-based consulting firm. Waldeck continues to provide research, consulting, and training for a variety of organizations in the automotive, real estate, and healthcare industries. Today, she regularly teaches undergraduate courses in business and professional communication, organizational communication, persuasion and social influence, research methods, and graduate seminars on training, consulting, and corporate communication skills for the healthcare industry.

Patricia Kearney (Ed.D., West Virginia University) is a Distinguished Professor of Communication at California State University at Long Beach. Her research and teaching, both theoretical and applied, focus on instructional communication, organizational training, and development. The former editor of *Communication Education*, Kearney has written a variety of textbooks and industrial training packages, and she has published more than 150 research articles, chapters, and commissioned research reports and instructional modules. She is listed among the hundred most published scholars and among the top fifteen published female scholars in her discipline. Kearney is the education director for Ross.Campbell, a Sacramento-based marketing and media production firm specializing in cause-related, social, and environmental issues. She teaches courses in business communication, training and development, instructional technology, and interpersonal relationships.

Timothy G. Plax (Ph.D., University of Southern California) is a Distinguished Professor of Communication at California State University at Long Beach. Plax is widely published, having authored college-level texts and over 150 professional articles and papers. With thirty years of experience in marketing research and message design, Plax is an authority on social influence and organizational communication. He has done extensive research and consulting on environmental topics including recycling, waste reduction, and pollution prevention. His clients include the California Air Resources Board, California Integrated Waste Management Board, California Department of Conservation, USA Funds, Sallie Mae, Gear Up, and more. Before joining the faculty at CSULB, Plax served as an internal consultant for The Rockwell International Corporation. Today he regularly teaches courses in organizational communication, social influence, and organizational leadership.

How to Use This Book and Its Online Components

This book is like no other. This is a book that you will experience. ***Business and Professional Communication in a Digital Age*** provides you with a set of innovative, engaging ways for you to interact with the content both here in the book and online. The combined experience includes fifteen chapters and sixteen digital modules. As you experience each chapter or module, you will encounter a variety of activities to bring the content to life. Using these activities will enhance your learning and appreciation for the information we provide. Look for these icons as you work your way through the book.

 Modules. Modules provide sixteen digital opportunities for you to experience additional information at your own pace. These components are designed with you, and your busy schedule, in mind. These modules, like the chapters, include self-assessments (Weigh In!), self-study activities (Visualize! Practice!), links (Check This Out and Link Out), and business case studies. If you want a brief module to help you prepare for a phone or video interview, we have one for you. If you haven't yet written a professional résumé, we have a module to help you write one. If you are concerned about getting a job that's the right fit for you, we have a module to help you make a good decision. And if you're suffering from job-search rejection as you're looking for work, we have a module designed specifically with you in mind. You'll find references to relevant modules as you navigate the book, and hyperlinks in the eBook—the digital version of this text. All sixteen modules can also be directly accessed from the CourseMate.

The following activities appear in both the chapters and modules, to give you the opportunity to interact with the concepts and keep exploring.

 Link Out. Explore the Web with this icon—it will direct you to more information about the topics in that section of the chapter or module. In Chapter 4, for example, you will have the opportunity to investigate which organizations are family friendly and all the benefits and perks that this label implies. In Module 11, read an article on how to harness the power of social media in your job search.

 Visualize! Practice! When you see this icon, you can complete activities that will help you visualize workplace situations and practice effective communication skills. In Chapter 10, for instance, you are asked to go online and generate some examples of the best and the worst sensory aids you've seen in presentations and discuss why audience members prefer interactive, media-rich presentations. In Chapter 4, you can analyze your personal and professional profiles that you can use to describe yourself and create the kind of impression you would like to leave in a job interview. Practice your citation skills in Module 6, and in Module 3 pick up the mic to learn more about specialized speeches.

 Weigh In! Look for this icon for online self-assessments of your communication skills. Complete these assessments to determine what you already do well and what areas you need to improve upon. In Chapter 6 you will be asked to complete a survey called "How Millennial Are You?" that examines your preferences in communication technology. This same chapter directs you to an assessment of your Twitter and Facebook habits. In Module 1, discover your business culture. In Module 5, examine your work-life balance.

 Check This Out. This icon signifies an activity based on a short video clips or web links of business examples that demonstrate particular principles or concepts from your readings. Following each presentation, you will be asked to respond to a series of questions probing your understanding of those online resources. In Chapter 3 you will be asked to watch and listen to a Suze Orman presentation, followed by a series of questions to check out your listening skills. Chapter 14 directs you to a video of a consultant who describes what she does for a living, followed by an opportunity for you to identify the kinds of consulting work you might be able to do. See a video résumé in Module 11, and explore audience data available online in Module 7.

In addition to these integrated activities, you'll find sample quiz questions tied to each of the chapters in the CourseMate. Use these quizzes to check your knowledge and to prepare for exams. The website will have other resources, such as Speech Builder Express, Speech Studio, a glossary of key terms, an enhanced eBook, a student workbook, Audio Study Tools chapter downloads, interactive video activities, and more!

Additional resources for students and instructors include

- ***Business and Professional Communication in a Digital Age* interactive video activities** include video clips, distinct from those provided in the chapters and modules, that reinforce ideas so you can see and hear how the skills you are studying can be used in various workplace circumstances. Then, answer the critical thinking questions that accompany each video and compare your answers to those provided.

- **The Speech Builder Express 3.0** organization and outlining program is an interactive Web-based tool that coaches you through the speech organization and outlining process. By completing interactive sessions, you can prepare and save your outlines—including a plan for visual aids and a works cited section—formatted according to the principles presented in the text.

- **The Audio Study Tools for *Business and Professional Communication in a Digital Age*** provide mobile content that offers a fun and easy way to review chapter content whenever and wherever. For each chapter of the text, you will have access to a brief communication scenario or speech example and a brief review consisting of a brief summary of the main points in the text and review questions. Audio Study Tools are available on the CourseMate. Audio Study Tools can also be purchased through CengageBrain (see below) and downloaded to student computers, iPods, or other MP3 players.

- **The Cengage Learning Enhanced eBook** is a Web-based version of *Business and Professional Communication in a Digital Age* that offers ease of use and maximum flexibility for students who want to create their own learning experience. The enhanced eBook includes advanced book tools such as a hypertext index, bookmarking, easy highlighting, and faster searching, and easy navigation. You get access to the enhanced eBook with the printed text, or you can just purchase access to the stand-alone enhanced eBook on CengageBrain.com.

- **The Speech Studio™ Online Video Upload and Grading Program** improves the learning comprehension in the business communication class. This unique resource empowers your instructor with a new assessment capability that is applicable to traditional, online, and hybrid courses. With Speech Studio, you can upload video files of practice speeches or final performances, comment on peers' speeches, and review your grades and instructor feedback. Instructors can create courses and assignments, comment on and grade student speeches with a library of comments and grading rubrics, and allow peer review. Grades flow into a light grade book that allows instructors to easily manage their courses from within Speech Studio.

- **The CengageBrain.com online store** provides you with exactly what students like you have been asking for: choice, convenience, and savings. A 2005 research study by the National Association of College Stores indicates that as many as 60 percent of students do not purchase all required course materials; however, those who do are more likely to succeed. This research also tells us that students want the ability to purchase à la carte course material in the format that suits them best. Accordingly, CengageBrain. com is the only online store that offers eBooks for up to 50 percent off, eChapters for as low as $1.99 each, and new textbooks for up to 25 percent off, plus up to 25 percent off print and digital supplements that can help improve your performance.

- *The Online Student Companion* by Diane Matuschka, University of North Florida, and Dr. J. Christopher Jolly, California State Unviersity at Long Beach offers chapter objectives and outlines, lists of important concepts that students can use to facilitate note-taking in class, skill-building activities, and self-tests. This workbook can be bundled with the text at a discount.

- *The Instructor's Resource Manual with Test Bank* authored by Dr. J. Christopher Jolly, academic specialist at the Bickerstaff Center for Student-Athlete Services at California State University at Long Beach, with the assistance of the authors of your book features teaching tips, suggestions for online instruction, sample course outlines, lists of useful media resources, detailed chapter outlines, skill-building activities, forms and checklists, and an extensive test bank.

- The *Power Lecture* **CD-ROM** contains an electronic version of the Instructor's Resource Manual, Exam View© Computerized Testing, predesigned Microsoft PowerPoint presentations, and JoinIn© classroom quizzing. The PowerPoint presentations contain text, images, and cued videos of student speeches and can be used as they are or customized to suit your course needs. These presentations are also suitable for i>clicker use, if desired.

- *Videos for Speech Communication 2011: Public Speaking, Human Communication, and Interpersonal Communication.* This DVD provides footage of news stories from BBC and CBS that relate to current topics in communication, such as teamwork and how to interview for jobs, as well as news clips about speaking anxiety and speeches from contemporary public speakers such as Michelle Obama and Senator Hillary Clinton.

- *Student Speeches for Critique and Analysis 2012* **DVD.** An abundant and diverse sample of student speeches is available in this eight-disc video set that features introduction, impromptu, informative, and persuasive speeches. The videos also include speeches by non-native English speakers as well as speeches containing visual aids.

- **The Flex-Text customization program** lets you create a text as unique as your course: quickly, simply, and affordably. As part of our Flex-Text program, you can add your personal touch to *Business and Professional Communication in a Digital Age* with a course-specific cover and up to 32 pages of your own content at no additional cost.

Contact your local Wadsworth Cengage Learning sales representative for more details.

Chapter 1

Contemporary Business and Professional Communication Competence:
What Does the Workplace Demand?

Jacob Wackerhausen/IStockphoto.com

Chapter Learning Objectives

After completing this chapter, you should be able to

- Explain the importance of competent communication in business and the professions.
- Understand the components of human communication.
- Describe communication as an interactive, simultaneous transaction process.
- Define communication competence.
- Describe what communication competence means in the business and professional context.
- Recognize common barriers to effective business communication.
- Describe the challenges of business and professional communication in the digital age.
- Identify the common forms of business and professional communication.

See also the modules that are relevant to this chapter:

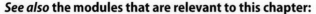 **1: How Do I "Get In and Fit In" to My Organization's Unique Culture?**
2: How Can I Practice Ethical Communication Behavior at Work?
4: What Do I Need to Know about Business Etiquette?
9: How Do I Navigate Office Politics?

Ron, a city government administrator in the parks and recreation department of a small Midwestern city, is feeling bombarded by information. In addition to the constant stream of people coming into his office needing information, help, or solutions to their problems, he receives up to 250 email messages a day. On top of that, he is expected to maintain Facebook and Twitter accounts—and update them regularly with his department's activities. He holds town hall forums for city residents once a month and has long lost track of how many voicemail messages he receives a week since the city required him to post his direct phone number (and email address) on the department website. The stress doesn't end when he goes home. Several nights a month, Ron is on call, when all after-hours calls are forwarded to his iPhone.

In addition to the pressure that Ron personally feels, he sees the effects of information overload on his staff. With less time for team meetings, he notices the staff relying more on email to discuss departmental issues—resulting in many misunderstandings and conflicts that Ron believes would never occur if people would just sit down and talk. But face-to-face communication is also often difficult in Ron's office. Because of the stress of communication overload, meetings and group discussions often result in conflict and disagreement.

Although Ron has always thought of himself as an excellent administrator and an effective manager of people, he sees no end to the problems in his office, and he is unsure what to do about them. Technology has been a tremendous asset to his department, but the problems that technology brings to the workplace are becoming very clear in the parks and recreation department.

Ron's dilemma is not unique. Information plays a critical role in today's business and professional environment. Now, it is more important than ever to be able to manage the vast amounts of information you are exposed to as well as to maintain productive relationships with your colleagues. In fact, the world's greatest business leaders have ranked effective communication in the workplace as one of the most important skills for professional success. In a 2009 presentation to Columbia Business School students, Bill Gates and Warren Buffett argued that strong communication skills may be even more important than the subject in which you got your degree or the amount and quality of technical training you've received.[1] The ability to communicate well is important for

- effective teamwork
- decision making
- problem solving
- organizing
- social networking, both in person and online
- relationship building
- the development of creative ideas
- and more

Communication is important in all kinds of industries, from service-oriented fields like travel, hospitality, real estate, and sales to highly technical fields like medicine and engineering. In fact, communication skills are becoming more important in industries that are thought of as more scientific and less communication-oriented. For example, Andrew Burroughs, a partner in the Silicon Valley engineering firm IDEO, recently commented, "We're looking for employees who are very smart technical contributors but who are also interesting, curious people who can communicate about a lot more than just technical matters."[2] The modern professional environment requires that "communicators" (such as people in sales, marketing, public relations, and human resources) have technical knowledge and that "tech" people (such as engineers, programmers, and designers) have the skills to interact meaningfully with others.

Whether you are searching for a job or attempting to succeed in a job that you already have, recruiters and hiring managers agree that the most important predictors of your success are related to the ability to communicate well.[3] But effective workplace communication is good not only for individual employees. It is also good for organizations as a whole: Functional and effective communication results in strong engagement by employees in their work and the organization's goals, employee satisfaction, positive organizational performance, increased shareholder dividends, decreased turnover, and a strong financial picture for the organization.[4] Harvard Business School professors Kleinbaum, Stuart, and Tushman sum up the importance of workplace communication: "Communication is central to the very existence of the business enterprise."[5]

This chapter explains what is meant by the term "business and professional communication." By understanding the essential components of communication, you can begin to evaluate why some interactions result in satisfying outcomes and why others result in frustration and misunderstanding. Furthermore, we examine the characteristics of competent workplace communication. We also take a look at the types of challenges business communicators face in today's information-intensive society. Finally, we introduce the most common types of communication you will take part in as a professional.

What Is Communication?

What is communication? We communicate all the time, so the answer may seem obvious. However, there is more to communication than many people are aware of. It is a complex, challenging process made up of a number of distinct components.

Communication Is a Complex and Challenging Process

Considering that we communicate so often and so automatically, we can experience a number of problems along the way. Indeed, human communication is a complex, but fascinating, activity that routinely presents some challenges.

Communication Is More Than Just Talking When you communicate with others, you use your cognitive and psychological resources to create, exchange, interpret, and respond to messages. For example, you may encounter people in the workplace who are very different from you, and as a result, you may have difficulty interpreting the meanings of what they say and do. Exemplifying this problem is the increase in sexual and racial harassment lawsuits as U.S. businesses have become more culturally diverse.[6] What you might consider appropriate and effective may be understood in a very different way by a co-worker—with sometimes dramatic and costly consequences.

Communicators Vary in Their Communication Skills and Comfort In any setting, including the workplace, people have different levels of communication skill, willingness to communicate, and anxiety about communicating. These variations contribute to the effectiveness or ineffectiveness of communication. People whose behaviors tell others "I'm willing to communicate with you" and who work to overcome their anxiety about communicating are perceived as more cooperative, more willing to solve problems, more likeable, and more credible in the workplace than those who seem unwilling or too apprehensive to communicate. Conversely, in business situations involving quiet people, problems tend to be solved less quickly and the decision-making process is often difficult. In addition, although there is no relationship between quietness and intelligence, quieter employees are often viewed as less competent than their more verbal counterparts.[7]

Problems Can Occur at Any Point During Communication—and Usually Do! Misunderstandings and conflict may also result from things that are out of the communicators' control. For instance, the structure of some organizations, like global companies, makes face-to-face communication with close colleagues infrequent. Other settings are so intense and stressful that even the most competent communicators are unable to cope effectively. For example, one of the authors of this book once provided consulting services to a medical center. The work at this center had become so stressful that communicators who had once been effective had stopped listening and were communicating aggressively and discourteously.

Business Settings Can Magnify Communication Problems The problems that characterize human communication in general seem to be more pronounced in business and professional settings. Noted organizational communication scholars Dan Modaff, Sue DeWine, and Jennifer Butler write that "as organizations develop, both productive

parema/iStockphoto.com

and unproductive features emerge, such as layers of hierarchy, opposing goals, struggles for power, use of technology, gender and cultural differences, reward systems, and control mechanisms."[8] In other words, when you interact with a variety of people and your relationships are complicated by workplace issues, communication can become difficult, confusing, and even scary.

Let's begin to better understand the communication process by looking at its various components. We'll start by examining a simple exchange between two people. Then we'll look at a more complex model that explains why there are so many opportunities for misunderstanding in business settings.

The Basic Communication Process Is Linear

The **linear model of communication** illustrates the most basic components of the human communication process. This model characterizes communication as a simple process in which a sender transmits a message to a receiver. **Figure 1.1** shows this model in action with a simple communication exchange between two people. In this exchange, the boss (the sender) says, "Nice work on the Kempster account, Julie" (the message), and Julie (the receiver) smiles in return. Five stages make up this simple exchange:

- **Stage 1: Deciding on the message.** A sender decides on a message to send to a receiver (or receivers) to achieve a desired goal. A **sender** is the source of a message. (In this case, the boss is the sender.) A **message** is the verbal, written, or nonverbal information sent from a sender to a receiver. (The message here is the verbal compliment the boss gives to Julie.) A **receiver** is the intended recipient of the message. (In this case, Julie is the receiver.)

- **Stage 2: Encoding the intended message.** The sender **encodes** the message, meaning that he translates thoughts and feelings into specific symbols that can be used to accomplish the intended goal. **Symbols** are words, sounds, and gestures that

FIGURE 1.1
The linear model, a basic communication exchange

Encoding the intended message — 2

Transmitting "information" — 3

Perceiving the information as a message — 4

1 — Deciding on the message

5 — Decoding and interpreting the message

"Nice work on the Kempster account, Julie."

MESSAGE

SENDER

RECEIVER

JGI/Blend Images/Corbis

Adapted from DeFleur, M. H., Kearney, P., Plax, T. G., & DeFleur, M. L. (2003). *Fundamentals of human communication* (3rd ed.). Boston: McGraw-Hill, p. 11.

represent ideas and feelings. In our example, the symbols the boss decided to use are Julie's name, the name of the project Julie was working on, and a widely understood form of praise: "Nice work."

- **Stage 3: Transmitting the message as information.** The message is transformed into physical information (in this case, verbal sounds) so that it can travel over a distance. The sender then decides on a channel for transmitting the message. A **channel** is the medium that carries the message from the sender to the receiver. Examples of channels are face-to-face communication, an email, or a phone call. In this case, Julie and her boss communicated face to face, and the boss transmitted his message with his voice.

- **Stage 4: Perceiving the information as a message.** The receiver attends to the physical information as it arrives and perceives the symbols used in the message. When you **attend** to a message, you use your senses to respond to stimuli in your communication environment. And when you **perceive** a message, you identify and classify that stimuli based on your knowledge, experience, and culture. In our example, Julie's response indicates that she attended to and perceived her boss's message.

- **Stage 5: Decoding and interpreting the message.** The receiver compares the incoming symbols with meanings stored in her memory and selects those that seem best for interpreting the message. In other words, she **decodes** the message, translating symbols into thoughts and feelings in an effort to understand the message. In our example, Julie interpreted the boss's praise positively and smiled. If Julie has received lots of praise in the past, she should have had no difficulty assigning the correct meaning to her boss's clear message!

Let's look at each of these stages in more detail.

The Sender Decides on a Message Whenever you initiate an act of communication, you have some goal in mind that helps you decide on the message you want to send. In our example, Julie's boss's goal was to give her positive feedback. Other common communication goals in business and professional contexts are

- to inform
- to influence
- to persuade others that we have a good idea
- to communicate a business story or narrative
- to negotiate conflict
- to develop a new relationship
- to improve an existing relationship
- to end a relationship
- to discipline or fire an employee
- to create opportunities for advancement and development
- to generate new ideas and better ways of doing things
- to comfort or support another person
- to deliver bad news
- to delegate tasks and responsibilities
- to provide honest and helpful feedback on others' performance or on business processes, procedures, and policies
- to motivate and inspire others
- to teach or train someone
- to sell a product or an idea

Of the many goals for communication, some are simple and obvious. For instance, in saying good morning to the person in the next cubicle, you probably don't have a complex goal. Rather, you are communicating because it's a routine, socially acceptable thing to do. But other goals are multilayered, vague, and difficult to understand. For example, when you ask your manager for a salary increase, having goals for the conversation and a strategy for achieving them is essential.

People often engage in this first stage of the communication process rather mindlessly. However, when they start the process without a clear goal, they may find it difficult to move effectively through the rest of the stages. Setting goals and communicating strategically in order to accomplish business objectives will be a major focus of this book.

The Sender Encodes the Intended Meanings Encoding can be a simple process, but more often it is quite complex. Selecting the right symbols can be difficult because you can never be sure if receivers assign the same meanings to those symbols that you do. For example, when Shani asked Jim to meet at 1:00 p.m., he responded, "Whatever," meaning "Whatever works for you, works for me." But Shani didn't share Jim's meaning for that particular symbol, *whatever*. She perceived his response as vague, curt, and dismissive. The process of encoding becomes even more complex when we consider

Link Out 1.1:
Working at Google

the many meanings assigned to nonverbal symbols, such as gestures, facial expressions, and postures.

Let's take a closer look at what *meaning* is, because this concept is central to the communication process:

- **First, meanings are subjective.** For example, for one person a performance appraisal, a common workplace event, may mean "an opportunity to obtain feedback about my job performance that I can use to improve and develop." But for another person, the meaning may be "an opportunity for my superiors to criticize me."

- **Second, the meanings you hold for objects, events, and ideas are closely related to your experiences.** For example, the person who has a negative attitude about performance appraisals may have experienced demoralizing appraisals in the past.

The notion that meaning is subjective and related to your experiences applies not only to objects, events, and ideas but also to the symbols (words) you use to label those objects, events, and ideas. For instance, Caitlyn has been turned down for several jobs recently because of her "lack of work experience." These words have taken on a negative meaning for her and elicit feelings of insecurity and defensive communicative responses.

Thus, we can define **meaning** as communicators' subjective responses to things they experience directly or to symbols used to label those experiences. Because of the subjective nature of meaning, you typically have no way of knowing what meanings a receiver will assign to your encoded messages. However, because you probably live and work among people who speak your language, you are able to communicate fairly effectively with them. This is because people who speak the same language have been taught rules for associating specific experiences with particular words. Even so, just because people in a group speak the same native language doesn't mean that they share the same meanings for every experience and symbol. The subjective nature of meaning is one of the features of human communication that leads to misunderstanding, especially in the diverse communities that make up the business world.

To explore meaning in terms of organizational culture, watch **LINK OUT 1.1: Working at Google**, a short video about a unique place to work. As you watch, consider how working at Google is different from working at other places. Even though Google seems like a great place to work, how could its culture be challenging for some communicators, especially those used to different kinds of organizations?

The Sender Transmits the Message as Information In order for a receiver to receive a message, the sender must transform it into information that spans a "distance."[9] That distance can be in the form of, say, the physical space between two people, two telephones, or two computers. The information moves physically across this distance as sound or light waves that represent verbal and nonverbal symbols. The information is in the form of stimuli that the receiver's sensory organs can detect. For example, when Julie's boss said, "Nice work," her ears detected the sound of his voice. If he had written the message in an email, her eyes would have detected his words as marks on a computer screen.

When transmitting information, communicators must consider which channel, or channels, would be most effective for transmitting the particular message. For example, some channels allow a more timely response than others—this would be an important

Alistair Berg/Digital Vision/Jupiterimages

consideration in a time-critical situation. Similarly, some channels allow receivers to ask questions more easily. If a message is complex and likely to prompt questions from the receiver, the sender should select a channel that allows the receiver to ask them.

Several channels are commonly used for business communication:

- the Internet (email, blogs, instant messages)
- online social networks (Twitter, Facebook, LinkedIn)
- the telephone (phone calls, voicemail messages, text messages)
- printed content (written reports, faxes, letters, magazines)
- face-to-face communication (conversations, public speeches, interviews, focus groups)
- mediated communication (television, radio, recordings)

We will consider the issue of channel selection further in Chapter 6.

The Receiver Perceives the Information as a Message *Perception* is a very important concept in understanding human communication in general and business communication in particular. It is a complex psychological activity. When a receiver perceives something, she is using her senses to see, hear, or feel a stimulus, and she then identifies the stimulus based on her knowledge and her cultural experience. For example, when you see a person taking a piece of paper from the tray of a fax machine, you have no trouble perceiving this activity as "receiving a fax." If someone didn't know that such a thing as fax machines existed, he would probably perceive the activity as something quite different—maybe that the machine was giving the person a gift.

Messages are often more complex than the simple message the boss sent to Julie, and receivers must exert more energy to perceive the information as a message intended for them. For example, some organizations send email "blasts" to customers that include myriad images, words, and perhaps even sounds. Customers must first attend to the complex information and then perceive it as a message that they're expected to respond to somehow.

Perception is of critical importance in human communication because receivers have to identify the symbols that make up a message before they can assign meaning to the symbols and decode the message.

The Receiver Decodes and Interprets the Message Decoding is automatic behavior that takes place almost instantaneously. You are able to receive and quickly interpret meanings associated with long clusters of words and complex patterns that a sender transmits. For example, when you hear the message "Be in the conference room at 8:30 a.m.," you don't need to spend a lot of time deciding what the pattern of the words and sounds imply and then interpreting what has been said. Rather, you perceive the message in an instant and head to the conference room at 8:30 a.m.

Nonetheless, decoding and interpreting the meaning of some messages can be challenging. The message may be very complex, the sender may use an unfamiliar language or dialect, you may be distracted by something else, or you may not have experience with the subject of the message. For example, a temporary administrative assistant might become overwhelmed in the first few days of a new assignment because the work is unfamiliar, she's not accustomed to the employees' communication style, or because she's excessively worried about impressing her supervisor. All these issues can make the process of decoding and interpreting messages more challenging.

Now that we've used a simple example to explore the basic components of the communication process, let's take a look at more complex exchanges and a more realistic model.

Beyond the Basics: Communication Is an Interactive, Simultaneous Transaction

Communication is rarely as simple as the linear model implies. Why? For one thing, not all interactions are two-person encounters like the one between Julie and her boss. You also communicate with teams and speak in front of large groups. You often communicate through other channels than simple face-to-face interactions. And rarely are the messages you perceive as straightforward and as easily interpreted as "Nice work." Rather, you must often interpret messages that have mixed meaning or meanings you do not understand. For example, a co-worker may give you instructions that are unclear or may deliver "Nice job" laced with a hint of sarcasm.

In addition, communication is not a simple one-way exchange in which the sender only sends and the receiver only receives. Communication flows back and forth between people as they engage in ongoing interactions. What communicators have said and done earlier; the subjective meanings they assign to words, events, and objects; and the channels they use for communication shapes what they say and how they interpret what is being said. A more sophisticated model of the communication process shows more interaction between the sender and the receiver.

People in a conversation constantly respond to each other, simultaneously initiating messages and sending responses back and forth. For example, after Julie's supervisor said, "Nice work on the Kempster account," Julie responded with a smile. In this case, Julie's smile served as *feedback*.[10] **Feedback** is the verbal or nonverbal message that the receiver returns to the sender as the receiver perceives and interprets the sender's message. You provide positive and negative feedback to other communicators all the time: You ask questions, you nod, you paraphrase the speaker's meaning to double-check your understanding, you praise, you criticize, and more. Julie's feedback, a smile, is a nonverbal gesture that

FIGURE 1.2
The simultaneous transactions model of communication

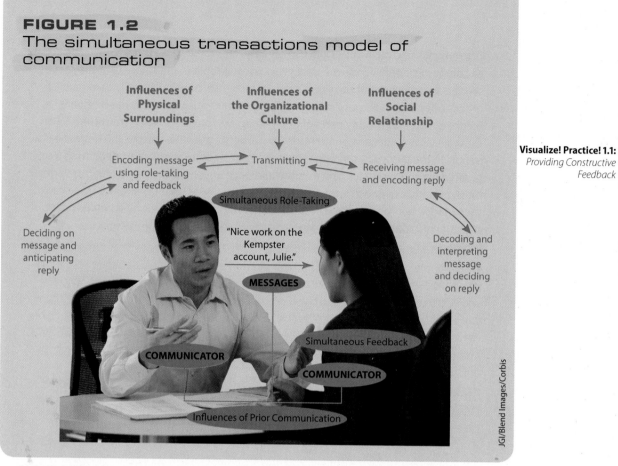

Adapted from DeFleur, M. H., Kearney, P., Plax, T. G., & DeFleur, M. L. (2003). *Fundamentals of human communication* (3rd ed.). Boston: McGraw-Hill, p. 18.

Visualize! Practice! 1.1: *Providing Constructive Feedback*

is universally recognized as a positive interpretation of what was said. Complete VISUALIZE! PRACTICE! 1.1: **Providing Constructive Feedback**. These scenarios will give you experience thinking through verbal and nonverbal feedback and its role in business situations.

This addition of feedback transforms the linear model into the **simultaneous transactions model**, shown in **Figure 1.2**. This more inclusive model shows that the sender and the receiver are undergoing the same kind of experience at the same time, or simultaneously. It implies that their exchange is a transaction, or an activity that mutually influences each of them in some way. These are the characteristics of communicators according to the simultaneous transactions model:

- **Communicators simultaneously encode and decode messages.** Senders don't *only* encode, and receivers don't *only* decode. Nor do receivers necessarily wait for a sender to encode a message before they begin decoding it. Rather, senders and receivers are both encoding and decoding all the time and at the same time. For example, in a sales presentation a salesperson (sender) must transmit a message that makes sense to the audience (receivers) about their needs. As the presenter explains the features of, say, a new model of printer, the audience decodes the explanation by considering their experiences with similar equipment, their reactions to the speaker, and their level of knowledge about the topic. They also encode their verbal and nonverbal responses, which the presenter continually decodes. For example, they frown or nod or they ask questions to elicit more information from the speaker.

- **Communicators simultaneously engage in role-taking and feedback.** Since all communicators decode messages and encode replies simultaneously, they act as senders and receivers at the same time. In this sense, they continually assume each other's roles. Even as a person speaks, she simultaneously assesses the receiver's feedback and may modify parts of her message as that feedback is transmitted. For example, as the salesperson mentions the printer's output capacity, she notices a few people in the audience sending messages by expressing nonverbal concern. As a result of receiving this feedback, she asks the audience questions and learns that the printer they currently use doesn't print an adequate number of pages per minute. She can then modify her message and emphasize her printer's speed as she continues her presentation. This continual role-taking and feedback keeps the transaction flowing.

- **Communicators are influenced by their prior communication experiences.** What people say and the way they respond during a transaction depend greatly on what has been said before. For example, when you speak to someone with whom you've had a conflict in the past, you tend to approach the situation differently than you would if that conflict hadn't occurred. Or when interpreting training content, you think about your previous experiences with this particular trainer. Was he helpful and accurate in the past? Or unclear? The answers to questions like these inform your understanding of the present situation.

- **Communicators are influenced by their physical surroundings and the channel used for communication.** People communicate differently in different places. For example, your tone may be more formal in a formal boardroom than it would be in a co-worker's cubicle. Similarly, people communicate differently depending on the channel. For instance, you may be more comfortable being assertive when using email than you are when standing in front of someone.

- **Communicators are influenced by their cultural situation.** What people say, to whom, and in what way is almost always influenced by *culture,* or an ongoing social situation that has its own set of behavioral rules. In the business context, communication is heavily influenced by *organizational culture,* or what life is like in a particular company or position. For example, people attending a board meeting of a *Fortune* 500 company have very different cultural rules for communicating than employees participating in a brainstorming session at a small company. People in different industries—lawyers versus engineers versus artists—also have different communication habits. Workplace norms such as formal versus informal dress codes, meeting participation styles, forms of address (such as first names versus "Ms." or "Dr." or "sir"), and frequency of communication all vary according to an organizational culture. To communicate effectively in the workplace, you must recognize and adhere to the norms of your organization.

- **Communicators are influenced by the relationship between them.** The type of social relationship between communicators, whether they are strangers or intimates, significantly influences their interactions. Workplace relationships such as those between clients and salespeople, supervisors and subordinates, mentors and protégés, and friends can strongly influence both the content of messages and the ways in which they are transmitted, received, and interpreted. The social expectations and rules of these various types of work relationships shape many aspects of exchanges. These aspects include the way messages are encoded or decoded, the effectiveness of assessments, the amount and kind of feedback, and even the amount of self-disclosure the sender and the receiver provide for one other.

The simultaneous transactions model provides a good general view that applies to a broad range of communication situations, relationships, and contexts. However, merely understanding the communication process isn't enough to ensure effective outcomes. To better understand why communication sometimes goes right and sometimes goes wrong, we need to look at the important concept of *communication competence*.

What Is Communication Competence in Business and Professional Settings?

What makes communication work? That is, what types of communication help us accomplish our goals? Although the success and failure of our efforts to communicate depend on a number of factors, one critical predictor of communication effectiveness is our communication competence. **Communication competence** is one's ability to "choose among available communicative behaviors to accomplish one's goals during an encounter."[11]

Knowing What's Appropriate

An important element of communication competence is your ability to sense what communication behaviors are appropriate in a given setting.[12] To determine what constitutes appropriate behavior in a business and professional environment, you must be able to analyze people, tasks, and situations. For example, say you work for an organization that values face-to-face communication and that tends to reserve email and other media for simple, routine communications. You would be violating organizational norms and making an *inappropriate* communication choice if you used email to discuss a sensitive or controversial topic.

Determining the appropriate communication approach is rarely simple. It can take many months, or even years, of working with people in an organization to learn the norms of the group and the members' expectations for your communication behavior and to assess the personalities and styles of your co-workers. But the sooner you can begin to observe and evaluate these aspects of your work environment, the sooner you'll experience success.

Putting Your Skills to Work

Throughout your school career, you've probably had plenty of practice analyzing people, tasks, and situations to determine appropriate communication behaviors. For example, you probably communicate differently with your friends than you do with family members, instructors, and classmates you don't know well. Apply your analytical skills to the workplace in order to learn what's appropriate communication with your co-workers, your bosses, and your clients.

A-Digit/istockphoto.com

Visualize! Practice! 1.2: *Mindful Business Messages*

Weigh In! 1.1: *How Competent Are You?*

Cultivating Communication Skills

A second important element of communication competence is skill.[13] You may be an insightful observer of communication norms and be able to easily detect what is appropriate, but you will have difficulty communicating competently if you lack effective communication skills. What kinds of skills are important in business and professional settings? To some extent, it depends on the setting. But we can begin by identifying some basic communication skills, all of which we'll discuss in this book: listening, eye contact, perspective-taking and empathy, conversation management, interviewing, persuasion, public speaking, global and intercultural communication abilities, and communication technology aptitude.

Being Motivated to Communicate

A final element of communication competence is motivation.[14] Even the most insightful, skilled communicators are sometimes unmotivated to communicate. People's motivation to communicate differs according to different communication behaviors and across time. For example, there may be days when you simply don't feel like making a presentation to a large audience. You may be bored with the subject of the presentation, you may be disinterested because you believe there isn't much incentive to do the presentation, you may be having a bad hair day, or you may be tired or hungry. That fluctuating degree of motivation affects others' perceptions of your business communication competence.

To assess your current level of communication competency, check out the self-assessment **WEIGH IN! 1.1: How Competent Are You?**

What Goes Wrong in Business and Professional Communication?

Even the most competent communicators can experience obstacles to their business communication goals. Some of these challenges are fairly typical communication problems.

Mindless Messaging

Sometimes people don't choose their words carefully, or they are not mindful of the nonverbal messages they send. For example, frowning while delivering a message may give another person the wrong impression of what was said and meant. Some communication interactions go poorly simply because you lack the resources to think through them carefully. When short on time and under stress, such as when you're trying to meet a deadline, you may be terse with others and fail to consider the most accurate ways to encode or decode your messages. Sometimes, you may react with anger or impatience instead of choosing your words carefully. When you communicate without being mindful of your goals and your audience, the result can be less than satisfying. To read about how to develop more mindful messages, check out **VISUALIZE! PRACTICE! 1.2: Mindful Business Messages**.

Ethical Dilemmas

Some communication situations test your ethical boundaries. For example, should you always tell the truth, even if the truth may hurt someone else's feelings? In an effort to avoid conflict, is it okay to be intentionally ambiguous or refrain from stating your opinion? Is office gossip okay? There are no right or wrong answers to those questions, but misunderstandings often result when communicators operate from different ethical frameworks. Someone who believes that she should always tell the truth, even when it hurts, may deeply offend another who believes that sometimes we should be protected from the truth. And although some research indicates that office gossip can be a productive form of business communication, some people resent it, and obviously people can be hurt by it. To think through the difficult issue of office gossip further, listen and respond to **VISUALIZE! PRACTICE! 1.3: Office Gossip**.

Self-Interest

The bottom line is that many business communicators operate from a position of selfishness. They will do and say whatever is in their best interest, even if it means distorting the truth or hurting others. Being involved with a competitive or, worse, a manipulative communicator can be challenging even for the most competent communicator. The office jerk, whether he or she is a bully, a manipulator, or simply an annoying communicator, is an unavoidable reality, and there is at least one in every workplace. To read more about dealing with the problem of workplace bullying, go to **VISUALIZE! PRACTICE! 1.4: Office Bullies**.

Communication Apprehension

Because you are enrolled in this class, you probably have an interest in and enjoy communicating—or at least want to enjoy it more. However, a great percentage of the population experiences fear about communicating with others—and even *thinking* about communicating with others. This fear can be a significant handicap in many communication situations. We will discuss communication apprehension further in a Chapter 8. In the meantime, consider the following examples of people who have high communication apprehension in the workplace. What might be some consequences of their apprehension?

Visualize! Practice! 1.3:
Office Gossip
Visualize! Practice! 1.4:
Office Bullies

Image Source/Jupiter Images

- Anthony rarely participates in his team's brainstorming sessions. Most of his team-mates think he's uncooperative. But really, he is very fearful of speaking up.

- Suzanne never volunteers to brief management on her department's activities. Speaking in front of her superiors gives Suzanne terrible anxiety. Her manager is beginning to wonder if Suzanne really contributes much, because she's the only member of the department he rarely hears from.

- Melanie feels isolated and alienated at work because she finds it difficult to initiate conversations with others. Even though her co-workers enjoy lunches out every Friday and happy hours once a month, Melanie has little fun and feels close to no one.

Incompetence

Many of your workplace colleagues will never have taken a course like this one. They may lack an understanding of the nuances of verbal and nonverbal communication, and they may behave in ways that surprise you or that seem counterproductive. They may lack the ability to listen well and can frustrate you with their inability to present information clearly and articulately.

Ineffective Use of New Media

Some challenges to effective business communication are caused by new media and by global organizing. Consider the following scenarios:

- Sheryl forwarded an email message to a colleague because she thought the message included information relevant to him. She neglected to consider the effect that other parts of the message might have on him—his feelings were very hurt by a part of the message he was never meant to see.

- Sean Facebooked about a project he was working on for his boss. The project was compromised when a competitor was able to read Sean's Facebook status updates because he had overlooked a security setting.

- Celia's new company has clients all over the globe thanks to the power of e-commerce. Celia didn't think about this fact when she set up the customer service phone center's hours. Now she's dealing with complaints that her company is unresponsive because "live" people are available to answer phones only between 8 a.m. and 5 p.m. Eastern Time in the United States.

- Kevin started an online discussion with four colleagues about a noncontroversial issue at work. The discussion quickly became heated when one of the participants interpreted one of the messages as a personal attack on her department's contributions. After numerous reply-to-all messages, Kevin had to end the online discussion and call everyone together for a face-to-face meeting to resolve the conflicts that had emerged. And the original issue still hadn't been discussed!

- Fran's boss expects her to leave her BlackBerry on all weekend so that she can respond to customer email. Her husband and children are feeling neglected because instead of enjoying her weekends with them, she's constantly looking at her phone and responding to messages. Communication in the family is suffering, and Fran and her husband have been fighting more than ever.

Although all of these individuals were communicating, you can see that *simply communicating is never enough*. Even your best efforts to communicate competently can still result in misunderstanding and conflict, which can prevent you from accomplishing your goals. This seems to be especially true when communicators use new media or communicate across cultures. So let's take a look at some of the challenges of business and professional communication in this contemporary digital, global age.

What Are the Challenges of Business and Professional Communication in the Digital Age?

Visualize! Practice! 1.5: *Mediated Comm—How Personal?*

Even though new technologies like the Internet, smartphones, social networking applications, and Skype make communication a more convenient task, these and other digital media can create problems if we do not use them appropriately. Similarly, although digital communication media make working with people all over the globe possible, we aren't necessarily prepared to work with those people if we lack cultural sensitivity. And, at the end of the day, if we're still both physically and psychologically connected to work through computers and smartphones, our personal lives are bound to suffer. We are much more likely to experience stress, burnout, and information overload as a result of this constant connection than people who can leave work behind from time to time. Let's take a look at each of these common challenges to business communication in the digital age.

Check This Out 1.1: *The Cons of Mediated Comm*

It Can Be Hard to Know When Face-to-Face Is Still Best

Take a moment to go to CHECK THIS OUT 1.1: **The Cons of Mediated Comm**. This video illustrates that although mediated communication is often quick and easy, it does have some drawbacks.

We have so many choices available when we need to communicate with others. For many of us, mediated communication such as email, texting, and instant messaging have become big parts of our communicative lives, and relying on them seems like the quickest, easiest choice. But what happens if the people you're trying to communicate with aren't as connected to their computers or smartphones as you are? You may end up waiting a long time for a response. When time is of the essence or you're in a crisis situation, new media are not always the best choices—unless quick responses are the norm in your business.[15]

In addition, media vary in their ability to transmit cues of "personalness."[16] Think about the various technologies you use and how personal they seem, meaning how well they simulate face-to-face communication. For instance, when speaking on the telephone, are you able to hear emotion better than you are when reading a text message? Similarly, when you sit in the same room with someone, you are able to see nonverbal messages such as frowning, eye rolling, and arm crossing. You can't detect those kinds of messages on a telephone call. To explore how personal some commonly used business media is, go to VISUALIZE! PRACTICE! 1.5: **Mediated Comm—How Personal?**

As a general rule, new media is a good choice for sending routine, simple information. But for complex, urgent, or controversial messages, face-to-face interactions may be better. Of course, there are exceptions to this rule that are unique to the cultures of different businesses. Research indicates that for business communication, being aware of when other communicators in your industry use technology and when they use face-to-face communication can help you make the right decisions about which medium to use.[17]

Link Out 1.2:
Thinking Intercultural Communication

Intercultural Sensitivity Can Be Difficult

Business and industry are becoming increasingly global as more organizations do business in other countries. New media not only make global business communication convenient and efficient, but they also often present you with the challenge of dealing with communicators who are very different from you. To communicate competently with people in other countries, you need to know about the values, language systems, and communication norms of their cultures. Additionally, you need to understand the economic and social conditions of their countries.

Intercultural communication is communication between and among individuals and groups across national and ethnic boundaries. Understanding the nature of this type of communication can help you interact more effectively with other business communicators. In large part, your dominant culture determines the way you communicate—how your beliefs influence what you say, what language system you use, and what gestures you use.[18] Your dominant culture also determines how you dress, how you use your time, the distances you use to interact with others, and how you make eye contact. All of these things can affect how others respond to you.

For example, Chinese people tend to be indirect in their communication and to understate their own accomplishments and successes. They learn to speak humbly. In contrast, people of European cultures tend to be more assertive and to show pride in what they do. Nonverbally, some Latinos and Latinas and some African Americans associate direct and prolonged eye contact with status and power, so looking steadily into the eyes of someone of higher status is a sign of disrespect.[19] Lack of awareness of intercultural differences like these can easily result in misunderstandings.

For more insights into how culture affects communication in the workplace, take a look at **LINK OUT 1.2: Thinking Intercultural Communication**, which features the research and thinking of one of world's leading experts on intercultural communication.

Intercultural communication can become especially problematic for business communicators when they begin to believe that the way people in their dominant culture communicate is the only or best way, or when they fail to learn and appreciate the cultural norms of people they do business with. In addition, businesspeople today can quickly find themselves in unfamiliar intercultural communication situations. They may not have expertise in how every culture handles every situation—in fact, they probably don't even know all of the norms of their own cultures! And people are sometimes so surprised by how other people communicate that they don't know how to respond effectively. Because of these challenges, intercultural differences are a common barrier to effective business communication in this global, digital age. We will revisit the challenges of intercultural and global communication throughout this book.

Stress, Burnout, and Information Overload Are Common

A third challenge to contemporary communication is how easily we can become stressed or burned out. Constant connection to others by way of smartphones, the Internet, and social networks can easily result in information overload, exposing us to more messages than we can process. The luxury of instant access to information and social exchange can quickly turn into a liability when your family communication suffers, when you interrupt engagements with friends to answer work-related text messages, or when you become

STOCK4B-RF/Jupiter Images

Link Out 1.3:
Managing Stress in College

so focused on work-related communications that you think of nothing else. Research indicates that a growing number of employees worldwide are feeling overwhelmed by the near-constant flow of email and text messages, and they feel pressured to respond to messages as soon as they receive them. In one study, some participants reported checking their email inboxes up to 40 times per hour, but monitoring equipment on their computers revealed that many actually *underreported* their obsessive email habits![20] Trying to keep up with information overload in the digital age can leave employees frustrated, tired, and unproductive.

Putting **Your Skills** to Work

Getting a college education can lead to stress, burnout, and information overload just as easily as having a job can. Try to start managing these challenges now, because life doesn't get any easier when you join the workforce! There are many resources online to help you manage stress—you can find one that might be helpful at **LINK OUT 1.3: Managing Stress in College**.

HOW TO AVOID BURNOUT

4x6/istockphoto.com

What Are Some Common Forms of Business Communication?

Subsequent chapters will introduce you to a range of verbal and nonverbal forms of communication that occur regularly in business and professional environments. Here is a preview of the forms of communication we will study.

Interviewing

Critical to finding employment, interviewing (Chapter 4) is a form of communication that gives many people a great deal of anxiety. An interview can land you a job, of course, but it should also give you insight as to whether the particular job is the right match for your skills and personality. You must be a competent interview participant in order to glean such important information from the experience. Knowing how to prepare for an interview, anticipating common (but important) questions, dressing appropriately, providing credible and articulate answers, and following up after an interview are all important dimensions of being a competent interview participant.

Relationship Communication

Although you may already be a competent interpersonal communicator, you will need to know how to apply the skills of relationship communication (Chapter 5) appropriately in the workplace. Knowing how to initiate, maintain, and sometimes even disengage from professional relationships will enhance your ability to succeed at work. Some of the common forms of relationships in the workplace include the ones you form with your peers, your supervisor, your mentor, your customers, and other individuals outside of the organization (such as suppliers and vendors). To successfully establish beneficial professional relationships, you will need to master skills such as small talk, self-disclosure, and affinity seeking. And you will need to understand the care and feeding of important workplace relationships in order to keep them healthy. Sometimes, when the costs outweigh the benefits of a particular relationship, you will need to know how to end it with minimal drama or negative consequences.

Mediated Communication

As we've discussed, new media can open doors for communicators. New media (Chapter 6) offer unprecedented convenience, timely access to useful information, and connections with people in distant places. But mediated business communication comes with challenges as well as benefits. For instance, video and telephone conferences are a cost-effective and convenient way to meet with colleagues in distant locations, but some of the traditional public speaking skills we've learned aren't effective when we use mediated channels.

Presentational Speaking

Most business leaders realize that presentation skills are key to business success, but many lack these skills or don't use them on a regular basis. This course will introduce you to some of the primary types of business presentations, including informative and persuasive presentations (Chapters 7, 8, and 9). You will learn the skills of knowing and understanding your audience, researching and preparing for a presentation, and creating

powerful introductions and conclusions that leave your audiences wanting more. Of course, excellent content doesn't go far if it's not delivered in an engaging manner. We will examine some delivery techniques that will help you create a positive impression with audiences. Finally, we'll discuss how you can engage business audiences with sensory aids such as PowerPoint, audio, and video (Chapter 10).

Group Discussions and Meetings

Intense group interaction is a fact of life in most contemporary business settings. However, if not carefully managed, this type of communication can easily result in conflict, misunderstanding, and poor focus. Effective group communication skills can help you maximize group output and minimize conflict and other negative by-products of teamwork (Chapter 12).

Meetings are another unavoidable reality of work (Chapter 11). Because many meetings are boring, unproductive, and a waste of participants' time, most people's reaction to them is "Not another one!" However, competent communication skills can make meetings productive. Knowing how to plan, facilitate, and appropriately participate in meetings can maximize their benefits.

Written Documents

As a professional, you will often be called upon to produce written communications (Chapter 13). Their various forms include proposals for projects, bids for jobs, emails addressing key issues of a particular project, executive summaries updating your boss on important issues, and technical descriptions of a process or product. For any type of written communication, you must know how to structure the information; select the right style, tone, language, and length; support the document with appropriate images; and create polished, error-free documents. When you create effective written documents, you will generate measurable business results, build your own credibility, and capture the attention of your managers and colleagues.

Consulting and Training

People well trained in business and professional communication are in a unique position to help organizations solve problems. Because so many business problems are related to the failure to communicate (or to communicate well), communication specialists, or consultants, are often called upon to diagnose and propose solutions to these problems. Consultants are trained to assess communication problems and design methods for improving ways in which individuals exchange and use information within business settings (Chapter 14).

One solution that consultants often recommend for business communication problems is training (Chapter 15). Training involves teaching people to improve particular job-related skills. More specifically, communication training helps people enhance their skills of relating to others, listening, speaking, and solving problems.

Now that you have a sense of what makes a truly effective and competent communicator, are you better able to relate to the frustrations Ron experienced in our opening scenario? The nature of competent business communication is evolving as we become more digitally connected to our jobs. New digital media play a dynamic role in the communication process, and we've come to rely on them heavily. Although these media are so promising in terms of achieving work-related communication goals, they also have shortcomings.

When you think of business communication as setting goals, exchanging messages in a transactive and simultaneous way, and anticipating challenges and misunderstandings, you can begin to approach a wide range of business communication tasks strategically. And in the process you can become a more competent communicator.

Use your Speech Communication CourseMate for *Business & Communication in a Digital Age* for quick access to the electronic resources that accompany this text. These resources include

Study tools that help you assess your learning and prepare for exams (*digital glossary, key term flash cards, review quizzes*).

Activities and assignments that help you hone your knowledge and build your communication skills throughout the course (*Visualize! Practice!, Weigh In!, Check This Out, and Link Out activities; modules; review questions*).

Media resources that help you explore communication concepts online (*Enhanced eBook*), develop your speech outlines (*Speech Builder Express 3.0*), watch and critique videos of sample speeches and communication situations (*interactive video activities*), upload your speech videos for peer reviewing and critique other students' speeches (*Speech Studio online speech review tool*), and download chapter reviews so you can study when and where you'd like (*Audio Study Tools*).

Key Points

- Effective communication is one of the most important skills for professional success.
- Communication is more than simply talking. Communication is a complex and challenging process because
  - ✔ Communicators vary in their skills and comfort.
  - ✔ Communication can cause misunderstanding and conflict.
  - ✔ Communication problems can be pronounced in business settings.
- The basic communication process is illustrated by the linear model. In this model,
  - ✔ A sender encodes a message by translating thoughts and feelings into symbols.
  - ✔ The sender then transmits the message through a channel to a receiver.
  - ✔ The receiver attends to message, perceives it, and then decodes it.
- A more sophisticated model of communication is the simultaneous transactions model. In this model,
  - ✔ Feedback flows between the sender and receiver continuously.
  - ✔ Senders and receivers both encode and decode messages simultaneously.
  - ✔ Their communication is influenced by a number of factors, such as culture and experience.
- An important predictor of communication effectiveness is communication competence. Communication competence is your ability to choose an appropriate communication behavior to reach your goals during an exchange.
- In the business and professional context, competent communicators know what's appropriate in a communication situation, cultivate their communication skills, and are motivated to communicate.
- Common barriers to effective business communication are mindless messaging, ethical dilemmas, self-interest, communication apprehension, incompetence, and ineffective use of new media.
- Challenges to business communication in the digital age are knowing when face-to-face communication is best, being interculturally sensitive, and managing stress, burnout, and information overload.
- Common forms of business and professional communication are
  - ✔ Interviews
  - ✔ Relationship communication
  - ✔ Mediated communication
  - ✔ Presentational speaking
  - ✔ Group discussions and meetings
  - ✔ Written documents
  - ✔ Consulting and training

Key Terms

attending (6)

channel (6)

communication competence (13)

decoding (6)

encoding (5)

feedback (10)

intercultural communication (18)

linear model of communication (5)

meaning (8)

message (5)

perceiving (6)

receiver (5)

sender (5)

simultaneous transactions model of communication (11)

symbol (5)

Questions for Critical Thinking and Review

1. Describe how communication competence can make you a more successful professional.

2. Why is communication a valuable skill, even for those in technical fields such as engineering or software design?

3. Think for a moment about the last time you felt misunderstood. Why do you think the misunderstanding occurred? Consider what meanings the other person may have assigned to what you said. How could you have taken better care to make sure that the other person understood you?

4. Explain the statement "Communication is more than just talking."

5. Create an example of communication between two people and label the parts of the message according to the five stages of the linear model of communication.

6. Describe a time when you were part of a group or team whose members had differing levels of communication skill and comfort. How did these varying levels affect (a) your satisfaction with the experience and (b) the group's ability to accomplish its goals?

7. In the simultaneous transaction model of communication, where does the most opportunity for misunderstanding exist? Why?

8. In what ways does the channel a communicator selects for transmitting a message influence the outcome of the interaction? Provide examples.

9. Think about your score on the Weigh In! quiz in this chapter, and consider the components of communication competence. In which are or areas do you need the most training and experience?

10. Review the challenges of business and professional communication in a digital age. Which ones have you already experienced? Describe a situation in which you experienced a challenge, and then explain how you could have handled the experience more competently. What choices would you have made differently?

Chapter 2

Communicating at Work:
How Can I Make Every Word and Gesture Count?

ACE STOCK LIMITED/Alamy

Chapter Learning Objectives

After completing this chapter, you should be able to

- Appreciate how verbal and nonverbal communication can affect your success at work.
- Use verbal and nonverbal communication to create and sustain a positive impression with your boss and colleagues.
- Identify verbal message strategies that will increase your communication competence.
- Identify nonverbal message strategies that will increase your communication competence.

See also **the modules that are relevant to this chapter:**

4: What Do I Need to Know about Business Etiquette?
14: How Do I Prepare for Phone and Video Interviews?
15: How Do I Manage Time as a New Professional?

"Do you think my boss likes me?" I don't think she does. She never answers my emails, and she doesn't return my phone calls. What do you think, Steve?"

"Why do you care, Mary, whether your boss likes you? Are you worried about losing your job?"

"No, that's not it. I just want her to show me some respect, to acknowledge my existence, and to define me as important around here."

"Why do you suppose the boss doesn't value you, Mary? What do you think you're doing wrong?"

"Nothing. But she complains that I'm high maintenance. She told the secretary that I ask too many questions, but I need direction. She said I don't follow through on my responsibilities. That's not true; she takes assignments away from me before I can get them done. She just likes to micromanage, that's all."

"Well, if you're right and her impression of you is wrong, you have your work cut out for you. From my experience, it's very hard to get someone to change their impression of you. How do you think the boss reached these conclusions about you in the first place?"

Steve is right to question what Mary might have said or done to contribute to her boss's negative impression of her. Impressions are not created in a vacuum. Instead, they are based on a whole host of verbal and nonverbal behaviors that communicate specific messages. What you say and how you say it influences how others form impressions of you. The problem is that most of these impressions are created quickly and based on very little information. Once created, these impressions become difficult, if not impossible, to change.

Mary is also right to worry that her boss's impression is an inaccurate one. People act on what they believe to be true about others. Knowing that her boss perceives her to be high maintenance, Mary is unlikely to receive the respect, acknowledgment, and sense of importance that she wants and maybe even deserves.

This chapter explores how your words and actions affect your successes and failures at work. Like Mary, you can benefit from knowing what verbal and nonverbal strategies will help you influence the impressions others form of you. One strategy we'll discuss is to select ahead of time the impressions you want others to hold and then to make and enact a plan to present yourself favorably in encounters that matter. Competent communicators draw on strategies like these to control how they are perceived.

How Can You Best Present Yourself in Encounters That Really Matter?

Presentation of self is the strategy of creating and sending verbal and nonverbal messages that tell others about the kind of person you are. The way you speak, dress, and behave communicates information about your personal qualities and your inner nature. From this information, others construct interpretations, understandings, and impressions about what they think you are really like. Similarly, as others form first impressions about you, you are forming your own impressions about them.

To help control the initial impressions your co-workers and supervisors have of you, plan to influence their evaluations in a particular way. Deliberately designing verbal and nonverbal messages to create a particular set of impressions is what sociologist Erving Goffman called **impression management**.[1] Managing your impression refers to *effective* self-presentation, and messages are effective when they cause others to evaluate you in the ways you desire. Because initial impressions and evaluations can be long-lasting and difficult to change, you need to manage your impression well in order to succeed professionally.

Researchers have spent considerable time studying how the impression management process works.[2] What does the research tell us?

- **First impressions are formed quickly.** In only a few seconds, we decide if someone is likeable, competent, and a good person—or not. We form first impressions quickly in an effort to feel comfortable with those we meet and to reduce uncertainty about new people and situations.

- **First impressions are based on limited information.** We form impressions based on the information available to us. This information comes from not only what we see but also what we have heard from others. In first encounters, we also tend to focus on characteristics related to our own personal preferences and biases. For instance, engineers may be biased in favor of someone who also has an engineering degree. What might be an engineer's first impression of a new co-worker who has a communication degree?

- **What people learn first about you influences, or biases, how they perceive subsequent information about you.** If people initially think you are friendly and easy to be around, they are likely to continue thinking that your humorous comments are entertaining. In contrast, if people have the initial impression that you are aloof, how might they perceive subsequent humorous remarks?

- **First impressions are easily generalized.** If others think you are smart, for instance, they are likely to generalize that impression and attribute other favorable qualities to you, such as skill and industriousness. If they think you aren't smart, they will likely perceive you as also being incapable, unskilled, and perhaps unreliable.

- **Some characteristics are more salient or more influential than are others.** Some characteristics can drastically affect how people perceive you. What characteristics are more salient or influential for you? For instance, if you discovered that someone smokes, would that change how you feel about that person? What if the person were overweight, or rich, dressed poorly or very well, were unkempt or fastidious, and so on?[3] What characteristics are salient in your impressions of others?

These research-based principles provide a good basis for the effective presentation of self in the workplace. The next task is to move beyond the research to developing practical strategies that will help you achieve the goal of managing how people at work perceive you.

Stephen Coburn/Used under license from Shutterstock.com

Select the Impression You Want to Make

An effective way to gain control over how others perceive you is to know your objective ahead of time. Simply ask yourself, "What impression do I want to create with this person?" The answer may be obvious—most employees want to create the impression of being highly competent, a team player, a hard worker, reliable, and easygoing. But don't worry if your answers seem obvious. Knowing clearly what impression you want to create is the first step in making it happen.

Defining the impression you want to make helps you design the most effective self-presentation strategy. Your strategy should help you communicate *characteristics that count* and that will be quickly perceived and unmistakably understood. We see politicians

Putting Your Skills to Work

From the time you were a baby, you've learned how to get what you need from the people around you. This is a natural, unconscious, and necessary skill. Often, how we go about getting what we need makes a powerful impression on others. Think about the impressions you've made on people over the years—when did others have positive impressions of you, and when did they have negative impressions? What can you learn from your insights that will help you cultivate skills to consistently make a good impression on others in the workplace?

Illustrious/istockphoto.com

do this all the time. When Barack Obama was running for president, he made sure he presented himself in ways that would appeal to the various groups he was trying to win over. He rolled up his shirtsleeves, took off his tie, and used local colloquialisms when he addressed a rural, Southern audience. When speaking to business executives, he was dressed in a conservative dark suit, a white shirt, and a narrow tie, and he relied on a more formal vocabulary. And occasionally, a photo op caught him shooting hoops and then eating burgers with friends while talking amicably with locals at the restaurant.

Make a Plan

Once you have identified the impression you need or want to create, come up with strategies to present that impression. Effective strategies of self-presentation consist of

- Verbal messages, or specific content delivered with a particular style and level of vocabulary.
- Nonverbal forms of communication such as clothing, mannerisms, gestures, posture, and demeanor.

Identifying the *best* verbal and nonverbal combination can be a challenge. Furthermore, you can never be sure what people might consider salient characteristics. In most business environments, a laid-back speaking style sprinkled with four-letter words, shaggy hair, sloppy clothing, and scruffy shoes will create negative perceptions. But some workplaces are looser about how you look and talk and require clothing that can get dirty. For example, if you're working among truck mechanics, a refined vocabulary, a tailored suit, neatly trimmed hair, and well-polished shoes might make exactly the wrong impression.

How do you know which strategies will ensure that your personal characteristics are perceived positively? Perhaps the best guide is common sense. Do not say or do anything that would cause others to form a negative impression of you.

One single checklist cannot be used as a game plan for all people in all work environments. But you can apply certain principles as you consider how to create a positive impression during an initial encounter:[4]

- **Carefully assess the person you are presenting yourself to.** Who is this person? What criteria will he or she probably use in judging you? If you're presenting yourself to your potential manager, what qualities are likely to matter most to her? What might she be looking for in a co-worker? How would she define an ideal employee?

- **Be honest about who you are.** Do not try to misrepresent yourself. Do not try to be someone you're not, even if you think that would make you more appealing. People can spot a cover-up very quickly. Even a minor falsehood can override your positive characteristics and cause others to perceive you unfavorably.

- **Consider the physical setting or context of the encounter.** Interactions with a new co-worker in her office should be more formal and deliberate than those that might occur later on in the company's lunchroom. Moreover, context often influences what kinds of topics and issues should and should not be discussed. Pulling out folders and initiating talk about a project during lunch will likely be met with groans and rolled eyes.

- **Use all available communication channels to get your positive qualities across.** Choose verbal and nonverbal channels—such as your appearance, timing, language choices, and posture—to communicate your positive characteristics.

- **Look closely for subtle feedback messages.** Listen and watch for how another person responds to you. Use this feedback to shift your strategy or to follow up on directions that seem successful.

Be deliberate in your planning. Be ready to present yourself honestly and divert attention from anything that might result in negative evaluations. When you carefully assess the people, the situation, the available channels, and the feedback you receive during an encounter, you're far more likely to present yourself effectively than if you just let things proceed spontaneously.

Enact and Evaluate the Plan

Once you have a plan, you'll need to put it into place. Just do it! Plans are meant to be used. Too many good plans are never implemented because people become anxious about them, they overlook an opportunity, or they forget to use them. But only imagining a planned interaction falls short of giving it a chance. Of course, no encounter will go exactly as planned. However, research on planned interactions shows that people who formulate a plan and operate from it come closer to actualizing their goals than those who do not plan.[5]

Another advantage to enacting a plan is that, after the encounter, you can step back and evaluate the plan's effectiveness. Begin by assessing the feedback you received, particularly the nonverbal cues. Did these responses support your objective? If so, you know you are on the right track. If not, change your plan. Sort out which elements worked and which did not work. Don't be discouraged if your plan doesn't seem to work immediately. Give your efforts sufficient time to influence how others perceive you. It may take several encounters to achieve your desired impression, particularly if you are attempting to change an existing impression.

Change Others' Negative Impressions about You

Sooner or later, you will have to confront a co-worker's or boss's negative impression of you, which may be based on earlier unfavorable encounters. You may decide it's important to change that impression, even though changing someone's entrenched convictions is a formidable task. Nevertheless, you can retrain people who have outdated or negative impressions about you, although it may take a while.

There are two key reasons why it is much more difficult to change a person's ongoing impression than it is to create a first impression.

- **It takes energy.** The person who has a negative impression must first erase the existing impression and then create a new one. To do this, he must disregard the earlier, well-remembered, and possibly viable perception of you. Recall that people form first impressions of others quickly and that they formulate those impressions based on a limited amount of information. Because this is a natural tendency, most people will want to resist the energy and inconvenience required to abandon an existing impression and create a different one.

- **It feels uncomfortable.** Humans tend to want to feel certain about things—uncertainty makes us feel uncomfortable. Forming initial impressions about others helps us feel more certain about who we are and how we should relate to others. Any attempt to change those impressions threatens to bring back that initial uncertainty and discomfort.

So what can you do? First, consider whether it is even possible to change the other person's impression of you. Second, is it worth the effort? Will changing that person's impression help you get your work done more efficiently or help you advance in the company? Assess the costs versus the benefits. For example, if you don't work very closely with someone who has a negative impression of you, or if her opinion doesn't affect your advancement prospects, or she will be retiring soon, it may not be that important to change her impression of you. Sometimes, changing someone's impression of you isn't worth the effort. And sometimes, the person's negative impression is so sturdy that it is virtually impossible to change. In those cases, don't even try! Part of successful self-presentation is being able to evaluate costs and benefits of trying to change someone's opinion about you.

Let's assume you feel change is possible and worth the effort. The process of changing an existing impression is similar to creating a new impression. First, consider your objectives carefully. Obviously, if a co-worker or supervisor perceives you negatively, your overall goal is to change that person's perception to a positive one. But beyond that, what are your specific goals? Do you have new personal or professional accomplishments you want your colleague to be aware of? Are you concerned that his impression of you lacks depth?

A common objective is to make a colleague aware of new positive accomplishments that he can add to what he thinks he already knows about you. For example, you may have special knowledge of Excel or be able to program a smartphone, repair the office copier, or install computer software. Perhaps you are well networked in the profession, never eat alone, and do cool things in your personal life that reflect well on the company. If such information can be linked to the interests of your colleague, so much the better. This new knowledge may open new avenues for communication that might displace or at least minimize unfavorable impressions.

Once you've determined your objectives, enact a plan to communicate the favorable qualities that you know others at work perceive to be true about you. Your plan will need to be long term, and you'll need to communicate your positive qualities over and over again but without belaboring the message. Use your actions and comments to show that others regard you favorably, respect your judgment, and believe you to be trustworthy. As with plans to create a first impression, be honest about who you are so you're perceived as ethical and credible, and remember to consider context, communication channels, and feedback.

The rest of this chapter addresses specific verbal and nonverbal strategies that can enhance your plans to influence your colleagues' impressions of you. Making every word and gesture count shows that you care about how you are perceived and that you are willing to work on it.

What Verbal Strategies Should You Use?

Selecting the right words and phrases begins with the impression you wish to make. Most of us would like others at work to see us as competent, smart, hardworking, diligent, responsible, ethical, and dependable. In addition, perhaps you want to be perceived as amiable, easygoing, approachable, nice, friendly, and warm. Or perhaps you would rather come across as powerful, resourceful, dominant, self-assured, and decisive. Your ability to cultivate whatever impression you desire is tied directly to what you say and how you say

Noel Hendrickson/Digital Vision/Jupiter Images

it. This section discusses verbal strategies that will help you come across as clear and un-ambiguous, strong and powerful, and inclusive rather than exclusive. Use these strategies in your oral and written communication, including briefings and reports, emails, memos, and conversations.

Speak to Be Understood

The root of many workplace communication problems is the inability to make ourselves understood. Rambling emails, complicated technical jargon, disorganized reports, and cluttered PowerPoint presentations can make communicators appear incomprehensible and, worse, incompetent. Here are some simple strategies to help you come across as clear, concise, and competent.[6]

- **Keep it simple.** Sometimes clear, simple words and concise phrases have the most impact. For example, if you use uncomplicated language to express complex thoughts, your listeners are more likely to grasp your ideas quickly. In fact, the juxtaposition of straightforward talk with complex thoughts communicates the thoroughness of your understanding. Use simple, everyday words to replace or complement long, difficult words and phrases. Short, concise, and even redundant phrases help prevent infor-mation overload, reduce ambiguity, and facilitate comprehension. But be sure to use vocabulary that is appropriate for your listeners. Be careful not to oversimplify to the extent that others perceive you as unintelligent. Work to be easy to follow without losing the integrity of your meaning.

- **Limit your use of jargon and acronyms.** Using technical terms unique to a particular work group or profession, or **jargon**, can convey your competence and is often convenient shorthand. Even so, use jargon only when you are sure your listeners are familiar with it. For example, communication professionals often use the following jargon in exchanges with each other but not at the grocery store or PTA meetings:

✔ Cognitive dissonance = confused

✔ Norm of reciprocity = if we self-disclose, others will disclose in return

✔ Disengagement = couples breaking up

✔ Affinity = liking

✔ Heterophily = dissimilar or different

✔ Reactance = saying no or being resistant to change

Similarly, use company **acronyms**, or words formed from the first letters of each word in a name or phrase, only if listeners will know what they mean. To understand how unfamiliar acronyms can impede communication, see how many of the following acronyms you can easily define. (See the key to this list at the bottom of this page.)

✔ COLA

✔ FT

✔ FTE

✔ LLC

✔ POP

✔ SKU

✔ UPS

✔ PL

✔ OPM

✔ COO

✔ COB

Too many acronyms and too much jargon can annoy receivers, prevent them from understanding a message, and can make the sender seem pompous or affected.

- **Be specific and clear.** Avoid using content-free language that is intended to be ambiguous. You've probably heard CEOs and politicians use this type of bloated speech to avoid answering potentially difficult or embarrassing questions. For example, U.S. Treasury Secretary Timothy Geithner resorted to evasive speech in a *Meet the Press* interview when host David Gregory asked him about the excessive bonuses given to AIG executives. Gregory asked if he was so outraged over the bonuses, why didn't he do something about it. Twenty seconds into his response, Geithner still had not addressed the question, claiming that his responsibility was first to fix the problems of the financial sector so that this wouldn't happen again in America, blah, blah, blah. With subsequent probing and a commercial break, Geithner finally provided a direct response—which is what he should have done in the first place.[7]

Occasionally, it's a good idea to be vague and ambiguous, particularly if a message is likely to unnecessarily alarm employees, clients, or customers. But more often, evasions are problematic. Comments that contribute nothing to the meaning of the

COLA: cost of living adjustment; **FT:** full-time; **FTE:** full-time equivalent; **LLC:** limited liability company; **POP:** point of purchase; **SKU:** stock keeping unit; **UPS:** United Parcel Service; **PL:** profit and loss; **OPM:** other people's money; **COO:** chief operating officer; **COB:** close of business message can reduce your credibility, and confuse listeners. In other words, stick to the adage: "Say what you mean and mean what you say."

Speak to Show Strength

Sometimes you will want to communicate an image of power and strength. You may want to command attention, influence others, gain respect, or communicate authority or expertise. To show strength when you speak, use power language and avoid unnecessary qualifiers, embed intense or animated language into your message, include concrete images, and choose the active voice.[8]

- **Use power language.** Some words and expressions are the opposite of power language and weaken a communicator's position and arguments. Notice how the italicized phrases seem to sap the strength from the following statements:

  ✔ *You probably know more about this than I do*—what font should I use for this report?

  ✔ *I think* U.S. stocks will face some turbulence in the weeks ahead.

  ✔ *This may not be right, but* current unemployment figures would indicate that the recession is not yet behind us.

  ✔ *I'm not sure, but I think* I deserve a raise.

  ✔ He is showing signs of improvement, *don't you agree?*

  By eliminating these qualifiers, you and your position will come across as stronger, more assertive, and more factual. With **power language**, others will assume that you know what you are talking about and that you have the courage of your convictions. Sometimes it is useful to communicate indirectly, using implication and suggestion, particularly if you are not confident in your opinion or you want to deliver a difficult message gently. But for most work-related encounters, unnecessary qualifiers only confuse or weaken your message.

- **Use intense, animated language.** An otherwise dull interaction can be made interesting with intense, animated language. Moreover, vivid language is a good tool for changing attitudes and behaviors. To illustrate, imagine that a co-worker wants to convince you to purchase and use i>clicker technology for employee training sessions:

  I heard about a new way for people to respond at training sessions. It's some kind of new technology that allows everyone to participate. I heard it was worthwhile—increases input and such. What do you think?

  Now imagine the same pitch but delivered with some intense, animated language—see how this persuasive appeal changes:

  I came across this amazing technology that really livens up your typical boring training session. Employees rave about it. They love it. It's called the i>clicker—it's simple to use, and it's 100% effective. Hundreds of companies use it worldwide, and thousands of employees are on board. Let's do it here. It's a winner.

  Notice how dramatic the contrast is between the two messages. Try substituting dramatic words for drab ones, using action words, employing unusual metaphors and similes, and offering descriptive detail.

- **Make images concrete. Imagery** is language that appeals to the senses of touch, taste, sound, sight, and smell to create concrete, realistic images. A car is easier to visualize and get excited about when you make it concrete: a Lamborghini or a Ferrari. The abstract idea "outstanding inventors" becomes more perceptible when you evoke specific names such as Steve Jobs and Steve Wozniak. Concrete language helps others picture or visualize your point. In addition, making abstract thoughts concrete helps others attend to and perceive your message.

President Barack Obama, well known for his presentational skills, relies heavily on concrete language to bring his messages home to the American public. Notice how he makes the problems with the economy concrete in a speech to a joint session of Congress in late 2009:[9]

> When I spoke here last winter, this nation was facing the worst economic crisis since the Great Depression. We were losing an average of 700,000 jobs per month. Credit was frozen. And our financial system was on the verge of collapse.
>
> As any American who is still looking for work or a way to pay their bills will tell you, we are by no means out of the woods. A full and vibrant recovery is still many months away. And I will not let up until those Americans who seek jobs can find them—(applause)—until those businesses that seek capital and credit can thrive; until all responsible homeowners can stay in their homes. That is our ultimate goal. But thanks to the bold and decisive action we've taken since January, I can stand here with confidence and say that we have pulled this economy back from the brink.

Emphasizing the economic problems of his early administration and the drastic action that he had taken to prevent further collapse, Obama spelled out for us in specific ways how his administration was intent on saving the country from financial collapse. Also note his use of intense, animated language. Can you identify specific words in his speech that make the message come alive?

- **Choose the active voice.** Grammatical voice refers to the relationship between the subject of a sentence and the action of the verb. In the passive voice, the subject receives the action. In the active voice, the subject performs the action. Consider the following statements:

  ✔ *Passive:* The meeting was facilitated by Larry.

  ✔ *Active:* Larry facilitated the meeting.

  ✔ *Passive:* The car was repaired by a highly qualified mechanic.

  ✔ *Active:* A highly qualified mechanic repaired the car.

  ✔ *Passive:* The employees were criticized by an upper-level manager.

  ✔ *Active:* An upper-level manager criticized the employees.

  Which of the statements in each pair expresses the idea with greater strength? By definition, active voice is stronger than passive. Using active instead of passive voice makes your language more concise, more exciting, and more inviting. And it makes your message more credible and engaging. Use the active voice whenever you have important discussions, written or oral.

  For practice converting passive statements to active, intense ones, check out **VISUALIZE! PRACTICE! 2.1: Passive to Active & Intense**.

Speak to Include, Not Exclude

The cultural diversity in the United States is greater than that of any other nation in history. As citizens of a nation that values diversity, we Americans strive for justice, equality, and harmony among all people.

Visualize! Practice! 2.1:
Passive to Active & Intense

Brand New Images/Getty Images

But because of our diversity, we also often experience conflict and misunderstanding. We have to work hard to acknowledge, respect, and, when possible, adapt to others who may think, feel, and behave differently from ourselves. One way we can do this is to speak to *include,* not to alienate or *exclude.* There are many strategies that can help us to modify our verbal messages to show our respect for and acceptance of others.[10] Underlying all these strategies is the use of **bias-free language**.

- **Use the labels others choose to identify themselves.** Can you identify culturally sensitive alternatives to the following labels?
  - ✔ Handicapped
  - ✔ Retarded
  - ✔ Old people
  - ✔ Midgets
  - ✔ Crazy
  - ✔ Criminal
  - ✔ Cheap

  Some people use words and phrases like these in their everyday conversations. But the people who are described by these labels are likely to regard them as offensive or hurtful. It's more respectful and effective to use the names that people use for themselves. Even though some people complain that "politically correct" terminology is sometimes taken too far in this society, keep in mind that speaking inclusively will add to the positive impression you want to create.

- **Don't mention group membership unnecessarily.** If group membership is relevant to your message, then include it. For example, the statement "Sarah Palin was the first female Republican candidate for Vice President" highlights a historically significant fact. But when group membership is not important, don't mention it. For instance, how relevant is it to refer to your boss as a "female boss"? How about a Middle Eastern accountant, a white male clerk, a Mexican CFO?

- **Use parallel labels.** Use similar labels for comparable groups. *Men* and *women* are **parallel labels**, whereas *men* and *girls* are not. Yet the term *girls* is often used to refer to females well beyond childhood. Consider the non-parallel labels *whites* and *nonwhites.* Why do some African Americans, Latinos, Asian Americans, and Native Americans dislike the label "nonwhite"?

- **Avoid using masculine terms as generics.** Refrain from using masculine pronouns as generic terms to refer to both women and men. *He* and *him* are not synonyms for *she* and *her.* It's easy enough to avoid the generic male pronoun by using the plural form instead (*they* or *them*) or pairing feminine and masculine pronouns (*she or he*). It's also inadvisable to use a false generic like *mankind* to refer to all human beings or *policemen* to refer to all law enforcement officers. It's better to talk about *people* or *humans* and *police officers.*

Speak to Stimulate Others' Interest in You

Certain words and phrases can reduce the perceived physical and psychological distance between communicators. We call this **verbal immediacy**. We often think of immediacy in terms of nonverbal behaviors, such as standing close to someone or maintaining eye contact. However, you can also develop immediacy verbally, for example, by using first names instead of titles or praising others.[11] When you use verbal immediacy strategies, you can trigger feelings of positive affect or liking and perceptions of closeness and inclusion. The more immediate you are with others, the more they will find you an attractive, friendly, and likeable communicator.[12]

Specific verbal immediacy strategies include

- asking questions
- initiating discussions
- replacing *I* and *you* with *we* and *us*
- being humorous
- soliciting feedback
- taking the time to communicate one on one
- sharing information about yourself (self-disclosure)
- using others' first names
- responding quickly and frequently
- praising, complimenting, and confirming others
- being attentive
- listening actively

People prefer to spend time with verbally immediate communicators because they find them warm and accepting, easy to talk to, and easy to understand. Using simple verbal immediacy strategies like these will help your colleagues feel closer to you and identify with you.

What are some other verbal strategies you can use to encourage others to like you? Explore some options in **VISUALIZE! PRACTICE! 2.2: Verbal Strategies to Create Immediacy**.

Visualize! Practice! 2.2:
Verbal Strategies to Create Immediacy

What Nonverbal Strategies Should You Use?

Verbal communication is clearly important in the workplace. Nonverbal strategies are equally important in managing others' impressions of you and developing positive relationships. In fact, few communication behaviors influence favorable impressions more than nonverbal immediacy behaviors. You probably already use a number of these nonverbal strategies, which can be as unwitting and spontaneous as distancing yourself from people you find unappealing. But once you become aware of how others perceive your nonverbal behaviors, you can begin to control these behaviors and, in turn, control how others perceive you.

Smile and Make Eye Contact to Connect

Making eye contact and using pleasant facial expressions are two of the most common nonverbal immediacy strategies. Smiling and looking directly at others communicate friendliness and approachability. Conversely, frowning and looking away communicate disregard and avoidance. Which communicator would you rather initiate contact with—someone who is smiling at you or someone who frowns and avoids eye contact?

Squaredpixels/iStockphoto.com

Dress to Fit In

People begin to form their impression of you before they even talk to you. They look you over, and they make judgments about how you look and what clothing you wear. Even if you believe that your attire has little to do with who you really are, many first impressions are based almost exclusively on personal appearance. Dressing neatly and professionally communicates credibility. And being well groomed shows others that you are a professional and someone to be respected.

Clothing is often associated with power and status. Historically, clothing has often distinguished people of higher and lower status. In fact, clothing is so strongly associated with rank that most employers have a dress code, ranging from formal to business casual to casual. Clothing can signal *who* you are, *where* you are in the organization (or where you would like to be), and *how* you feel at a given time.

Clothing can even affect your ability to obtain a good job. A job applicant's clothing can indicate status, power, and ability and can affect the outcome of the interview. As a recent study indicates, clothing is especially critical for women who lack the financial resources to buy appropriate job-related clothing. As a result, a number of programs have been designed in the past few years to provide office attire to poor women entering the workforce.[13] For example, the international nonprofit organization Dress for Success has helped thousands of disadvantaged women worldwide find and keep jobs by providing them with professional attire and a network of support.[14]

A quick search at Amazon.com reveals over five thousand books advising employers and employees how to dress for success in the workplace. With all the books, online sources, and other references available, it's not difficult to learn how to dress appropriately for the workplace. Advice ranges from how to select professional-looking pants, shirts, and suits to how to wear makeup, jewelry, belts, and shoes. Recommendations are typically based on types of company culture, dress codes, or norms. Dressing for success also requires good grooming, such as keeping clean, smelling good, and wearing an appropriate hairstyle. Whether you think appearance is important or irrelevant, people often make assumptions about your credibility and personal characteristics based on what you wear. Looking put together and dressing professionally are important aspects of fitting into a workplace.

For practice determining what is appropriate business casual attire for women and men, complete **VISUALIZE! PRACTICE! 2.3: Dress for Success**.

Gesture to Illustrate and Emphasize

The study of gestures used to communicate meaning is called **kinesics**. Gestures can be classified as four types: adaptors, affect displays, emblems, and illustrators.

- **Adaptors** are unintentional hand, arm, leg, or other body movements used to reduce stress or relieve boredom. Examples include chewing on a pencil, tossing your hair, drumming your fingers, and jiggling your foot. Most of us are unaware of our adaptors, yet others are quick to notice them. Adaptors can communicate the impression that you are nervous, insecure, or unprepared—messages you probably do not want to convey. Learn to be aware of and minimize your adaptors. They are not your friends.

- Some nonverbal actions or behaviors substitute for verbal language. People may express meaning with **affect displays** by using facial expressions to communicate disgust, hostility, or joy. **Emblems** are more straightforward and have a direct verbal translation that is widely understood, such as twirling an index finger in the air like a lasso, blowing a kiss, or cupping an ear and leaning forward. Although an emblem may seem perfectly clear to you, not everyone may understand it. Some emblems are ambiguous or so new that people in a different age group or a different part of the country may not be familiar with them. And keep in mind that the meanings of emblems can vary from culture to culture.

- **Illustrators** are hand and arm movements that enhance or reinforce your verbal messages. An example is counting aloud while putting up one finger, then two. What nonverbal illustrators could you use to enhance the following verbal messages? *p. 40* →

Visualize! Practice! 2.3:
Dress for Success

Putting **Your Skills** to Work

Take a moment to think about why you dress the way you do. Are you trying to fit in? If so, what group do you want to fit in with? Are you trying to be provocative or shocking? Why? However you dress, consider how the way you look influences the impression you make on people who are important to you. Now imagine you have your dream job. To fit in with your dream colleagues and make a good impression, do you feel you'd have to change anything about how you look now?

A-Digit/istockphoto.com

Pete Souza/White House/Handout/CNP/Corbis

In many Middle Eastern cultures, pointing the sole of your shoe at someone is an insulting emblem. Consequently, this photo of President Obama talking to Israeli Prime Minister Netanyahu caused a lot of controversy in the Middle East.

VERBAL MESSAGES

✓ Come on, let's go.

✓ Be quiet.

✓ Wait, just a minute.

✓ My raise was this big.

✓ Did you get my point?

✓ No!

✓ I'm glad to meet you!

Because illustrators communicate nonverbally what you're saying verbally, they're used for emphasis or to add intensity. Illustrators help to create the impression that you are dynamic and decisive. To demonstrate how helpful illustrators can be, try giving directions somewhere without using them.

Recognize the Implications of Time

Some people are always late, no matter how hard they try to be on time. Others are so punctual that they tend to be annoying. Our society is preoccupied with time—just count the number of clocks in your home, car, and office, and don't forget to include your laptop and cell phone. And yet, our individual tolerances for early or late schedules are remarkably different. For example, "owls" work best at night and drag in late to work in the morning. They have difficulty relating to "sparrows" who wake up early, even without an alarm.[15] In addition, owls become more functional as the day wears on, whereas sparrows are ready for a nap by mid-afternoon.

The study of **chronemics** encompasses not only our rules, individual beliefs, and personality differences associated with time but also how people schedule what they do and what time means to them. For example, what does a manager mean when he says the meeting will begin at noon? Most people would assume that the meeting will start promptly at 12:00, but others might assume that the meeting will include lunch and social time first, which would affect their arrival time.

Misunderstandings about time are commonplace because of such imprecise meanings and because of our individual attitudes about time. Some people take time literally. When they say, "Just a minute," they are asking you to wait exactly one minute. Others might think of time more flexibly and expand that minute to an hour or more.

Organizations can also be imprecise about meanings associated with time. For example, some organizations offer employees flextime, or flexible starting and quitting times with emphasis on project completion rather than hours clocked. But some organizations that offer flextime may expect employees to put in the same degree of face time that they would if they worked a regular schedule, requiring them to be seen and available whenever needed. Given this conflict between policy and expectations, misunderstandings are likely to occur.

Even if we realize people have different attitudes about time, we tend to judge other people's punctuality by our own personal time preferences. For example, managers who are highly punctual are likely to be intolerant of employees who are late.

For more about time in the workplace, see **MODULE 15: How Do I Manage Time as a New Professional?**

Use Your Voice to Mean What You Say

As you've no doubt experienced, *how* you say something can be as important as *what* you say. Your voice often communicates your emotions and state of mind, such as whether you are happy, sad, confident, nervous, bored, or angry. The study of nonverbal uses of the voice is called **vocalics**. Nonverbal cues like pitch, tone, rate, volume, and accent all make a difference in how verbal messages are interpreted. Based on vocalics, we assign personal and social qualities to people who talk differently than we do, such as status, regional affiliation, intelligence, laziness, and level of education. What attributes might you assign to a co-worker who has a Southern drawl? How about to someone who talks rapidly and with a Brooklyn accent?

We typically prefer a speaker who uses a lot of vocal variety, because variations in volume, pitch, and rate help convey meaning. Varying vocal cues also keeps us alert and attentive and helps us discern what the speaker finds important and unimportant. Paying careful attention to your vocal variety will give you greater control over how others perceive what you are trying to say.

Perhaps no other vocal variation has more impact than *pause time,* or the strategic use of silence. A pregnant pause before or after a phrase can add special meaning and emphasis. Many communicators feel awkward using pause time and fill the gaps with "uh," "er," and "you know," which only distracts from their message.

Learn to be comfortable with silence and use it to your advantage. For example, use a lengthy pause before you begin a meeting or some other meaningful work encounter. Stop and pause immediately before you intend to say something especially important or memorable. Take off your glasses, if you wear them. Lean forward. Look at everyone in the room. Then proceed. You will find that pause time captures everyone's attention and builds suspense.

Sit, Walk, and Stand to Communicate Confidence and Attitude

Sitting up straight, walking with purpose, and standing tall while pulling your shoulders back and your stomach in all communicate self-confidence and a particular attitude. In fact, the word *attitude* originally referred to posture, particularly a defensive posture

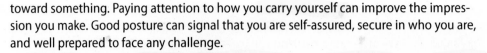

toward something. Paying attention to how you carry yourself can improve the impression you make. Good posture can signal that you are self-assured, secure in who you are, and well prepared to face any challenge.

Recent research reveals that good posture has a positive effect on us as well as others.[16] Researchers discovered that people who were told to sit up straight were more likely to believe what they wrote about their qualifications for a job than those who slumped over the desk. (Imagine the implications of this research for test-taking. Would you be more confident about your answers on a mid-term exam if you were sitting up straight while taking the test?) Self-assurance comes not only from your thoughts and attitudes but also from how you carry yourself. The better the posture, the more confident you appear—and the more confident you become.

Value Others' Personal Space to Show Respect

Space and distance are among the most subtle aspects of nonverbal communication. Both can influence others' impressions of us. The study of meanings associated with the use of space and distance is called **proxemics**. The two significant uses of space in the workplace are territoriality and personal space.[17]

Territoriality refers to fixed or semifixed space that you claim or stake out as your own. Some territory belongs exclusively to you. Other territory you share with friends or family. And still other territory is only temporarily yours. Regardless of the level of exclusivity, people respond to invasion of their territory as if they have a right to that space. Your primary territory at work may be your office or a particular leather chair or desk. Should others encroach on your rightful domain, you may feel frustrated, angry, or even hostile. Examples of shared and temporary forms of territory are a favorite parking spot or a particular seat at a conference table. Even though you have no rightful claim to such public territories, you may behave as if you do.

Respecting others' territory in the workplace is very important. When it comes to office space, people become very territorial about invaders. So when you enter a co-worker's office, knock and ask permission to enter, don't "borrow" a notepad without asking, never rummage through someone's desk, and do not log onto someone else's computer. When visiting someone in her office, do not assume that it's okay to eat your lunch there, do not move things around, and do not leave anything behind.

Personal space refers to the immediate zone you carry around with you during your daily interactions with others. It's like a bubble that contracts and expands as you move, depending on where you are, who you are with, and what you are doing. According to anthropologist Edward T. Hall, the degree of personal space you allow with others is determined by the nature of your relationship, the topic being discussed, and factors such as gender, age, and cultural background.[18]

The more intimate the relationship, the less personal space people require. For work relationships, we expect others to give us between 4 and 8 feet—what is commonly referred to as the social or consultative zone. A space greater than 8 feet typifies the formal relationship between a speaker and an audience. At the other end of the spectrum, a space smaller than 4 feet implies a personal relationship, such as a friendship. It is difficult to discuss topics of any intimacy across more than 3 or 4 feet, so communicators move closer to do so.

In the workplace, people provide their superiors, such as their supervisors, with more personal space than they do their peers or subordinates.[19] The personal space increases as

MIXA/Alamy

the status difference increases. So you probably give the company president more space than you do your immediate supervisor. Moreover, only the person with higher status and more power can decide to decrease personal space. In other words, your boss may choose to move closer to you to discuss a personal issue with you—you cannot be the first to move closer. Similarly, your boss may choose to invade your office by leaving a file on your desk or by using your telephone—you may not do the same in her office. Violating this rule of personal space can result in some kind of sanction against the offender. It's safest to remember that the appropriate distance between two people is almost always determined by the more powerful person in the relationship.

Touch Judiciously

Touching others in the workplace is touchy business.[20] Touch is perhaps the most misunderstood form of communication, with all sorts of interpretations assigned to it. Social scientists refer to the study of touch as **haptics**. How touch is interpreted or understood is due to many factors, including personality, gender, culture, status, and context. Who gets touched, where, when, and how make a difference in the meaning that is assigned to the act.

Touching can transmit messages with meanings ranging from the most tender and significant to those that are offensive. Shaking hands or gently gripping the forearm are common at work and are generally understood to be welcoming and acceptable. But holding hands or extending a hug may raise eyebrows!

Some people are touch avoiders, who would never touch a stranger or a co-worker and who feel uncomfortable with gratuitous pats, hugs, and kisses. Others are touch approachers, who just can't seem to wait to get their hands on people.[21] Which type are you? Because everyone has a different touch threshold, you would be wise not to assume that everyone at work will welcome an occasional pat on the back, touch on the arm, or a warm hug.

In addition, the cultural norms that govern touching differ from country to country. The United States is a "low-contact culture," and Americans seem particularly nervous about or avoidant of touch. Even so, there are cultural and ethnic groups in the country that are just the opposite, who appreciate and value touch.[22] Can you think of examples of ethnic groups in the United States that tend to be touch approachers? Touch avoiders?

Likewise, touch between men and women may be unwanted or misunderstood. When women touch clients or colleagues, they risk being misperceived as flirtatious. Female employees can interpret touch by a male supervisor as threatening. The courts are full of sexual harassment suits because co-workers were insensitive to one another's personal boundaries. (Chapter 5 has further discussion of sexual harassment in the workplace.)

Status also plays an important role in who initiates touch, with higher-status people much more likely to touch lower-status people than the reverse.[23] Even so, both managers and employees are cautioned against touching that goes beyond a handshake, a hand on the shoulder, or a pat on the back. Take heed: Be thoughtful about your use of touch at work.

For more about effective and considerate nonverbal communication at work, see **MODULE 4: What Do I Need to Know about Business Etiquette?** For more about nonverbal communication and video interviews, see **MODULE 14: How Do I Prepare for Phone and Video Interviews?**

By now, you may better appreciate why Mary's suspicions that her boss doesn't like her could become a real problem for her. Her professional success depends on how she presents herself. She would be wise to give serious thought to Steve's question: "Why do you suppose the boss doesn't value you, Mary? What do you think you're doing wrong?" Moreover, she must recognize that changing her boss's negative impression about her will be difficult, requiring many attempts, persistence, and time. But by implementing a plan that includes various verbal and nonverbal communication strategies, Mary may be able to influence her boss to regard her more favorably.

When you think about your own self-presentation as a professional, remember that it's better to make a good first impression than it is to try to change a negative impression later on. Determine what impressions you would like to cultivate in your work environment, and remember that your ability to manage those impressions depends on what you say and how you say it. You now have at your disposal a number of simple, effective verbal and nonverbal strategies that will allow you to make the best possible impression.

Use your Speech Communication CourseMate for *Business & Communication in a Digital Age* for quick access to the electronic resources that accompany this text. These resources include

Study tools that will help you assess your learning and prepare for exams (*digital glossary, key term flash cards, review quizzes*).

Activities and assignments that will help you hone your knowledge and build your communication skills throughout the course (*Visualize! Practice!, Weigh In!, Check This Out, and Link Out activities; modules; review questions*).

Media resources that will help you explore communication concepts online (*Enhanced eBook*), develop your speech outlines (*Speech Builder Express 3.0*), watch and critique videos of sample speeches and communication situations (*interactive video activities*), upload your speech videos for peer reviewing and critique other students' speeches (*Speech Studio online speech review tool*), and download chapter review so you can study when and where you'd like (*Audio Study Tools*).

Key Points

- From the verbal and nonverbal messages you send, others form impressions of you. This process is called presentation of self.

- You can influence the initial impressions your co-workers and supervisors have of you. This process is called impression management.

- To present yourself effectively in the workplace, select the impression you want to make and then make a plan. An effective plan includes these steps:
  - ✔ Carefully assess the person you are presenting yourself to.
  - ✔ Be honest about who you are.
  - ✔ Consider the physical setting or context of the encounter.
  - ✔ Use all available communication channels to get your positive qualities across.
  - ✔ Look closely for subtle feedback messages.

- Make the effort to change another person's negative impression of you if you feel the benefits of doing so outweigh the difficulty of the process.

- There are several verbal strategies you can use to encourage others to form a good impression of you:
  - ✔ Speak to be understood by speaking simply, avoiding unnecessary jargon and acronyms, and using clear and specific language.
  - ✔ Speak to show strength by using power language, animated and intense language, concrete examples, and the active voice.
  - ✔ Speak to include rather than exclude by using bias-free language. Use the terms others use to identify themselves, don't mention group membership unnecessarily, use parallel labels, and avoid masculine terms as generics.
  - ✔ Speak to stimulate others' interest in you by using verbal immediacy strategies to encourage positive feelings and perceptions of closeness and inclusion.

- There are several nonverbal strategies you can use to encourage others to form a good impression of you.
  - ✔ Smile and make eye contact.
  - ✔ Dress appropriately to fit in.
  - ✔ Gesture to illustrate and emphasize, and avoid inappropriate or distracting gestures.
  - ✔ Recognize the implications of time.
  - ✔ Consider that how you say something is as important as what you say.
  - ✔ Use good posture to communicate confidence.
  - ✔ Show respect for other people's personal space.
  - ✔ Touch judiciously and appropriately.

Key Terms

acronyms (33)	**jargon** (32)
adaptors (39)	**kinesics** (39)
affect displays (39)	**parallel labels** (36)
bias-free language (36)	**personal space** (42)
chronemics (40)	**power language** (34)
emblems (39)	**presentation of self** (27)
haptics (43)	**proxemics** (42)
illustrators (39)	**territoriality** (42)
imagery (34)	**verbal immediacy** (36)
impression management (27)	**vocalics** (41)

Questions for Critical Thinking and Review

1. Research on impression formation suggests that we consider some attributes more salient than others when we form our perceptions of a person. Name three attributes that are salient to you in your initial encounters with others. To what extent do you think your focus on those attributes is prejudicial or unfair? How might you use this realization to more accurately assess others?

2. Managers often judge their employees on how they use time. For example, we once had a colleague, Elizabeth, who always arrived late to work and left early. Her performance appraisal was negatively affected by her lack of punctuality, even though she was efficient and got the job done. How do you suppose the manager felt about time? How did the manager's and Elizabeth's attitudes about time probably differ? How are status and time related? What advice might you have given Elizabeth to help her change her manager's negative impression of her?

3. When Mary complained to Steve that her boss may not like her, Steve's first impulse was to ask, "Why do you care, Mary, whether your boss likes you?" Use what you now know about impression formation and management to answer Steve's question.

4. Research on proxemics reveals that gender influences personal space needs.

    a. Who needs more space: Boys or girls? Women or men?

    b. Who requires more space: Male–male pairs or female–female pairs?

    c. When a man and a woman who are strangers approach each other on the sidewalk, who gives up personal space first: The man or the woman?

    d. Who is more likely to face an interaction partner: A woman or a man?

    e. Who is more likely to react negatively, even aggressively, to crowding: Men or women?

    f. Who is more likely to be a space invader: Children or adults?[24]

    (See the answers to these questions at the bottom of this page.)

5. People often have difficulty remembering others' names. What are some strategies you use for remembering the name of someone you just met? How important is a name to someone? If we know a person's name is important, why is it so difficult for us to recall names?

6. In the last five years or so, many workplaces have opted out of casual Fridays and re-instituted more formal dress codes. Why do you suppose employers granted casual-dress days in the first place? What reasons might companies give for requiring more formal dress at work? What impressions are created with business dress codes, and how might those impressions influence not just clients and customers but also the employees themselves? For a comedic look at this issue, you might watch Season 5, Episode 24 of *The Office*, "Casual Friday."

a. Males do, whether they are boys or men. Men are known to expand, and women seem to contract. Why do you think this is?

b. Male–male pairs require more space. Why do you think this is?

c. The woman is more likely to move aside. Why do you suppose this is the case?

d. A woman. What does more directly facing your partner communicate to others?

e. Men. Why is that?

f. Children are more likely to invade everyone's space. Why do you suppose this is so?

Art Kowalsky/Alamy

Chapter Learning Objectives

After completing this chapter, you should be able to

- Understand how listening can affect your success at work.
- Identify what good listeners do differently from poor listeners.
- Differentiate between active and passive listening.
- Appreciate the reciprocal listening responsibilities of senders and receivers.
- Recognize that good listening begins with your self-concept.
- Hear your self-talk and manage its filtering effects.
- Prepare a listening plan to increase your effectiveness at work.

See also the modules that are relevant to this chapter:

 1: How Do I "Get In and Fit In" to My Organization's Unique Culture?
14: How Do I Prepare for Phone and Video Interviews?

Module 1:
How Do I "Get In and Fit In" to My Organization's Unique Culture?

Module 14:
How Do I Prepare for Phone and Video Interviews?

Harry is having some communication problems with a rather difficult co-worker named Fred.

Fred is one of those guys who argues over everything. Even the simplest idea triggers a squabble. After complaining about Fred to his friend Mary, he tells her, "Maybe I'll talk to Hector about the problem I'm having with Fred."

"Why talk to Hector? He's not even your boss, Harry. What can he do to help?"

"Hector listens, that's why. He's attentive, he asks good questions, and he seems genuinely concerned about me and what I do around here. I consider him a good listener and mentor."

"What does Hector do that I don't do?"

"It's hard to put into words, Mary. With Hector, I always get the sense that what I'm saying is the most important thing on his mind at that moment. I have his total and complete attention. When I come to him with a problem, he makes time for me. I never feel rushed."

"And I don't do that for you?"

"Honestly? Few people are really good at listening. Hector is a really good listener. It's hard to put into words, but it's a special skill!"

Hector sounds like one of those rare individuals who knows how to make people feel as though no one is more important than they are and no issue more pressing than the one they are talking about. Making people feel like they have all your attention and that they have it for as long as they like is worth money.

Harry may have some difficulty describing why Hector is so effective as a listener, but like most of us, he probably has little problem spotting poor listeners.[1] When employees at a Midwestern petroleum plant were asked to differentiate good from poor listeners at work, most could readily agree who were the bad listeners, but good listeners were much more difficult to identify. In explanation, the researchers claimed that "bad listeners were easy targets. That is, when you're bad, you're bad, and everyone knows it."[2] One of the reasons good listeners were harder to identify might be that there are so few of them.

This chapter examines how listening can affect your success at work. By understanding how good listeners differ from poor listeners, you can begin to evaluate how well *you* listen. Your ability to listen well begins with your self-image: How you see yourself and how you feel about yourself at work influence what you hear and how you interpret it. Although your listening effectiveness depends primarily on how well you listen to messages you receive, both senders and receivers are reciprocally responsible for listening. If they know their listening responsibilities, both senders and receivers are more likely to understand each other's messages accurately. To help you improve your listening skills in the workplace, this chapter ends with a step-by-step plan you can follow to fulfill your listening responsibilities.

Just How Important Is Listening at Work—Really?

Academics and business professionals alike rank listening as one of the most important skills for professional success:[3]

- We devote over half of our communication time to listening—we listen to people talking face to face and over the phone as well as listening to radio, television, and music.[4]
- With recent technological advances, including computer-mediated discourse, voice-mail, videoconferencing, and Skype, we now have more choices about how to listen.[5]
- Research reveals that employees' work performance and communication competence are judged largely on their ability to listen effectively. Moreover, employers rank listening as one of the most important skills when they are making decisions about entry-level employment and promotions.[6]
- Study after study demonstrates the importance of listening during the interview process.[7]

Perhaps no profession relies on listening skills more than the health care industry.[8] Effective listening is a significant predictor of patient satisfaction and patient compliance: Patients report greater satisfaction with oncologists who actively listen when making treatment decisions, they are more willing to carry out prescribed treatments, and they are less likely to file lawsuits against physicians who have good bedside manners, which, of course, includes empathic listening skills.[9] Moreover, both the doctor–nurse relationship and the nurse–patient relationship are influenced by good communication skills, with listening cited as the most important.[10] On the flip side, poor listening skills in the health care profession can be potentially life-threatening. In one study, for instance, physicians interrupted within the first 18 seconds in almost 70 percent of patient interviews. As a result, in 77 percent of those interviews, the true reason for the patient's visit was never revealed![11] Fully two-thirds of malpractice cases are tied to breakdowns in communication, with 13 percent of the families claiming that their physician would not or did not listen.[12]

In fact, it's hard to conceive of any profession where listening isn't critical. Yet listening skills are missing from the curriculum in elementary, intermediate, and secondary schools as well as from most colleges. Course work in listening is not required in higher education, and even basic communication courses devote less than 10 percent of their instructional time to listening training.

Nonetheless, you stand to gain a great deal from learning how to listen effectively. Listening serves four different purposes: to acquire information, to screen and evaluate what you hear, to simply enjoy or relax, and to get along with others.

- **Listen to acquire information.** Some messages are more important than others. For example, when your supervisor explains how to put together the annual report, you listen carefully because you need the message content to carry out the task. But if your supervisor mentions that his relatives are visiting, you'll probably consider the message unimportant and dismiss it.

If a message is complex, we may need to hear it or some variation of it many times. Listening repeatedly helps us better comprehend and retain the information.

- **Listen to screen and evaluate what you hear.** If you tried to listen to every message that you're exposed to, you would certainly suffer information overload.[13] Indeed, many corporate surveys have found that information overload is a major problem for employees.[14] In the workplace, you must be able to sort through a daily flood of messages and select for more intense listening those that are accurate and important to you.

- **Listen to enjoy and relax.** Listening can also be recreational. Most of us enjoy listening to our iPods, watching and listening to TV, and socializing with our friends. At work, you probably engage in recreational listening whenever your job becomes too intense, difficult, or overwhelming—in other words, when you need a break and a diversion. Engaging in this type of relaxed listening is useful and important for mental health, but it may become problematic if you are too relaxed about listening to discussions that are important to getting a task accomplished.

- **Listen to get along with others.** It's not an exaggeration to say that your personal and professional success depends on how effectively you listen. To win friends and influence others, you need to listen well. Other people appreciate it when you listen attentively because that signals your interest in them and what they have to say. At work, you need to pay attention to what co-workers say and participate actively in conversations.

It pays to polish your listening skills. Effective listening allows you to make a good impression in job interviews, to better understand work assignments, and to turn in high-quality work. In addition, listening effectively helps you establish and maintain

Radius/SuperStock

Visualize! Practice! 3.1:
Does Listening Include Talking?

Check This Out 3.1:
How Well Do You Listen?

good relationships with your co-workers, clients, and bosses.[15] And your ability to listen well will have benefits for your social and personal life, helping you to meet people, enjoy the company of friends, maintain family ties, and build intimate relationships.

To get a sense of your listening abilities, listen to the audio provided in **CHECK THIS OUT 3.1: How Well Do You Listen?** Do you listen as effectively as you think you do?

What Do Good Listeners Do Differently from Poor Listeners?

It's easy to recognize when someone is listening to you rather than tuning you out. Poor listeners look disinterested, and they probably believe that listening just happens. In contrast, good listeners look like they are listening, and they understand that listening is an active process that takes effort. Good listening, then, implies a deliberate use of effective listening behaviors.

Take a minute to check out some specific nonverbal and verbal listening behaviors in **VISUALIZE! PRACTICE! 3.1: Does Listening Include Talking?** Which of these behaviors do you implement when you're listening to others?

Good Listeners Make an Effort to Listen Actively

Passive listening is what most people do. They receive messages on autopilot, without exerting much, if any, effort and without concern for what is being communicated. People listen passively for any number of reasons, ranging from boredom, disinterest, and apathy to fatigue and illness.

Active listening is the process of making a conscious effort to pay full attention to and comprehend the message being communicated. When you listen actively, you not only increase your ability to understand the message, but you also encourage the sender's enthusiasm and appreciation.

Putting Your Skills to Work

Do your friends come to you first when they have a problem they'd like to talk about? Do others see you as being a concerned and caring person? Are your teachers or bosses impressed that you don't need to be told twice to get things done right? You may be a good listener, and people respond positively to your interest in them and what they say. Use this chapter to help you hone the skills you already have!

A-Digit/istockphoto.com

Some people and topics may be inherently more interesting to us, and thus, it's easier to listen to them actively. But you won't be interested in every message that you need to comprehend. To become a more effective listener at work, try to find at least one interesting thing about each person you interact with. This will help you listen more actively. And once you begin to listen to someone actively, you cannot help but become more interested in what is being communicated.

Active listening is especially important for disagreeable or uncomfortable interactions. Listening well is often a beginning point to resolving misunderstandings, disagreements, and even conflicts in the workplace.

Good Listeners Look Like They're Listening

Active listening is not always visible. What, then, are the actions, expressions, and other signs that tell you someone is a good listener?[16]

- **Good listeners focus their full concentration on the communicator.** Poor listeners are easily distracted, allowing their attention to wander. During a face-to-face encounter with a colleague, a good listener will shut off his phone; a poor listener will take the call every time. A good listener will turn away from the computer screen to listen; a poor listener will multitask with instant messages.

- **Good listeners use their bodies to communicate openness and receptivity.** Poor listeners use their bodies to close off exchanges. Whereas good listeners will sit with arms open, lean forward, and face the communicator, poor listeners might cross their arms, lean backward, and look away from (or through) the communicator.

- **Good listeners use facial expressions to communicate interest.** Poor listeners look bored. Good listeners will nod their head, make eye contact, and smile appropriately to encourage further talk time. Poor listeners might look bored, unhappy, or preoccupied, showing disinterest in both the communicator and the message.

Looking like a good listener contributes to effective listening in at least two ways: First, if you're a good listener, you reward the person communicating with you. When the person talking to you perceives you to be a good listener, he is likely to feel better appreciated and understood. He'll feel encouraged by the encounter and will continue the conversation. And if you seem confused or ask for clarification, he knows to make the effort to adjust the message. Thus, accurate exchanges are more likely with good than with poor listeners.

Second, good listening behaviors actually compel you to listen better. Looking motivated and making an effort to listen has a way of transforming even the most unwilling listener to one who is engaged in the exchange.

To illustrate, Sharon, a customer relations representative for the last twenty years, is showing signs of burnout with her job. Lately, she's discovered that the unhappy customers are starting to sound alike. Based on what you've learned about listening, what would you recommend?

You might advise Sharon to behave in ways that show she is actively listening. A deliberate attempt to change her listening behaviors is key to her transformation. If Sharon starts to look like she's listening, she will not only *appear* to be a good listener, but she will in fact become a good listener again.

track5/iStockphoto.com

Who Is Responsible for Listening?

Up to this point, we have talked about listening primarily as something that receivers do. This is not the whole picture. Even though receivers carry most of the burden for listening, effective communication requires that both senders and receivers adapt and respond to one another. Both parties share the responsibility for good listening.

Successful adaptation to each other in a communication encounter involves **sender–receiver reciprocity**.[17] Feedback tells a sender how the receiver is interpreting the transmitted message (Chapter 1). When both communicators simultaneously send and receive messages and constantly adapt to each other's feedback, they are engaging in sender–receiver reciprocity.

To illustrate, let's assume that you begin to explain to your assistant how to upgrade his word-processing software. He perks up and listens, causing you to become more systematic in your explanation. You make a joke about Internet search engines, and he grins, which makes you smile. If he says something you like, you nod in agreement, which motivates him to provide more of the same kinds of comments. Or the interaction may go another way, with your assistant mentally formulating a rebuttal to your reasons for upgrading his software again. Anticipating his rebuttal, you may work at incorporating counterarguments into your message.

Senders Are Responsible

As the sender of a message, you have several responsibilities:

- **Know what content you want to communicate before you actually say it.** Have you ever noticed how some people seem to leave no thought unuttered? They talk and talk with little thought to what they are saying, how they say it, and most importantly, whether they should say it. Poorly designed messages can be confusing and unwelcome. We cannot be expected to listen carefully to senders (or managers) who give no thought to the messages they transmit. For example, some bosses require employees to do things that they have never done themselves, so they fail to fully understand all that is involved in the assignment.

- **Carefully consider the way the message should be communicated.** The way a message is communicated affects the way the message is received. The sender needs to select the way to send the message that will best help the receiver interpret its full and nuanced meanings. This consideration is particularly important when email is one of the possibilities. Emails are limited to only the words on the page. A phone conversation or an office visit may be more appropriate for complex or sensitive messages that might require feedback, repetition, and nonverbal cues.

- **Ensure that the message is appropriate for the context or occasion.** The context can control both how a message is interpreted and whether it will be listened to at all. Whereas a discussion about the merits of the generation-skipping transfer tax may be appropriate for a lawyer's or accountant's office, it would not be for a wedding toast or a PTA meeting. Similarly, disclosing a message about your wild weekend in Vegas could be interpreted negatively at the office.

- **Design the message with the particular receivers in mind.** Senders who give no thought to the receivers of their message may use words that their receivers cannot understand, phrasings that are inappropriate, or even words that arouse suspicion or hostility. Using company acronyms and technical jargon when conversing with a prospective client makes little sense. Relating a dirty joke to a casual co-worker may incite disdain and undermine the sender's reputation. In short, insensitive and offensive language significantly reduces listening effectiveness.

- **Be mindful about the possible implications of the message.** Senders must consider the consequences of a message before they transmit it. An old saying is that "you can't unring that bell." When we say the wrong thing, our message is seriously undermined. For instance, a supervisor who constantly gives an employee critical negative feedback in an effort to get her to change may instead cause her to give up and quit. A patient may overhear a young internist complaining that if it weren't for sick people, she'd love her job. Too many times employees wish they could unsend an email. (An experimental feature of Gmail is the "undo send" button that allows the sender a few seconds to stop a message en route. If only communicators could do the same!)

Receivers Are Responsible

As the receiver of a message, you have several responsibilities:

- **Make an effort to listen.** Not all messages are created equal. For example, office gossip, although interesting, is much less important to attend to than discussions about the agenda for an upcoming staff meeting. Once you decide which messages are worth listening to, you can focus your attention on them.

    Choosing what messages to attend to is an ever-increasing challenge. More and more office workers rely on iPods or other portable music players to blot out unwanted noise (and messages) while they work. They claim it helps them to focus and increases their productivity. However, the music may interfere with their ability to listen actively on the phone or during face-to-face encounters. Similarly, workers are often distracted by messages that are delivered via smartphones like BlackBerry and iPhone. Checking

Weigh In! 3.1:
What Are Barriers to Listening?

text messages during a meeting while supposedly listening to co-workers is not only annoying to others but also decreases the potential for understanding decisions made during the meeting.

- **Consider the physical and social context of the message.** Context affects how a message is transmitted and received. Hearing about a possible promotion at a social gathering warrants a different interpretation and response than hearing about it in your supervisor's office. How seriously should you listen to a co-worker's praise of your accomplishments at a party in front of friends, as opposed to that same praise at a formal staff meeting? To be an effective listener, you need to be able to recognize the effect of the communication context to understand the meaning of a message.

- **Give the sender a fair hearing.** Messages sent by highly credible senders are almost universally listened to, but other senders may have a harder time. For example, you may be more inclined to listen to someone who has fifteen years' experience on a work project than to someone who just started. Even so, as a receiver you are obligated to give all senders a fair hearing. Someone can contribute meaningfully to a conversation even when she is new to the issue. You also need to make an effort to listen to senders who are difficult to listen to. In short, it's good idea to evaluate the content of the message before dismissing the sender out of hand.

- **Provide the sender with feedback.** Senders need to know whether they are communicating their intended message. As a receiver, you can provide nonverbal feedback with nods, smiles or frowns, gestures, and eye movements to signal what you understand or fail to understand. Verbal feedback—such as asking a question, expressing agreement or disagreement, or repeating in your own words what you understood the sender to say—helps the sender achieve greater accuracy.

- **Manage your response to the message being communicated.** Make every attempt not to overreact to what someone says or how she says it. Think about what she is saying before reacting to it. Inappropriate or preemptive responses can decrease listening effectiveness. If someone at work disagrees with your point of view, you might too quickly assume that he has it in for you, when in truth, he may simply disagree. Jumping in before the he is finished talking, becoming defensive or adversarial, yielding to your emotions, or hearing only what you want to hear are all barriers to your ability to listen and truly understand his message. If you can suspend judgment until you fully appreciate what he is saying, you will be a more responsible listener.

Senders and receivers together, then, jointly assume responsibility for effective listening. Like any good relationship, it takes two to make it work. Senders can do a great deal to help listeners understand, but they can't do it alone. Receivers must be active participants in the exchange, but they can't do it alone either. Senders and receivers have the responsibility to help each other make sense of their encounter.

A number of barriers prevent people from listening well. See what they are in **WEIGH IN! 3.1: What Are Barriers to Listening?** Find out which of these barriers both college business students and experienced business practitioners identify as the primary barriers.

tmarvin/iStockphoto.com

How Does Self-Talk Influence How You Listen to Others?

What you bring to an encounter influences your ability to listen. Perhaps nothing is more critical to understanding another person than the personal experiences and histories that you and that person bring to an interaction. What you each bring to the table—who you are, what you know, what you think about yourselves—affects how you interpret and make sense of what you hear.

Most interpersonal experts agree that communication begins with the self.[18] How you see yourself, or your **self-concept**, consists of a relatively stable set of perceptions that you hold about yourself. Evolved over your lifetime, your self-concept becomes defined through many of your social interactions with others. How your parents, friends, teachers, and co-workers respond to you gives you information about who you believe yourself to be. In turn, how you perceive yourself, everything you believe about yourself, affects how you filter or process incoming information.

Self-awareness, or knowing who you are conceptually, is influenced by how you evaluate your image of who you think you are. **Self-esteem** is how you feel about or evaluate the characteristics that define you—such as your intelligence, your capabilities, your physical appearance, and your professional, social, and personal roles. Do you see yourself as attractive? If so, *how* attractive? Do you think you are smarter than the average person? How capable are you to do the kind of work you want to do for a living? How successful are you? How successful do you believe you can be? How prestigious is your career choice? How meaningful is your life's work? How you answer these and similar evaluative questions reveals your self-esteem.

Evaluate yourself in relation to others with **WEIGH IN! 3.2: Are You Smarter Than the Average Person?** How self-aware are you?

Self-Concept and Self-Esteem Affect Self-Talk

Both self-concept and self-esteem influence not only your thoughts about yourself but also your self-talk. **Self-talk** is the internal dialogue you engage in throughout your daily activities. You are constantly thinking about and making sense of your actions and experiences as you encounter them. Self-talk is a running commentary on everything you do and experience. This inner voice also determines how you perceive and respond to every message you hear.

Some self-talk is positive; other self-talk is negative. Some self-talk is reasonable; other self-talk misrepresents reality. Whatever the nature of the self-talk, it influences how you listen, perceive, and process what others say and do. Consider how the following positive self-statements might filter the way you would respond to a performance appraisal by your immediate supervisor:

"I believe I am well qualified to do this job."

"I know more than he does about this."

"I'm good at what I do."

"One thing for sure, I'm a hard worker."

"I get along well with everybody at work."

"I'm glad I wore a suit today."

Weigh In! 3.2:
Are You Smarter Than the Average Person?

Next, consider how these negative self-statements might influence how you would respond to the performance appraisal:

"I hate what I'm wearing today."

"I wish I were a better writer."

"I'm too nervous. I'm sweating!"

"This interview can't be good."

"I should be looking for another job."

"I don't like this job anyway."

Self-Talk Affects How You Process Information

Knowing that self-talk influences how you interpret what you hear, you probably would choose to engage in positive self-talk during that hypothetical performance appraisal situation. When you engage in positive self-talk, you are more likely to seek understanding, be open to criticism, and make the suggested changes in how you work. With negative self-talk, on the other hand, you are likely to listen to the appraisal from a defensive perspective, selectively perceiving everything your supervisor says as personal attacks rather than as recommendations for improvement.

Because of the harmful effects of negative self-talk, authors of popular self-help books advocate replacing it with positive self-statements. Therapies, such as cognitive restructuring or cognitive behavior therapy, are designed to change people's cognitions through positive self-talk. And yet, recent research reveals that substituting positive for negative self-statements can backfire for some people and make them feel even worse.[19] Individuals with low self-esteem reported feeling worse when repeating positive self-statements than those who did not. Positive self-talk seemed to work only for those who already felt positively about themselves—those with high self-esteem. The researchers reasoned that people with low self-esteem may feel that positive self-talk is untrue and only underscores how awful they really are.

Replacing negative self-talk with positive self-statements works, then, for people with relatively high self-esteem. At times, however, you may be unable to successfully substitute positive thoughts for your negative self-talk. Whenever that happens, be aware that your negative talk is likely to distort what you hear. To be a better listener in such situations, try these strategies:

- Check for misunderstandings. Don't make assumptions.
- Check for objective facts versus personal opinions. Ask for clarification.
- Check your perception further. Ask for further explanation.
- Check your self-talk. Try to figure out why you are reacting defensively or with anger.
- Check to see how much of what you think you hear is a function of you, the sender, and how much is the message itself.
- Check to see if your responses are rational or emotional.

Becoming a better listener, then, requires recognizing how your self-talk influences your ability to process information accurately. Take a look at your self-talk to see whether you are listening effectively—or potentially distorting what you hear.

What's a Sound Listening Plan?

You can use all that you have learned about how to listen well to make a listening plan for yourself. This series of steps will improve your listening skills and your ability to interpret messages more accurately.[20]

Suppose you are going on a trip with your colleague Al, whose favorite topic is himself. You have a three-hour flight, and you're dreading it. But your boss has asked the two of you to go to a meeting related to a project you will be working on together. She'd like you to get to know Al because she feels you could learn a lot from him. This project is important to your career development, so you decide to create a listening plan to help you get the most out of your interactions with Al. These are your eight steps.

Step 1: Be Mindful of Your Self-Talk

Much self-talk makes sense and is worth heeding. If you know you have a long flight with Al and have to spend two days with him at a conference, it's reasonable to make these kinds of self-statements:

> "I need to prepare for this meeting."

> "I had better pull together some questions about our project so I have something to talk about with Al."

> "I'll need to select the right clothes to wear."

Other self-talk is positive and will help you face the flight and meeting with confidence and hope:

> "I'm able to connect really well with all kinds of people."

> "I've always done well at work, which is why my boss asked me to work on this project with an experienced person."

> "I can probably learn some useful things from Al."

Radius Images/Corbis

But some self-talk is negative and self-defeating and can undermine your ability to listen effectively:

"I'm going to say something stupid to Al and embarrass myself."

"Al will see me as too young and inexperienced to be taken seriously."

"I've never been to a meeting that's this important, and I don't know what to do when I get there."

Once you become aware of the content of your self-talk about this encounter, it will be easier to control your thoughts and behavior. By logically examining the basis for your self-talk, you can begin to pull away from the more negative comments and focus more on what you do well.

Step 2: Mentally Prepare to Listen

To be open to a sender and receptive to what he says, you often must warm up and prepare to listen. Anticipate the need to expend effort, assess the speaker's intent, be ready to give feedback, understand the implications of the context, and recognize the dangers of overreacting.

How might you mentally prepare yourself to listen to Al during your flight? You've brought your earbuds along, but you want to dedicate at least part of the trip to listening to him. Recognize that Al talks so much about himself because his primary communication objective is probably to impress others, including you. So why not let him? Be ready to give him affirmations and confirmations, both verbally and nonverbally. You may find that the context of close quarters while traveling is conducive to self-disclosure. You may learn that Al has much to offer as a person. You may even learn something you did not know about Al that you like. Mentally preparing to listen to Al will likely minimize any overreactions you might have and open up some possibilities for meaningful exchange.

Step 3: Concentrate and Commit to Listen

Ask yourself, "How much do I need to concentrate on what this person is trying to say?" A good listening plan requires that you listen actively rather than passively. But it also allows you to vary your level of concentration. Remember that you don't need to give all messages the same level of attention.

With Al, you may find that after some talk about his favorite topic (me, myself, and I), he moves on to another issue. He focuses on the upcoming meeting to market the company's product, the latest version of the Kindle ebook reader. Because this topic is highly relevant, your attention heightens and you recalibrate your level of effort to listen. You will likely move from passive to active listening. Making a commitment to listen to this new topic changes your level of concentration.

Step 4: Look Like You're Ready to Listen

Good listeners engage in specific overt behaviors that lead senders to believe they are truly listening. Give Al your full attention. Pull out the earbuds, put down your ebook, and focus on Al as if he were the only person on the plane. Turn your body in his direction. Sit with your arms uncrossed, lean forward in his direction, and make an effort to face Al. Now look like you are interested in what he is saying: Give him some eye contact, nod when you understand or agree, and smile when he needs reassurance.

Recall that active listening behaviors not only communicate interest to the sender but also ignite your interest in what he is saying. You will find that these active listening behaviors will both make Al happy and motivate your continued efforts to listen.

Step 5: Encourage the Other to Talk

You want to know all you can about the new Kindle before the meeting. Al will likely talk your ear off about it if you encourage him to do so. You can encourage him nonverbally with smiles and head nods. You can also use simple verbal prompts like "Go on" or "Tell me more."

Which of the following comments and questions will likely encourage Al's interactions with you, and which will discourage them?

"You always have such good ideas, Al."

"That's right."

"You need to think that through a little more."

"We've already tried that."

"Sure. I agree with you."

"Nope. I don't think so."

"Why do you think so?"

"I didn't know that."

"Yeah, I already know that."

Now can you think of comments that might discourage Al from returning to the topic he really wants to talk about, himself? Perhaps the best advice is not to say anything at all. Rather than encourage talk, simply remain quiet. Eventually, Al will stop talking and you can plug into your nano.

Step 6: Search Actively for Meaning

In this step you look for clues to what the person is trying to say. Take into account the person's background, personal and psychological characteristics, special mannerisms, possible connotative meanings, and implications of the context or setting. You might also consider experiences you may have had with this person, what others have told you about him or the issue, and what you already know about the topic. If you are unsure of the sender's meaning, provide feedback and request further details. Trying to understand the purposes of the sender's choice of words and phrases, nonverbal cues, and syntax or grammar may require that you understand cultural differences between you and the sender as well as grasp how your personal prejudices may distort the message.

Let's say Al brings up his favorite topic again. When searching actively for meaning in his message, you might take into account his level of insecurity and his high need for approval. Moreover, you might consider these facts: He is much older than you; he has been with the organization for more than thirty years; he ranks only as middle management; and he has few friends and even fewer family. What clues do these factors reveal about the underlying meaning in his messages with you? What other information might you gather to help you better interpret what he wants to communicate?

Step 7: Make an Effort to Keep Listening Actively

Sometimes as a conversation unfolds, the motivation to be an active listener subsides, and you start to lose focus and distort or misunderstand the message altogether. Most of us have experienced such difficulty while listening for any length of time.

Listening actively over time is a little like psyching yourself up to run a marathon. Many runners have lost races because they failed to sustain momentum to carry them through to the end. In the context of listening, if your level of listening deteriorates before the interaction is finished, you will likely miss something critical.

How might you do that with Al? Avoid slipping into a coma or a more passive manner of receiving. Remember that you need to understand what Al can tell you about marketing the new Kindle. Avoid daydreaming, and dismiss all distractions. This may require you to change your behavior: Sit up straight, lean forward, breathe in, breathe out, make eye contact, and make any other shifts to keep you awake and attentive.

Step 8: Suspend Judgment

The final step in a sound listening plan is to avoid prejudging the sender or the message. It is not easy to separate your feelings about a person and all of the labels and categories she or he might represent from the meanings inherent in a message. However, if you can recognize your personal biases, you can take them into account in your listening plan. With this insight, you can limit their influences on your objectivity.

Al is an easy target for biases. You have already determined things about him that you do not like: He is insecure and self-focused. You may have also labeled him a loser simply because he has no real power in the organization. Finally, you may find him old and out of touch with the newer technologies that excite you, a person who grew up in the digital age. Now how might you put aside all these biases so that you might more objectively attend to what Al has to say? Even old, insecure, and powerless employees can have valuable insights. By suspending judgment, you may find that Al has something to offer you and the company.

In overview, this eight-step listening plan may seem complex. Indeed, it may not be possible to put all eight steps into action at the same time. A sensible way to begin using the plan is to master one or two steps at first, and incorporate additional steps later. As you add more steps, knowing how to listen effectively will become second nature.

Putting Your Skills to Work

YOU POSE AN INTERESTING QUESTION!

It's not always easy to listen when you'd rather be doing something else. And it can be even tougher to put together a conscious plan to listen—after all, that takes a lot of effort. But you already use many of the skills outlined in this chapter's sound listening plan when you pay attention in a class you don't particularly like. You may be bored or confused, but you make an effort to listen anyway because you know the class is important to your education.

A-Digit/istockphoto.com

After reading this chapter, you should have more ideas about how to help Harry in our opening vignette explain why Hector is so special as a listener. Even though you have never seen or heard Hector communicate, you might predict that he assumes responsibility for listening. He regards listening as an active process. He knows how to convey, verbally and nonverbally, that he is listening. You might suspect that Hector's self-talk is positive, providing the kind of filter that helps him empathize with Harry, listen carefully and thoughtfully to Harry's concerns, and help Harry think things through. It's safe to say that Hector has probably worked through many of the steps of the sound listening plan.

Effective listening is one of the most important of all communication skills, but doesn't necessarily come naturally. Rather, people learn how to be good listeners. Learning to listen well takes time and practice. You can improve your listening skills by implementing the plan for strategic listening outlined in this chapter and by remembering that your ability to listen effectively is directly related to the amount of effort you exert.

Use your Speech Communication CourseMate for *Business & Communication in a Digital Age* for quick access to the electronic resources that accompany this text. These resources include

Study tools that will help you assess your learning and prepare for exams (*digital glossary, key term flash cards, review quizzes*).

Activities and assignments that will help you hone your knowledge and build your communication skills throughout the course (*Visualize! Practice!, Weigh In!, Check This Out, and Link Out activities; modules; review questions*).

Media resources that will help you explore communication concepts online (*Enhanced eBook*), develop your speech outlines (*Speech Builder Express 3.0*), watch and critique videos of sample speeches and communication situations (*interactive video activities*), upload your speech videos for peer reviewing and critique other students' speeches (*Speech Studio online speech review tool*), and download chapter review so you can study when and where you'd like (*Audio Study Tools*).

Key Points

- Listening is one of the most important skills for professional success.
- Listening serves four key purposes:
  - ✔ To acquire information
  - ✔ To screen and evaluate what you hear
  - ✔ To simply enjoy or relax
  - ✔ To get along with others

- Good listeners use two effective listening behaviors routinely:
  - ✔ They make an effort to listen actively. Active listening is the process of making a conscious effort to pay full attention to and comprehend what is being communicated.
  - ✔ They look like they're listening by focusing their full concentration on the communicator, using their bodies to communicate openness and receptivity, and using facial expressions to communicate interest.
- Poor listeners rely on several ineffective listening behaviors.
  - ✔ They listen passively, receiving messages without exerting much effort and without concern for what is being communicated.
  - ✔ They are distracted, and they multitask instead of focusing on the communicator, use their bodies to close off exchanges, look away from the communicator, and appear bored, unhappy, or preoccupied.
- Senders and receivers are both responsible for listening. When a sender and a receiver successfully adapt to each other during a communication encounter, they experience sender–receiver reciprocity.
- Senders of a message have the responsibility to
  - ✔ Know what content they want to communicate before they say it.
  - ✔ Carefully consider the way the message should be communicated.
  - ✔ Ensure that the message is appropriate for the context or occasion.
  - ✔ Design the message with the particular receivers in mind.
  - ✔ Be mindful about the possible implications of the message.
- Receivers of a message have the responsibility to
  - ✔ Make an effort to listen.
  - ✔ Consider the physical and social context of the message.
  - ✔ Give the sender a fair hearing.
  - ✔ Provide the sender with feedback.
  - ✔ Manage their response to the message being communicated.
- Your self-concept and self-esteem influence your self-talk, or the internal dialogue you engage in continuously. Your self-talk can be positive or negative, and it influences how you listen and perceive what others say and do.
- Your self-talk also influences how you process information. Being mindful of how your self-talk influences your ability to process information can help you become a better listener.
- A sound listening plan is a series of steps to improve your listening skills and your ability to interpret messages more accurately.
  - ✔ Step 1: Be mindful of your self-talk.
  - ✔ Step 2: Mentally prepare to listen.
  - ✔ Step 3: Concentrate and commit to listen.
  - ✔ Step 4: Look like you're ready to listen.
  - ✔ Step 5: Encourage the other to talk.

✔ Step 6: Search actively for meaning.

✔ Step 7: Make an effort to keep listening actively.

✔ Step 8: Suspend judgment.

Key Terms

active listening (52)

passive listening (52)

self-awareness (57)

self-concept (57)

self-esteem (57)

self-talk (57)

sender–receiver reciprocity (54)

Questions for Critical Thinking and Review

1. Why is it so hard to listen to some communicators but not to others? What can senders do to make listening worthwhile and easier for listeners?

2. Suppose you are leading a meeting and no one appears to be listening. What can you do? Suppose someone else is leading the meeting and no one is listening. Do you have a responsibility to help out this person? What can you do?

3. Do you have any stereotypes about people whose religious background is different from yours? How do you feel about people who smoke, who have chronic bad breath, or who never pay their fair share of a bill? Under what circumstances might these (or other) biases interfere with your ability to listen well to them? What can you do to prevent such barriers to listening?

4. To what extent is suspending judgment until after an entire message has been heard an ethical responsibility of listeners? What principle is involved here? Is it unethical to prejudge communicators? Can anyone truly suspend judgment of others?

5. Is it true that smart people make better listeners? Why or why not?

6. In this chapter you learned that good listeners *look* like they are listening. Can good listening behaviors be faked? Would faking it ever be a good thing? Have you ever faked good listening behaviors in the college classroom? Why did you do so? Do you believe your teacher knew you were faking it?

7. Do you usually listen to music while studying or working? Does music help or hinder your ability to concentrate? Would you call this kind of listening *active* listening or *passive* listening?

Chapter 4

The Job Interview:
How Do I Get the Job?

Chapter Outline

Why Do Organizations Need Job Interviews?

- Interviews Supply Organizations with a Competent Workforce
- Interviews Screen Applicants
- Interviews Match People with Organizations
- Interviews Yield Idiosyncratic Information about Applicants
- Interviews Minimize Turnover Rates

What's the Best Way to Interview Job Candidates?

- Prepare for the Interview
- Facilitate the Conversation
- Conclude on a Positive Note

What's the Best Way for Job Candidates to Interview?

- Prepare for the Interview
- Pay Attention to the Basics
- Make a Good First Impression
- Sell Yourself
- Check for a Good Fit
- End the Interview
- Follow Up after the Interview

What Will You Be Asked and How Should You Answer?

- Some Questions Are Predictable
- Some Questions Are Illegal, But You Need to Respond Anyway
- Some General Rules for Answering Questions

Christian Kieffer/Shutterstock.com

Chapter Learning Objectives

After completing this chapter, you should be able to

- Identify the reasons that organizations need job interviews.
- Appreciate how the interviewer can make or break your interview.
- Prepare effectively for job interviews.
- Anticipate questions likely to be asked during job interviews.
- Strategically answer typical job interview questions.

"Hey, Ty, how did your job interview go today?"

"I don't know—not so good. I felt good when I arrived, but when I sat down at the table and looked at the interviewer, I felt the sweat beading on my face. Things just didn't seem to go very well, Sheree. I thought I was well prepared, but now I'm not so sure. The interviewer didn't give me much feedback on my answers, and he didn't say anything about my chances of getting the job. He didn't even tell me when they are going to make a hiring decision."

"I'm surprised, Ty. You were well prepared for that interview. You shouldn't be so hard on yourself. If things really didn't go that well, it may not have had anything to do with you. Maybe you got a bad interviewer. Maybe the questions he asked were bad. Or maybe you just weren't the right fit for this particular job. Or maybe your perceptions are wrong. You probably did a great job, they loved you, and they'll call you tomorrow with a job offer. Tell me more about the interview. Give me some specifics. What do you think you did right rather than wrong during the interview?"

"Okay, Sheree. I think I came across as knowledgeable about the company. I believe that my answers were thoughtful and on target. And when I wasn't sure how to answer a particular question, I didn't try to fake it—I was honest and gave the best answer I could."

"Well, Ty, it sounds to me like you did a good job."

Sheree's ideas about what may have happened in Ty's interview are good ones. How you perform in a job interview and the outcome of that interview are tied to a number of factors. Even though some of what happens during an interview is out of your control, you can anticipate many of the questions and plan how to present yourself.

This chapter discusses what you need to know to prepare for and effectively navigate a job interview. In the first section, we'll consider the reasons that organizations conduct employment interviews. Next, we will examine how a good interview should be conducted, whether you are the interviewer or the job candidate. Last, we'll take a look at the questions likely to be asked during a job interview and how you can answer them thoughtfully. Like Ty, you can benefit from knowing more about what makes job interviews effective. This knowledge can make all the difference in whether or not you eventually land that dream job.

Why Do Organizations Need Job Interviews?

Walk into any work environment, look around, and what do you see? People working. Organizations begin and end with people working at jobs. These employees did not simply appear out of nowhere. Virtually everyone working was interviewed before he or she was hired. Moreover, whether someone working is eventually terminated, resigns, is replaced, or a new position is created and filled with a new employee, the job interview is central to the hiring and re-hiring of employees.

In its most basic definition, the **employment interview** is a face-to-face encounter designed to evaluate whether an applicant is suitable for a particular position in an organization.[1] Because all employees enter an organization through job interviews, these interviews must be managed properly. To a large extent, an organization's success depends on the quality of its employment interviews.

Interviews Supply Organizations with a Competent Workforce

The bottom line of most businesses is to make money so that the business can sustain and survive over time. It is only by hiring good employees that an organization can make money. No business can succeed without employees to complete the activities that are required to run it and produce the product lines or services. Nor can a business be successful with employees who have been hired arbitrarily, without regard for how well suited they are for their jobs.

In addition, all organizations require that money be made to pay the overhead costs of running the business. A delicate balance exists between overhead and profit. No business can survive for very long when costs continually exceed profits. Perhaps the single largest overhead cost for any business is pay and benefits for its workforce. Having the most qualified workforce, then, is essential.

Sustainability and profitability, then, are two primary reasons why effective interviews are so important. The failure to effectively interview job candidates while considering a standard set of job criteria can result in hiring unqualified employees. And no manager, however good she may be, can possibly manage employees who cannot do their jobs because they're incompetent. Moreover, recommending that an unqualified applicant be hired based on an interview that was ill-conceived, went badly, or was poorly conducted can have long-term negative implications for an organization.

Interviews Screen Applicants

Job interviews are a form of assessment. Like all other types of assessment, interviews require planning and design:

- Specific skills are defined, and candidates are recruited.

- Application forms, résumés, cover letters, letters of recommendation, and sometimes tests are all examined as sources of information to determine the first level of elimination in the applicant pool.

- Once the pool has been narrowed, decisions are made to bring in or phone candidates for further consideration.
- Interview questions are generated according to the target job description and applicant profile in order to gain additional information about the applicant's abilities and suitability.

Many organizations spend a great deal of money and time with the initial screening process, even hiring recruiters and headhunters for higher-level job vacancies. All of this is done to assemble the best possible list of finalists to interview.

Interviews Match People with Organizations

Beyond meeting the objective qualifications for the job, candidates must fit into the culture of the organization. The interview provides an opportunity for interviewers to describe the organization's culture and for candidates to assess whether that culture will work for them. These are some typical culture concerns:[2]

- What is the hierarchy of the organization? What does the organizational chart look like?
- How is staff managed?
- How are decisions made—collaboratively or individually?
- Do employees have private offices or share open work spaces?
- What is the overall communication style of the organization? Is it open or closed? Informal or formal?
- How committed are employees to the organization?
- How do employees relate to each other? What social opportunities are available and institutionalized?
- Is flexible scheduling an option, a norm?

Answers to these and other questions about the company's culture help match candidates with particular work environments. Job seekers should use the interview to assess

AP Photo/Guillermo Tapia

how compatible the organization is with their personal values and preferences. At the same time, a good interviewer can evaluate the extent to which the candidate will fit into the company culture.

See Chapter 5 for more about company culture.

Interviews Yield Idiosyncratic Information about Applicants

Even with extensive screening of job candidates, only the face-to-face conversation with the finalists can reveal "people data." Talking with a candidate in person allows the interviewer to make judgments about the individual's social skills, self-confidence, maturity, trustworthiness, honesty, level of commitment, enthusiasm, motivation, and more. The interviewer gets a sense of who this person really is. No one wants to hire an individual sight unseen; interviewers want to be able to form a firsthand impression of each candidate.

Interviewers look for personal characteristics or lifestyles that might limit a candidate's ability to sustain a long-term relationship with the company. These kinds of data come in many shapes and sizes. During an interview, for instance, a candidate might reveal greater concern for vacation time than for the job itself. She might seem distracted, disinterested, or humorless. She might lack enthusiasm about the company or the job. She might complain or express anger about a previous job or employer. All these revelations could be deal breakers—but this information can be gained only in an interview, not on any form, résumé, or letter.

Interviews Minimize Turnover Rates

Handled competently, a good interview can result in hiring an employee who will be loyal, committed, and happy to stay with the company long term. This function of an interview cannot be understated, because the costs of replacing an employee range from 30 percent to 150 percent of the yearly salary of that position. Direct costs can include severance pay, outplacement fees, litigation, screening and evaluating new candidates, time spent interviewing, relocation and travel, signing bonuses, and training. Indirect costs of an employee's departure include the temporary loss of productivity, disruption of team or company morale, and perhaps even the loss of customers or clients.[3] Here is one illustration of how dramatic employee turnover costs can be:

> If your firm has a turnover rate of 25% (about the national average) and employs 40 employees each earning $25,000 annually, your costs of turning over 10 of these employees over the course of a year will be at least $125,000![4]

Avoiding high turnover rates makes good business sense. So one goal of the interviewing process should be identifying not only the best-qualified candidates but also those who are most likely to stay with the organization over time.

What's the Best Way to Interview Job Candidates?

Research findings reveal that the validity of an interview depends on a high degree of structure.[5] And yet, far too many organizations fall short of that objective, relying instead on unplanned and unstructured interviews.[6] When interviewers allow interviews to just happen, employers and candidates can be left feeling short-changed and frustrated. The consequences of haphazard interviews are well documented.[7]

In an unstructured interview, the interviewer typically

- Does most of the talking.
- Tends to make the hiring decision within the first four minutes of the interview.
- Fails to gather relevant information about the candidate beyond the résumé.
- Asks illegal or inappropriate questions that frequently violate Equal Employment Opportunity (EEO) laws.
- Reveals personal biases and prejudices.[8]

The best interviews are well planned and highly structured. The interviewer must take the time to prepare sufficiently for the interview, facilitate the conversation with the candidate to gather all the relevant information, and eventually summarize, reflect, and recommend a hiring decision.

Prepare for the Interview

To ensure that the interview process is as fair as possible, interviewers must carefully and thoughtfully plan for it. They must think about what the perfect person for the job would be like and develop a set of questions to ask in every interview. They must then become familiar with the material submitted by each candidate.

Develop an Ideal Applicant Profile Before interviewing any candidate, the organization must determine the specific skills and personal qualities required for the position. In other words, the interviewer must know what she wants. What is the job description? What skills are required? What personal attributes might best fit the position, the team, and the company?

Generate a List of Questions Questions serve the purpose of information gathering. But during an employment interview, you can't ask just any question that comes to mind. All questions should be job related, carefully written, and approved by the relevant teams in the organization. Extraneous and illegal questions are often eliminated in this way.[9] The skillful use of planned, vetted questions can yield relevant data upon which to make good hiring decisions.

The list of questions prepared for the interview is called the **interview protocol**. These questions are designed to be reliable and valid. **Reliable questions** are those that are standardized and asked of every candidate in every interview for the position. Only with reliable questions can the interviewer objectively compare and evaluate the candidates. Asking the same questions of every candidate also eliminates inadvertent or deliberate discrimination.

Valid questions are those that accurately reflect the skills and qualities required for the position. These questions do not stray into areas that might be illegal or unethical; instead, they focus directly on the particular requirements for the job. These requirements are often called **bona fide occupational qualifications (BFOQs)**. BFOQs should address only the candidate's educational background, work experience, work qualifications, special skills and pertinent physical abilities, and personality characteristics that have a *direct* bearing on the job itself.[10]

As much as possible, questions should also be open-ended. Closed-ended questions are useful for tests and questionnaires, but open-ended questions prove more useful for a face-to-face interview. **Closed-ended questions** are answered by choosing from two

Module 16:
What Makes a Winning Cover Letter and Résumé?

Visualize! Practice! 4.1:
Asking Open-Ended Questions

or more alternatives, such as a simple yes or no. **Open-ended questions** allow candidates to answer in an unrestricted way, providing as much information as they want. With open-ended questions, the interviewer allows candidates to talk more and to reveal more about themselves.

For practice generating open-ended questions, check out **VISUALIZE! PRACTICE! 4.1: Asking Open-Ended Questions**.

Become Familiar with the Candidate's File If applicants have made it through the screening process to the interview, their qualifications deserve thoughtful consideration. Unfortunately, the following interview scenario is all too common:

> Mr. Jarvis invited Fariba to sit down and asked her if she had brought another copy of her résumé. (He had misplaced hers on his desk.) He asked her again for her name, what position she was interested in, and where she went to school. Fariba was a bit put off by his lack of preparation and interest in her as a candidate. She wasn't so sure this was the right company for her.

What is wrong with this scenario? What would you recommend to Mr. Jarvis in future interviews? Thoroughly familiarizing himself with the candidate's file prior to each interview would be a good start. He should take the time for each of these steps:

- **Read the cover letter.** A good cover letter reveals the candidate's level of interest in the job, calls attention to relevant aspects in the candidate's background, and provides a first impression of the candidate's credibility.

- **Study the résumé.** Résumés provide contact information and specifics about education, work experience, and awards and honors. There's no need to discuss this background information during the interview. Instead, the interviewer should probe for details about how the candidate's background relates to the job. The résumé might also suggest common interests and facilitate friendly, open interactions.

- **Read and evaluate letters of recommendation and any other supporting materials.** These kinds of letters often provide character references, testimonials of the candidate's personal and professional attributes, and other relevant observations about the candidate's abilities and work ethic.

- **Know the file inside and out.** Finally, and most important, interviewers should be so familiar with each candidate's file that they come across as personable, approachable, and being knowledgeable about the candidate. Critical to this impression is learning and saying the candidate's name when greeting him or her.

For more about cover letters and résumés, this time from the candidate's point of view, check out **MODULE 16: What Makes a Winning Cover Letter and Résumé?**

Facilitate the Conversation

Interviews are not interrogations. Rather, they are conversations guided by the interviewer. The more the interview resembles a friendly conversation, the more likely both the interviewer and candidate can accomplish their objectives. How can the interviewer make this happen?

Establish Rapport The first and perhaps most important task for the interviewer is to put the candidate at ease. The more important the interview, the more likely the

Sean Locke/istockphoto.com

candidate will be anxious and uncomfortable. Anxiety and discomfort typically prevent the candidate from presenting his or her best possible self. Starting with some small talk, focusing on mutual interests or background (see the résumé), and spending some time just getting to know each other sets the tone for a productive and meaningful interaction. Describing the purpose, nature, and length of the interview as well as explaining why the candidate was selected for the interview further reduces uncertainty.

Sell the Company Remember that the candidate is also interviewing the employer. The interviewer may be the only company representative the candidate will talk with before deciding whether to take the job. Thus, the interviewer establishes the first and perhaps most long-lasting impression of what the company represents. The interviewer, then, must come across as friendly and professional. Moreover, the interviewer must provide a realistic, yet positive image of the organization, the position, and the people who work there. By the end of the interview, the candidate should leave with the impression that this company would be a great place to work.

Stick to the Protocol Sticking to the interview protocol prevents the interviewer from asking irrelevant or illegal questions and from drifting off topic. In addition, because the interview is scheduled for a limited amount of time, the protocol ensures that all the necessary questions are asked and answered. The protocol should allow for the interviewer to ask follow-up questions throughout the interview, such as "Why do you think so?" or "Then what happened?" The interviewer must not only stick to the protocol but also be careful not to make any false promises about the job, promises that could be construed as binding contracts about benefits or salary, for example.

Encourage the Candidate to Ask Questions In any good conversation, both participants feel comfortable asking and answering questions. The candidate should have ample opportunity to ask about the position, the company, and any other relevant topic. Interviewers can signal to the candidate that they expect such inquiries by asking, "What do you want to know about this position or the company more generally?" Prepared candidates come to an interview with their own questions in mind. Absent such questions, the interviewer might assume justifiably that the candidate has made little effort to prepare for the interview and has little or no interest in the job.

Listen Actively As you have seen, good listening takes effort (Chapter 3). Active listening allows the interviewer to acquire essential information and to evaluate what the candidate says. The interviewer's interest should be evident throughout the interview, expressed by leaning forward, smiling, nodding, making eye contact, and commenting on what the candidate reveals. If several candidates are being interviewed for a position, the interviewer should take notes about each one, jotting down impressions, facts, and special concerns.

Common advice to interviewers is to stick to the 70/30 rule: talk 30 percent of the time and listen 70 percent. The candidate needs to do most of the talking, and the interviewer should spend most of the time listening. How else will the interviewer collect information?

Conclude on a Positive Note

Because the interviewer is responsible for leaving the candidate with a positive impression of the company, interviewers should plan the conclusion as well as the questions. The interviewer needs to conclude the interview with some indication of when the hiring decision will be made and when and how the candidate will be informed.

Even if the interviewer determines early on that the candidate is not a good fit for the position, the interviewer is obligated to give the candidate a fair hearing and complete the interview as if the candidate were still viable. The candidate may be unsuitable for this particular position, but she could be a good choice for another position in the future.

Immediately after the candidate leaves, the interviewer's next task is to look over his notes, add additional observations, and jot down an overall impression of the candidate and the interview. With multiple candidates and multiple interviews over multiple days, forgetting specifics is likely. Documenting each interview provides reminders of each candidate's performance, forms the basis of hiring recommendations, and helps in defending hiring decisions.

What's the Best Way for Job Candidates to Interview?

So, you have a good résumé and an excellent list of references. The next hurdle is the interview. You're almost there, right? You made it through the first screening of the applicants. You're qualified for the job. The problem is that other candidates are also lined up for interviews. Any one of the finalists could do the job, but who will get the offer? Lots of very qualified people are interviewed and yet remain unemployed. Somehow, you will have to find a way to stand out from the others. What must you do to make an interviewer perceive you as special, unique, and worthy of the job? In this section we will show you how you can make this happen.[11]

Prepare for the Interview

Even though interviews are basically a conversation, they require planning. Just as good interviewers plan for the interview, you need to plan as well if you hope to obtain a job offer. Reaching this objective requires that you prepare, prepare, and prepare some more.

Visualize! Practice! 4.2:
Your Personal and Professional Profiles

Develop a Personal Profile Begin your preparation by analyzing yourself. Identify your personal strengths and weaknesses by creating a **personal profile**. Are you reliable, motivated, hardworking, and mature? Are you willful, resistant to change, and unable to accept criticism? Do you learn easily, enjoy reading, and work out every day? Take inventory of who you are. You might even ask someone you trust to give you some candid feedback.

Be honest with yourself as you assess your strengths and weaknesses. One of the most common interview questions is, "Tell me about yourself," or "How would your best friend describe you?"[12] From your personal profile, you can quickly select a number of positive key words and phrases to use to describe yourself. Another frequent question is, "What would you say are your two greatest weaknesses?" Be prepared to identify a personal weakness that you might explain or are currently addressing. Ideally, this weakness will have no relation to the job you are seeking.

Develop a Professional Profile Next, inventory your professional qualities and assets by creating a **professional profile**. To some extent, your résumé reflects your professional profile. But what is missing from that document are answers to questions like "What unique experiences or qualifications separate you from other candidates?" and "What major professional obstacle did you have to overcome this year?" To develop your professional profile, answer the following types of questions:

- What special skills and talents would you bring to the job?

- Are you, for example, fluent in Spanish, competent in Excel, or an exceptionally good listener?

- Are you good at public speaking, writing research reports, or computing low-level statistics?

- Have you had a lot of experience working with diverse groups, participating in teams, or leading large or small groups?

Once you begin your inventory, you may be surprised at how many professional skills you have!

For help taking stock of your personal and professional strengths and weaknesses, complete VISUALIZE! PRACTICE! 4.2: **Your Personal and Professional Profiles**.

Do Your Research Every resource on interviewing advises candidates to investigate the company thoroughly. The most obvious source for accessing this information is the Internet. Look up the company website. Most medium-sized and large companies have websites filled with information about their organization, conveniently organized by topic. Many organizations advertise their perks and benefits, such as on-site day care and workout facilities. And some organizations, such as government agencies and some nonprofits, even provide information about salary. Sometimes you can even locate the names, bios, and résumés of employees—an important way to find out about your interviewer and the kinds of people you might end up working with.

Take, for instance, the Boeing Company. Google "Boeing" and the first entry you'll find is its home website. The website tells you that they are the "world's leading aerospace company and the largest manufacturer of commercial jetliners and military aircraft combined. Additionally, Boeing designs and manufactures rotorcraft, electronic and defense systems, missiles, satellites, launch vehicles and advanced information and communication systems." Did you also know that Boeing operates the Space Shuttle and International Space Station? Look to its website to find out anything you want to know about Boeing (and then some).

You can often also find good information about smaller organizations. For example, the official website for Chipotle Mexican Grill has a rather interesting story about its founder and CEO, Steve Ells. You will also learn that Chipotle serves only meat that comes from animals that were raised in a humane way and were never given antibiotics and hormones.

Other possible sources for information about a company and a position are people you know who currently or formerly worked there, clients or customers of the company, and the company's human resources department. Feel free to make an appointment or stop in to speak with company representatives or staff. Whatever sources you use, take good notes and study what you have learned. Commit to memory key names, interesting projects, and some history about the company. Be prepared to use this kind of information during the interview. The more familiar you sound about the company, the more knowledgeable and impressive you will appear. An added bonus to this research is learning enough about the organization to determine if it is a good match for you.

If you have children, you may want to investigate whether a company is "family friendly" by going to **LINK OUT 4.1: Family Friendly Companies**. Discover if the organization offers scholarships, day care, flextime and other benefits or perks. All or most of this information is available on the Internet.

Adam Gault/Jupiter Images

Anticipate the Questions Do your homework and consider answers to the questions you will probably face during your job interview. If you simply Google "interview questions," you'll find almost 36 million sites that discuss typical interview questions. These questions range from simple to complex, legal to illegal, and easy to tough. Anticipating what you will be asked allows you the luxury of thinking about what answers you would like to give. Later on this chapter, we'll discuss a number of questions that are likely to be asked during your interview.

Practice Your Answers Take the time to prepare and practice the answers you want to give. Consider this a dress rehearsal. It may be simple enough to answer the easy questions; it's the difficult, illegal, and uncomfortable questions that need strategic preparation. Moreover, practicing your answers allows you to prepare *how* to say what you want to communicate. You will want to impress upon the interviewer that you are confident, competent, and sincere. Later in this chapter we offer some suggested answers that you might use during your preparation and practice.

Make a List of Questions to Ask If you have done sufficient research about the organization, the position, and the people who work there, you may have answered most of your questions about the job. Even so, interviewers expect and want candidates to ask questions, and you will be judged by how thoughtful your questions are. Take the time, then, to generate five or six questions. You can always add to the list as you move closer to the actual interview.

Stewart and Cash, prominent communication authorities on interviewing, maintain that "not having any or having too few questions is a major common mistake of applicants."[13] They further suggest that good applicants should ask open-ended questions: These questions should focus on the organization, the position, and, most importantly, the interviewer's own opinions. In contrast, unsuccessful applicants use closed-ended questions and ask about miscellaneous or irrelevant issues. To see the difference, consider which of the following questions are more likely to create a favorable impression with an interviewer:

1. "Do you like working here?"
2. "What is the overriding management style of this organization?"
3. "What holidays do we have off?"
4. "What's a typical working day like?"
5. "Is this the kind of organization where people stay long term?"

If you selected questions 2 and 4, then you have a good sense of what kind of questions to ask during your interview.

Just as important as knowing what to ask is knowing what not to ask. Stewart and Cash argue convincingly that good candidates should avoid asking questions about salary, vacation, retirement, and promotions at the initial interview. These kinds of questions should be saved for *after* the job offer. They also suggest that questions whose answers can be easily found online or in the organization's publications should be avoided.

For more dos and don'ts about preparing questions to ask during an interview, check out **VISUALIZE! PRACTICE! 4.3: Do You Have Any Questions?**

For more about preparing for interviews, see **MODULE 14: How Do I Prepare for Phone and Video Interviews?** For a detailed discussion about why you should wait until after you've been offered a job to ask about salary and benefits, see **MODULE 12: What's the Best Way to Negotiate a Compensation Package?**

Module 14:
How Do I Prepare for Phone and Video Interviews?

Module 12:
What's the Best Way to Negotiate a Compensation Package?

Visualize! Practice! 4.3:
Do You Have Any Questions?

Pay Attention to the Basics

Making a good impression at the interview depends on many things. Even the smallest detail can make the difference in how an interviewer will respond to you. Here are some tips for making the best possible impression:

- **Don't be late for the interview.** In fact, you should arrive fifteen minutes early. Find out what kind of traffic to anticipate around the time of your interview and leave early enough to account for it.

- **Know where you're going.** Find out exactly where the interview will take place, including the room or suite number. Go online and map out the location, identifying the specific building. Also figure out where to park and bring coins for a meter if there isn't a nearby parking garage or lot. Remember to map out how to get from the parking area to the building where you're interviewing.

- **Bring extra résumés.** Pack three extra copies of your résumé just in case the interviewer or others who may attend the interview need one.

- **Plan for small talk.** Think about safe, easy topics that you can introduce into the conversation, such as the weather, traffic patterns, or perhaps comments about the unusual landscaping or layout of the facility. Whatever the topic of your small talk, be positive and keep the conversation light.

- **Consider your appearance and personal hygiene.** The interviewer's first impression will be based on how you look. Millions of websites provide information about what you should plan to wear to a job interview. Several you might find helpful can be accessed through LINK OUT 4.2: **Virginia Tech Tips for Interview Attire**, LINK OUT 4.3: **Dressing for Interview Success**, LINK OUT 4.4: **About.com's Tips for Interview Attire 1**, LINK OUT 4.5: **About.com's Tips for Interview Attire 2**, LINK OUT 4.6: **What Women Should Wear to an Interview**, and LINK OUT 4.7: **What Men Should Wear to an Interview**.

  In terms of personal hygiene, give priority to the basics:
  - ✔ Shower before the interview.
  - ✔ Wash your hair.
  - ✔ Use a liberal amount of deodorant.
  - ✔ Clean and trim your fingernails.
  - ✔ Brush your teeth and freshen your breath.
  - ✔ Wear subtle perfume or cologne (if any).
  - ✔ Shave (if applicable).
  - ✔ Make sure your clothes are clean and pressed.
  - ✔ Shine your shoes.
  - ✔ Tone down the makeup (if applicable).

Yuri Arcurs/Shutterstock.com

Make a Good First Impression

Making a good first impression is a crucial step in any productive relationship (Chapter 2). This applies even to the temporary relationships you form during an interview. First impressions are formed quickly, and they are based on limited information. Moreover, what others observe first about you influences everything else they discover subsequently about you.

Carefully monitor how you come across during the first few minutes of contact with the people who are involved with your interview. Very often, the interview begins with the secretary's or assistant's impression of you. This is the person who makes your appointment and directs you to the interviewer. More importantly, this person typically provides feedback to the interviewer—after you leave. Be mindful, then, of how you behave with this person. Be relaxed, engage in brief small talk, and wait patiently. Smile and nod, thank this person by name for any courtesies, and thank him or her again after the interview as you leave.

First impressions are also formed by the simple things you do when you meet the interviewer. Smile, offer a firm handshake, be seated when directed, sit up straight, look like you are listening, make and sustain eye contact, and try not to yawn. In other words, look confident, comfortable, and professional.

Sell Yourself

Your résumé may *tell* the interviewer all that you can do. But it's in the interview that you have the opportunity to sell your skills, interest in the company, and desire to work hard or assume responsibility. Be your own best advocate! Be yourself, and don't be intimidated. Now is not the time to question your abilities or qualifications. Keep in mind the personal and professional profiles you prepared for the interview. What qualities and strengths can you project so that you come across as the right person for the job?

Your goal is to persuade the interviewer that you bring an advantage. Help the interviewer appreciate that what you'd bring to the company would add value to the organization. Explain how your background and qualifications suit you for the job. Let the interviewer know that you want this particular job and no other and that you want to begin working at the company right now. By the time the interview is over, the interviewer should have a good idea of why you should be the candidate the company hires.[14]

Check for a Good Fit

You also need to use the interview to find out if this is a good company and a good position for you. However much you may need and want a job, little is worse than working at the wrong place and with the wrong people. A newspaper columnist observed, "**Misemployment** happens when people work at jobs that do not match their skills or their interests—when people are working at the wrong jobs."[15] Misemployed people do not enjoy going to work, are probably not all that productive in their jobs, and are frequently absent. They are also likely to influence the general morale of the workplace. Unfortunately, many of the misemployed do nothing about their situation. In a sense, taking the wrong job or choosing the wrong career is like being married to the wrong partner.

So, before you get too far into the interview process, ask yourself these questions:

- Am I going to be happy working here and doing this?
- Will I look forward to coming to work every day?
- Do I fit in here?
- Is this what I really want to do?
- Can I see myself working here for a long time?

Seriously consider whether this organization and this job are right for you. Use the interview to assess whether you and this job will be a good fit.

Link Out 4.8:
Sample Thank-You Letters

Link Out 4.9:
About.com Thank-You Letters

Link Out 4.10:
Thank-You Notes

End the Interview

After the interviewer signals the close of the interview, stand and shake hands. Thank the interviewer for taking the time to talk with you, using his name and maintaining eye contact. Tell him how much you enjoyed your conversation. If you are still interested in the position, say so directly with a statement such as "I remain very much interested in this position." If the interviewer doesn't offer the information, ask when a hiring decision will be made and when the organization will contact you. Keep in mind that you are being evaluated as long as you are in contact with the company's employees, such as if your interviewer or another employee escorts you to your car or drives you to your hotel or airport.

Follow Up after the Interview

Immediately following the interview, jot down some notes about your conversation with the interviewer. Assess your performance. What did you do well? What went wrong and why? What did you learn? Be as specific and objective as you can. Also record both personal and professional items that you can use in a subsequent conversation or a follow-up thank-you note.

Write a brief, professional thank-you note within twenty-four hours of the interview. A handwritten note through the regular mail is always better than an email. In this note, express your appreciation and re-emphasize your interest in the position. For a memorable thank-you letter, highlight some connection you made with the interviewer. Mention something you have in common or refer to some personal topic that came up. For example, during the interview you may discover you have a friend in common. You could mention in the letter, then, that you contacted your friend and she said how pleased she was that you two had met.

Several websites provide examples and templates of thank-you letters. You can use them to draft and personalize your own letters. See **LINK OUT 4.8: Sample Thank-You Letters**, **LINK OUT 4.9: About.com Thank-You Letters**, and **LINK OUT 4.10: Thank-You Notes**.

Putting Your Skills to Work

Even if you've never interviewed for a job, you gained some experience with the interview process when you applied for college. You probably researched which college would be the best fit for you. And you may have discovered that only some schools require an admission interview. But even if your school didn't require an interview, you still used your college application, essay, or portfolio to make a good impression and to sell yourself. All these skills will be useful when you start applying for jobs.

mark wragg/istockphoto.com

By now, you can see why some writers argue convincingly that getting a job can be a full-time job. What happens before, during, and immediately after an interview all makes a difference in whether or not you will get an offer.

What Will You Be Asked and How Should You Answer?

Visualize! Practice! 4.4:
Possible Answers to Commonly Asked Questions

As we've discussed, a résumé or job application may provide the employer an objective description of experience and abilities, but the face-to-face interview provides information about personal characteristics, attitudes, and motivation. During an interview, the interviewer can gather nonverbal information, observe the candidate thinking things through, and get a sense of who the candidate really is. Some questions are straightforward and elicit basic information. But others are subtle, designed to access information about the candidate's personality, attitudes, and behaviors.

Some Questions Are Predictable

Not only should you try to anticipate the questions you are likely to face during an interview, but you should also think about why any particular question will be asked. Understanding the reason behind the question allows you to formulate a clear, thoughtful, and suitable response. For example, what do you suppose an interviewer is looking for when she asks, "Why do you want this job?" Perhaps she wants to know how serious you are about this job and how much thought you have given to the position. Or perhaps the organization is suffering from high employee turnover, and the interviewer wants to ensure that whoever is recommended will take the job and stay. If the latter is the case, you would want to emphasize how reliable you are and ready to commit yourself to the company, the job, or the product.

Let's take a look at reasons why interviewers ask twelve standard questions. After this list, Table 4.1 offers two options to answer each of these questions. Decide which option in the table is the most appropriate and effective answer for each question. **VISUALIZE!** **PRACTICE! 4.4: Possible Answers to Commonly Asked Questions**

1. **"Tell me about yourself."** This question seems very general, but employers use it to draw information from candidates about how they see themselves and, more importantly, how they present themselves. Is the candidate too self-assured and arrogant, or is she confident and realistic about herself?

2. **"How would your best friend describe you?" "How would your last boss describe you?"** Most candidates will answer such a question by listing the qualities they believe the employer wants to hear. This makes sense, but be honest. A good interviewer might follow up with the question, "Do you mind if I contact your friend (or boss) and see what he says?" Focus on the positive, but be realistic.

3. **"What would you say are your two greatest weaknesses?"** The interviewer is looking for answers that not only reveal weaknesses but also how you plan to overcome them. Some sources argue that revealing any weakness is problematic. However, we all have weaknesses and should be aware of them. Identifying what you are doing to overcome them or how you are turning them into advantages can be interpreted favorably.

4. **"How do you handle stressors on the job?"** Every job causes stress, so no interviewer is going to believe a candidate who denies experiencing stress. The

David C Ellis/Getty Images

interviewer wants to learn what positive strategies you employ to reduce stress, such as reading or physical exercise.

5. **"What are your short- and long-term goals? Where do you want to be in five years?"** These questions are designed to elicit personal and professional goals that demonstrate your work–life balance, drive, motivation, and whether you are forward thinking. Answers to these questions reveal your level of ambition and whether you take a proactive approach to your career.

6. **"What type of work environment do you prefer?"** Because work culture varies considerably across organizations, the interviewer wants to know whether you are suited for this particular workplace. In other words, to what extent will you fit into the organization?

7. **"Why should we hire you?" "Why do you want to work here?"** A candidate who cannot answer this question readily and enthusiastically will not get a job offer. Respond by describing what you can do for the organization, how well suited you are for this job, and how much you'd like to work there.

8. **"How organized are you?"** Employers like their employees to be organized. No candidate is going to say he is disorganized. So provide a specific explanation or example of how you stay organized.

9. **"Why are you leaving your current job?"** No matter the circumstances, you should never complain about your current position. It's better to say you are looking for opportunities for advancement and new challenges.

10. **"In what ways do you raise the bar for yourself and others around you?"** All candidates like to tell interviewers that they set the highest standards for themselves and others, but you should answer this question by identifying specific standards you've set for yourself and how you've motivated others. Moreover, answers to this question can reveal the extent to which you are a team player or a leader.

11. **"Tell me about two memorable projects, one success and one failure. To what do you attribute the success and failure?"** Good candidates are people who know why they succeeded or failed. They are able to analyze, evaluate, and articulate what they did right—and what they did wrong.

12. **"What unique experiences or qualifications separate you from other candidates?"** This question allows candidates to reveal additional information about their qualifications that are specifically relevant to the job. The question might also reveal what qualities and experiences the candidate values.

Link Out 4.11:
50 Standard Interview Questions

Link Out 4.12:
100 Standard Interview Questions

Link Out 4.13:
1,000 Standard Interview Questions

These questions are typical for most job interviews. But anticipating and preparing answers for others, particularly ones that pertain to your particular industry, is a good way to give yourself an advantage over your competition.

A number of online sources offer some of the more typical questions and reasons they are asked.[16] Try **LINK OUT 4.11: 50 Standard Interview Questions**, **LINK OUT 4.12: 100 Standard Interview Questions**, or **LINK OUT 4.13: 1,000 Standard Interview Questions**. Although we recommend these links, don't try to memorize answers to every question. Focus on questions that you are likely to encounter.

Some Questions Are Illegal, But You Need to Respond Anyway

Federal and state laws prohibit employers from asking certain kinds of questions during job interviews. These equal employment opportunity (EEO) laws are designed to protect candidates from questions that might be discriminatory or prejudicial. Even so, you may find interviewers asking unlawful questions out of ignorance or some sense of power. Regardless of the intent, these questions pose a dilemma for candidates.

What is the best answer when illegal, prejudicial questions are asked?[17] Begin first by determining how discriminatory the question is. Some questions are minor and can be easily answered. One way to do that is to simply deflect the question with humor.

Putting Your Skills to Work

Anticipating interview questions and practicing answers is like studying for a test. You can usually anticipate what your instructor is going to test you on, and in order to do well on the test, you at least draft the answers you plan to give. This is especially true for oral exams!

A-Digit/istockphoto.com

TABLE 4.1
Possible Answers to Commonly Asked Interview Questions

Question	Which answer is more appropriate and effective?*
1. Tell me about yourself.	**Option 1** I just graduated from one of the top ten business programs in the country. As you might expect, I have the best training available, and I'm highly marketable. I'm looking around at options. **Option 2** I just completed my degree, and I'm anxious to get to work. I've studied hard to get the basics; I've taken course work that has prepared me for this position, and I just finished an internship working alongside someone who did this kind of work.
2. How would your best friend describe you? How would your last boss describe you?	**Option 1** I believe they would characterize me as hardworking, but easy to get along with. I'm also diligent and responsible. They might also tell you that I am honest and keep my commitments. **Option 2** They would probably describe me as a water-walker. They would tell you that I stand out from the rest, and that you would be lucky to have me work here.
3. What would you say are your two greatest weaknesses?	**Option 1** My husband accuses me of being too punctual; we arrive early or on time to every social event. And yet punctuality has always been an asset for my job. **Option 2** I can't think of any weaknesses important to how I work. I guess I have a weakness for chocolate.
4. How do you handle stressors on the job?	**Option 1** I'm not the kind of person who stresses out over every little thing. My mother describes me as mellow and easygoing. **Option 2** Some level of stress works for me. I find it motivating and, at times, exhilarating. That said, too much stress can be negative and demotivating, so when I begin to feel overly anxious, I take a long walk.
5. What are your short- and long-term goals? Where do you want to be in five years?	**Option 1** In the future, I see myself continuing to work here but moving on to supervision. I like working with people, managing others, but I also recognize the need to gain experience first. **Option 2** I don't like to think about tomorrow. I tend to be more now-oriented. I take things one day at a time.
6. What type of work environment do you prefer?	**Option 1** I like my work environment to be highly structured. I like to have my own office and my own space. I work best in quiet places. **Option 2** I am flexible. Tell me about your work environment here. What's it like?

(*continued*)

7.	Why should we hire you? Why do you want to work here?	**Option 1** I've looked around at a lot of companies, and I believe this organization is the right place for me. I believe I can make a home here and contribute meaningfully. I have the skill base that you need. I am qualified, and I'm ready to begin work. **Option 2** I'm sure that there are a lot of candidates like me, just out of school. I'm hoping that you will give me a chance to prove myself. I will work very hard if I get this job. I really need a job right now—I have a lot of student loans to pay back.
8.	How organized are you?	**Option 1** I'm pretty organized. I like my desk cleaned off at night before I go home so that I'm ready to begin work the next day. I like knowing where everything is; everything should have its place. **Option 2** I've always thought that a messy desk is a sign of creativity and intelligence. Besides, I know where everything is. If someone asks, I can pull just the right file from under the stack on my desk.
9.	Why are you leaving your current job?	**Option 1** I'm bored, and I don't particularly like my boss. I never feel all that appreciated. I need to move on. **Option 2** I'm looking for new opportunities and new challenges. I've learned as much as I can from this job, and now it's time to move on. I will miss the people where I work, but they want me to succeed, and they are encouraging me to seek new opportunities.
10.	In what ways do you raise the bar for yourself and others around you?	**Option 1** I don't like to set expectations for myself or others. I find that when I do, I'm disappointed. This way, when things go really well, I'm surprised and happy. **Option 2** I typically set high standards for myself. I'm willing to work hard to meet those standards, too. The fact that I do set high standards helps others do the same.
11.	Tell me about two memorable projects, one success and one failure. To what do you attribute the success and the failure?	**Option 1** I can't think of any failures, but I was able to complete my last project well ahead of schedule and the boss was pretty excited. Things just seemed to fall in place when I was working on that. **Option 2** Sometimes I learn more from my failures than from my successes. Regardless of the project, I try to step back and figure out what we did right and wrong—and more importantly, why and how would I do it differently next time. For example, ...
12.	What unique experiences or qualifications separate you from other candidates?	**Option 1** If you look at my résumé, you'll find that I have all the qualities you need for this position. I'm a college graduate; I have good letters of recommendation; and I'm available. **Option 2** I know you've looked at my résumé, but what bears repeating is the internship experiences I have had. Because of those experiences, I have a pretty good idea of what's required to do this job, and I'm confident that I can do this.

*Best answers: 1. Option 2; 2. Option 1; 3. Option 1; 4. Option 2; 5. Option 2; 6. Option 1; 7. Option 2; 8. Option 1; 9. Option 2; 10. Option 2; 11. Option 2; 12. Option 2

Link Out 4.14:
Illegal Interview Questions?

Weigh In! 4.1:
What Questions Are Illegal to Ask?

Another way is to answer the question briefly, and then redirect the interview to another, separate issue. How might you deflect or redirect these unlawful questions:

"How old are you?"

"What does your husband/wife do?"

You might answer the first one, "How old are you?" by saying, "Old enough to get the job done!" or asking, "Does age make a difference in this position?" To the second question, "What does your husband or wife do?" you might respond, "My husband/wife is very supportive of whatever I do." If you're unmarried or you're in a same-sex relationship, you can say, "I don't believe my marital status will affect my ability to fulfill the responsibilities of this position."

Sometimes discovering the interviewer's intent helps you formulate your response. To uncover intent, you can ask (in a nondefensive way), "Why do you ask?" or "Can you clarify how that relates to my ability to handle this job?"

Other questions are more discriminatory, such as "Do you have any disabilities?" or "Have you ever been arrested?" You may choose not to answer these questions at all, and instead, you may need to politely remind the interviewer that the question is not relevant to the qualifications for this particular position. Try these responses: "I'm not really comfortable answering that question" or again, "Why do you ask?" Quickly change the topic, then, and avoid further discussion of the issue.

To test your knowledge of illegal interview questions, complete the self-assessment WEIGH IN! 4.1: **What Questions Are Illegal to Ask?** And check out LINK OUT 4.14: **Illegal Interview Questions** to find out why certain questions are illegal and what interviewers should ask instead.

Some General Rules for Answering Questions

Now that you have anticipated the variety of different questions you might be asked during an interview, and you have some ideas about how you want to answer each of them, you are almost ready for your interview. We would like to leave you with some final advice on how to approach questions during your interview. These guidelines will help you frame the conversation in ways that will reinforce the impression that you are thoughtful, sincere, hardworking, and the best possible candidate for the job.[18]

- **Listen carefully to the question.** Ask for clarification if you're unsure. You might even repeat or rephrase the question before answering.

- **Pause before answering.** Good answers should be thoughtful and sincere. Pausing communicates the care you are taking to answer effectively.

- **If you do not know the answer, be honest and say so.** Make your response simple and direct: "I don't know. I would have to think about it."

- **Avoid tangents.** Limit your answers to what is asked and what is pertinent to the question. Try not to go off on tangents or tell long stories that might move the interview off track. Remember that you have a limited time to sell yourself.

- **Provide concrete examples.** You may need to illustrate or demonstrate particular qualities, such as your integrity, problem-solving skills, and perseverance. The more concrete you can make your examples, the better.

- **Be confident and stay calm.** Every candidate is anxious about being interviewed. Your calm and composure can communicate maturity and confidence.

Make every effort to avoid nervous mannerisms; instead, smile and sit with an open, relaxed posture.

Module 11:
How Do I Use Social Media for Professional Networking?

Module 13:
How Do I Deal with Job Search Rejection?

The interview is your final and most important marketing tool. The conversation gives you an opportunity to find common ground with the interviewer. For example, discovering that you both went to the same high school, grew up on a farm in the Midwest, or root for the Chicago Cubs gives you an advantage in making a positive first impression, and a lasting one. Anything you can say or do to make the interviewer comfortable with you, to reduce his uncertainty or anxiety about you will give you an advantage over other candidates.

For more tips about conducting an effective job search, see MODULE 11: **How Do I Use Social Media for Professional Networking?** and MODULE 13: **How Do I Deal with Job Search Rejection?**

By now you have a good idea how important an employment interview is to the employer and to the job candidate. No wonder Ty anguished so much over his interview. Sheree gave him good counsel to evaluate how he did during the interview. Like so many of us, Ty probably overemphasized what he thought went wrong in the interview, without also thinking about what he did right. Taking the time to evaluate his performance will help Ty do an even better job at his next job interview.

Appreciating how interviewers prepare for an interview should provide you with insight into your own planning for a job interview. Recognizing what interviewers are looking for and how they process candidate information will help you prepare strategically. Even so, whether you get the job offer depends on many factors, some of which are beyond your control. You may be the best qualified candidate, you may have all the right credentials, and you may have dazzled the interviewer—but no call and no job offer. Don't take it personally. The right people don't always get the job—the first time. Stay in the game; a job will be yours eventually.

Use your Speech Communication CourseMate for *Business & Communication in a Digital Age* for quick access to the electronic resources that accompany this text. These resources include

Study tools that will help you assess your learning and prepare for exams (*digital glossary, key term flash cards, review quizzes*).

Activities and assignments that will help you hone your knowledge and build your communication skills throughout the course (*Visualize! Practice!, Weigh In!, Check This Out, and Link Out activities; modules; review questions*).

Media resources that will help you explore communication concepts online (*Enhanced eBook*), develop your speech outlines (*Speech Builder Express 3.0*), watch and critique videos of sample speeches and communication situations (*interactive video activities*), upload your speech videos for peer reviewing and critique other students' speeches (*Speech Studio online speech review tool*), and download chapter review so you can study when and where you'd like (*Audio Study Tools*).

Key Points

- The employment, or job, interview is critical to an organization for a number of reasons.
  - ✔ Interviews supply organizations with a competent workforce.
  - ✔ Interviews screen applicants in order to assemble the best possible list of finalists for the position.
  - ✔ Interviews match people with organizations, ensuring a good fit.
  - ✔ Interviews provide "people data" about applicants, such as verbal and nonverbal skills, that are not found in applicants' files.
  - ✔ Interviews minimize employee turnover rates by assessing a candidate's suitability for the job and the organization.
- The best interview requires that *both* the interviewer and the interviewee are well prepared.
- Effective interviewers prepare for the interview by
  - ✔ Developing a profile of the ideal candidate for the job.
  - ✔ Generating a list of reliable, valid, open-ended, and legal questions to ask during every interview for the job.
  - ✔ Becoming familiar with each interviewee's file by studying the résumé and reading and evaluating letters of recommendation and other supporting materials.
- Effective interviewers facilitate friendly conversations with the candidates.
- Finally, effective interviewers conclude the interview on a positive note, leaving the candidate with a positive impression of both the interviewer and the company.
- Effective job candidates prepare for the interview by
  - ✔ Developing both personal and professional profiles of themselves.
  - ✔ Researching the company.
- During the interview, effective candidates
  - ✔ Pay attention to the basics, such as arriving on time and dressing appropriately.
  - ✔ Make a good first impression.
  - ✔ Sell themselves, helping the interviewer understand why they're the best candidate for the job.
  - ✔ Evaluate whether the company and job will be a good fit for them.
  - ✔ End the interview professionally.
- Finally, effective candidates follow up after the interview by assessing their performance during the interview and by sending a thank-you letter to the interviewer.
- Anticipating and answering questions is the key to all interviews. Because most questions are typical, common, and predictable, candidates can plan ahead, strategically managing the impression they want to make.

Key Terms

bona fide occupational qualifications (BFOQs) (71)

closed-ended questions (71)

employment interview (68)

interview protocol (71)

misemployment (79)

open-ended questions (72)

personal profile (75)

professional profile (75)

reliable questions (71)

valid questions (71)

Questions for Critical Thinking and Review

1. This chapter discusses how to conduct a good job interview, but many interviewers approach the interview in a more haphazard way. How would you change the way you prepare for an interview if you knew the interviewer was inept at interviewing? What interviewer mistakes might you anticipate, and how might you turn an ineffective interview around by assisting the interviewer?

2. How can you be sure if a job is a good fit for you? How important is a good fit when you don't have a job now and no other prospects are in sight? Should you take a job even if you know you will leave it as soon as a better one comes along? What is your ethical responsibility toward the interviewer?

3. A good interviewer is advised to talk for only 30 percent of the interview time, allowing the candidate to talk the other 70 percent. When you're a candidate, why might it be in your best interest to encourage the interviewer to talk more? What do you know about the principles of interpersonal communication that might influence the amount of time you talk about yourself during the interview?

4. Even though it's the primary responsibility of the interviewer to establish rapport during the interview, what are some ways you, the interviewee, might help to make that happen? How can you help the interviewer become as comfortable with you as soon as possible?

5. Why are the topics of salary, health benefits, perks, and vacation time best left to discussions after a job offer has been made? What might be the consequences of addressing such topics during the interview?

6. What if your work experience is limited to serving in a restaurant or a bar? How do you apply this type of work experience to jobs you are more likely to want after you graduate, such as office jobs?

7. Because job interviewers might be unaware of what a communication studies major or minor really means, how would you translate this degree to a business work environment? To what extent does a background in communication studies influence what you might emphasize in your personal profile? In your professional profile?

Chapter 5

Relationships in the Workplace:
How Do I Get Along?

Dmitriy Shironosov/Shutterstock.com

Chapter Learning Objectives

After completing this chapter, you should be able to

- Appreciate the importance of initiating and maintaining good relationships with people at work.
- Identify factors that influence your ability to get along at work.
- Use a variety of communication strategies to promote good relationships in the workplace.
- Better manage diverse relationships at work.
- Better manage challenging relationships at work.
- Know how to sustain a good relationship with your boss.

See also the modules that are relevant to this chapter:

1: How Do I "Get In and Fit In" to My Organization's Unique Culture?
4: What Do I Need to Know About Business Etiquette?
9: How Do I Navigate Office Politics?
11: How Do I Use Social Media for Professional Networking?
15: How Do I Manage My Time as a New Professional?

Module 1:
How Do I "Get In and Fit In" to My Organization's Unique Culture?

Module 4:
What Do I Need to Know About Business Etiquette?

Module 9:
How Do I Navigate Office Politics?

Module 11:
How Do I Use Social Media for Professional Networking?

Module 15:
How Do I Manage My Time as a New Professional?

"I've always enjoyed working. I like what I do. But I haven't always liked the people I work with. It's not the job—it's the people that make my job difficult," Leandra complained.

"I know just what you mean," Carlos empathized. "I have a boss right now who is always on me to do more, more, more. She just doesn't seem to understand how much time it takes to do each project I am assigned. All I seem to do is multitask. I hurry to meet deadlines, and the quality of my work suffers as a result. I know my work would be better if she didn't pressure me so much."

Leandra looked surprised. She had a manager who was very supportive. She looked up to him as a mentor. "I have a great boss, Carlos. We have a really good relationship. It's not my manager that's the problem for me; it's my co-workers. I work around some really eccentric types, and they're difficult to read sometimes. I never know how to act around them," Leandra explained. "I don't think they like me, Carlos. Some days I dread going into the office."

"I know what you mean, Leandra. I need to work; I need the money. It would sure make my life a lot easier if I had your boss—and not mine."

Leandra and Carlos realize that getting along with the boss and co-workers is critical to what they do every day. Thinking about work as simply "doing your job" oversimplifies what's required to do a job well and undervalues the importance of interpersonal relationships in the workplace. No meaningful work can be accomplished without the participation and support of many other people. This chapter explores how you can best get along in your workplace and make working more productive, enjoyable, and sustainable.

Although most people have been trained in how to do their job, they have not been educated in how to initiate and sustain good relationships with people at work. This chapter will help you identify reasons why you might get along with some people you work with and not others. By appreciating the factors that influence your ability to get along, you will be better able to choose specific communication strategies to promote good working relationships. As Leandra aptly noted, some relationships are more difficult to manage than others. This chapter will prepare you to meet challenges of work relationships with co-workers, clients, and bosses.

Perhaps no relationship is more important than the one with your boss; this chapter will teach you how to gain and keep your boss's approval. Rather than looking for a new boss, Carlos might benefit from learning how to get along with the boss that he already has.

Why Are Good Relationships Important in the Workplace?

Unless your financial situation is highly unusual, you will likely spend most of your adult years working. Why do you have to work? Work provides you with a salary so that you might pay for food, shelter, and all of life's other necessities and luxuries both large and small. Work also often gives you a sense of purpose and a feeling that you're contributing to society. Although working does not guarantee you wealth or happiness, it is important to sustaining both a healthy physical and emotional existence for yourself and your family.

Since early childhood, you have been getting ready for a life of work. Around the time you were playing alongside other children in the sandbox, you began to train for a lifetime of working with people. Unfortunately, that's where you began encountering people who didn't play nice. For example, some children found sharing difficult. Others got away with being verbally and physically aggressive, pushing other children out of what they presumed was their own personal sandbox. Unchecked, these early patterns of relational behavior may result in communication difficulties later on in life, and these people may have trouble operating in harmony with their bosses and co-workers.

Other skills are formally taught in elementary and secondary school, but communication skills are seldom offered. What you know about relating to others you probably learned through fairly automatic and habitual daily interactions with family, peers, and other role models. Unfortunately, what you learned might be wrong, and you may not even be aware of it. As a result, you may have learned to communicate in ways that don't always work that well for you. You may have also learned along the way some very good communication habits. But if you don't understand which strategies work and which don't work, you will not know how to manage communication challenges competently. To one degree or another, then, many people end up relationally and communicatively insecure, limited, or worse—incompetent.

Communication competence is critical to your ability to develop and sustain relationships at work. Competent communication can make the difference in getting and keeping a job, being promoted or fired, finding yourself undermined or supported, and completing or failing to complete work assignments. Virtually all the work assignments you have in your life will require the assistance and cooperation of other people. No meaningful job can be completed in total isolation from other people. Those who do not work well with others, then, learn very quickly that they have to find ways to overcome their relational and communication inadequacies. Even if you are already a competent communicator, you may work with people who do not share these skills. In order to be a truly effective communicator at work, you will need to know how to relate to co-workers and superiors who may not know how to relate to you. Let's look a little closer at why it's important to develop good relationships in the workplace.

You Spend a Lot of Time with Others at Work

College graduates holding a full-time job work, on average, eight hours per day, five days per week and sometimes on weekends and holidays.[1] During an average workweek you will have to interact frequently with others. Your workdays will involve depending on, working with, operating side by side, and, importantly, getting along with co-workers, supervisors, and subordinates.

We spend a lot of our work time communicating with others. Whether they are administrators, technicians, or professionals, people spend about 70 percent of their time at work communicating, and of that 70 percent, two-thirds is spent talking. Interestingly, observational data reveal that people tend to underestimate the time they spend talking at work and overestimate the time they spend reading or writing.[2] Because you will spend so much of your work time relating to others, it is in your best interest to continually develop and hone your communication skills.

Visualize! Practice! 5.1:
How Do You Spend Your Time?

How do you spend your time? To assess how much of your time you spend working, studying, or relaxing, check out **VISUALIZE! PRACTICE! 5.1: How Do You Spend Your Time?**

1. What percentage of time did you spend working this past week?

2. What percentage of time did you spend studying this past week?

3. What percentage of "leisure" time did you spend enjoying?

Does it surprise you to learn that most U.S. workers only enjoy, on average, between five and six hours per day doing leisure activities—and most of those are spent watching TV?

Source: American time use survey summary (2009, June 24). Bureau of Labor Statistics. Retrieved February 1, 2010, from http://www.bls.gov/news.release/atus.nr0.htm

Pleasant Working Relationships Are Better Than Unpleasant Ones

Study after study points to human issues as the primary source of employees' dissatisfaction.[3] Even though money may motivate and reward hard work, experts agree that money has the power to do only so much. Beyond some threshold of needs being satisfied, money fails to sustain long-term motivation and satisfaction in the workplace. Conflict, tension with a co-worker, or a misunderstanding with the boss can undermine even the

Fuse/Jupiter Images

most lucrative job. Research on organizational life indicates that unpleasant work relationships lead to employee stress, inability to coordinate tasks, and employee turnover.[4] No one likes to go to work feeling uncomfortable or anxious about the possibility of a difficult encounter. We would all rather approach our work life looking forward to our exchanges with people. Although good relationships at work may not be sufficient to keep you at a low-paying job, bad relationships will likely drive you away from a high-paying position.

Much of Your Work Requires That You Collaborate with Others

Putting people with shared interests and concerns together often leads to the sense that "we are all in this together." Talking about a project as *ours* rather than *mine* often leads to greater buy-in or commitment to the solution that evolves. Working collaboratively requires us to cooperate in ways that enable us to work together long-term to solve complex problems. Building teams, working in groups, and participating in committees are standard procedures in most organizations today. Effective, productive organizations cannot exist without people being able to work together in teams building consensus, making decisions, and solving problems.[5]

Friendships Often Evolve from Work Relationships

There's an old saying: "You can never be *friends* with people you work with." Opponents of workplace friendships claim that they promote socializing at the expense of productivity and foster cliques and exclusivity. But proponents assert that workplace friendships offer opportunities for critical feedback that only friends can provide, increased collaboration and cooperation, and a more enjoyable environment.

Recent research supports the proponents' position: Having close friends at work boosts employees' satisfaction by 50 percent.[6] Gallup interviews reveal that people "who have a best friend at work are seven times more likely to be engaged in their job. They get more done in less time. They also have fewer accidents, have more engaged customers and are more likely to innovate and share new ideas."[7] Yet most companies discourage their employees from developing close relationships. Fully one-third of the managers and supervisors polled by Gallup agreed with the adage "familiarity breeds contempt." In truth, familiarity reduces people's uncertainty about each other, and discovering similar attitudes and beliefs often leads to liking or friendship.[8] Preventing or discouraging workers from becoming close erodes employee satisfaction and undermines productivity. Instead, researchers advise company managers to find ways to promote workplace friendships.[9]

What Factors Influence Your Ability to Get Along at Work?

People come together at work to achieve a goal by collective action that one person acting alone could not achieve. Organizations have objectives that cannot be fulfilled without people communicating and interacting together in some coordinated way. Over time, people within an organization work out some stable set of rules and expectations that define how they are supposed to communicate with each other and regulate their behaviors in order to coordinate their actions to attain the organization's goals. This set of understandings defines what is expected of each employee, what will be not be tolerated, and what will be rewarded. These understandings define who is to do what; who will have more power, authority, prestige, and rewards; and what will happen to an employee who does not do what the others expect and want. These understandings and expectations define the relational pattern of each social organization.

It can be difficult to understand an organization's relational pattern without observing over time how the individuals within the organization are relating to each other. Such an observation would reveal at least four kinds of regularities. In every organization, large or small, these four regularities or factors influence how employees think, act, and relate to each other at work:

- **norms** that all members of the organization are expected to follow
- **roles** or specialized functions for each member of the organization
- **ranks**, or hierarchy, that prescribe levels of authority
- **controls** that members use to reward desired contributions or punish deviations[10]

Norms Define What's Acceptable

Rules that every member of an organization is expected to follow are called norms. These norms define when and where workers assemble for staff meetings, what kinds of behaviors communicate respect or disrespect, when humor is okay (and when it is not), what titles are used and when, and so on. In some organizations, the norms for dress, office romance, use of space and equipment, and the like are written out as formal policy, printed in a company handbook, and distributed to all members. Other norms are implicit and informal, but members are required to learn and appreciate them nevertheless. Knowing and following the rules enable you to adapt to and get along with others who are also expected to follow the rules.

Roles Define Your Job

Like actors in a play, each member of an organization performs some specialized role or set of behaviors that complements the roles of others in the effort to achieve the organization's objectives. If each employee's role is understood and accepted, the members can act effectively as a team. Roles in an organization are usually clearly defined and labeled. Common labels for roles in an organization include boss, supervisor, manager, director, secretary, administrative assistant, janitor, clerk, and foreman or forewoman. You are hired into a role when you enter an organization. Your role may change over time as you are promoted or repositioned in the company. Adhering to your role identity at work enables you to do your part as a member of the team.

Ranks Define Your Position

Some people in an organization play more critical or more honored roles than others. People assume different ranks within the same organization. Some members have more authority, power, prestige, income, skills, and education. Such rankings are often accepted by most, if not all, employees of a given organization. Ranks define hierarchical levels of management and non-management. These rankings can be visually depicted in organizational charts that define levels of leadership. People lower in ranks are often expected to show deference to and follow the instructions of those in higher ranks. Recognizing your own and others' ranks within an organization influences your ability to communicate effectively.

Controls Regulate Your Behavior

Controls maintain an organization's norms, roles, and ranks—its pattern of social organization. Employees who fail to carry out or who deviate from the organization's

Module 1:
How Do I "Get In and Fit In" to My Organization's Unique Culture?

Module 9:
How Do I Navigate Office Politics?

expectations will likely be sanctioned in some negative way, ranging from a verbal reprimand, a frown from the boss, open complaints, conflict, or social exclusion to a negative performance appraisal, a letter of reprimand, temporary leave without pay, or probation to termination. On the other hand, if an employee performs above and beyond what the organization's members expect, verbal, nonverbal, and material rewards might be used to recognize that contribution. Positive sanctions include smiles of approval, compliments, pay raises, promotions, parking privileges, or a bigger office—with a window. Social controls, then, consist of the administration of positive and negative sanctions in order to maintain the pattern of social organization. Such controls ensure that everyone moves to effect the company's goals. Following the rules and procedures of an organization enables you to fit in and get along.

For more about productive relationships within a company's culture, check out **MODULE 1: How Do I "Get In and Fit In" to My Organization's Unique Culture?** And for more about approaching a company's norms, roles, ranks, and controls in ways that benefit your career, see **MODULE 9: How Do I Navigate Office Politics?**

What Strategies Will Help You Play Well with Others?

Communication researchers have identified a number of strategies people use to successfully initiate and sustain interpersonal relationships. Social scientists have done extensive research on strategies that people use to try to get others to respond favorably to them.[11] Dozens of strategies seem to work, at least some times. Moreover, several strategies can be used at the same time, resulting in thousands of possibilities for achieving affinity. Clearly, there's no shortage of ways to get people to like you. Implementing them requires a conscious, deliberate decision to do so. Here, we'll discuss the strategies we consider to be the most important in helping you influence how others respond to you.

Initiate Relationships

If you want a relationship at work, take the initiative. Approach someone, say hello, and engage in some small talk. This is where it starts—by simply making contact in a nonthreatening way. A simple greeting and the power of small talk should never be underestimated. Striking up a conversation with someone you do not know begins with eye contact and hello. Safe topics for initial conversations are the weather or sports; avoid issues and topics that could be controversial or risky. Remember: your goal is to initiate a relationship, not to offend a co-worker. Small talk provides the social framework for what can become a meaningful friendship over time. In spite of its apparent superficiality, small talk is critical to the development of interpersonal relationships at work. Even if you feel like you are too busy, make it a point to engage in small talk with people you see at work every day.

Communicate Respect

Ask people at work how they would most like to be treated, and they are likely to say, "With dignity and respect." Perhaps no issue is more important to sustaining good working relationships than communicating respect for each other. Showing respect validates others' importance to you and to the task. We all desire to be valued and accepted by others. And the reciprocity principle suggests that if you give respect, you will receive respect. So how can you communicate respect? Begin by listening actively to what others say. Ask for their input and opinion. Acknowledge their points of view. Confirm their value. Give them credit

Golden Pixels LLC/Alamy

for their ideas. Be inclusive: encourage their active participation on the team. No matter their background, ethnicity, race, religion, age, or sex, be respectful in your interactions with co-workers. Never disparage, insult, or demean what they say or do, privately or publicly. Focus more on what your co-workers do right than what they may do wrong.[12]

Be Trustworthy

Trust is the basis of all good relationships. When people trust you, that means they believe you are honest and reliable. Without trust between co-workers, little is doable. Trusted co-workers feel more comfortable with each other. They do not question each other's motives or ambitions. Instead, they feel like they are working toward a common goal. For people who do not seem particularly trustworthy, you might proceed as though they are.

Demonstrating trust is the first step in building and sustaining a trusting relationship. Good working relationships all come down to trust. Can you trust your co-workers to respond to you sensitively when you need their help and support? Can you be confident that they will continue to like and support you when you make a mistake or fail? Can you believe that they will understand when you admit you do not know how to do something and need help? If you can answer yes to all of these questions with conviction, then you can assume the relationships are trusting ones. At the same time, you need to ask yourself if your co-workers would similarly answer yes about you.[13]

Be Careful What You Reveal

Even though you are likely to develop friendships in the workplace, you will need to monitor what information you share. Because there is often a fine line between personal friendships and work relationships, it is easy to become confused between what is acceptable to disclose and what is not. Some topics should be avoided at work.

In the business environment, what you say affects how you are perceived as an employee or a manager. If you disclose, for instance, that you are taking medication for an anxiety disorder, your manager might mistakenly assume that you will not be as able to

Visualize! Practice! 5.2:
*Are You Being
Confirmed?*

cope with challenges as other employees. Moreover, your employer might perceive you as an expensive, high-maintenance employee. What are topics that you might want to avoid discussing with your boss or co-workers? Consider these:

- gossip, particularly gossip about people at work
- salary information, how much money you make
- intimate details about your personal life
- politics and religion
- hangovers and wild weekends
- personal problems at home
- racial or ethnic remarks, jokes, or slurs
- negative views about your colleagues or boss[14]

Be selective in what you reveal, and always consider the work-related implications of what you say—even with those colleagues you consider to be close friends.

Confirm or Praise Others

It is human nature to notice what is wrong or out of the ordinary more than what is right or typical. Even so, you can refrain from pointing out others' errors. At the same time, you can choose to notice and praise people for doing something well. Everyone likes to feel that others value what they do, particularly at work. When people feel validated, they have a greater sense of well-being and self-worth. You can affect how people feel by the kinds of messages you use. **Confirming messages** reinforce a person's value, whereas **disconfirming messages** undermine or attack a person's self-worth.

Behavioral social scientists have long advocated the use of positive reinforcement. They know that praise works; punishment does not. Employees and managers both respond favorably to positive feedback. People like to feel valued; praise or confirming messages help to make that happen. The principle of positive reinforcement is simple: immediately reinforce any behavior you want increased or repeated. Ignore any behavior you don't want to continue (unless, of course, the behavior is likely to cause harm to self or others).

Researchers have examined the effects of confirming messages in families, at school, and in a variety of other contexts, and they concluded that confirming others may be the single most important factor in individuals' mental health and overall well-being.[15] Even though most managers recognize that praise can motivate employees, few of them apparently make praise a high priority. In an often-cited study by Gerald Graham of Wichita State University, 58 percent of the employees surveyed said that their managers seldom if ever praised them, and only 19 percent ever received public praise at work.[16] How many confirming messages have you received recently? Take a minute to assess those messages with **VISUALIZE! PRACTICE! 5.2: Are You Being Confirmed?**

Recall confirming messages that a supervisor, coworker, classmate, or teacher has communicated to you in this past week.

1. How did those messages feel?
2. How did you respond?
3. How many did you recall?
4. How many do you *wish* you had received?

Praise comes in many shapes and sizes, ranging from an easy smile or nod to a formal written commendation placed in your personnel file. Different positive behaviors warrant different types of praise. The more consequential the positive behavior, the more substantial the praise should be. Look for opportunities, big and small, to give praise. When someone meets a difficult deadline, when a colleague helps you complete a task or pitches in when needed, or when your manager makes a good decision, give praise. Praise should be immediate, specific, warranted, and sincere. Here are some examples:

Visualize! Practice! 5.3:
Confirming Others

"I like the way you handled that."

"I have confidence in your ability."

"I'm proud of you for trying."

"You did a great job on this project."

"That's a good question."

"I know that I can depend on you to do this right."

"These results show a lot of hard work. Thank you!"

"You get high marks on this task."

"This is definitely an A project."

"You managed that difficult encounter well."

Now it's your turn. What confirming messages could you use to praise the people in your life? Take a minute to create those messages with **VISUALIZE! PRACTICE! 5.3: Confirming Others**.

Generate five confirming messages that you would use to praise a coworker, classmate, teacher, or boss.

1. _____

2. _____

3. _____

4. _____

5. _____

Caution: Not all behavior warrants praise or confirmation. At times you may not want to confirm. At times, you may need to call out an employee's or co-worker's inappropriate behavior and offer suggestions for change. Co-workers who fail to complete their tasks, arrive consistently late to work, or engage in office gossip should not be confirmed for what they do or fail to do. You may choose to ignore the behavior altogether, or you can offer constructive criticism or feedback on what they might do differently. When giving criticism, be careful to avoid disconfirming messages that hurt and devalue the individual. Here are some examples of disconfirming messages:

"Why are you always late?"

"Your work on this project was really subpar."

"You have a bad attitude."

"You never seem to get along with your co-workers."

"Why do you complain so much?"

How might you recast these disconfirming comments into constructive, helpful feedback? For instance, instead of "Why are you always late?" you might say, "When you are late for work, it affects all of us. How might you restructure your schedule to ensure that you arrive to work on time?" Now try recasting the remaining disconfirming messages into constructive messages.

Be Open to Criticism

Much of our behavior at work is scrutinized and subject to evaluation. That's the nature of work; we are paid to perform, and how much we are paid often depends on the quality of our performance. Criticism is often used to provide employees with guidance about how they might better perform. Criticism, then, should be a welcomed opportunity for improvement and advancement.

Even so, no one likes to be criticized. Criticism implies that our performance is less than perfect. Disconfirming messages are particularly hard. Try not to take disconfirming messages personally. Go beyond the words and focus on the communicator's intent. Neither giving nor receiving criticism comes easily.

Some criticism is informal and spontaneous, and other criticism is part of the performance appraisal process. Either way, you will need to be prepared to respond to criticism in constructive ways. How you handle unfavorable or evaluative feedback affects how you are perceived. In fact, how you respond to criticism influences your credibility at work. Try to respond with grace and dignity. Here are some ways to do that:[17]

- **Listen carefully.** Allow others to provide you with the full picture of what they see and want from you. Do not interrupt. Think about what the message means. Avoid building mental defenses against what they say; try not to prematurely dismiss or deny the validity of all or part of their criticism.

- **Ask for clarification.** If you are unsure about what is being said, ask questions. Find out exactly what you should have done and still need to do. Repeat what you hear as you understand it, and ask for confirmation.

- **Look confident.** Nonverbal behaviors can leak information about how you really feel. These unwitting behaviors are easily misunderstood as well. Be careful how you sit and

Putting Your Skills to Work

...THE RESOURCES YOU SUGGESTED HAVE REALLY HELPED...

Being open to criticism isn't always easy. But you're probably already applying this skill now. For example, you've already learned how to be non-defensive and open to criticism when you're able to listen to and learn from feedback that your teachers or peers have given to you following a speech you gave in class, or perhaps a paper you wrote for a course.

A-Digit/istockphoto.com

look while listening to criticism. Folded arms may signal defensiveness, arrogance, or resistance. Lack of eye contact may communicate apathy or disregard. Sit erect, make eye contact, and maintain an open and relaxed posture.

- **Keep things in perspective.** Criticism, right or wrong, accurate or inaccurate, should be seen in the broader context of who you are and what you know you can do. Just because you performed less than optimally this time, you should not generalize the criticism to all your work performance. This is one event, one criticism. Moreover, the criticism may not be accurate or legitimate. Consider the messenger: Perhaps this evaluation says more about the critic's own selective perceptions and organizational experiences. You may want to check with others to determine how reliable the criticism is before assuming it is valid.

Yes, criticism is hard to take, but following these simple practices should make the evaluation process a little more helpful and manageable.

Taken together, these basic communication strategies will go a long way toward helping you get along with others at work. That said, you also need to be mindful of the diversity of your co-workers. By being aware of your different characteristics and backgrounds, you can better appreciate your colleagues and gain greater control of your workplace interactions. In the next section, we'll discuss specific communication strategies for a variety of work relationships.

For more about playing well with others, check out **MODULE 4: What Do I Need to Know About Business Etiquette?**

How Do You Manage Diverse and Difficult Relationships?

Whoever you interact with at work, the potential exists for a relationship. Relationships based on an organization's norms, roles, ranks, and controls are common in the workplace. Most typical are relationships between superiors and subordinates, between mentors and protégés, among colleagues, with clients or customers, and even romantic relationships. Organizations often define the types of relationships, and the organization's culture defines the way the relationships function. Because positive working relationships are important to both personal and organizational well-being, it's important to recognize the different types of relationships you are likely to encounter at work and their potential challenges.

Despite your best efforts to get along, conflicts with co-workers will occur. Research shows that 60 to 80 percent of all difficulties in an organization stem from troubled or strained employee relationships.[18] Managers report spending an estimated 25 to 40 percent of their time on employee conflicts.[19] At the same time, employees rate getting along with managers and co-workers as their greatest challenge—and highest priority.[20] In this section, you will begin to appreciate a variety of differences among co-workers and challenges that you may encounter during your own work life. Being able to effectively relate to people of different ages, genders, and cultures can help you avoid conflict and enjoy more productive relationships with your co-workers.

Communication accommodation theory helps us understand how to interact with people who are different from us. One of the most prominent proponents of this theory, Howard Giles, explains that when people communicate, they often adjust their style of communicating to match the communication style of the other.[21] This is called **accommodation**. When talking to a child, for instance, adults often change their speech

patterns to accommodate those of the child by speaking more slowly and using simple words. By doing so, adults attempt to convey a sense of warmth, compatibility, and similarity. Accommodation is more likely when the people communicating like each another, want to connect, or intend to show agreement. However, this type of communication can be perceived negatively if the receiver looks at the adaptation as insincere, mocking, or condescending, or as an attempt to come across as overly familiar.

Whereas accommodative messages can reduce perceived differences between individuals, non-accommodative messages can increase perceived differences. Communicators can *converge* (or accommodate) to show liking, or they can deliberately choose to *diverge* (or avoid accommodating) to show dislike or to communicate distance, status, or power.[22] Remember communication accommodation theory when you want to increase or decrease perceptions of attraction, status, agreement, or similarities between you and your co-workers. Being able to adjust your communication style will help you facilitate and manage diverse and challenging relationships at work.

Intergenerational Relationships

If you've been out of school and working for a while, you may notice that the new generation of workers seems a bit different from your own generation. You may worry that their expectations are too high, they demand too much too soon, and they want everyone in the workplace to abandon paper and rely exclusively on technology. If you are new to the corporate life, you may be bewildered at the norms and rules established by the older generations of workers. You may wonder why they are so slow to innovate, why they rarely take vacation time, and why they work so hard for such little return.

Much has been written in the popular literature about Generation Y (also known as the Millennials, the Net Generation, and the Echo Boomers), who were born between approximately 1977 and 1994. Like other generations (such as the baby boomers and the Gen Xers), Gen Yers are heavily influenced by the events, music, politics, technology, and pop culture of their time. Certainly, no generation of workers is more educated or more technologically savvy than the Gen Yers. Growing up with smartphones, laptops, the Internet, texting, email, instant messaging, YouTube, instant news, iPods, and hundreds of TV channels, Gen Yers rely extensively on electronic media for news, entertainment, study, and social networking. And technology use is likely to continue increasing. According to the Kaiser Family Foundation, children between 8 and 18 today consume an average of 7 hours and 38 minutes of media per day, or more than 53 hours per week.[23] In other words, children today spend as much time using media as most adults spend at work. Consider these statistics:

- 66 percent of these kids own cell phones.
- Besides using cell phones to talk, children use cell phones 49 minutes per day to access TV, music, and games.
- 76 percent of them own iPods or MP3 players.
- TV viewing is up, with children watching 4 hours and 29 minutes per day.
- 74 percent of high school students have a social profile online (such as Facebook or MySpace), and they spend 22 minutes per day visiting social Internet sites.

Visualize! Practice! 5.4: *Multi-tasking with Technology*

Consider some of the effects of the increased use of technology among Gen Yers with VISUALIZE! PRACTICE! 5.4: **Multi-tasking with Technology**. It's not always as effective as you might think.

1. On a scale of 1 to 10 (1 being *least* effective and 10 being *most* effective), how effective are you at multi-tasking? How easy is it for you to talk on your cell, instant-message a friend, and read your email all at the same time?

    Least effective   Most effective

      1   2   3   4   5   6   7   8   9   10

A recent Stanford study reveals that heavy media multi-taskers are much worse than low multi-taskers at getting the job done. In fact, heavy multi-taskers had trouble filtering out important information from unimportant information, and they were unable to remember as much as low multi-taskers.

Source: Gorlick, A. (2009, August 24) Media multi-taskers pay mental price, Stanford study shows. *Stanford University News.* Retrieved February 1, 2010, from http://news.stanford.edu/news/2009/august24/multitask-research-study-082409.html

2. On a scale of 1 to 10 (1 being *least* capable and 10 being *most* capable), how capable are you of talking on the phone and driving at the same time?

    Least capable   Most capable

      1   2   3   4   5   6   7   8   9   10

Drivers using cell phone are four times more likely to have a serious car accident that results in hospitalization.* Moreover, in a controlled laboratory study, cell phone drivers were as bad, if not worse, than drunk drivers.**

* News release: 1st evidence of effects of cellphone use on injury crashes (2005, July 12). *Insurance Institute for Highway Safety.* Retrieved February 1, 2010, from http://www.iihs.org/news/2005/iihs_news_071205.pdf
** Strayer, D. L., Drew, F. A., & Crouch, D. J. (2006). A comparison of the cell phone driver and the drunk driver. *Human Factors,* 48, 381–391.

Reliance on technology is not the only difference between Gen Y and generations before them. Researchers have found that over the years, workers have changed gradually in ways that influence how they view work and how they interact with others.[24] More emphasis on leisure time and a balance between work and family life, increased self-esteem and narcissism, greater anxiety and depression, and more concern for wealth, looks, status, and autonomy—all these changes are likely to affect how Gen Yers behave and respond to others at work.

So how do co-workers from different generations get past these differences and communicate effectively with one another? Critical to effective communication between generations is the ability to accommodate what you say and how you say it. Interestingly, older people are often perceived as *underaccommodative* in their encounters with younger people, while younger people are perceived as *overaccommodative* with their elders.[25] Either way, the potential for intergenerational miscommunication is high.

For instance, older people are perceived to hold and express negative stereotypes about the younger generation, they do not seem to appreciate the younger generation's needs and wants, and they tend to brag about "the good old days." So you might expect younger people to find conversation with older people difficult and disagreeable. Yet research reveals that these kinds of underaccommodative comments by older people are not intended to demean younger people but to assert the elders' continued vibrancy and relevance. On the other hand, younger people are often perceived to be talking down to their elders, evidenced by slowing their speech, smiling excessively, nodding and other apparently condescending behaviors. In reality, these overaccommodative attempts are likely born out of the younger peoples' desire to nurture or to be attentive than to patronize, denigrate, or demean.[26]

Communicating effectively between generations requires that younger and older people work to better accommodate one another and to translate or seek to understand when the other over- or underaccommodates. As it turns out, generational differences are often perceived to be much greater than they actually are. Looking beyond the popular literature, researchers have documented similarities among the generations in the workplace, noting that many perceived differences in values, for instance, are likely a function of age, status, and longevity in the organization.[27]

In addition to accommodating our speech to them, we should make a point of interacting more often with people outside our generational group, moving beyond our comfort zone. Discovering and focusing on similarities, or what you have in common with one another, will often override assumptions about differences. Perhaps most important to effective intergenerational communication is seeking each other's advice and help. For older workers, reaching out to Gen Yers for help designing an effective webpage, navigating the Internet, or learning to use the company's latest smartphone makes good communication and work sense. For younger workers, asking more experienced co-workers to explain the origins of current policies as well as the more informal rules and asking for mentoring can only make their work more productive.

Women and Men at Work

Not until the late 1800s did women find their way into the workplace outside the family home. Today women make up 46.5 percent of the labor force in the United States, with projections of even greater representation in the future.[28] Obviously, it's in everyone's best interest for men and women co-workers to relate effectively. Knowing how to accommodate each other can make working together easier and more productive. In order to be able to accommodate the other gender appropriately, you need to reflect first on how women and men communicate.

No innate, or biological, differences account for how women and men communicate differently. But how children are socialized influences how they relate and, more importantly, how they perceive others to communicate. Women and men are a product of their socialization. Throughout their lives, they learn to view the world differently and to think and behave in particular ways. Growing up male implies being part of a masculine culture, and growing up female means being a member of a feminine culture. When men and women don't behave in gender-appropriate ways, they often encounter negative reactions.

As a member of a feminine culture, a woman is often expected to place a high priority on personal relationships and to provide support, show compassion, and nurture others. To achieve symmetry or equality, women often "match experiences"[29] to show others they have felt the same way or the same thing happened to them. Because women value being polite, showing respect, and acting courteously, they "avoid criticizing, outdoing, or putting others down."[30] In contrast, men, as members of a masculine culture, are expected to give high priority to individual success and achievements, appreciate competition, assert themselves and challenge others, and control or dominate interactions.

How might these stereotyped gendered differences influence how women and men communicate with each other at work? Given the demands of the workplace, men may fail to appreciate women who they perceive as weak and unsure of themselves, and women may respond negatively to men who they perceive as attempting to dominate or self-promote. Recognizing differences in their values or priorities is one way for men and women to begin accommodating one another. Men may need to appreciate that women give support ("I like how you handled that situation"), communicate a sense of equality when working on tasks ("Let's try to analyze this problem *together*. How should *we* begin?"), and share the success of joint achievements ("We did a really good job on this project. I couldn't have done it without you"). Women may need to assert themselves while affirming their male co-workers' abilities ("I know that you already know how to do this. Let me give it a shot this time"), promote their own successes ("I feel really good about the work I did on this project"), and engage in more powerful talk by using fewer qualifiers (*maybe* and *perhaps*), tag questions ("don't you agree?" or "isn't that so?"), and intensifiers ("very, very happy").[31] Women and men respect each other more when they try to accommodate each other's communication styles.

The failure to accommodate often leads to miscommunication and misunderstandings. At the extreme, it can lead to sexual harassment. In recent years the U.S. Supreme Court has identified behaviors that might be perceived as hostile or victimizing, including telling off-color jokes, discussing explicit sexual conduct, using demeaning or inappropriate terms ("honey" or "babe"), or using crude or offensive language.[32] Perhaps no other kind of work relationship requires greater efforts to accommodate than the one between genders. The consequences of not doing so can be damaging to the organization—and potentially illegal.

Romantic Relationships at Work

Although most organizations discourage romantic relationships between co-workers, only a few organizations (about 30 percent) report having policies prohibiting them.[33] Nevertheless, many companies frown on office romances because they want to avoid allegations of sexual harassment and acts of retaliation after bitter breakups. Both employers and employees strongly agree that romances between supervisors and their subordinates are unhealthy. However, relationships between colleagues of equal status are perceived more positively.[34]

Regardless of company policy, co-worker romances are likely for several reasons: First, more women are working in the office alongside men. Second, with work hours steadily increasing over the last two decades, both men and women are spending more time together at work. Third, proximity, shared interests, and similar work values are predictors of attraction.[35] It's no wonder, then, that about 40 percent of employees today report involvement in a workplace romance at some point during their career.

The consequences of workplace romances can include marriage, divorce, sexual harassment, decreased morale and productivity, stalking, and even workplace violence. Co-workers may gossip about the romantic couple, complain of favoritism, attribute questionable motives, and exhibit signs of jealousy.[36] Whether you are involved with someone at work or you work with couples who are involved, these relationships should be managed so that they do not adversely affect the workplace morale.

Work–family border theory provides a contemporary view of the workplace environment that does not separate the work domain from one's personal life. This theory views work and life as two separate domains with permeable borders that individuals move in and out of throughout any given day.[37] People become **border crossers** as they move from work to home and back again. These domains overlap considerably for workplace romances, making the distinctions between work life and personal life arbitrary and less meaningful.

Accommodating co-workers in a romantic relationship requires rethinking an older paradigm that views romance and work as two separate and distinct entities. We can no longer prohibit office romance, nor do we seem to want to these days.[38] People are more tolerant of personal relationships at work, particularly when so many experience work romances themselves. In general, human resource professionals agree that when they learn about an office romance, they should simply keep an eye on the situation. Both employees and managers suggest that they should be on the lookout for potential "problematic behavior" and, when necessary, "talk to the employees involved" and "monitor conflict" and "productivity." In addition, a number of employees argue that romantic relationships should be supported, for example, by offering common vacation time.[39]

Two authors of this book, Dr. Plax and Dr. Kearney, are married to each other and work together at the same university. As marrieds who have been border crossing for thirty years, they have worked out a series of rules for how they want to relate to each other at work. Perhaps these simple rules will help you as you manage your own workplace romance.

Edw/Shutterstock.com

- **Rule 1:** Treat each other the way you would treat any other professional colleague at work—with respect and professionalism.
- **Rule 2:** Avoid using terms of endearment or making nonverbal contact that might make others feel awkward or embarrassed.
- **Rule 3:** Disclose the nature of the relationship. Attempts to hide or keep secret the relationship only invites distrust.
- **Rule 4:** Keep personal conflicts at home. Sharing marital conflicts only makes colleagues feel uncomfortable.
- **Rule 5:** Retain your own separate professional identity. Insist that others respond to you as individuals, not as a unit. Ensure that phone and email correspondence remains separate. Invitations, promotions, praise, pay raises, and assignments should be given to the deserving individual, not to the couple.

Visualize! Practice! 5.5:
A Rule for Managing Workplace Romance

Visualize! Practice! 5.6:
A Rule for Accommodating Workplace Romance

Complete **VISUALIZE! PRACTICE! 5.5: A Rule for Managing Workplace Romance** to come up with a sixth rule for managing your own (hypothetical or real) workplace romance.

Write your own sixth rule for how to manage your own (hypothetical or real) intimate relationship with someone you work with.

Rule 6: _____

At the same time, accommodate co-workers who are romantically involved. Consider these possible rules:

- **Rule 1:** Recognize and confirm their personal and working relationships.
- **Rule 2:** At the same time, treat them as separate individuals. Do not assume they will think, feel, or behave the same way on important issues.
- **Rule 3:** Do not assume or behave as though one individual is the conduit for information or messages to the other.
- **Rule 4:** Avoid making comparisons by pointing out differences and similarities between the two individuals.
- **Rule 5:** Negotiate your relationship with each person separately first—and then together.

Complete **VISUALIZE! PRACTICE! 5.6: A Rule for Accommodating Workplace Romance** to come up with a sixth rule for accommodating a (hypothetical or real) relationship between two people you work with.

Write your own sixth rule for how you would respond to someone you know at work who is involved with a coworker or boss.

Rule 6: _____

Co-workers with and without Children

Many companies today have implemented policies and practices that support the ever-increasing numbers of working parents, including flextime, telecommuting, job-sharing, subsidized maternity or sick-child leave, family health insurance plans, and compressed work weeks. Some even provide lactation rooms, on-site day care, and parenting 101 seminars. *Working Mother* magazine regularly provides a list of the one hundred most family-friendly companies, with Abbott Laboratories, Allstate Insurance, American Express, AOL, Bank of America, and Bayer beginning the list.[40] Providing family-friendly work

Weigh In! 5.1:
Workers with and without Children

environments has proved cost-effective, often resulting in lower rates of absenteeism, reduced stress levels, and increased productivity.

Even so, many American companies fail to provide the perks that benefit parents, particularly for workers in lower-paying positions (such as servers or secretaries).[41] In addition, a challenge many working parents face is the scarcity of after-school programs, leaving a gap in childcare from 2:00 or 3:00 p.m. until 6:00 or 7:00 p.m., amounting to 15 to 25 hours a week that children are left without supervision. Parents are fighting long and hard for organizations to help them meet challenges like these and flexibly border-cross the work-family domains.

In the meantime, workers without children are showing signs of discontent over the family-friendly policies that are beginning to pervade the workplace.[42] Although recognizing the special demands facing working parents, they feel they are being taken advantage of. They argue that the compensations provided to parents are not similarly applied to them. These compensations include the ability to select vacation days at times that most benefit parents (such as during the summer and school holidays), miss work days and appointments for prenatal care or to take children to doctors, and prioritize shift assignments. In addition, working parents are given more perks and financial benefits, such as more generous subsidies for family health care plans, child care assistance, and pregnancy or parental leaves.

Workers without children are increasingly calling for child neutrality in the workplace, demanding greater equity and equivalent compensation packages (equal pay for equal work). Perhaps most contentious for workers without children is the presence of children at work, who become distracting and problematic, particularly when co-workers are forced (or asked) to become babysitters. What are your thoughts about the differences between workers with children and those without? Explore your thinking with **WEIGH IN! 5.1: Workers with and without Children**.

In this module, we refer to parents and non-parents as coworkers with and without children. Others impose labels of *child-burdened* and *child-free*. What connotations or meanings do these labels communicate? What other terms might you use? Why do you suppose your authors chose to avoid using the term *child-less*?

No Kidding! International* is a nonprofit social organization that caters solely to singles and couples who do not have children. Founder Jerry Steinberg wanted to reach out to people who were tired of parents alienating those who did not have kids, for whatever reason. This is a club for those seeking child-free friends. Is this a club you would like to join? If so, why? If not, why not?

* No kidding! The international social club for child-free couples and singles. Retrieved February 1, 2010, from http://www.nokidding.net/

Given that co-workers with and without children hold two very different perspectives, they should hold discussions at work in a joint attempt to make their work–family life crossovers more doable and equitable. Cafeteria-style benefit packages[43] may provide one of many solutions palatable to both types of workers. These packages provide workers with an allowance or budget for them to choose alternative benefits and perks that can be selected for multiple reasons, such as family care or fitness programs. Some packages allow workers to flexibly take time off from work without providing specific reasons, allowing individuals to use their days to attend child functions or to run errands, ski, or play with the dog. Here are some other, more concrete strategies:

- Limit when and how often co-workers talk about toddlers, prenatal care, and baby clothes.
- Host baby showers for co-workers outside the workplace, lessening the pressure for every co-worker to attend and give a gift.

- Support parents' efforts to balance their work–family domains. Offer to switch schedules when the need arises.

- Ask about parents' children (it is their favorite topic, after all).

- Be understanding and sympathetic when child-care emergencies happen.

- Offer some kind of compensation to those without children who assume co-workers' responsibilities when parents must leave work, arrive late, or leave early (such as gift certificates, schedule trading, and working extra hours on their behalf).

- Ensure that work-sponsored social events reflect the interests of both workers who have children and those who don't.

- Be sensitive to the fact that more and more adults are choosing not to have children, lacking a compelling reason to have them, disliking or fearing children, enjoying a child-free lifestyle, or preferring pets. Broaching topics of interest to them is a good idea.

Visualize! Practice! 5.7:
Equity between Workers with and without Children

To come up with some additional strategies for creating greater equity between workers with and without children, check out **VISUALIZE! PRACTICE! 5.7: Equity between Workers with and without Children**.

Generate three additional approaches to creating greater equity between coworkers who have children and those who don't.

1. _____
2. _____
3. _____

Culturally Dissimilar Co-workers

Most researchers contend that the greater the similarity between co-workers in terms of demographic characteristics such as race, age, ethnicity, culture, and gender, the more attracted co-workers are to one another. Such attraction or liking often results in greater work cohesion, productivity, job satisfaction, and other desirable work-related outcomes. Similar individuals tend to identify with each other, seek each other's company, and interact more. Conversely, dissimilar co-workers often have difficulty relating to each other, dwell on differences, and avoid (or worse, confront) each other.[44] And yet, contemporary workplace environments are highly diverse, particularly in our global economy, and we are reminded as Americans to expect and embrace diversity.

When managed appropriately, diverse workers can increase overall work performance, productivity, and quality. By bringing fresh ideas, providing new perspectives, and challenging the status quo, a diverse work group can be highly desirable for the bottom line.[45] Workers' demographic or cultural dissimilarity, as it turns out, matters most at the early stages of their relationship, decreasing in importance as they interact over time.[46] As workers come to know one another, they share more and more information and discover individual or unique similarities.

Because we tend to disassociate from, avoid, and even feel alienated from people we perceive to be different from us, you have to work hard to minimize these differences between you and your co-workers. To be even more effective, try to interpret perceived differences not as challenges or problems but as assets that might enhance the work group's performance. In other words, appreciate someone's differences and redefine them as positive or interesting attributes. Changing how you look at someone will influence how you behave toward and work with that person.

Visualize! Practice! 5.8:
*A Challenging
Co-worker*

Bob Daemmrich/PhotoEdit

Perhaps most fundamental to working with diverse others is recognizing the human tendency to **stereotype**. You must never assume that just because a person is a member of a particular social or demographic group, he or she necessarily shares all the cultural characteristics attributed to it. There is often as much diversity *within* groups as there is *between* groups. So be open to exceptions and individual variations at all times. Also keep in mind our almost-inescapable tendency to be **ethnocentric**. In other words, we all have a tendency to believe our own cultural background is and should be the baseline against which all other groups should be judged. We are inclined to judge people who are unlike ourselves by our own cultural standards.[47] How fair or open-minded is that?

Challenging Co-workers

In a recent survey, 29 percent of respondents indicated that they work with someone who is rude or unprofessional.[48] With job uncertainty, increased debt load, and excessive work demands, worker stresses have resulted in what the popular media term "desk rage." Workers have become grumpy, irritable, and short-tempered. Almost half of American workers today report being yelled at and verbally abused, with one in four admitting that they were driven to tears.[49] No one is immune: Desk rage extends across businesses, social classes, and levels of employment.

Desk rage is not the only challenge you are likely to face at work; some co-workers are simply difficult to work with. Some workers continually miss deadlines or show up to work late. Others are disagreeable, disorganized, or undependable. Some co-workers talk too much or not at all, and others are antagonistic, condescending, or self-promoting braggarts. To explore a case study of a challenging co-worker and how you might respond to her, check out **VISUALIZE! PRACTICE! 5.8: A Challenging Co-worker**.

Jessica is a recent graduate from Berkeley. She's young, smart, ambitious, attractive, and fun. Here's the problem: Even with all that, she's very insecure. She's afraid that she'll be "found out" as not knowing as much as a Berkeley grad should know! Consequently, she works very hard at hiding her weaknesses and limitations. For instance, it would never occur to her to ask questions, to seek guidance or help, or to admit that she'd didn't know something. Adding to her level of insecurity is the fact that she is in a managerial position, supervising 25 people who have been with the company for 15 years and more. Their response to Jessica is predictable: They don't like her, they don't trust her, and they don't have faith in her abilities. Jessica suspects that she is not well-liked and respected by her workers.

1. What advice would you give to Jessica? List three strategies she could use to remedy this situation with her employees.

   a. _____

   b. _____

   c. _____

2. What advice would you give to her employees? List three different strategies her employees might use to help Jessica better manage them.

   a. _____

   b. _____

   c. _____

Even though there are no one-size-fits-all rules for relating to challenging co-workers, a few simple rules may help you navigate your interactions with these people:

- Be open and mindful of each other's apparent differences.
- Don't overreact to what challenging co-workers say or do.
- Be patient with the co-workers' anxieties and be respectful of their feelings.
- Ask challenging co-workers questions about themselves; give them opportunities to impress you.
- Acknowledge them when they do something good or correctly.
- Be a good listener; communicate a real interest in them and their work.
- Include challenging co-workers in group discussions; treat them as important members of your team.
- Appreciate the fact that it takes time to develop relationships with challenging co-workers.
- Give them your undivided attention; restrict difficult or challenging interactions to one-on-one encounters.

Rules are tools to use when needed. Keep in mind that sometimes a rule will work with an individual, and sometimes it won't. Just because a rule doesn't work on one occasion doesn't mean it won't work in another context or at another time. Don't throw away a rule simply because you tried it once and it didn't work. Rules can be useful. Having a set of rules to employ strategically allows you the flexibility to interact with even the most difficult co-workers.

Difficult Clients and Customers

Working with the public has its challenges. Any number of reasons might cause a client or a customer to become angry, upset, or confused. As a customer yourself, you have probably experienced these emotions or more—and for good reason. Customers are most likely to become difficult with waiters, attendants, salespeople, and other types of service providers when

- Their needs are not being met.
- They are being treated unfairly.
- They feel no one is listening to what they are saying.
- They are given the runaround.
- Promises are not kept.
- No one seems to care.[50]

Perhaps the best way to get along with clients and customers is to avoid treating them in ways that you wouldn't want to be treated. But if the client becomes difficult, there are two simple strategies you can use to diffuse the situation and meet his or her needs.[51]

- **Listen and empathize.** Angry or frustrated customers first need to vent. They want you to listen and understand what they are going through. They need and want you to confirm the reality of their situation or problem. Allow them to tell their story, ask them questions, and validate their experience. Let them know that what they are feeling is understandable and justified.

- **Apologize and resolve.** Once the problem is clear and you completely understand it, apologize on behalf of your organization. As the representative of the organization, you need not admit to any wrongdoing, but you can apologize for their bad experience. Saying "I'm sorry that this happened to you" goes a long way toward diffusing a client's anger and frustration. But an apology is not enough. You need to go further by working with the client to resolve the problem. Find ways to work through the issues. Develop a plan. Reassure her that you will follow through to make sure the solution works.

Others who have written on this topic offer similar strategies, such as "connect, correct, and close"[52] or "strategize, acknowledge, clarify, resolve, and check back."[53] Common to all these approaches is the acknowledgment of what the client is experiencing or feeling and a sincere effort to resolve the problem. When you effectively manage difficult customers, they feel that you really care about them, they gain confidence in your organization, and you have the satisfaction of knowing that you made a difference.[54]

For information about making your relationships work for you, check out **MODULE 11: How Do I Use Social Media for Professional Networking?**

How Do You Sustain a Good Relationship with Your Boss?

Perhaps no relationship is more important than the one you have with your boss. Getting along with your boss has its obvious benefits, and yet, according to a recent Gallup poll, 24 percent of workers would fire their current boss if they could.[55] Day-to-day interactions with bosses are a problem for many employees, who in one study rated such interactions as "less enjoyable than cleaning the house."[56] In another study, employees were asked what constitutes a bad boss:

- 39 percent said that bad bosses didn't keep their promises.
- 37 percent indicated that their boss didn't give them credit.

- 31 percent reported that their boss ignored them ("the silent treatment").
- 27 percent claimed that their boss made negative comments.
- 24 percent said their boss invaded their privacy.
- 23 percent reported that their boss often blamed them to cover up their own personal mistakes.[57]

Bad bosses are more common than any of us would like, and they are often responsible for high rates of employee turnover. In addition, employees with bad supervisors are at a higher risk for heart attacks, and people who suffer from bad bosses take more sick leave.[58]

If bad bosses are not be good for you, good bosses are the opposite. A Gallup survey of about 8 million people discovered that workers who agreed with the statement "My supervisor, or someone at work, cares about me as a person" were more productive, more likely to stay with the organization, and more engaged (that is, they felt a connection with the company).[59] The best managers appear to be those who are not only competent at their assignment or task but also experts in knowing who their employees are as people and as workers. Good bosses will keep you engaged, productive, and committed. They will find ways to bring out the best in you, make you feel important and valued, and mentor you as you develop professionally.

Working for a good boss is easy to do. The problem occurs when you don't have a good boss and you're stuck (at least until you find other employment) with a bad or mediocre manager. Working with a bad boss will require that you make some changes. Yes, *you* will have to change. The only way you can manage a bad boss is to change how you relate to her or him. Your first impulse might be a negative one: to confront your boss and tell her what you don't like and how she needs to change. But that impulse would be wrong. Remember that your goal is to get along, not to blame or criticize.

Developing a positive relationship with your supervisor begins with trust. If you want to be trusted, you will first need to show that you are worthy of that trust. Keep your commitments. Do what you say you will do, and do it when you say you will do it. When you are reliable and your boss can count on you, trust is established. Although trust is essential to a good relationship with your boss, you may also want to try these strategies:[60]

- Prioritize what your boss wants and needs. Discover what is important to him and make that your priority, too.
- Find ways to help your boss be successful, efficient, and productive, and then help her do that.
- Allow your boss to mentor you; ask for help and guidance. Many bosses like to feel needed and appreciated, and others like to teach.
- Be sensitive to your boss's moods and habits. Determine when it's a good time to approach her and when it's not.
- Try matching your boss's work style or orientation. If he likes to get into work early, then you might do the same.
- Identify the standards of work quality that your boss requires. Some bosses are perfectionists and want to see only final copy; others would rather see and work with first drafts. Don't assume that your standards for excellence are the same as his.

Given what you have learned in this chapter, what advice might you give to Leandra and Carlos? Let's begin with Leandra. Recall that she has problems with her colleagues at work. She doesn't believe that they even like her. As a result, she is probably distancing herself from them, avoiding them at lunchtime, failing to ask them for help, and providing them with no signs of wanting to get along. Although avoidance may be a natural tendency when you feel you're not liked, Leandra should do just the opposite. She needs to make an effort to reach out to her co-workers, say hello, and strike up brief conversations throughout her work day. Important to her relational success is providing her co-workers with confirming messages that are sincere and believable. It will be difficult for her colleagues to ignore her or be unpleasant to her when she is being so rewarding and confirming to them.

Carlos seems to think he has one of those bad bosses we talk about this chapter. Whether his perception is legitimate is not the issue here. Carlos would benefit by trying to better accommodate his boss by using some of our suggested strategies. If his boss burdens him with too many tasks at once, Carlos might ask his boss to help him prioritize the list and negotiate more realistic deadlines. Carlos believes that he could turn in higher-quality work with more time; however, his boss's standards for quality may be different from Carlos's standards. Asking for clarification about standards and expectations would help Carlos's efforts to satisfy his boss. To the degree that Carlos meets his boss's now-clarified expectations, their working relationship will improve.

By now, you have a greater understanding of the factors that influence how people relate at work, and you have at your disposal a variety of communication strategies that can help you initiate, develop, and sustain good working relationships. Organizations are highly complex environments. They survive in large part because of the people who make them function. Employers and employees who learn to effectively get along and relate well together facilitate a highly productive work environment and an enjoyable work

Putting Your Skills to Work

Establishing a trusting relationship with your boss is like establishing a trusting relationship with your instructors and classmates. Do what you say you'll do, and do it when you say you'll do it. You already use this skill when you attend all your classes, turn your assignments in on time, show up for meetings when you say you will, and so on.

YOU POSE AN INTERESTING QUESTION!

A-Digit/istockphoto.com

experience. Keep in mind that every workplace contains a highly diverse mix of individuals. Strategically approaching relationships at work can give you greater control over how you spend your day. Remember: pleasant work relationships are better than unpleasant ones. So let's just try to get along.

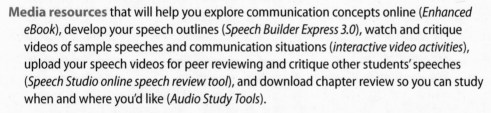

Use your Speech Communication CourseMate for *Business & Communication in a Digital Age* for quick access to the electronic resources that accompany this text. These resources include

Study tools that will help you assess your learning and prepare for exams (*digital glossary, key term flash cards, review quizzes*).

Activities and assignments that will help you hone your knowledge and build your communication skills throughout the course (*Visualize! Practice!, Weigh In!, Check This Out, and Link Out activities; modules; review questions*).

Media resources that will help you explore communication concepts online (*Enhanced eBook*), develop your speech outlines (*Speech Builder Express 3.0*), watch and critique videos of sample speeches and communication situations (*interactive video activities*), upload your speech videos for peer reviewing and critique other students' speeches (*Speech Studio online speech review tool*), and download chapter review so you can study when and where you'd like (*Audio Study Tools*).

Key Points

- Sustaining pleasant and productive relationships in the workplace is important for several reasons:
  - ✔ You spend a lot of your time in the workplace.
  - ✔ Unpleasant work relationships can lead to stress, ineffective performance, and employee turnover.
  - ✔ Good relationships contribute to more effective and collaborative work groups and teams.
  - ✔ Friendships often evolve from work relationships.
- Communication competence, or the ability to interact with others effectively and appropriately, contributes to productive relationships at work.
- A number of factors influence your ability to get along with others at work:
  - ✔ All organizations create rules and expectations that define how employees must interact with one another in order to attain the organization's goals. These rules and expectations are known as norms, roles, ranks, and controls.
  - ✔ Norms are rules that everyone in an organization is expected to follow.
  - ✔ Roles are specialized activities or functions that each member of an organization fulfills, typically defined by the jobs members do.

- ✔ Ranks are hierarchical roles that define status, authority, and power in an organization.
- ✔ Controls are positive and negative sanctions used to maintain the norms, roles, and ranks within an organization.

- There are a number of strategies you can use to successfully initiate and sustain workplace relationships:
  - ✔ Initiate relationships.
  - ✔ Communicate respect.
  - ✔ Be trustworthy.
  - ✔ Be careful what you reveal.
  - ✔ Confirm or praise others.
  - ✔ Be open to criticism.

- Getting along with a diverse group of co-workers can be challenging and sometimes leads to conflict. To facilitate and manage diverse and challenging relationships at work, co-workers can match their styles of communicating. This is called accommodation.

- No workplace relationship is more important than the one you have with your boss, so it's important to develop a productive way of working with him or her.
  - ✔ Show that you are trustworthy by doing what you say you will do, when you say you will do it.
  - ✔ Prioritize your boss's wants and needs.
  - ✔ Find ways to help your boss be successful, efficient, and productive.
  - ✔ Allow your boss to mentor you.
  - ✔ Be sensitive to your boss's moods and habits.
  - ✔ Try matching your work style with that of your boss.
  - ✔ Identify the standards of quality that your boss requires.

Key Terms

accommodation (101)	**ethnocentric** (110)
border crossers (106)	**norms** (95)
communication competence (92)	**ranks** (95)
confirming messages (98)	**roles** (95)
controls (95)	**stereotype** (110)
disconfirming messages (98)	

Questions for Critical Thinking and Review

1. Do you have children? How does having children or not having children influence your work life? How much consideration should co-workers who do not have children be expected to provide co-workers who have children?

2. To what extent do you think Gen Yers under- or overaccommodate older generations? Can you think of concrete examples that demonstrate each? On the other hand, what do older people do that suggests their unwillingness to accommodate Gen Yers?

3. In your work experiences, have you ever had a bad boss like the ones described in this chapter? What specifically did your boss do that made him or her so bad? When you become the boss, what will you do differently from that bad boss?

4. In this chapter, we argue that having close friends at work is a good thing. Under what circumstances might we be wrong about that?

5. What are the implications of having a romantic relationship with your boss versus with a co-worker? Can you ever see yourself getting involved with a boss or a supervisor at work? Why or why not?

6. What controls operate in your workplace? In other words, what rewards and negative sanctions are applied for good and bad work behavior? Are these controls reasonable and fair? What controls would you use to replace these existing ones?

Chapter 6

Mediated Communication:
How Can New Media Help Me at Work?

Chapter Outline

What Are New Media?
- New Media Are Digital
- New Media May Involve Networking
- New Media Allow Information Exchange and Communication

What Are Some Assumptions about New Media?
- New Media Allow for More Information and Communication
- New Media Remove the Barriers of Time and Space
- New Media Enable Globalization
- New Media Provide New Opportunities for Interaction

How Does Mediated Communication Differ from Face-to-Face Communication?
- New Media Can Limit Effective Role-Taking
- New Media May Limit Feedback

How Do You Select the Right Medium for Work-Related Communication?
- Understand Your Goals and the Nature of Your Message
- Consider the Characteristics of Your Audience
- Assess the Strengths and Weaknesses of the Available Media
- Ensure the Dynamic Interplay among Your Audience, Media, and Message

How Do You Use New Media in Ways That Will Attract, Not Alienate?
- Email
- Text Messaging
- Videoconferencing
- Social Media

iceteaimages/Alamy

Chapter Learning Objectives

After completing this chapter, you should be able to

- Define *new media*.
- Understand what it means to be a digital native.
- Know the challenges of being a digital native and interacting with digital immigrants.
- Understand the nature of mediated communication and how it differs from face-to-face communication.
- Identify and describe some forms of new media commonly used in the workplace.
- Practice the norms of socially acceptable new media use.
- Select the appropriate media for a given communication task.

See also the modules that are relevant to this chapter:

   4: **What Do I Need to Know about Business Etiquette?**
11: **How Do I Use Social Media for Professional Networking?**
14: **How Do I Prepare for Phone and Video Interviews?**

Module 4:
*What Do I Need to
Know about Business
Etiquette?*

Module 11:
*How Do I Use Social
Media for Professional
Networking?*

Module 14:
*How Do I Prepare
for Phone and
Video Interviews?*

Laura recently graduated from college. Like

most people her age, Laura was more than comfortable using a variety of technologies to communicate with others, to find and manage information, and even to promote herself and her skills. She had maintained a Facebook page since she was very young and watched most television shows at Hulu.com instead of on network TV. Many of her friends created original YouTube content, and she enjoyed watching it. Texting and Facebook messaging were her primary ways of staying in touch with friends, and she'd even tried online dating. When she began looking for her first job after graduating, she not only completed most phases of her job search online, but she even used Skype for a preliminary interview with the company she ultimately went to work for.

So when Laura started her new job, she wasn't surprised at how much technology was available. A good portion of her training took place via the Internet. She was assigned to a virtual learning community for sharing ideas, best practices, successes, and failures with like-minded colleagues. Because members of her team worked all over the globe, including from their homes right in Laura's city, videoconferencing and audioconferencing were regular activities.

One thing that did surprise Laura was the flexibility her employer gave her to work from home or from her family's vacation home in the Arizona desert. Last winter, she worked from home for four months on a flexible schedule so that she could train for an Ironman triathlon. New media enabled her to stay connected to the people and information that were critical to her ability to perform her job—whether in the office or away.

Who wouldn't love this arrangement? For the most part, Laura was quite happy with her job. Because of the power of new media, she had been able to pursue and achieve one of her lifetime dreams—to finish a triathlon. She had more time to spend with friends and family than most people she knew, and she got to work in sweats and slippers more often than not!

However, Laura had some nagging misgivings about it all. When she did need to head to the office and actually meet with people, she

(continued)

Weigh In! 6.1:
Are You a Digital Native?

check this out

sometimes felt awkward. In some ways, after having communicated virtually so much, she felt like she was losing her ability to communicate competently in face-to-face situations.

And sometimes, she felt as though the boundaries weren't clear enough between "work" and "home." Sometimes she'd work well into the evening while her husband ate dinner and watched television alone. And because she sometimes worked from that vacation home in the desert, when she took a true vacation, her co-workers expected that she'd still be connected and available.

Like Laura, you are probably what experts refer to as a **digital native**.[1] In other words, you grew up with digital technologies like computers, the Internet, mobile phones, and MP3 players. (People who had to learn to use these digital technologies as adults are called **digital immigrants**.) By the time you leave college, you will probably have exchanged close to a half million emails and text messages, played over 5,000 hours of video games, and have accumulated about 10,000 hours of talk time on a mobile phone. Like 75 percent of your classmates, you probably have a social network profile, and one in five of you has posted a video online.[2] You've probably never used a typewriter, never had pictures "developed," and you don't remember a time when you couldn't buy an individual song from the Internet to play later.

In addition to being comfortable with digital media, you probably expect access to such media to be convenient and quick. You may not even remember dial-up Internet and probably become easily frustrated with slow connections that don't handle audio and video well. You're probably unproductive or are even unable to work if your Internet connection is disrupted. You may be surprised that some people don't use text messaging or carry their phones with them all the time.

Communication technology makes life easier for digital natives like you, and it connects you to family, friends, and colleagues in important ways. To learn just how much of a digital native you are, take the quiz **WEIGH IN! 6.1: Are You a Digital Native?** adapted from the Pew Research Center's quiz "How Millennial Are You?" in its study *Millennials: A Portrait of Generation Next*.[3]

Regardless of how much of a digital native you are, you will need to be prepared for a technology-intensive workplace. You will also need to be prepared to interact with people who are more or less fluent than you are when it comes to new media use. And you will need to be able to make competent choices when choosing media—and know when face-to-face communication might still be the best alternative. This chapter will encourage you to learn and think critically about the ways in which new media are used in the workplace and will help you answer the question, "How can new media help me at work?"

What Are New Media?

The term *new media,* rather than *technology,* is the most accurate description for the kinds of communication media you'll find in the contemporary workplace. Because the nature of technology changes over time, the term *technology* has no fixed meaning. At one point in time, ballpoint pens, typewriters, and fax machines were all "new technologies." However, the term *new media* is fairly stable in its meaning.

A **medium** is a device that moves information over distance or through time so that people who are not face to face can communicate. A medium can be anything from a handwritten letter to a text message, as long as it moves information across distance. *Media* is the plural form of *medium*. **New media** is a term that encompasses the digital or networked information and communication technologies that have emerged since the later part of the twentieth century.[4] Examples include the Internet, computer games, CD-ROMs, DVDs, email, instant messaging, mobile phone and smartphone technology, and computer multimedia such as video, animation, and audio. New media does *not* include forms of media that are not digital, such as fax, film, television, and paper-based publications.

Furthermore, the term *new media* implies more than just a device or a medium; *new media* connotes the creation and maintenance of social ties and communities through interaction. For example, the Internet is no longer just a place you go for information. It's a place you go to interact with others, often about the information you find there. And it's not just a place you go to buy something. It's a place you go to buy, rate, and chat with others about purchases.

New Media Are Digital

Digital media are electronic and operate on digital codes. When information, such as text, photographs, or video, is digitized, a vast amount of it can be stored in a very small space. For example, think of the SIM card in your mobile phone. It's about the size of your fingernail—and yet it can store thousands of images, email messages, contact information, and even documents. Thus, new media, because they are digital, offer the opportunity to create, store, and access huge amounts of information, often at the press of a button.

New Media May Involve Networking

Networking is the interconnectivity of digital devices and by extension, of the people who use them. For example, networks enable co-workers to access documents from one another's computers. The Internet itself is a network that permits access to any user with a connection.

New Media Allow Information Exchange and Communication

Traditional communication media—such as television—do not enable information exchange. For example, the traditional evening newscast is a one-way transmission of the day's news. There is no interactivity or exchange involved. In contrast, new media facilitate information exchange and interaction. For example, Facebook provides users with storage space for photographs and facilitates communication among members of the site. Blogs are a vehicle for exchanging information about a topic and for interacting through comments and responses about the topic. An increasing number of shopping websites allow consumers to rate products and exchange comments about them. For example, professionals who are in the market for business equipment and computer software often use cnet.com. The social, interactive nature of the site enables consumers to make informed choices by reading about others' experiences and opinions about featured products.

Table 6.1 highlights some of the common channels for business and professional communication that meet the definition of new media.

TABLE 6.1
New Media in Business

Channel	Description
Email	• One of the most common forms of computer networking. • Originally developed so that scientists could easily communicate with one another. • Now universally used for business and personal correspondence. • Messages are sent from one person's device to another's nearly instantaneously.
Website	• A collection of web pages, images, video, text, and other digital material. • Used by businesses and individuals to communicate information, interact with clients and consumers, and to help promote a brand or image.
Videoconferencing	• Interaction among colleagues and clients facilitated by television technology. • A cost-effective way to conduct meetings and an alternative to bringing people from distant locations together face to face.
VoIP and Skype	• Voice over Internet protocol (VoIP) enables communicators to use the Internet to make telephone calls. • Business communicators use VoIP for both one-on-one and audioconference calling. • Skype is a popular example of VoIP software that also enables videoconferencing over the Internet rather than with television technology.
Webconferencing	• Live meetings, training, and presentations conducted over the Internet. • In a webconference, each participant sits at his or her own computer and is connected to other participants via the Internet. • A popular variation is the webinar. Webinars can be used for one-way transmission of information to others with questions and answers at the end. For example, corporations often use webinars to share quarterly financial reports with stockholders. • Some webinars are more interactive and facilitate audience polling and other forms of dialogue among listeners and speakers.
Mobile (cell) phones	• A portable device used for mobile communication, including voice calls and text messaging. • Smartphones, such as the iPhone or some BlackBerry models, are advanced mobile phones that offer email capability, Internet access, Wi-Fi, an ebook reader, applications that help users track everything from Facebook activity to calories consumed to their favorite team's score, and even an operating system for viewing and editing documents.
Virtual learning communities or online communities of practice	• Internet-based communities in which online interaction among participants replaces classroom-based, face-to-face, instructor-led training. • Some are based on a particular profession or industry. Others are solely based on the desire of participants to learn from each other.
E-learning	• Employee training via CD, DVD, or a business computer network. • Trainees interact with a training website by clicking on links, responding to open-ended questions, and taking assessments. • Differs from virtual learning communities in that trainees can't communicate with one another.

(continued)

Text and instant messaging	• The exchange of brief written messages between mobile and portable devices over either cellular networks or the Internet.
	• Images, video, and sound may also be exchanged.
	• May also be used to interact with automated systems, such as voting via text for *American Idol* contestants.
	• In business, products and services can be ordered via text messaging technology. Similarly, advertisers and service providers can text mobile phone users about promotions, payment due dates, and more.
Social networking sites	• Websites that focus on building social relationships and networks among users.
	• The best-known examples are Twitter, Facebook, MySpace, and LinkedIn.
	• In business, social network sites may be created for specific disciplines or industries to facilitate information exchange and relationship building.
Virtual organizations	• The ultimate use of new media in business. Virtual organizations transact business through electronic media with little or no face-to-face interaction among colleagues or customers.
	• A virtual business would have no centralized office but, rather, a group of employees connected by a computer network for communication and information-sharing.
	• One example of a virtual business is Amazon, which uses the Internet to sell products to and interact with its customers. Some of its employees work face to face, but others are connected virtually.

What Are Some Assumptions about New Media?

Business writers and social critics have written a great deal about the implications of new media for society in general and for workplace communication more specifically. Let's look at some of the major assumptions about new media and discuss what they mean in terms of business and professional communication.

New Media Allow for More Information and Communication

Think about how much physical space it would take to house all the information on the Internet if the Internet didn't exist. The fact that new media enable us to store and retrieve information conveniently has actually resulted in our creating far more information than existed in pre-digital times. For example, before digitization and new media, we stored information in encyclopedias consisting of several printed volumes. In the post-digital age, we have Wikipedia. Can you even begin to guess how many printed volumes it would take to publish the contents of Wikipedia in traditional format? Similarly, businesses can easily access and use data about their customers by capturing information via a company website. In the pre-digital age, customer data were simply not as easy to come by or to access.

Additionally, new media have increased how much and how often we communicate. Think about how easy it is to fire off an email or a text message about a single thought at any point during the day. Now imagine a world in which you'd have to write a letter, pick up the telephone, or wait until you saw the receiver of your message in person. You would probably engage in far less communication than you do in the post-digital world. Thanks to new media, we communicate more frequently with people at greater distances than we did in the pre-digital era.

Visualize! Practice! 6.1:
Time and Space: No Longer a Problem?

Weigh In! 6.2:
How Often Do You Communicate with New Media?

In a recent consulting role, Jennifer Waldeck, an author of this text, experienced another example of how new media encourage increased communication in business settings. She was involved in the development of an online community for automobile dealership managers. Managers of similar-sized dealerships in non-competing markets were grouped anonymously. In those communities, members shared financial data, marketing and sales best practices, and other confidential information that they would have been reluctant to exchange in traditional face-to-face or mediated forums. But the data they shared were helpful to the growth and development of one another's businesses. And it only occurred because of the power and benefits of new media.

Assess your use of new media with **WEIGH IN! 6.2: How Often Do You Communicate with New Media?** How does your use of new media affect the volume of information and communication you deal with every day?

New Media Remove the Barriers of Time and Space

Again, think of the prehistoric time in which people had to use mail or a delivery service if they wanted to send documents to a colleague in California from their office in Florida. At best, the materials would arrive the next day. With new media, however, time and space for business communicators has disappeared. Those same documents can be digitized, uploaded, attached to an email, sent to California, and downloaded by the recipient in seconds, rather than hours or days.

Consider the advantages of new media with **VISUALIZE! PRACTICE! 6.1: Time and Space: No Longer a Problem?** How does your use of new media affect the volume of information and communication you deal with every day?

Additionally, new media's ability to remove the barriers of time and space have changed what it means to work. In 1990 and before, for most people "going to work" meant going to a physical place away from home and interacting face to face with a boss and co-workers. But now a number of businesses let their employees work from home or some other location. What makes this possible? New media, of course. Think of the media

Belinda Images/SuperStock

that enable people to be productive from just about anywhere: smartphones, laptops or notebook computers with Internet connections, remote access to data files on corporate servers, and more. New media is replacing the daily commute for many people in much the same way that Laura worked from her vacation home in the opening scenario for this chapter. Are you interested in telecommuting? Take a look at LINK OUT 6.1: **Telecommuting** to propose a work-at-home arrangement to your boss.

New Media Enable Globalization

In many ways, the emergence of new media has allowed professional organizations of all sizes to become global in their communication and reach. New media enable us to exchange information, blogs, photos, music, video, and other user-generated content with people all over the world. As a result, businesses are able to expand their activities beyond the boundaries of their own communities, states, and even countries. For instance, employees of a company in California may find themselves on a webconference with people in Israel, Great Britain, and Alaska. And instead of selling products in a local storefront, a company's reach can extend across the globe.

Consider your possible role in an increasingly global business environment with CHECK THIS OUT 6.1: **Are You Ready for Globalization?**

New Media Provide New Opportunities for Interaction

One of the most profound characteristics of new media is their potential for social interaction. Blogs, podcasts, wikis, and online social networking are all ways that people can generate web-based content, interact about that content, and exchange sometimes valuable information and ideas. The interactivity of new media may be something as simple as giving a thumbs-up or thumbs-down rating on an article. Or interactivity may be more complex. For instance, wikis allow numerous people to collaboratively produce an article, website, or knowledge database. Elsewhere, Amazon recommends material to users based on ratings they've given to products they purchased previously, and users of Yelp .com inform others of their experiences with local businesses.

Business and professional communicators have learned to leverage the power of new media that promote interaction, often referred to as **social media**. For instance, a company may create a Facebook fan page to promote its brand or product. Or it may create a YouTube video and tweet about a company event or promotion to create buzz in the hopes that it will go viral. Allowing people to feel connected to an idea, brand, or organization through social media is a way of building loyalty and name recognition for businesses and their products, innovations, and ideas. Read more about how businesses have used one social media service, Twitter, to communicate with the public by checking out LINK OUT 6.2: **Huge Brands Use Twitter**, LINK OUT 6.3: **Twitter for Business**, and LINK OUT 6.4: **Twitter & Business Success Stories**.

Research indicates why social media can be so useful to businesses for creating awareness and buzz: nearly half of all Facebook and Twitter users check their accounts *during the night* or first thing in the morning. Close to 80 percent of users check the sites at least once throughout the day. And 28 percent of iPhone users check their Facebook accounts *before getting out of bed in the morning.*[5] Another report indicates that 67 percent of consumers who follow a brand on Twitter are likely to buy that brand, and 79 percent are likely to recommend a brand that they follow to others.[6] Thus, these new media provide powerful communication vehicles for business messages.

Link Out 6.1:
Telecommuting
Link Out 6.2:
Huge Brands Use Twitter
Link Out 6.3:
Twitter for Business
Link Out 6.4:
Twitter & Business Success Stories

Check This Out 6.1:
Are You Ready for Globalization?

Visualize! Practice! 6.2:
*Why Is Role-Taking
Important?*

Weigh In! 6.3:
*How Much Do You
Interact with New
Media?*

Assess how much you use new media to interact with others by taking the quiz
WEIGH IN! 6.3: How Much Do You Interact with New Media? Are you like the average Facebook
or Twitter user?

How Does Mediated Communication Differ from Face-to-Face Communication?

Mediated communication is the use of various media to facilitate communication between senders and receivers. In many ways, mediated communication is similar to face-to-face communication. The primary similarity is that both forms of communication require a sender and a receiver. For instance, an email exchange begins with a sender, who has to formulate an initial email message so that a receiver can interpret it. So that the receiver can interpret the sender's message, the sender must follow the rules and requirements of written expression when writing the email. New media—such as mobile telephones, Skype, e-learning, and text messaging—also rely on the basic elements of human communication: oral and written symbols (words), nonverbal cues and signals, and the transactional creation of meaning (Chapter 1).

But mediated communication differs from face-to-face communication in some significant ways. One primary difference is that both the sender and receiver must have a certain amount of technical expertise. For example, to send an email you must know how to use the email interface. In addition, communication researchers have long suggested that the medium a communicator chooses for a particular message affects how that message is received and interpreted. And the way we move messages across distance sometimes also alters their nature. Some media alter messages greatly; others have only a slight impact. Let's explore these ideas in more depth by taking a look at the two main ways that new media can alter the communication process.

New Media Can Limit Effective Role-Taking

Role-taking, critical to face-to-face interactions, allows senders and receivers to assume each other's roles so that each can make predictions about how the other will interpret and respond to messages (Chapter 1). For example, the salesperson who has done his homework on a prospective client should know enough about her business and her current needs to deliver a sales presentation she'll respond positively to. If the sender knows the receiver well and can anticipate subtle ways in which she will interpret a message, role-taking can facilitate a productive interaction.

Consider why role-taking is so important to face-to-face communication with
VISUALIZE! PRACTICE! 6.2: Why Is Role-Taking Important?

However, role-taking can be difficult when senders use new media forms. For example, when the human resources director sends an email blast to remind all employees about the company dress code, he can't possibly predict the reactions of each recipient of the email. Some employees may simply feel they're informed, whereas others may feel attacked because they interpret the email as a reprimand. Role-taking can even be a challenge for people who know each other well. For example, when a sender uses instant messaging to joke about something her close colleague said in a meeting that struck her as funny, she cannot know for sure if the recipient is in a good or bad mood, or if he is responding to her gentle teasing with humor or sarcasm.

Many new media, such as email and text messaging, lack "personalness." As a result, messages can be interpreted in multiple ways. When used effectively, new media keep people informed, expedite work, and connect people across distance. But often, mediated communication also leaves receivers with too many questions, and those questions can cause problems.[7]

Assess how effective you are at role-taking by taking the quiz **WEIGH IN! 6.4: Does My Role-Taking Help Others Understand Me?**

Weigh In! 6.4:
Does My Role-Taking Help Others Understand Me?

New Media May Limit Feedback

When new media is used, feedback may be limited, untimely, or inadequate. For example, in a face-to-face training session, the instructor can sense a great deal of immediate feedback from learners. Nonverbal cues such as yawns, laughter, or confused expressions convey to the trainer how her message is being received. However, those cues can't be observed in an online training session. In this way, mediated training may not be as rich in feedback as face-to-face training.

The timeliness of feedback depends on whether we use synchronous or asynchronous media. **Synchronous media** allow for an instantaneous reply from another communicator. For instance, when two people are online using instant messaging at the same time, the communication is synchronous. Each communicator can ask questions, get instant feedback, and immediately confirm that his messages are received and understood. Conversely, **asynchronous media** enable communication and collaboration outside the constraints of time and place.[8] For example, email is asynchronous when you send a message and have to wait for a response because, say, the receiver is not at her desk or is not responding to email at the time. When you rely on asynchronous media, feedback may not be as timely as it would be if you used face-to-face communication.

Because communicators use so many new media and are exposed to so many mediated messages, they sometimes may fail to provide the kind of feedback that others would appreciate or find useful. Managers are especially likely to provide inadequate

Will Rennick/Mazdaguy03/iStockphoto.com

feedback because they tend to be overloaded by more information than most employees—they receive an overwhelming amount of information each day. Let's take a look at an email exchange that reflects how information overload may result in inadequate feedback.

From:	frustrated.employee@gmail.com
To:	busy.boss@yahoo.com
Date:	March 30, 2010, 11:16 AM
Subject:	Miscellaneous issues

Hi Jon,
I'm writing to find out if we've heard anything back from Lucas on the new contract. Are there any modifications necessary? Also, have you had time to consider my vacation request? Thanks very much.

Rob

From:	busy.boss@yahoo.com
To:	frustrated.employee@gmail.com
Date:	March 30, 2010, 4:47 PM
Subject:	RE: Miscellaneous issues

Nothing from Lucas. Got your vacation request.

In what ways is Busy Boss's feedback inadequate? How would you rewrite the boss's reply to be more responsive to Frustrated Employee? Could Frustrated Employee have written his email differently to maximize the chances of an adequate response from Busy Boss?

In our global era, face-to-face communication is not always possible or practical—that's why people rely on new media so much. Later in this chapter, we will suggest some ways to make the most out of communication using new media. But first, let's take a look at factors to consider in selecting media for business messages.

How Do You Select the Right Medium for Work-Related Communication?

New media are here to stay. They have changed our lives in numerous positive ways and have maximized our potential to stay informed and successfully connect with others. But with so many media available for business interactions, how do you choose the one that is most likely to help you accomplish your goals? And when would face-to-face communication be best?

Understand Your Goals and the Nature of Your Message
Whenever you communicate in a business setting, be mindful of what you are trying to accomplish (Chapter 1). Some communication goals are more complex than others and may require a type of media that can handle complexity.

- If your message would be better understood if it were accompanied by an image, select a medium that can accurately transmit visual cues.

- How quickly do you need your message to be received? When a message is urgent and you're certain that the recipient is able to access email or text messaging, those might be quick ways to communicate.

- How much control do you wish to exert over how the recipient interprets your message? If you want to help shape the receiver's perceptions of you and your message, you might want to use the most interactive medium available or even face-to-face communication. Messages that can easily be misinterpreted should be communicated with a medium that allows for feedback and perception checking.

Visualize! Practice! 6.3:
How Would You Use New Media to Communicate with a Colleague?

Consider the Characteristics of Your Audience

Understanding the characteristics of a recipient of a mediated message is similar to analyzing your audience before making a business presentation. What do you need to know about the recipient in order to send an effective message? For example, what is your relationship to this person in the organizational hierarchy? Does he have more or less status than you? People with high status in organizational settings tend to receive more messages than do others. With that in mind, what approach would you take? How would you decide to communicate with that person? What medium would you select and why?

If you'd like to explore these questions online, complete the activity **VISUALIZE!**
PRACTICE! 6.3: How Would You Use New Media to Communicate with a Colleague?

What's the nature of your relationship to the recipient? Formal or informal? A person with whom you have a formal relationship may find a text message or Facebook friend request from you inappropriate. Also consider her communication style and willingness to use new media. Opinion leaders and innovators in organizations tend to be "early adopters" of new media, meaning they are among the first to buy and use new media for communication. If your boss is an early adopter, she will likely be positively disposed to any communication that is conducted using new media. What are some cues you could use to determine a person's willingness to use new media if you don't know the person well?

Putting Your Skills to Work

Have you ever waited until "just the right time" to tell somebody something? To put your message in the best possible light, you probably considered your communication goals, the nature of your message, and the unique characteristics of your audience. You can use these same skills to decide which is the appropriate new media to use to communicate with your colleagues and bosses.

Andy Cook/istockphoto.com

Visualize! Practice! 6.4:
Consider Another Person's Willingness to Use New Media

If you'd like to consider this question online, complete the activity **VISUALIZE! PRACTICE!** **6.4: Consider Another Person's Willingness to Use New Media**.

Further, consider what media your intended recipient has access to. For example, if your boss is traveling and only accessing email on a smartphone, avoid sending long messages or ones with complex attachments until she returns to the office. What are the recipient's personal preferences regarding communication media? For instance, a supervisor might make clear to his employees that he prefers face-to-face meetings to email. A colleague might dislike online social networking and just prefer to catch up with associates from other companies by phone or at professional meetings.

Assess the Strengths and Weaknesses of the Available Media

Examine four criteria to assess the strengths and weaknesses of a particular medium for communication:[9]

- First, does the medium **allow for instant feedback**? When the message may be unclear or equivocal, instant feedback is important because it allows communicators to more quickly arrive at shared understanding.

- Second, does the medium **allow the communicator to send multiple cues**—such as facial expressions, tone of voice, and verbal inflection? When communicators detect such cues, they are better able to determine whether their messages are being perceived accurately.

- Third, does the medium **allow communicators to use natural language**, similar to what they would use in a face-to-face conversation? Email allows communicators to be fairly conversational, while text messaging relies on a lot of acronyms and symbols. The more ambiguous or complex the message is, the more important it is to engage in normal, natural conversation.

wavebreakmedia/iStockphoto.com

- Finally, does the medium **have personal focus and qualities**? Messages are always transmitted and interpreted more accurately and clearly when communicators can express emotion and feeling.

Ensure the Dynamic Interplay Among Your Audience, Media, and Message

There are no firm rules regarding media choice in the business setting. Much like the success of your face-to-face communication, the effectiveness of media use rests on your ability to recognize what's appropriate in a given situation and your skill at practicing the appropriate communication behaviors.

Visualize! Practice! 6.5:
What Are the Norms for Using Media in Your Business?

Visualize! Practice! 6.6:
Lean versus Rich on Your Campus

One way to effectively judge the relationship among audience, media, and message is to examine the norms for media use in your organization or industry. Communication research suggests that people use and evaluate communication media based on how those around them use and think about media.[10] For example, if a decision maker in the marketing department hears from a trusted colleague that "Twitter is a waste of time for creating brand awareness," she may develop a similar negative attitude. Therefore, it's wise to be aware of how the majority of communicators in your environment are using new media and then use them in similar ways.

Consider these ideas further by interviewing a working professional regarding the norms for media use in his or her business. **VISUALIZE! PRACTICE! 6.5: What Are the Norms for Using Media in Your Business?** provides the types of interview questions you might ask.

You can also make an effective media choice by evaluating a medium's *richness*. Communication media vary in their capacity for resolving confusion, solving disagreements, bridging multiple or competing interpretations of a message, and facilitating understanding.[11] **Rich media** are those most capable of facilitating understanding among communicators, and **lean media** are the least capable. Rich media also happen to be the ones that are most similar to face-to-face communication, because they have the capacity to communicate nonverbal information, affect and emotion, and quick feedback.

It's difficult to say which media are richest, because that can vary from situation to situation based on an organization's norms. For instance, Skype can be considered a rich medium because it allows communicators to interact verbally and nonverbally in a synchronous fashion, much like face-to-face communication. However, if you use this medium with a colleague who doesn't like it, you aren't likely to achieve the kind of understanding you'd hoped for.

Assess how lean or rich the media used for communication is on your campus with **VISUALIZE! PRACTICE! 6.6: Lean versus Rich on Your Campus**.

How Do You Use New Media in Ways That Will Attract, Not Alienate?

Once you have selected a particular medium for your message, you will need to use it *appropriately*. There are some ground rules to keep in mind as you use new media to communicate in the business context.

Email

Email should be used thoughtfully for three reasons. First, following the rules of business email etiquette will give you and your message *credibility*. This credibility will enhance the likelihood that your message will be read, understood, and acted upon as you hope it will be. Second, thinking about your email message will improve the *efficiency* of your communication. Efficient emails maximize the chances that recipients will take the time to read your messages thoroughly without becoming annoyed. Third, good email etiquette can *protect* you and your company. Email is a risky form of communication. Your messages can be forwarded to unintended recipients without your knowledge, saved and used in a damaging way later, or simply lost in cyberspace without ever reaching the target recipient. Using email judiciously is a simple way to CYA (cover your rear).

Here are tips for business email etiquette:

- **Be concise.** Keep your email short, simple, and easy to read. Reading a message on the computer screen is more difficult than reading a printed document.

- **Create a meaningful subject line.** Some email users sort their incoming mail based on keywords in the subject line. Make your subject line brief, relevant, and informative to the recipient.

- **Make it personal.** Use the recipient's name in the message and, where possible, refer to something you know about this person. For example, at the end of an email you might write, "And by the way, congratulations on your daughter's graduation from college. What a milestone!" These small social gestures can help facilitate and sustain positive relationships.

- **Answer promptly.** A good practice is to respond to email within one business day. If you don't have an answer, acknowledge the email and let the sender know that you are working to obtain one. Give the sender an estimate of when you might respond.

- **Answer all questions, and anticipate future questions.** One of the most pressing problems that business communicators face is a lack of time. You can help save others time by carefully answering all the questions they asked in an email. This will preempt the need to contact you again about the same issue, so you will avoid wasting that person's time (and potentially irritating him or her).

  Additionally, if you can anticipate future questions, the other person will be impressed and grateful. For example, if a customer asks if your company uses direct billing, you could simply answer that question. But you could also anticipate that his next questions will be, "What are the billing terms, how do I order, and how do I pay?" So if you not only answer the original question but also include a link to your company's order site, your customer is sure to be appreciative.

- **Use proper grammar, spelling, and punctuation.** Violating the basic rules of articulate writing detracts from your credibility as well as that of your company. Proofread your email and use the spell check function.

- **Do not write in capitals.** You will be perceived as aggressive and ill-mannered.

- **Pay attention to structure, layout, and font.** Text can be more difficult to read on a computer screen than on paper. Use white space, separate paragraphs with spaces, and use a simple black font (e.g., Arial or Times New Roman). Avoid using a decorative background; plain white is best.

- **Avoid ambiguous abbreviations and emoticons.** Use of "smileys" is unprofessional in the business setting as are some abbreviations (such as LOL or ROTF). Unless an abbreviation or acronym is relevant to your business, avoid using it.

- **Read email before you send it.** Proofread it for technical errors and anything that could be misunderstood or inappropriate. Once it's sent, you can't undo damage easily. Moreover, when someone's email message frustrates you or angers you, you should wait to reply. Replying immediately is almost sure to lead to an ongoing and perhaps escalating conflict.

- **Do not use email to discuss confidential information.** Assume that your email will be forwarded or read by others.

- **Don't send offensive content.** Never send or forward email that contains sexist, racist, obscene, or libelous remarks. You and your company could be held responsible in a court.

- **Do not send unnecessary attachments.** Attaching logos and business cards to your email is unnecessary. Avoid sending large files; compress attachments whenever possible.

- **Do not forward a message or attachment without permission.** You may be infringing on copyright laws or violating a colleague's trust.

- **Do not overuse the "reply to all" command.** Only include people in your address list who really need to see your message. Do not use "reply to all" to incite gossip or to heighten others' emotions.

- **When sending an email blast, use the "bcc" function.** Do not make email addresses visible to all recipients. This compromises their privacy and also detracts from your goal of communicating in a personalized fashion via new media.

- **Always follow your company's email policies.** These are created for a reason and provide you with important guidance on how to use email successfully in your work environment. Failure to adhere to company email policies can have negative consequences.

For more about email etiquette, see MODULE 4: **What Do I Need to Know about Business Etiquette?**

Putting Your Skills to Work

You probably use very different communication styles when emailing and texting your friends versus your parents and teachers—most people do. After all, you and your friends have shared experiences, inside jokes, and mutual concerns that your parents and teachers wouldn't necessarily understand. You're able to adapt your messages in order to communicate in ways that don't alienate people. This skill will come in handy when you're in the workplace, communicating with all sorts of people—co-workers, bosses, clients, and more.

A-Digit/istockphoto.com

Text Messaging

Although text messaging is quick and efficient, use this medium only if you're sure the recipient of your message also uses it regularly. Even if you and everyone else in your organization regularly use text messaging, it is not a universally used form of communication. Although about 75 percent of mobile phone users worldwide use text messaging (often referred to as SMS, for short message service, in countries outside the United States), only a little over half of U.S. mobile phone users text.[12] And not all mobile phone plans include a data package; some people pay a premium for text messaging. In this case, you run the risk of annoying the recipient and costing him or her money.

Here are tips on how to use texting effectively and courteously:

- **Keep text messages brief and informal.** Do not use text messaging to discuss important, sensitive, or controversial topics that deserve a richer form of interaction.

- **Avoid abbreviations and slang.** In business communication, avoid using abbreviations or text slang, such as "u" for "you."

- **Text only routine messages that don't need to communicate emotion.** It's hard to interpret tone or mood from a brief text message. Therefore, reserve text messaging for only the most routine messages. For example, texting may be an appropriate way to remind someone of a meeting or let someone know that you are running late. A text is an inappropriate channel for delivering criticism or informing someone of a new policy.

- **Consider others' usage habits and schedules.** Don't assume that just because you are awake, available, and have your phone near you that the recipient of your message will too. There are times when people cannot respond to text messages. When in doubt, follow up your text message with a voice call or voice message.

- **Be considerate of the people around you.** Don't compose a text while involved in a face-to-face conversation with someone else.

Mark Hatfield/iStockphoto.com

- **Don't text during meetings.** In most cases, texting during a meeting or presentation is as rude and unacceptable as taking a voice call. If you are expecting an urgent message, put your phone on "quiet" or "silent" mode and watch for the indicator light. Let the meeting facilitator or presenter know ahead of time that you may need to leave to respond to a message. Reserve this action for only the most urgent situations.

Videoconferencing

Videoconferencing saves business communicators money and time, allows them to develop richer relationships than they might over the telephone, and enhances their ability to share ideas. But this form of new media can have drawbacks as well—especially when users don't follow some essential ground rules.

If you are planning or facilitating the videoconference:

- **Test equipment in advance.** Avoid frustration and wasted time by making sure you know how to use the equipment and that it's working properly.

- **Follow good meeting etiquette.** Use an agenda and provide it to participants in advance. Begin and end on time. Introduce all participants to one another.

- **Be enthusiastic about the event as well as the technology.** Research indicates that one key opinion leader can make videoconferencing a successful initiative for an entire company.[13]

If you are participating in a videoconference:

- **Make sure people both in and out of the room can hear the conversation.** Speak loudly and clearly. Avoid making unnecessary background noise. Don't interrupt or talk over people.

- **Don't forget that with this medium, nonverbal communication counts.** Make eye contact with both the camera and the other participants at your location. Dress as you would for a face-to-face meeting.

- **Refer to people by name.** When some people are in the room and others are on camera, it's not always easy to see who is talking to whom. Referring to meeting participants by name clarifies who's being addressed.

- **Minimize distractions.** Turn off pagers, mobile phones, and watch alarms. Don't leave the room unless absolutely necessary.

For more about using videoconferencing in a specific business context, see MODULE 14: **How Do I Prepare for Phone and Video Interviews?**

Social Media

Social media include social network sites, social news sites, and blogs. Examples include Facebook, Twitter, YouTube, Digg, and LinkedIn. Although sites like Facebook and Twitter were created as sites for social, rather than business, communication, these powerful new media have been leveraged for business and professional purposes in a big way. Additionally, professionals use business-oriented networking sites such as LinkedIn to promote themselves and to connect with others. And social media sites like YouTube host video advertising for some products and services that is never seen anywhere but the Internet.

Social media have changed the way information is disseminated in the workplace; how organizations hire, screen, and interview prospective employees; and how products, ideas, and services are marketed and sold. Blogger Tamar Weinberg observes in her *Ultimate Social Media Etiquette Handbook*[14] that anytime we use the Internet, and social media in particular, we leave behind our "digital signature."

Here are some tips for ensuring that your presence in the Internet community is a positive one:

- **Make sure your "friends" know who you are.** Don't request that users of social network sites become your "friend" without introducing yourself if there is any chance that you're not known to them. You wouldn't just walk up to someone and start talking to them without providing some type of introduction, would you?

- **Save one-on-one conversations for other media.** Avoid using your Twitter feed or Facebook wall as a chatroom for conversations that are exclusively between you and another user. Use email or instant messaging instead.

- **Save gaming for your social contacts only.** Don't invite professional contacts on social network sites like Facebook to participate in games. Many will view these invites as spam.

- **Remember that not everyone wants to mix the professional and personal.** Some users of social networking sites aren't interested in business or professional networking. They consider these media to be purely social. If you're looking to establish a professional connection, consider LinkedIn rather than Facebook.

- **Don't turn your profile into a blatant promotion for your company or brand.** Most users of sites such as Facebook and Twitter understand that the sites can be used for professional as well as social networking. However, they will not respond well to a profile that's been created with the obvious purpose of gathering business leads.

- **Use your own name, not the name of your company.** Remember that it's generally considered poor form to respond to articles and blog posts with the name of your business (e.g., Bert's Bakery) instead of your name (e.g., Bert).

- **Keep your address books private.** Don't join a social network site and then allow the site to send invites to your entire Gmail, Yahoo! Mail, or Hotmail address book when requested.

- **Don't be a spammer.** Never leverage your social media connections to send spam or direct email.

- **Always think about the consequences of your participation on a social site.** Personal attacks, unflattering stories and photos, racial slurs, profanity, and other negative communication do not reflect well on your professional identity. Potential employers and clients will look at your social profiles and draw conclusions about you from them.

- **Do not put others' jobs and careers at risk.** For example, don't tag photos of them heavily intoxicated or doing something illegal or socially unacceptable.

- **Don't say or do anything online that you wouldn't do in a face-to-face setting.** You may feel anonymous and powerful when using the Internet, but the consequences of your online behavior are likely to haunt you. For example, no one likes someone who constantly talks about and promotes herself in person—and they don't like that person online, either.

For more about using social media for connecting with other professionals, see

MODULE 11: How Do I Use Social Media for Professional Networking?

mi
modlink

linkout

visualize

weigh
in

check this
out

One of the most difficult aspects of new media use in business settings is the fact that the rules change. New media rapidly evolve in their sophistication and in their uses. For example, less than ten years ago, most workplaces frowned upon employee use of the Internet during business hours. Now, those same organizations would lose competitive advantage by preventing workers' access to the information and opportunities for collaboration that the Internet offers. As new uses for new media evolve, so do the guidelines for using them effectively and appropriately. We have provided you with some of the most current thinking on the use of new media in business, but pay attention to emerging norms for use of new media in your chosen profession.

The emergence of new media has created entirely new work and communication styles for many people. The growing number of communication choices enables us to now work together across space and time so that geographic location is becoming a less relevant consideration for business problem solvers and decision makers. In addition, as employees have learned to communicate effectively and appropriately using new media, researchers have found them to be more engaged in their work and more committed to their organization's goals and mission. Similarly, as business enterprises have leveraged new media, they have experienced increased financial performance and shareholder dividends and decreased turnover.

Yet, despite the numerous advantages of our connected workplaces, people still experience difficulties using new media for mediated communication. Technologies may fail, we may make the wrong media selection, or we may not be understood. For example, you may be a digital native working and communicating in a land of digital immigrants and encounter conflict and confusion as a result. Or you may be accustomed to using new media for your social communications but not familiar with acceptable professional norms for text messaging or social media. But now, armed with what you've learned in this chapter, you have a better understanding of how to use new media in the business context skillfully, in ways that will bring about creative, productive ideas and relationships through communication.

Use your Speech Communication CourseMate for *Business & Communication in a Digital Age* for quick access to the electronic resources that accompany this text. These resources include

Study tools that will help you assess your learning and prepare for exams (*digital glossary, key term flash cards, review quizzes*).

Activities and assignments that will help you hone your knowledge and build your communication skills throughout the course (*Visualize! Practice!, Weigh In!, Check This Out, and Link Out activities; modules; review questions*).

Media resources that will help you explore communication concepts online (*Enhanced eBook*), develop your speech outlines (*Speech Builder Express 3.0*), watch and critique videos of sample speeches and communication situations (*interactive video activities*), upload your speech videos for peer reviewing and critique other students' speeches (*Speech Studio online speech review tool*), and download chapter review so you can study when and where you'd like (*Audio Study Tools*).

Key Points

- Regardless of your comfort level, experience, or skill with new media, you will need to be prepared for a technology-intensive workplace.
- New media are digital, networked information and communication technologies that have emerged since the later part of the twentieth century.
  - ✔ Examples include the Internet, computer games, DVDs, email, instant messaging, and mobile phones.
  - ✔ New media help create and maintain social ties among communities of people.
- Certain characteristics of new media are significant for business and professional communication.
  - ✔ New media allow for increased information and communication.
  - ✔ They also remove the barriers of time and space, enabling people to be productive from just about anywhere.
  - ✔ They provide increased opportunities for social interaction.
  - ✔ Finally, new media allow professional organizations to become global in their communication and reach.
- Mediated communication differs from face-to-face communication in key ways that may reduce the accuracy of messages and how messages are perceived, prevent "personalness," and limit important feedback.
- Effective business communication is partially dependent on your ability to select the right medium. In order to use the appropriate media, you must
  - ✔ Understand your goals and the nature of your message.
  - ✔ Consider the characteristics of your audience.
  - ✔ Assess the strengths and weaknesses of the available media.
  - ✔ Ensure the dynamic interplay among your audience, media, and message.
- When you use new media, use it in a mindful way that attracts and interests rather than alienates others.

Key Terms

asynchronous media (127)	**medium** (121)
digital immigrant (120)	**networking** (121)
digital media (121)	**new media** (121)
digital native (120)	**rich media** (131)
lean media (131)	**social media** (125)
mediated communication (126)	**synchronous media** (127)

Questions for Critical Thinking and Review

1. What competitive advantage do you believe digital immigrants have in the contemporary workplace? How about digital natives?

2. In what ways do you believe digital immigrants might be handicapped as communicators in the contemporary workplace?

3. Would you prefer to experience job-related training in a traditional face-to-face classroom setting or online in a Web-based format? Why? What are the advantages and disadvantages of each training format?

4. In this chapter, we argue that the Internet has evolved from a source of information into a more interactive and community-oriented forum for communicating. Explain what we mean by this and provide a few examples.

5. What are some of the ethical dilemmas involved in the use of Facebook for business networking? Do you believe that Facebook and Twitter should be used for professional purposes, or should they be reserved for social interaction? Why?

6. When thinking of online communication, is it truly possible to differentiate between personal and professional communication? Why or why not?

7. Describe a time when you experienced communication or information overload. How did you cope? What did you learn as a result of that experience? What are some strategies you could use in the workplace for managing the stress associated with communication overload?

8. Are there any new media discussed in this chapter that you believe are inappropriate for business communication? Why or why not?

9. How do you think norms for the use of new media develop in business settings? How might a newcomer begin to learn what is and is not acceptable use of new media?

10. Select one of the media (e.g., email, text messaging, Facebook) discussed in this chapter that you believe is most often misused or abused by communicators. Explain why you selected that medium. List three to five rules you believe people should follow in using this medium to avoid the problems you have observed.

Chapter 7

Giving Presentations:
How Do I Prepare to Tell My Story?

Chapter Outline

Why Are Speeches Best Delivered as Stories?
- The Characteristics of a Good Story
- Business Presentations Told as Stories

What Type of Business Presentation Best Fits Your Purpose?
- Sales Presentations and Proposals
- Briefings
- Team Presentations
- Specialized Business Presentations

How Do You Begin Your Presentation?
- Analyze Your Audience
- Analyze Your Speaking Environment

How Do You Build Support for Your Ideas?
- Establish Credibility
- Consider the Different Types of Support
- Select Only the Best Supporting Material

How Do You Organize Your Presentation?
- Understand the Importance of Organization
- Get Ready to Organize
- Select the Best Organizational Framework

Jon Feingersh/Iconica/Getty Images

Chapter Learning Objectives

After completing this chapter, you should be able to
- Appreciate the narrative approach to presentational speaking.
- Differentiate among the most common types of business and professional presentations.
- Identify key characteristics of your target audience.
- Consider features of the presentational context.
- Select appropriate supporting materials.
- Develop an organizational framework for your presentation.

Renee drives to work with a knot in her stomach that she can feel all the way up to her throat. Today's the day she will be presenting a proposal for her first project idea since joining the company. Although she's been thinking about this idea for months, she has a palpable sense of apprehension as she finally walks toward the conference room with her colleagues. She thinks to herself, "I'm doomed. Why did I need to come up with a new idea? Why couldn't I just go with the flow and work on other people's ideas?"

Renee has given project presentations before, but this is her first formal presentation in this company. All the senior management—including the CEO—will be there. And if that weren't enough to intimidate her, Renee ran out of time before she could put together an appealing presentation and rehearse it because she had spent so much time perfecting her idea. She hopes she won't babble!

This chapter focuses on pre-presentation activities that will help you avoid some of the problems that Renee is facing. You will learn to approach business and professional speaking strategically by defining your speaking purpose, selecting the most appropriate type of presentation, analyzing your audience and speaking environment, researching your topic to find effective supporting materials, and organizing your presentation.

In later chapters, you will continue to build your understanding of crafting and delivering business and professional speeches by exploring informative presentations (Chapter 8), persuasive presentations (Chapter 9), and sensory aids (Chapter 10). By applying what you learn, you will see how Renee and other professionals can deliver presentations that have impact!

Why Are Speeches Best Delivered as Stories?

Who doesn't love a good story? As children, we all had our favorites that we wanted to hear over and over again. As we got older, a good story was one that made us laugh. And as we entered adulthood, a good story was one about an experience we could relate to.

What makes a good story? Good stories are entertaining, make sense, and arouse our attention. Often, a good story leaves us wanting to hear more and thinking about its topic even after the story has ended. Good stories are sometimes dramatic, sometimes suspenseful, sometimes funny, and sometimes tragic. But regardless of the tone or the topic, a good story grabs our attention and holds it.

Imagine the success you could experience at work if you delivered presentations, proposals, briefings, and technical reports in much the same fashion that you tell a good story at the dinner table or during happy hour! Recent research on business speaking has revealed the power of approaching a presentation as an opportunity to tell a good story.[1] For example, in her work on effective communication for trial attorneys, communication professor Sunwolf writes that a defense lawyer is most successful when he learns to tell the defendant's story. According to her research, juries respond positively to a defendant's story when it is told in a way that allows the jury to connect with that person.[2] Similarly, taking the opportunity to frame your business presentation as a good story helps you to excite, involve, and captivate your audience—instead of simply talk at, and possibly alienate, your listeners.

Stop for a moment and think about the characteristics of a good story. What catches your attention and keeps you listening when someone is telling a story?

The Characteristics of a Good Story

From a literary perspective, good stories have the following qualities:

- A topic of interest and significance to listeners.
- A plot that plays out over time, reflecting the complexity of many situations and problems.
- Elements of drama that make the story vivid and interesting. Often, the drama emerges not from the story's content but from the way the speaker tells the story.
- A definable beginning, middle, and end.
- An appropriate setting.
- Characters that are interesting and easy for listeners to relate to.
- A conflict, which at some point climaxes, and then, typically, is resolved. The resolution is realistic to listeners.[3]

At this point, you are probably thinking, "I came here to get a solid business communication education, not become a literary expert!" But human beings have relied on stories as the basic tools to exchange information and understand each other for thousands of years. In professional situations, when much is at stake and understanding is critical, why not use the communication tool that listeners are most comfortable with? Author Gordon Shaw made a strong case for the narrative approach to public speaking in an essay on business communication effectiveness: "We dream, not in bullet points, but in narratives and stories."[4] Let's look more closely at how a business presentation can be shaped as a story.

Business Presentations Told as Stories

Traditional public speaking can be dull and is usually delivered by a single person with little, if any, audience interaction or engaging media support. Accustomed to television and movies that feature informative, compelling, and entertaining stories with a variety of heroes and experts, people may have lost their patience with traditional public speaking

Deklofenak/Shutterstock.com

and boring PowerPoint slides. Thus, John Brown, director of Xerox's Palo Alto Research Center, calls storytelling the "core presentation skill in the digital age."[5]

Communication scholars have argued that our use of interactive media influences what we prefer and expect in public speaking experiences. The Internet, email, online communities, and social networking sites all promote interaction, personal expression, and collaboration. Every day, we are exposed to media with sophisticated graphics, sound, and video—all of which contribute to an expectation that *all* our communication experiences, including public speaking, should be similarly exciting! Audiences crave a presentation that is easy to understand yet substantive, very relevant, interactive, and media-rich.[6]

But stories are not only entertaining. Communication scholar Walter Fisher argues that compelling stories are also persuasive.[7] Fisher argues that we accept some messages and reject others based on our evaluation of the reasoning that the speaker uses. Legal, scientific, and medical data are common rational forms of evidence, but they are not the only, or even prevailing, forms of proof upon which we rely. Instead, Fisher argues, we are essentially storytellers. Therefore, we respond more strongly to narratives that resonate with our experiences than to other, more rational forms of evidence. In other words, to be convincing, you will need to develop a story to which your audience can relate.

Historically, public speaking has been studied apart from communication, as if it were so different from everyday interactions that it was not be guided by some of the same principles. Recently, however, communication scholars have begun to examine the effectiveness of more conversational and personalized approaches to making a presentation—approaches that have been proved effective in the study of relational communication. Much business communication is about relationships (Chapter 5), so doesn't it make sense to approach a business presentation to an audience as you would a conversation in a more personal relationship?

For example, when Dave, who provides staffing and financial consulting for companies in the automotive industry, speaks to a prospective client about his services, he often tells a story about a business similar to his prospect's. After establishing similarity and capturing his listener's attention, he includes details of the other company's problems before his arrival and then illustrates how the company took his recommendations and improved its bottom line. He talks about the emotional impact that both the losses and the ultimate gains had on the business owner and the employees—in terms that his listener can relate to, because she perceives the company in the story to be like hers. She feels similar to the characters in the story and can relate to the key events and conflicts that Dave mentions.

Good stories are a powerful way to communicate with business audiences because they are entertaining, attention-getting, and often motivate listeners to change. Earlier, we looked at the characteristics of a good story. Now let's take a look at a more specific list of characteristics. In the business and professional context, good stories

- Are **realistic**. Listeners must feel that the story rings true and is actually happening or could happen in their profession.

- Are **relevant and have value**. Listeners should leave your story with one or more lessons that they can apply in solving their own business problems.

- Are **coherent**. Good stories make sense. They are easy for the listener to follow and understand.

- Are **interactive**. Excellent storytellers are responsive to their listeners and use listener feedback to measure the reality and relevance of their presentations.

- Have **sustainable take-away lessons**. Listeners remember good stories for their endings. In other words, the end of your story should have enduring value for your listeners.

These principles apply to any type of business presentation, including sales presentations, briefings, team presentations, and special occasion speeches.

Putting Your Skills to Work

You tell some sort of story every day, right? When you tell a story, you tell it in a way that makes sense to listeners, that makes them interested in listening to you, and that includes a point you're trying to make—even if the point is that something funny happened to you on the way home from work. All the skills you use to tell a good story are skills you can use to deliver an effective presentation.

A-Digit/istockphoto.com;
4x6/istockphoto.com

What Type of Business Presentation Best Fits Your Purpose?

One of the first and most critical tasks for any business speaker is identifying the general purpose of the story that needs to be told. The **general purpose** of a presentation is its broad goal: to inform, to persuade, or to commemorate or accept. Having a clear understanding of your general purpose for your presentation will help you to select appropriate content, meet your audience's expectations, and appropriately inform, influence, or entertain your listeners. Identifying your general purpose answers the question, "Why am I speaking about this topic for this particular audience and occasion?"

Here's an example. Sometimes, even in sales situations, a speaker may take a "soft" approach and simply inform the audience about the product's features, leaving a persuasive pitch for a later presentation. For example, at a meeting of professors who research the process of software development, you might choose to simply inform your audience about software that ordinarily you try to persuade people to buy. You inform rather than persuade because your audience isn't in the market for new software. Rather, they want to learn about new developments in the software industry that their students should know about. Thus, to align your general purpose with the needs of the audience, your purpose should be to inform.

One helpful strategy for identifying your general purpose is to identify the *type* of presentation that will best meet your needs and goals. Let's take a look at the most common types of business presentations.

Sales Presentations and Proposals

One of the most common types of business presentations is the **sales presentation**, which is an attempt to persuade clients or customers to purchase a product or service. The hallmark of excellent sales presentations is a narrative approach, using conversational skills such as active listening, clarity, enthusiasm, solution orientation, and a focus on your audience (rather than yourself or even your product or service) to convey your message.

Sometimes you will need to propose, or pitch, an idea to members of your own organization. A **proposal** motivates action and commitment to ideas or behaviors. Here are some examples:

- Andrew, who works in the marketing department of an investment bank, must propose a new advertising campaign and persuade bank officers to allocate funding for it.
- Lynne, who works in the research department of a newspaper publisher, must present to her colleagues a plan to switch from daily print publication to an online-only format.
- Becky, the director of human resources for a health maintenance organization, is preparing a proposal for a new recycling and energy conservation policy that she will present to her superiors.

Like conventional sales presentations, effective proposals are designed to build positive regard and eventual commitment for an idea, either within an organization or among outside clients and customers.

Briefings

Briefings are short, structured informative overviews of highly specific or technical information, packaged appropriately for the intended audience. Effective briefings showcase facts in a way that allows the audience to quickly understand and apply them. Here are some examples:

- Zack, lead engineer for a yacht manufacturing business, must present a ten-minute briefing to his team on the results of a product test that took two weeks to complete.

- Frank, director of production for an auto parts manufacturer, is preparing to brief his boss on his department's quarterly safety record.

- Valerie, the office administrator for a university communication department, must explain a new scheduling policy to department faculty.

- Jake, who designs instructional packages for a professional training company, must determine the most efficient way to brief his manager on his progress related to an important project.

Briefings are often used to provide listeners who are not involved with your day-to-day work tasks—such as managers, work groups other than your own, and clients—with complex, important information in a short amount of time.

Team Presentations

Working in teams and groups is an inherent part of professional life (Chapter 12). You will be involved in group work frequently throughout your career, and as part of your group membership, you may have to speak publicly before an audience. **Team presentations** may be either persuasive or informative, and they are different in some respects from the kinds of speeches you make as an individual. They require a great deal of preparation, which can be difficult when group members have competing schedules and needs, different areas of expertise, and sometimes even different geographic work locations. As a result, group members must understand and follow through on their individual roles in order to achieve a seamless, organized team presentation.

Two types of team presentations are used commonly in the business and professional context:

- A **symposium** is a public presentation in which several people deliver short planned speeches about some topic to an audience. Often each speech represents a slightly different perspective on the overall theme of the symposium. The symposium is common at academic, business, and professional meetings and conferences, where experts are brought together to present their research and thinking on a particular topic. Typically, there is little interaction among individual speakers during a symposium.

- The **panel discussion** is a public presentation in which a moderator manages interaction among panel members about a particular problem or topic. In panel discussions, the moderator first organizes and then facilitates the members of the group. No planned speeches are delivered.

Team presentations not only require speaking skill, but they also require leadership by individual group members (Chapter 12). Team members must work together to organize the presentation, help accomplish the planning and preparation, and maintain a collaborative attitude throughout the preparation and delivery process.

Specialized Business Presentations

At one time or another, you may be asked to present an award to a colleague, accept an award yourself, introduce a guest, give a toast or a roast, or any number of other **special occasion speeches**. Even though these types of speeches can be delivered in informal or social situations at work as well as at formal events, remember that business speaking must always remain professional. When identifying your general purpose, remember that everything you say—and how you say it—reflects on your credibility as a professional. Avoid off-color humor, anything that listeners may perceive as inappropriate or offensive, and always be sensitive to the expectations of your audience. For example, a speaker presenting an award at a ceremony must be sensitive to the fact that the audience wants to see the person receiving the award succeed. There's nothing worse than listening to an award presenter talk about herself instead of about the award recipient!

For more about specialized business presentations, see MODULE 3: **How Do I Give Specialized Presentations?**

How Do You Begin?

Identifying what type of presentation best suits your general purpose is a great first step in developing your presentation. However, you need to consider a number of other factors in defining your approach. These include the nature of your audience, its size, the time of day and the time allotted for your presentation, the seating capacity and physical arrangement of the room, and its sound and lighting capabilities.

Analyze Your Audience

To impress your audience—whether it's an audience of one or one hundred—you need to understand them and their attitudes toward you, your opinion, your product, your employer, and so on. This is true whether you're speaking to a large or small audience, peers or managers, or to sales prospects or existing customers.

LUKE MACGREGOR/Reuters/Corbis

FIGURE 7.1
Checklist of audience analysis activities

☐ Have you reviewed your presentation in light of the age range of your listeners? What examples and evidence will they recognize and find relevant?

☐ Do you address the concerns of both your male and female listeners?

☐ Are you prepared to sensitively handle objections that listeners may have about you or your presentation?

☐ Have you considered how appropriate your approach is in relation to listeners' work or professional roles?

☐ Are your explanations, examples, and vocabulary at a level that is appropriate to the audience's sophistication and education?

Your audience is central to all the decisions you make about preparing and delivering your presentation. **Audience analysis** requires the systematic gathering of information about your intended audience: Who are these people? Why are they here? What are they interested in? What stake do they hold in the reason you are speaking? These can be complex questions to answer in the business environment, where personal interests, politics, and scarce resources can all affect how audience members anticipate and receive your presentation.

Here are some specific questions to help you determine who your listeners are. Also see **Figure 7.1** for a checklist of activities that will help you analyze your audiences.

- How many men and how many women are there in my audience? Is my audience mostly male, mostly female, or evenly mixed?

- How old are the audience members? What is their approximate age range?

- What specialization or area of the industry/company do my audience members represent?

- What ethnic and co-cultural affiliations are represented in this group?

- What is the education level of my audience members?

- What is my audience's current level of knowledge about my topic?

- What experience does my audience already have with the issue I'm going to speak about? Do they view the issue favorably or negatively?

The answers to these questions can help you form a general impression of your particular audience and whether you need to adjust your topic or approach to fit its demographics. In other words, try to get an idea of who these people are, what they are like, and what they might interest them, and how much time they are likely to have to listen to your presentation. For example, an audience analysis would give you an idea of whether audience members will be inclined to participate in the recycling program you are proposing as a cost-reducing measure for your company or whether they might be interested in buying stocks or treasury bills. The larger your audience is, the more challenging your audience analysis task will be. But any effort you make to frame your presentation with some information you have about them will contribute to your effectiveness.

You must also determine what biases, if any, your listeners might have toward you or your presentation. One of the most important lessons you can learn as a speaker is that people tend to evaluate messages in terms of their own attitudes, beliefs, and values, and not yours, the speaker's. So you are far more likely to sustain your listeners' attention if you know their feelings about your topic, you as a speaker, and other factors related to your presentation. For instance, is your presentation taking them from an important project, thus irritating them or stressing them out?

Recall Renee from the opening of this chapter. She is preparing to pitch a new project proposal to important colleagues. She knows that because of office politics, some audience members will want her to succeed and others will want her to fail. But Renee has carefully considered the attitudes that members of her audience will have toward her and her idea. For example, she knows that Gary from accounting won't like the idea at first because of its expense. Elaine from PR will be attracted to the project because it could result in good publicity for the company. And she believes that Barb might react negatively because she and Renee have had a number of interpersonal conflicts in the past year. So she has built into her speech statements, explanations, and examples that will appeal to Elaine and that will help to overcome Gary's and Barb's objections. Anticipating your audience's attitudes before you make a presentation can help you deflect negativity and capitalize on favorable attitudes.

To read another example of how a speaker handled a business presentation—this time not as well as Renee did—check out **VISUALIZE! PRACTICE! 7.1: Case Study: Jeff's Presentation**. After you read about and analyze Jeff's presentation, consider the six things every presenter must know about sales prospects.

For more about gathering all the information necessary to accurately analyze your audience, see **MODULE 7: What Methods Can I Use to Analyze My Audience?**

Analyze Your Speaking Environment

In addition to determining the demographic characteristics and attitudes of your audience, you must evaluate the features of your **speaking environment**, such as the size of your audience, the physical setting for your presentation, the time and length of your presentation, seating capacity and physical arrangement of the room, and sound and lighting. Managing these features effectively gives you credibility and motivates your audience to listen to you. To determine how best to prepare, package, and deliver your presentation, consider the following questions:

1. **What is the size of the audience?** The larger the group, the more difficulty you will have interacting with your audience. With a lot of audience members, you will need to be creative to engage them, plan where to position yourself, and consider how you will need to adjust your voice to be heard. For example, you may need the aid of a microphone, so you'll need to make sure one is available and that you know how to use it.

2. **What is the presentation schedule and how much time is available to speak?** How receptive your audience is to your presentation is affected by the time at which your presentation is scheduled and its length. For example, people gathered at breakfast, lunch, or dinner meetings come to a speech with more than one agenda. They may want to listen to you, but they also want to eat and socialize. Similarly, speaking too long or finishing too quickly can interfere with audience members'

Module 7:
What Methods Can I Use to Analyze My Audience?

Visualize! Practice! 7.1:
Case Study: Jeff's Presentation

schedules, negatively affecting your effectiveness and the impression you make. Very little will irritate your listeners more than the perception that you don't value their time. Do everything you can to start your speech promptly and to stay within the time allotted you, always leaving time for questions and comments.

These are typical lengths for the various presentation types:

- Sales presentations and briefings: 15 to 20 minutes
- Presentation to your manager: 1 to 10 minutes
- Toast: 1 to 2 minutes
- Award acceptance speech: 3 to 5 minutes

3. **What is the seating capacity and physical arrangement of the room?** How will audience seating be arranged? Will it be the traditional theatre/lecture-style seating arrangement, or will attendees be seated at round tables? Will you be able to change the arrangement of the room to better suit your needs? Where will you be positioned? At a head table? On a stage? Or can you roam around as you talk? Also, consider the atmosphere of the room: The feel of a boardroom is different from that of a banquet hall and even more different from that of an office or cubicle—although all of these can be settings for business presentations.

4. **What will the sound and lighting be like?** Will people in the back of the room be able to hear you as well as people seated in the front? Will the lighting be dim enough so that any projected images or slides will be visible, yet bright enough for listeners to take notes and see you?

5. **What other characteristics should you consider?** Every presentation occurs in a particular context. For example, you might be the last speaker on a panel of five. How might that affect your audience's willingness and ability to listen to you? Or you might precede or follow a speaker who is more dynamic or better known than you are. Your listeners may be affected by some unusual event in their environment, such as a financial crisis within the company or the resignation of a key leader. Addressing and acknowledging these kinds of issues during your presentation, even briefly, will help you build a sense of goodwill and connection with your audience.

How Do You Build Support for Your Ideas?

For any type of presentation you make, you must support your speech with evidence that ensures your information and arguments are credible and defensible. **Evidence** is made up of facts and of experts' opinions. **Experts** are people who, through education, training, or experience, have special knowledge about a particular subject. Draw heavily on what experts know by conducting interviews and researching books, magazines, industry publications, magazines, the Internet, and other sources of information. In addition, consider your own expertise and personal knowledge. Help build support for your ideas by ensuring that you and the evidence you use are credible, appropriate, and tailored to your audience.

Establish Your Credibility as a Speaker

Even if you are widely perceived as an authority on your topic, you must still use supporting evidence in order to maintain credibility. Even experts need to prove their arguments—that's how they continue to be recognized as experts. Assume that your audience will need to be convinced. Speak clearly about your own experiences, knowledge, or expertise, but also be sure to use the opinions and experiences of other experts to demonstrate that your ideas are supported by a diverse group of authorities.

The way you present yourself also affects your credibility. Audience members can see you as a physical object the minute you walk into a room or move to the podium. All eyes are on you, and everyone assesses what they see and hear. What you communicate non-verbally during those first few seconds is your audience's first impression of your credibility.

One way to appear credible and believable is to project confidence. Audience members look for signs of apprehension, but don't let them see any. They need to feel comfortable with you and to know that you can handle the speaking situation confidently. Looking composed, then, is critical to appearing credible (Chapter 1). The more apparent signs of composure include smiling, nodding, making prolonged eye contact, and using slow, deliberate movements. Concentrate on looking calm and composed even before you give your presentation. Then, once you are in front of your audience, take a moment to pause. Sweep your eyes across the audience, taking notice of all the faces in the room. See audience members as individuals. Smile, nod, and say hello. Then, begin to tell your story.

Your credibility also depends on your physical appearance and what you wear (Chapter 2). Clothing and grooming send powerful messages. Dressing sloppily in a professional setting causes most audiences to form an immediate negative impression of you. But dressing appropriately and being well groomed show that you have made an effort to look good for a professional occasion. Audiences appreciate the time and trouble you take to present the best possible you.

Consider the Different Types of Support

Just what should you look for when gathering research materials? Begin by reading general discussions and opinions about your topic. Then gather specific materials that you can use as evidence to support your information and arguments. These different kinds of supporting materials can be used for different purposes and audiences:

- **Facts and data.** Statistical data and physical evidence are very powerful, particularly for people from certain disciplines, such as the sciences and engineering. For example, some audiences need to know what is true most of the time for most people or how often a particular phenomenon occurs, in what location, and under what circumstances. Individuals who prefer facts and data over personal experiences as evidence will be more likely to accept your ideas as credible if you provide them with this type of support. Without facts and data, some audience members, because of their education, training, or profession, may perceive your experiences or examples as representing only unique or unusual cases.

- **Stories and examples.** Not all evidence must be grounded in hard, objective facts to make your case. Some types of support provide a more personal feel and are particularly well suited to a presentation told as a story. These types of support include expert testimonials, eyewitness accounts, human interest stories, quotable phrases, and real-life examples.

For more about facts, stories, and quotations, see Chapter 8.

Michael Newman/PhotoEdit

Select Only the Best Supporting Material

As a professional, you are likely to have access to a great deal of supporting material to use in presentations. In order to use your research time most effectively and find the most appropriate material, you need to know where to begin your research, what information to skim or omit, and when to end your research. You can accomplish these goals by taking the time to assess the relevance, recency, and credibility of your materials.

- **Relevant evidence** is information that is directly associated with your topic. If evidence isn't relevant to your topic and your audience, don't use it. Although you might run across an incredibly good quotation, a really funny story, or a fascinating statistic, use it only if it is directly related to your topic and will be understood by your audience. Don't make the audience try to guess how supporting materials fit within your presentation—your job is to make that clear to them.

    Take, for instance, Chris, a pharmaceutical company sales representative. In preparing his presentation for doctors about a newly approved cancer drug, he learned a great deal about pancreatic cancer—one of several types of cancer that the drug was designed to attack. Chris spent much of his presentation discussing the causes and symptoms of pancreatic cancer. Although the doctors were impressed with his knowledge of pancreatic cancer, they left the presentation knowing very little about his company's drug. The evidence Chris chose to use was only indirectly relevant to his product. Chris's supporting materials would have been more effective if he had opened with a compelling story about a family affected by cancer and then discussed the potential his company's drug had for helping similar families.

- **Recent evidence** is information about your topic that cannot be considered outdated. Audiences are more willing to consider your evidence valid if it is recent. But how recent is "recent"? In this information age, yesterday's news—perhaps even this morning's—can be outdated. However, some evidence stands the test of time. For example, five-year-old scientific reports published in journals are often still valid because a new study of the topic hasn't been conducted. As a professional, you must know your topic well enough to determine how quickly the facts about it are changing.

- **Credible evidence** is consistent with other known facts and comes from sources that are known to be credible. The sources of your support must be acknowledged experts in their field and should reflect a sense of impartiality and fairness.

  For example, imagine giving a presentation about the safety of SUVs in rollover accidents. Most audiences would consider supporting materials from companies that manufacture SUVs to be less credible than support from, say, the National Safety Council. Car manufacturers have a financial interest in selling SUVs, so they are not necessarily impartial when it comes to vehicle safety. In contrast, the National Safety Council is a nonprofit, nongovernmental, and nonpartisan public service organization with 54,000 member companies. It's not interested in selling cars and it partners with businesses, so it's more likely to provide impartial information about road safety.

  Credibility is particularly important for Internet resources. Anyone can post information on the Web—true or false, good or bad. Nevertheless, the Internet is a rich resource if you know how to evaluate the credibility of the information you find there. Table 7.1 provides some guidelines.

TABLE 7.1
Evaluating Information from the Internet

What question should you ask yourself?	Why should you ask yourself this question?
What is the source of the information? Who is the author or sponsor of the site?	• Websites maintained by government agencies, professional organizations, and established news organizations are likely to present trustworthy information. • Many other groups and individuals post accurate information, but consider your sources carefully. Carefully verify information from wikis (such as Wikipedia) and blogs—information on these sites may lack objectivity or accuracy. • If you can't identify the sponsor of a website or verify an author's credentials, don't use the information in your presentation. • Pay attention to where you are on the information superhighway. Even if you start out at a trustworthy site, the click of the mouse can send you to an untrustworthy site.
How often is the site updated?	• Look for clues that indicate how recently the site has been updated. • If the topic you are researching is time sensitive, look for sources that are updated frequently.
Does the site promote a particular viewpoint or product? Are there obvious reasons for the bias?	• Websites whose authors or sponsors have a financial interest in a topic may not provide unbiased information about that topic. • Be wary of sites that appear to have an ax to grind.
What do other sources say about your topic?	• To validate a piece of information, check out other sources—books, experts, other websites. And never base an entire presentation on information from a single Internet source. • You are more likely to obtain and recognize quality information if you utilize several different sources.

Module 6:
"You Gotta Have Style": Using APA and MLA Styles

Module 2:
How Can I Practice Ethical Communication Behavior at Work?

Visualize! Practice! 7.2:
Audrina's story

As you conduct research to collect support for your presentation, keep careful records of where you obtain your information and what sources you consult. Write down when you are quoting or paraphrasing from a particular source. Careful note-taking at this point will make it easy to be accurate and ethical when you deliver your presentation, and it will help you avoid inadvertently plagiarizing the work of others.

Check out Speech Studio to see how other students use facts, stories, and quotations in their speeches. Or record a speech you're working on, upload it to Speech Studio, and ask your peers for their feedback. What feedback could you use to fine-tune your supporting material before you give your speech in class?

To learn more about using recognized styles to report references and cite sources in your presentations, see **MODULE 6: "You Gotta Have Style": Using APA and MLA Styles**. For more about avoiding plagiarism, see **MODULE 2: How Can I Practice Ethical Communication Behavior at Work?**

How Do You Organize Your Presentation?

VISUALIZE! PRACTICE! 7.2: Audrina's story Audrina was preparing to present to the editor her first proposal for her own feature article as a staff writer for a prestigious fashion magazine. However, she runs into a common snag that a lot of public speakers struggle with.

Audrina considered a variety of topics based on her own experience as a young woman interested in fashion trends. She studied the demographic, sociographic, and psychographic profiles of the magazine's readers. She conducted telephone interviews with a sample of subscribers. What immediately struck her was the dark secret of so many fashionable women: the massive amounts of debt that they incur attempting to copy the ever-changing styles of international supermodels and celebrities. She decided to pitch a story to the editor about the dangerous pattern of credit card use and abuse that so many people fall into all in the name of looking good.

With her topic established, Audrina began her research. She considered her own spending habits, and her attempts to rationalize $125 for the latest shoes or $400 for this season's "must have" handbag—on a staff writer's salary. She also interviewed a spokesperson from Consumer Credit Counseling who provided her with some statistics on women and credit card debt. She talked with a psychologist who specializes in shopping addictions and was even able to gain access to several of the psychologist's clients who gave her some fascinating insights into the worst kind of fashion crisis: overspending, overcharging, and the inability to pay monthly bills. Finally, she compiled data from statistical abstracts, government publications like the Fair Credit Reporting Act, and books by experts on the subject of shopping addiction and credit card debt. Now, she had to put together a coherent presentation for the magazine's editorial staff that would convince them that the story merited publication.

With all the compelling information she had collected, Audrina should have been ready to pitch her story and get the green light. But she had a problem: She'd accumulated too *much* material: interview notes and tapes, books, photocopied materials, websites, and even photographs. How could she organize and condense all the information into a persuasive seven-minute story proposal that would engage and excite the editorial staff?

You may encounter similar difficulties when preparing for a presentation. After gathering a lot of information from the Internet, the library, and other sources, all of which relates to your topic in some way, you then need to sift through the information, select the right pieces, and organize them in some logical format. Let's look at some concrete strategies for sorting through and organizing information for your presentations.

Understand the Importance of Organization

When you organize your presentation, you put your ideas and supporting materials together into some logical manner. An organized presentation is very important both to you as speaker and to your audience members as listeners.[8] Organizing your presentation helps you remember your ideas and deliver your presentation coherently, and it helps your audience follow the logic of your information and arguments.

- **Benefits for the speaker.** Speakers who organize their presentations effectively are able to stay on course and engage their listeners. They should have little fear of losing their place, omitting important information, misquoting facts, repeating themselves, or wandering from point to point and losing their audience's attention. In addition, organized presentations are associated with perceptions of greater speaker credibility.[9] In other words, the more organized your presentation is, the more credible you will appear to your audience.

- **Benefits for the audience.** If you just discuss your ideas randomly, with no organization at all, audience members won't be able to follow along and they'll conclude that you don't know what you are talking about! Although little research has been done on the effects of speech organization, what does exist supports the claim that audiences rely on you to tell your story in some organized way.

  ✔ Research shows that audiences prefer organized presentations to disorganized ones.[10] That same research also indicates that audiences tolerate a small degree of disorganization. This is good news for speakers who may need to backtrack when they omit something or who have to forego a point when time runs out.

  ✔ The more disorganized a speech is, the more difficulty audience members will have understanding the speaker's message.[11]

  ✔ Recently, experts in presentation development have suggested that in the era of Facebook and YouTube, both a visual component and a personal story are important to creating a sense of organization for your audience.[12]

Get Ready to Organize

The first steps in organizing your presentation are to stop researching, begin thinking about how you want to present your ideas, and consider how to organize your ideas in a way that will appeal to the widest audience.

- **Stop researching.** Like Audrina, you may have discovered a mountain of facts, testimonials, definitions, statistics, and examples. At some point, you must stop gathering information and quit reading. Don't let yourself be overwhelmed by the data. Instead, begin to make decisions about what information is truly necessary and what information you should discard. Remember to choose information that is relevant to your topic, recent, and credible.

- **Arrange your thoughts.** Begin to arrange your ideas in some systematic way. This initial arrangement is unlikely to be your final organizational scheme—it may be very rough, but it will be a start. Organizing a speech may require two, three, or more attempts before you are ready to present your thoughts in a truly helpful way.

- **Consider how you'll appeal to the widest audience.** Just as some class lectures are easy for you to understand while others seem confusing, business presentations can make sense to some audience members but not to others. To begin organizing your story for the widest variety of listeners, arrange essential information in a way that will allow *you* to understand what you're trying to say. This will help you help *your audience* understand what you mean to say. Determine where you're going with your speech, and then create a clear path for getting there.

Select the Best Organizing Framework

What may seem organized and logical to one individual may appear disorganized to another. For example, the groups people belong to influence how they make sense of the information they are presented with in a public speaking context. Consider Lori, who works for a nonprofit organization that provides medical care to children in third-world countries. As a result of her interest in aiding people experiencing hardship and tragedy, she may prefer a presentation that integrates narratives about individual experiences. Conversely, Maxwell is a geologist, so he may prefer a more linear framework, organized around verifiable facts and objective data.

Robert B. Kaplan is credited with the concept that individuals organize their ideas using different frameworks as a function of their language and cultural affiliations. Kaplan noticed that nonnative speakers of English wrote paragraphs and essays very differently than native English speakers. The ideas in the essays he examined were not organized according to the linear patterns of the typical Euro-American but rather with alternative organizational schemes.[13]

Putting Your Skills to Work

AND SO, IN CONCLUSION...

Audiences expect professional public presentations to be organized coherently, just as you expect your instructors to present their lectures in a way that you can follow and understand—and just as your instructors expect you to organize your essays and research papers! An organized speech is similar to a good essay in that it's a coherent presentation of ideas. However, like a good lecture, it's meant to be listened to and not read.

A-Digit/istockphoto.com;
4x6/istockphoto.com

Interestingly, we also know that people adapt the ways in which they listen to and process information based on particular situations and their own experiences—such as what kinds of mass media they consume and how often.[14] Most of us have become accustomed to rich visuals and sounds streaming across our computers, through the advertising we are exposed to, and the shows and films we view. Through cell phones, instant messengers, and other media, we have the constant opportunity to interact with others through technology. Consequently, we have developed new interaction and listening habits and patterns. We *expect* speakers to invite our interaction and to dazzle us with impressive audio, video, and animation.

To help you determine your personal preferences regarding organizational frameworks, complete the survey **WEIGH IN! 7.1: What Type of Organizational Framework Do You Prefer?** This survey assesses your cultural preferences as well as your experience with interactive media.[15]

Let's take a look at two common organizational frameworks people use to make sense of information: linear and configural.

Linear Framework Not too long ago, we would have suggested that if you were educated in the United States, you are probably more oriented to and comfortable with a **linear framework**. However, the way people learn about logic and organization appears to have changed dramatically in the past several years in the United States. Even so, a linear framework is still preferred and privileged for most business presentations and briefings.

A presentation with a linear framework follows a straightforward pattern:

1. The speaker lays out the basic argument or thesis by previewing each main point.

2. The speaker discusses the main points in detail, one at a time. These points are organized in some linear pattern—chronological, spatial, topical, problem–solution, or cause and effect. See Table 7.2 for a description and example of each of these patterns.

Weigh In! 7.1:
What Type of Organizational Framework Do You Prefer?

Yuri Arcurs/Shutterstock.com

TABLE 7.2
Linear Patterns of Organization

Pattern	Description	Sample speech outline organized according to this pattern[16]
Chronological	Organizes a speech according to a sequence of events or ideas.	I. In the past, speech-recognition software was so prone to error that it was easier to just type what you wanted to say. II. Today, Google's powerful systems allow faster and more accurate processing of speech sounds. III. In the future, Google wants its speech-recognition technology to be so good that users can work with any online application just by speaking to their phones.
Topical	Allows speaker to divide a topic into subtopics about different aspects of the larger topic.	I. Android's speech-recognition technology allows users to successfully handle many types of computing tasks verbally, such as getting directions and translating foreign languages. II. Android's technology works so well because Google has created systems that allow for the analysis of huge stores of information.
Spatial	Arranges ideas in terms of location or direction.	I. The top of the phone displays a menu of icons that allows you to access various features, including the speech-recognition feature. II. The main screen displays the message or command you've spoken into the phone. III. The bottom of the screen allows you to send or cancel your message or command.
Problem–Solution	Organizes a speech by identifying a specific problem and then outlining a solution.	I. In the past, speech-recognition software made you speak slowly and was so prone to error that it was easier to just type what you wanted to say. II. Although today's top-of-the-line software allows you to use your normal speaking voice, it is still slow and uses a lot of your phone's computing power. III. Google has solved these problems by moving the processing from the phone to the Internet, using Google's own servers to process speech sounds.
Cause and Effect	Describes a cause-and-effect relationship between ideas and events.	I. Google's unique infrastructure—which enables computers to store, analyze, and manage vast amounts of information—caused a giant leap forward in speech-recognition technology. II. The effect is a far more positive experience for Android users who want to take advantage of the phone's speech-recognition feature.

3. The speaker relies heavily on facts and data to clarify, illustrate, and support each main point. Supporting material comes from traditional experts—people with advanced degrees, established reputations, and highly recognizable names—as opposed to everyday people who may have experience with the issue.

4. The speaker uses words and phrases called transitions and signposts to connect the main points and the supporting ideas. A **transition** is a phrase that links one main point to another. A **signpost** is a word or phrase that signals the organization of ideas, indicating where a speaker is in a speech or highlighting an important idea. See Table 7.3 for examples of common transitions and signposts used in speeches. See if you can add to these examples by completing VISUALIZE! PRACTICE! 7.3: **Transitions & Signposts**. You can also use this activity to access a list of more sample transitions and signposts.

5. The speaker concludes with a summary of the main points and, if applicable, an explicit call for some kind of action or response from audience members.

A presentation organized in a linear fashion can be likened to a recipe: a series of ordered ingredients and steps that must be followed precisely if the result is to be successful.

Visualize! Practice! 7.3:
Transitions & Signposts

TABLE 7.3
Examples of Transitions and Signposts

	Examples	Used in a sentence
Transitions	• Along the same lines • On the other hand • Now that you understand • Let's turn to • In addition to • Moreover • In short • Now let's discuss • Once you've done . . . , you're ready to move to • This all boils down to one thing	• *Now that you understand* that an effective resume should allow an employer to quickly scan for important information, *let's look at* some strategies for making your resume easy to read. • *In addition to* causing problems in the workplace, working too many hours can cause conflict at home.
Signposts	• Let me begin by • Next • First . . . second . . . third • My primary concern • You'll want to listen to the next point • Let me repeat that statistic for you • The important thing to remember is • What follows is • In conclusion	• *The important thing to remember* is that handling an ethical dilemma in the workplace requires sensitivity and effective communication. • *Let me repeat that statistic for you*: Fully 70 percent of doctors interrupted patients within the first 18 seconds of the visit.

Let's look at an example of a speech excerpt organized according to the linear framework in **VISUALIZE! PRACTICE! 7.4: Chase's Presentation**. This is from Chase's training presentation to the sales team of a local health club on how to be more persuasive with prospective members.

There are three basic reasons why people purchase gym memberships.

The first and most common reason is because they want to look good. People recognize that regular exercise results in greater muscle tone, less fat, and even clearer skin tone. Emphasizing these benefits with prospects will result in more sales.

The second reason why people join gyms is to improve their internal health. People who fear heart disease, cancer, and stroke will respond to the evidence that regular exercise can help prevent these maladies. Be sure to have this evidence on hand when meeting with a potential club member.

And third, people join health clubs because they want an opportunity to socialize with others and meet people. When working with a potential member, point out that the gym is a great place to meet like-minded people who share similar interests. Give prospects a schedule of planned mixers hosted by the club so that the social aspect of working out is clear.

Understanding the three primary reasons why people join gyms and addressing them in your sales pitches will result in more memberships.

Chase clearly and systematically lays out the three basic reasons people join gyms. Notice how he previews his three major points and then ticks off each one by signaling with the signposts *first, second*, and *third*. Step by step, he tells the audience the order of reasons (most common to least common) that people buy health club memberships. By organizing his message in this progressive manner, Chase actively helps the audience to follow along.

For an example of a speech organized with a linear framework, access **LINK OUT 7.1: Sample Linear Speech**. This informative speech, "The Four Ways Sound Affects Us," was given by Julian Treasure, chair of the Sound Agency and author of *Sound Business*, at the TEDGlobal 2009 Conference.[17]

Configural Framework Whereas a linear framework is direct and straightforward, a **configural framework** is more indirect. Speakers using a configural framework are not likely to preview their main points or spell out a specific conclusion. Instead, much like the hit cable TV show *The Sopranos* did in the series finale, these speakers allow their audiences to draw their own conclusions.

With a linear framework, the speaker is largely responsible for helping the audience understand the message.[18] By contrast, some individuals and cultures tend to find such direction and assistance unnecessary, boring, and even demeaning, preferring instead that the speaker give them credit for being able to figure out the message on their own.[19] Other research demonstrates that people may become overloaded by too many facts presented in a linear format.[20] As more people become accustomed to the visual and interactive strategies of new media, they may come to prefer the configural framework, which is less straightforward and allows audience members to work more to determine the meaning of a message.

For example, the display about the Watergate scandal at the Richard Nixon Presidential Library was revamped to have a configural approach. The library's director, Timothy Naftali, told the *Los Angeles Times* that the gallery will be "an interactive . . . experience.

HBO/courtesy Everett Collection

You'll be able to navigate through this story yourself. It'll be up to the visitor to [view all the materials] and decide, 'Did Nixon order the coverup? What were the abuses of power? What role did partisan politics play in Richard Nixon's downfall?' [As director,] I'm not going to answer those questions. It's not up to me."[21] In other words, like a speaker attempting to create an interactive, configural story, Mr. Naftali presented a wide variety of materials on the Watergate incident, allowing the public to draw its own conclusions.

Little research has been done about the types of patterns that characterize the configural framework, but we do know that this framework is not characterized by linear patterns. Here's what else the research tells us:

- A presentation organized with a configural framework usually requires more audience engagement than one organized with a linear framework does. The speaker is not solely responsible for the message. Rather, the listener must also actively construct and create meaning.[22]

- A speaker using the configural framework does not spell out his purpose and main points for audience members. Instead, listeners must rely on what they already know about the speaker and the topic to interpret the presentation.

- Speakers explore issues from a variety of tangential views or examples. Links among main points may not be made explicitly. Direction is only implied.

- Finally, configural organizational patterns often rely more on speaker self-disclosure through personal examples and the act of drawing out comments and participation from audience members. Research indicates that the growing preference for this form of evidence may be a by-product of the growing popularity of interactive media such as blogs and social networking sites. These forms of communication encourage us to be more self-expressive and to appreciate others' self-expression in all kinds of communication situations.[23]

Table 7.4 provides descriptions of some patterns used within the configural framework: narrative, web, problem–no solution, and multiple perspectives.

TABLE 7.4
Configural Patterns of Organization

Pattern	Description	Sample speech outline organized according to this pattern

Narrative	Organizes a speech using a story or series of stories to convey an idea.	I. I am the head of development at a nonprofit agency that fights poverty, and I'm also a volunteer firefighter in my town.
		II. When I fought my first house fire, I really wanted to make a difference in someone's life.
		  A. A volunteer who arrived at the scene before I did was assigned the job of rescuing the homeowner's dog from the burning house—I was stunned with jealousy!
		  B. I was assigned the job of getting the homeowner a pair of shoes—not exactly what I was hoping for.
		  C. But a few weeks later, the homeowner wrote the fire department, thanking us for saving her home.
		  D. The act of kindness she noted above all others was that someone had even gotten her a pair of shoes.
		III. All acts of generosity and kindness matter, whether they're on a monumental scale or an individual basis.
		  A. Don't wait until you make your first million to make a difference in somebody's life.
		  B. Not every day offers us a chance to save a life, but every day offers us a chance to affect one.
		  C. So get in the game—save the shoes![24]

Web	Emanates from a core idea. Each specific idea, branching from the core, illuminates or extends the central point. The speaker begins with a central idea, examines a related idea, and then returns to the central point.	I. The paparazzi should show restraint in their coverage of celebrities, particularly those who don't seek attention.
		  A. Arnold Schwarzenegger's "secret" son should be left alone.
		  B. This boy never asked to be put in the situation he's in.
		II. Disrespectful of others' needs for privacy, irresponsible photojournalists are putting their targets' lives in danger.
		  A. Princess Diana was involved in a high-speed chase by paparazzi, resulting in her death.
		  B. Most people believe that the princess would be alive today if the paparazzi hadn't followed her.

Problem-No Solution	Focuses on the breadth and depth of a problem to alert listeners about a significant problem. Often used for an audience that is uncertain or opposed to your position. Can also be used to promote a dialogue about possible solutions.	I. Throughout the world, we have too few women leaders, both in government and in professional life.
		  A. Women systematically underestimate their own abilities, which leads them to fail to negotiate effectively for themselves or feel comfortable with their successes.
		  B. Women take on more household responsibilities than men do, so they are more likely to drop out of the workforce when there is a need for one partner to stay at home (e.g., for childcare).
		  C. Women don't always take advantages of promotions or new opportunities because they anticipate having to leave the workforce temporarily to have children.
		II. Women of my generation won't see an increase in their numbers at the top, but I'm hopeful that future generations—including my daughter—will be able to.[25]

(continued)

Pattern	Description	Sample speech outline organized according to this pattern
Multiple Perspectives	Systematically addresses many sides and positions of an issue.	I. There are a number of ways in which a person can get a college education, regardless of their life situation. A. Many people take the traditional route and go straight to college from high school, like I did. B. Others find that life circumstances keep them from taking the traditional route, and they opt for alternative paths to an education. 1. My brother joined the military after high school, wasn't happy in a traditional university setting after returning to civilian life, and found success pursuing an online business degree. 2. A friend of mine decided to stay home and raise a family rather than go to college, later decided she also wanted a career, and obtained an associate degree in early childhood education from her local community college. C. Still others decide to return to college in order to change careers after having been in the workforce for many years. 1. These people can save money by first fulfilling general requirements at a community college and then transferring to a four-year school. 2. Or they can continue to work and obtain an online degree in their off hours. 3. Or they can take advantage of the traditional four-year college experience. II. All these approaches should be valued and encouraged equally because all offer valid paths to a college education.

Let's take another look at Chase's presentation to the gym's sales staff, this time organized within a configural framework:

> Have you ever noticed that the same person may have multiple reasons for joining your club? Although we tend to think of working out as a way to get healthy, some people come to the gym to meet people and for something to do. Sometimes people sign up because they've had a health scare or have lost a close family member to disease—nothing like a reality check to send someone to the local gym. Has anyone ever heard a particularly interesting story about why a prospective member is interested in signing up? Tell us about it. *[Chase takes a comment from an audience member, who shares a brief personal example.]*
>
> But of course if you can tell a prospective member that she's going to look better as a result of working out, you typically can close the deal. I remember when I first got into this industry, I was stunned at the number of men and women alike who failed to see any benefit to working out other than that it enhanced their physical appearance. There is so much more to gain from a gym membership.

In this example, Chase does not preview his main points. Instead, he assumes his audience members will be able to impose their own structure onto his presentation. In

Link Out 7.2:
Sample Configural Speech 1

Link Out 7.3:
Sample Configural Speech 2

Visualize! Practice! 7.5:
Pros & Cons of Linear and Configural Presentations

addition, he subtly suggests his main points rather than explicitly delineating them as progressive steps. In these ways, he invites interactivity among his audience's members—they must be more actively engaged to figure out his purpose, understand his main points, and help construct meaning. In fact, Chase invites his audience to insert some of their own meanings by soliciting their personal experiences in the context of his talk. Also notice how he approaches his topic from a variety of angles, using evidence, stories, and personal testimony, including his own experiences and the example offered by one of his listeners.

For an example of a speech organized with a configural framework, access **LINK OUT 7.2: Sample Configural Speech 1**. This informative speech, "Tough Truths about Plastic Pollution," was given by artist and activist Dianna Cohen at TED Talks, April 2010.[26]

For another example, go to **LINK OUT 7.3: Sample Configural Speech 2**. In this video a manager discusses branch goals with his staff. Clearly, he knew a lot about his employees before this planned interaction. But he also is interested in conversing with his listeners during his presentation. Notice how he not only solicits audience feedback but also incorporates his listeners' comments and responses into the presentation in meaningful ways.

Use Different Organizational Patterns to Organize Your Story You can organize your presentation in a variety of ways. The particular organizational pattern you select need not depend *entirely* on the framework you or your audience prefers. Selecting an appropriate pattern (or combination of patterns) depends on your industry, your topic, and your own framework preference.

Fortunately, you can count on your audience members to make sense of your presentation in their own way. Research indicates that audience members can make sense out of a wide variety of organizational patterns, regardless of their cultural background, information-processing habits, or media exposure. Studies have shown, for example, that nonnative English speakers who prefer the configural framework are able to recall the major points and premises of content organized linearly at about the same rate and frequency as native speakers.[27]

Although no comparable research has examined how accurately people who prefer the linear framework can recall information presented configurally, theorists interested in the influence of new media suspect that technology has made us all a bit more configural than we were a few years ago. In his book *Beyond Bullet Points*, business consultant Cliff Atkinson speculates that as a result of our near-constant exposure to and use of interactive, dynamic media, we've begun to think more creatively and communicate more expressively—and less linearly.[28] Other writers point out that the point-by-point linear speech is an outdated form that lacks drama, visual interest, and eloquence—and that like a customized, interactive website, a configural narrative accompanied by creative visual support allows you to better express your identity and connect with your audience.[29] What are your thoughts about each of the frameworks? Check out **VISUALIZE! PRACTICE! 7.5: Pros & Cons of Linear and Configural Presentations** to voice your opinion.

Audiences are likely to reorder and prioritize the information in ways that make the message most meaningful to them while discarding or ignoring information they find redundant or meaningless. Although speech organization does affect message comprehension, audiences can decipher and make sense of unfamiliar and seemingly mildly disorganized presentations. Audiences likely to have problems interpreting the message only when it is highly disorganized and its points are apparently offered at random.

Creating an outline will help you organize and then deliver your speech most effectively. See **MODULE 8: What's the Best Way to Organize and Outline My Presentation?** to learn how to create a useful outline.

Although Renee was nervous about her presentation, she was confident that she had completed some of the most important tasks associated with business speaking. She knew what her general purpose was and exactly what type of presentation she needed to deliver to accomplish that purpose. She knew enough about her audience and the speaking environment to ensure that audience members were comfortable and both physically and mentally ready to listen to her. And, importantly, she knew her topic inside and out. She had gathered enough appropriate supporting materials to convince her audience that her project idea was a winner. Lastly, she organized her speech using a framework and organizational patterns appropriate for her audience.

Use your Speech Communication CourseMate for *Business & Communication in a Digital Age* for quick access to the electronic resources that accompany this text. These resources include

Study tools that will help you assess your learning and prepare for exams (*digital glossary, key term flash cards, review quizzes*).

Activities and assignments that will help you hone your knowledge and build your communication skills throughout the course (*Visualize! Practice!, Weigh In!, Check This Out, and Link Out activities; modules; review questions*).

Media resources that will help you explore communication concepts online (*Enhanced eBook*), develop your speech outlines (*Speech Builder Express 3.0*), watch and critique videos of sample speeches and communication situations (*interactive video activities*), upload your speech videos for peer reviewing and critique other students' speeches (*Speech Studio online speech review tool*), and download chapter review so you can study when and where you'd like (*Audio Study Tools*).

Key Points

- Delivering a business presentation as a good story helps you excite, involve, and captivate your audiences.
  - ✔ Delivering a speech as a story reflects the fact that interactive media impact what today's audiences prefer and expect from speakers: interaction, personal expression, and collaboration.
  - ✔ Compelling stories are also persuasive because audiences tend to respond to narratives that resonate with their own experiences.

- In the business and professional context, good stories have several characteristics.
  - ✔ Good stories are realistic.
  - ✔ Good stories are relevant and have value for audiences.
  - ✔ Good stories are coherent.
  - ✔ Good stories are interactive.
  - ✔ Good stories have memorable take-away lessons.
- Having a clear understanding of the general purpose for a presentation helps you select appropriate content, meet your audience's expectations, and appropriately inform, influence, or entertain your listeners.
- A helpful strategy for identifying a general purpose is identifying the type of presentation that will best meet your needs and goals. The most common types of business presentations are
  - ✔ Sales presentations and proposals
  - ✔ Briefings
  - ✔ Team presentations, such as symposiums and panel discussions
  - ✔ Special occasion speeches
- A critical step in speech preparation is audience analysis, or the systematic gathering of information about an intended audience. You must also evaluate your speaking environment, including the size of the audience, physical setting for a presentation, and so on.
- Build support for you and your ideas by using evidence that is credible, appropriate, and tailored to your audience.
  - ✔ Establish your own credibility as a speaker.
  - ✔ Consider the different types of support: facts and data, and stories and examples.
  - ✔ Select only the best supporting material, ensuring that it is relevant, recent, and credible.
- Organize your presentation appropriately so that you remember your ideas, deliver your presentation coherently, and help audiences follow the logic of your information and arguments.
- Select the organizing framework that best suits your presentation and your audience's needs and goals. There are two common organizational frameworks speakers use to make sense of information: linear and configural.
  - ✔ The linear framework is a clear and fact-based approach to organizing a speech that follows a straightforward pattern: preview main points, discuss one point at a time, and summarize each point.
  - ✔ The configural framework is an approach to organizing a speech that is relatively indirect, relies on speaker self-disclosure, allows the audience to engage with the speaker, and asks audience members to impose their own structure and meaning onto the presentation.

Key Terms

audience analysis (148)

briefing (145)

configural framework (160)

credible evidence (153)

evidence (150)

experts (150)

general purpose (145)

linear framework (157)

panel discussion(146)

proposal (145)

recent evidence (152)

relevant evidence (152)

sales presentation (145)

signpost (159)

speaking environment (149)

special occasion speech (147)

symposium (146)

team presentation (146)

transition (159)

Questions for Critical Thinking and Review

1. Which type of supporting material is most important to you: statistical data or your own personal experiences? What about others you know? Why do you believe this is true?

2. Choose a current event from the business section of a newspaper, magazine, or website. Can you redefine this event as a story? Who are the characters? What is the plot? Come up with a way to tell this story that you think will be more interesting to your classmates than the original way it was presented. What strategies would you use to make this or other seemingly dull topics engaging or fascinating for your audience?

3. What type of framework—configural or linear—is easier for you to comprehend? Why?

4. How might the formality of a business speaking situation influence the way you define your approach? Explain.

Chapter 8

Giving Presentations:
How Can I Best Present My Ideas at Work?

Chapter Outline

What's the Central Message of Your Presentation?
- Identify Your Specific Purpose and Thesis Statement
- Provide a Format for Your Story

What's the Best Way to Begin Your Presentation?
- Demonstrate Your Credibility with the Topic
- Compel Your Audience to Listen
- Preview Your Story

What's the Best Way to End Your Presentation?
- Signal the End of Your Story and Summarize Your Points
- Compel Your Audience to Remember You and Your Message

What Strategies Will Help Your Audience Understand and Remember?
- Keep It Simple
- Keep It Concrete
- Be Repetitive and Redundant
- Elicit Active Responses
- Use Familiar and Relevant Examples
- Use Transitions and Signposts

How Do the Experts Do It?

Sample Student Speech: Informative

Paul Springett C/Alamy

Chapter Learning Objectives

After completing this chapter, you should be able to
- Develop a central idea and framework for your presentation.
- Compel the audience to listen to your presentation.
- Compel the audience to remember you and your message.
- Incorporate strategies to make your informative presentation easily understood and remembered.
- Analyze and evaluate others' informative presentations.
- Prepare and deliver an effective presentation to inform others.

See also the modules that are relevant to this chapter:

> **2: How Can I Practice Ethical Communication Behavior at Work?**
> **3: How Do I Give Specialized Presentations?**
> **6: "You Gotta Have Style": Using APA and MLA Styles**
> **7: What Methods Can I Use to Analyze My Audience?**

Module 2:
How Can I Practice Ethical Communication Behavior at Work?

Module 3:
How Do I Give Specialized Presentations?

Module 6:
"You Gotta Have Style": Using APA and MLA Styles

Module 7:
What Methods Can I Use to Analyze My Audience?

Melvin, a senior director of a mid-sized, high-tech company, knows how to give a good briefing.

Recently Melvin's organization decided to move employees from a traditional fixed schedule to flexible work schedules. Melvin's task was to brief employees about the merits of this decision, along with the plans for implementing flextime.

He began his briefing with some background explaining the genesis of this decision. He noted that Hewlett-Packard was the first company to institute flextime, in 1973. Since then, about a third of all U.S. employees use some form of flexible scheduling. Melvin quickly moved to an explanation of how flexible work schedules would benefit his audience. He emphasized the most obvious benefit, how flextime will accommodate those who want a better balance between their work and personal lives. Then he explained how this decision would benefit the company, too, by retaining employees, reducing overhead costs, and meeting the needs of customers and clients in different time zones. He noted that similar companies have opted for flexible schedules and found that the decision worked well for them.

Finally, Melvin overviewed the implementation plan, ensuring that everyone would know how it would work. Before closing, Melvin invited employees to ask questions and raise potential concerns. The briefing turned into an open forum for interaction between management and employees.

Melvin concluded by first reviewing the plan and then by reassuring his audience that "this plan will be good for you; it will be good for our families; and it will be good for our company."

Melvin's briefing was well received. He followed much of the advice of communication researchers and scholars who know what's involved in preparing and giving a good briefing.

- For one thing, he did some background research about flextime, including its historical basis and how other companies, similar to his own, had incorporated flextime successfully.

- In addition, he emphasized the benefits of flextime to his employees first and to the company second. He understood that good briefings are audience-centered.
- And he encouraged his audience to participate in the briefing to ensure greater understanding of and eventual buy-in to the company's plan.

This kind of briefing may look easy, but it's not. And yet, people give briefings all the time in companies, both large and small. Unfortunately, many briefings invite more controversy and uncertainty than closure—think of how much controversy White House press briefings can generate! Knowing how to give a good briefing will help you to stand out among the rest and ensure that your message is both understood and well received.

This chapter provides the basics for what you need to know to prepare and deliver a good briefing.[1] Briefings are only one type of informative presentation, and the principles and ideas presented in this chapter apply to other types of informative business presentations as well, including reports, lectures, training presentations, and demonstrations. Other chapters also build your understanding of crafting and delivering business and professional speeches: Chapter 7 (preparing to speak), Chapter 9 (persuasive presentations), and Chapter 10 (sensory aids).

The first section of this chapter considers how you can convey the central idea of your informative presentation by identifying what you want your audience to learn and then providing an appropriate framework for your presentation. The next two sections are devoted to making the beginnings and endings of your presentations compelling—effective introductions and conclusions make all the difference in gaining audience attention and leaving a positive impression. Next we offer a variety of practical strategies to ensure that your audience will understand and remember your message. Finally, this chapter concludes with examples of professionals who effectively apply these principles in their efforts to inform.

What's the Central Message of Your Presentation?

Informative presentations can provide new and unfamiliar information, extend what the audience already knows, or update old information about a topic or an issue. Many times, presentations help the audience view an issue in a different way. You might think that informing people in any of these ways can't be all that difficult. After all, isn't it merely a matter of telling them what they need to know? Once they hear it, they will understand it and learn it.

But it's not really that simple. Too many managers and supervisors assume that telling equals learning. However, informing others requires more than merely telling. According to organizational communication consultant John Kline, the biggest mistake that speakers make is focusing on what they want to tell listeners rather than on *what they want their listeners to think, feel, and do*.[2] Effective speakers consider how the story they want to tell relates to what their audiences need. They then prepare a presentation that tells the story in a way that will appeal to and be understood by their audiences. That starts with identifying why you want to tell the story, what the central message of your story is, and how you will present the story in a format that is easy to follow.

Identify Your Specific Purpose and Thesis Statement

All presentations begin with some general purpose (Chapter 7). In the case of a briefing, the general purpose is to inform. Then what? If you don't know up front what you want to accomplish, your audience may not respond to your presentation as you would like. Decide what you want from your audience. In the process, you will come up with your **specific purpose**, which identifies what you want your audience to know, believe, or do. You can identify your specific purpose by answering the question, "What do I want my audience to think, feel, or do as a result of my presentation?" Begin your answer with "I want to inform my audience (for example, the boss, president, co-workers, customers, clients) about . . ." Limit your specific purpose to one clear and simple sentence. Think back to Melvin's briefing about flextime. When he was preparing his speech, he decided that his specific purpose was this:

> I want to inform the employees about the company's plan to implement flextime.

To further clarify your intent, you can develop a **thesis statement**. A thesis statement is a concise summary of the central message of your speech. It states your most essential points and acts as a sort of road map of what you plan to say to the audience to accomplish your specific purpose. Like your specific purpose statement, your thesis statement should be specific, clear, and concrete. For example, Melvin's thesis statement might read something like this:

> Implementing flextime benefits both employees and the company for several reasons: it helps employees better balance their work and personal lives, and it helps the company to retain employees, reduce overhead, and meet client needs.

See Table 8.1 for more examples of specific purposes and thesis statements for informative presentations.

TABLE 8.1
Specific Purposes and Thesis Statements for Informative Presentations

Specific purpose	Thesis statement
I want to inform my customers why the speech-recognition technology of Google's Android phone is effective.	Android's speech-recognition technology allows users to successfully handle computing tasks verbally, because Google's systems allow for the analysis of huge stores of information.
I want to inform the board of directors of my company why there are so few women leaders in the corporate world.	There are too few women leaders in the corporate world for several reasons: women underestimate their own abilities, many women leave the workforce to take care of household responsibilities, and they don't always take advantage of promotions because they anticipate having children.[3]
I want to inform my son's high school class about the many ways in which they can obtain a college education.	You can obtain a college education by going to a traditional college directly from high school, by earning an associate degree from a community college, by earning an associate degree first and then transferring to a four-year college, or by pursuing an online degree.

Provide a Format for Your Story

Virtually every informative speech relies on the same basic format, whether it's a classroom lecture or a televised public service announcement, a briefing updating your boss about a project you're working on or a nontechnical training presentation on a new retirement plan. All organized informative presentations, whether structured with a linear or configural framework, have some kind of identifiable introduction, body, and conclusion. You always begin with opening and introductory remarks, follow with your main points and supporting materials, and then conclude with a summary. In other words, you tell them what you're going to tell them, then tell them, and then tell them what you've just told them.

- **Tell 'em what you're going to tell them.** The introduction to your presentation should first compel your audience to listen by demonstrating your credibility and providing some kind of attention-getter. Let your audience know what makes you an authority on your topic and why they should listen to you. In addition, gain and maintain their attention. After all, if audience members don't pay attention or, worse, if they are bored and disinterested, how will they learn or comprehend what you have to offer? Once you have the audience's attention, provide a brief overview of the main points.

- **Tell 'em.** The body of the speech covers the main points and subpoints of your message. Most presentations focus on no more than three main points or themes. More information than that usually results in information overload, which translates into audience confusion and boredom. Be selective when you consider what major points you want to address.

- **Tell 'em what you just told them.** Conclude your presentation with a brief summary that wraps up your central message. Provide a succinct review of your main points and then end memorably with, for example, some kind of dramatic comment or a creative connection to your opening remarks.

Xinhua/eyevine/Redux

Apple CEO Steve Job provides a good example of a narrative, informative presentation with his 2005 Stanford University commencement address. Access a video of his speech with **CHECK THIS OUT 8.1:** **Steve Job's Commencement Address**.

Now that you have an overview of the basic format for an informative presentation, let's look at some specifics regarding your introduction and conclusion.

Module 3:
How Do I Give Specialized Presentations?

Check This Out 8.1:
Steve Job's Commencement Address

What's the Best Way to Begin Your Presentation?

What you say and do during the first few minutes of a presentation can make all the difference in how your audience will respond to you and what you have to say. First impressions are formed quickly and often on the basis of very little information (Chapter 2). Audience members begin to form first impressions of you as soon as you are introduced. What the host says about you, how you dress, what you look like, and how you stride to the podium all enter into the impression others form about you. But it's those opening remarks, the introduction to your speech, that seem to make all the difference in how they choose to listen and perceive you and your message. That's a lot of pressure, but you can plan ahead to maximize your success. In the first few minutes of your introduction, plan to accomplish three objectives:

1. Establish and demonstrate your credibility with your topic.
2. Compel your audience to listen actively.
3. Preview your story.

Demonstrate Your Credibility with Your Topic

In many professional environments, especially if you're asked to speak by an organization other than the one you work for, you will be introduced by someone who will describe your credentials and validate your expertise. From that point on, building and maintaining credibility is your responsibility. The audience needs to hear from you exactly what qualifies you to speak on the issue. Your expertise may derive from your education and your professional background and your personal experiences. In addition, most accomplished speakers rely on their own personal testimony. To define your own expertise, ask yourself, "Why or how am I an expert on this topic?" Here's why audiences consider the following speakers credible with their topics:

- Steve Jobs speaks credibly about the iPad by being one of the first users of the technology. His position in the company, his background as an e-inventor, and his ability to speak meaningfully about the iPad all contribute to how audiences define and respond to him.

- You might perk up and listen to Ben Cohen and Jerry Greenfield speak on a topic that has to do with ice cream or how to create a successful dynasty of ice cream parlors.

- Katie Couric's experiences as a mother and a successful career woman might similarly compel you to listen to a speech about the importance of women having a career to fall back on in case they need to support their children by themselves.

Because Steve, Ben, Jerry, and Katie are all experts in their related field, they come across as believable in the stories that they tell.

For more about being introduced by another speaker (and introducing a speaker yourself), see **MODULE 3:** **How Do I Give Specialized Presentations?**

Link Out 8.1:
Compelling Introduction

Visualize! Practice! 8.1:
Personal Story

Visualize! Practice! 8.2:
Emotional Appeal

Compel Your Audience to Listen

To be an effective storyteller, you need to give the audience a reason to listen. It's up to you to determine the reason why audience members should listen to you, and then to tell them that reason. Audiences like to listen to good stories, and good stories are relevant and have value for the listeners (Chapter 7). The more personally relevant your story and your reasons for telling it are to audience members, the more likely they will feel compelled to listen to you. For a good example of a speaker who compels his audience to listen, see LINK OUT 8.1: **Compelling Introduction**. In this video, Dr. Robert Portnoy motivates his audience to listen to his speech on relationship-building in an organization by first discussing the "costs of conflict" to "your company." Notice in this brief introduction how audience-centered his reasons are for his presentation.

You can also motivate your audience to listen by using dramatic devices such as personal stories, emotional appeals, humor, rhythmic repetition, famous quotations, or startling facts and statistics.

Personal Stories Tell a personal story to let the audience get a sense of who you are beyond your resume or credentials. Make sure your story relates to your topic in a way that makes it personal and meaningful to you and your audience. Here's how Tim used a personal story to introduce his presentation on the importance of knowing what you want when selecting a career:

> I have such vivid memories of my parents being laid off time and time again, always searching for the next job. They were constantly preoccupied with getting and then keeping a job. Even as a small boy, I worried about the family's finances. It didn't take long for me to learn that money was tight—and important to have. I knew not to ask for money. And I knew what it felt like to go without birthdays, Christmases, and vacations. Because of those early memories and anxieties, I chose a profession where I knew job security was ensured.

Write your own personal story for a presentation on this same topic or on a topic for a speech you plan to give in class. You can complete this activity with VISUALIZE! PRACTICE! 8.1: **Personal Story** and email your response to your instructor if requested.

Emotional Appeals Appealing to feelings and emotions is another way to connect with your audience. Depending on the topic, you may want to incite fear, guilt, anger, passion, pity, love, or other emotional responses. Whatever emotion you intend to evoke, it should foster empathy or shared feelings between you and the audience. Emotional appeals are also useful for concluding a presentation. Sometimes emotional appeals far outweigh the impact of logic or reason. When people feel emotional about an issue, they are more likely to feel connected with you and the message. Notice how Fariba used emotional appeals to encourage her colleagues at work to give aid to victims of a recent earthquake:

> Thousands of children have been left homeless and suffering. They need medical supplies, food, water, and shelter. They need our help, yours and mine. Let's show these families that we are the kind of organization that cares about people in need.

Write your own emotional appeal for a presentation on this same topic or on a topic for a speech you plan to give in class. You can complete this activity with VISUALIZE! PRACTICE! 8.2: **Emotional Appeal** and email your response to your instructor if requested.

Humor Humor is an excellent way to begin or end a speech. It's is a way to show your boss that you have a good sense of humor and that you like what you do. Of course, your attempt at humor should be genuinely funny, and it must be relevant to your topic. And never, ever use inappropriate or offensive humor—there's no faster way to turn off an audience. To determine humor that's appropriate for your audience, be sure to analyze your audience before you deliver your speech (Chapter 7).

Mike's speech on time management included this humorous one-liner[4]:

> Punctuality is important but the problem with being punctual is that there's never anyone around to appreciate it.

Mike also used this one-liner in the same speech:[5]

> Nothing makes me more productive than the last minute.

For some humorous quotes that can be used in a variety of business presentations, check out **LINK OUT 8.2: Funny Business Quotes**. And for tips on using humor effectively, access **LINK OUT 8.3: Tips for Using Humor in Speeches**.

Repetition Repetition of a word or phrase adds rhythm to a speech and draws attention to your topic. With repetition, you invite the audience to focus on and become engaged in your speech. Here's how Dani concluded her speech with a series of phrases designed to motivate her colleagues to reach higher:

> If you think you can succeed, you can succeed, and you will succeed. But first, you have to dream.

Why don't you try it. How might you complete this series of phrases in a speech on productivity?

> We want . . .
> We want . . .
> We want . . .

Link Out 8.2:
Funny Business Quotes

Link Out 8.3:
Tips for Using Humor in Speeches

Putting Your Skills to Work

Using emotional appeals is a natural thing to do. When you call in sick to work, you probably hope to elicit feelings of sympathy from your boss. And when you tell your friends about how that guy on the freeway cut you off, you hope they'll feel as angry as you do so that they can really understand how frustrating the experience was. Listeners often respond well to responsible emotional appeals, because humans are emotional creatures and we can all relate to emotional experiences.

A-Digit/istockphoto.com

Visualize! Practice! 8.3:
Repetition

Stephen Bulley/Alamy

You can complete this activity with **VISUALIZE! PRACTICE! 8.3: Repetition**.

Famous Quotations Using familiar sayings or borrowing quotations from famous speakers, politicians, and entertainers is a popular and effective way to begin or end a presentation. Occasionally, a particular thought or phrase can capture a message precisely. How might you incorporate these famous quotes into a presentation at work?

> I've always worked very, very hard, and the harder I worked, the luckier I got.
> —Alan Bond, businessman[6]

> It's not so much how busy you are, but why you are busy. The bee is praised, the mosquito is swatted.
> —Catherine O'Hara, actress[7]

> Twenty years from now, you will be more disappointed by the things that you didn't do than by the ones you did do.
> —Mark Twain, author and humorist[8]

> Failure is the opportunity to begin again, more intelligently.
> —Henry Ford, industrialist[9]

> Well, if you pick a fight with somebody that's smaller than you and you beat them, where's the honor in that?
> —Carol Moseley Braun, U.S. senator and ambassador[10]

Startling Facts and Statistics Facts and statistics can further entice an audience to listen, assuming these data are startling and interesting, not boring. Moreover, the facts should be easy to understand, and they should apply to your message. Remember: the audience only has one opportunity to hear and process your message, so keep it simple and be brief. Take a look at the following facts and statistics and indicate which ones you think would amaze an audience and which would be likely to bore them.[11] See the answer key at the bottom of this page. Why do you think the ones that aren't considered interesting might bore an audience? After making your choices, reflect on why some information is inherently more interesting than other types of information. Why do you think that is?

1. Ninety percent of the population report anxiety about meeting new people.

2. People have to repeat your name at least six times before they can remember it.

3. Ninety-five percent of your customers will come back if their complaint is resolved immediately.

4. An estimated 50 to 80 percent of all life on earth is found under the ocean surface, and the oceans contain 99 percent of the living space on the planet. Less than 10 percent of that space has been explored by humans. Eight-five percent of the area and 90 percent of the volume constitute the dark, cold environment we call the deep sea. The average depth of the ocean is 3,795 meters. The average height of the land is 840 meters.

5. It only takes about seven seconds for a customer to decide whether she likes you.

6. Ninety-two percent of salespeople give up their efforts after only four turndowns.

7. Coca-Cola was originally green.

8. Every time you lick a stamp, you're consuming one tenth of a calorie.

9. What do bulletproof vests, fire escapes, windshield wipers, and laser printers all have in common? All were invented by women.

10. *Cardisoma guanhumi* is a circumequatorial species found throughout estuarine regions of the Caribbean and Central and South America, including Columbia, Venezuela, the Bahamas, and Puerto Rico. Within the United States, it is limited to the Gulf of Mexico and coastal Florida and is rarely found more than 8 kilometers from the ocean.

11. In every episode of Seinfeld there is a Superman somewhere.

12. On average, people fear spiders more than they do death.

13. One-third of high school graduates never read another book for the rest of their lives.

14. Forty-two percent of college graduates never read another book after college.

15. In 1980, book sales decreased by 10.17 percent; in 1990, book sales further decreased by 3.24 percent—but only for fiction, not nonfiction. Nonfiction sales that year rose by 2.97 percent, making the total sales reduction only about 0.27 percent.

16. Seventy percent of all the books published today make no profit at all.

17. Eighty percent of U.S. families did not buy or read a book last year.

18. Seventy percent of U.S. adults have not been in a bookstore in the last five years.

19. Twelve percent of children age 7 to 10 prefer to read online; another 12.82 percent prefer to listen to a book on tape; and 17.83 percent would rather not read at all and instead watch TV. These data change as children age, with teenagers, age 13 to 18, reversing this trend. Of course, exceptions exist and trends change with time.

20. Banging your head against a wall uses 150 calories an hour.

Answers: 1. amazing; **2.** amazing; **3.** amazing; **4.** boring; **5.** amazing; **6.** amazing; **7.** amazing; **8.** amazing; **9.** amazing; **10.** boring; **11.** amazing; **12.** amazing; **13.** amazing; **14.** amazing; **15.** boring; **16.** amazing; **17.** amazing; **18.** amazing; **19.** boring; **20.** amazing

Each of these strategies can be used to invite and entice your audience to listen. These same strategies can also be employed in the conclusion to your speech. You can tell a personal story or appeal to audience members' emotions in ways that can leave them believing in some cause or feeling excited or sympathetic.

 Check out Speech Studio to see how other students use dramatic devices in their speeches. Or record a speech you're working on, upload it to Speech Studio, and ask your peers for their feedback. What feedback could you use to fine-tune your introduction before you give your speech in class?

Preview Your Story

The third important function of an introduction to a speech is to provide a brief **preview** of what will follow ("tell 'em what you're going to tell them"). The purpose of previewing your presentation is to help the audience organize what's to follow in some systematic way.

The preview always comes at the end of the introduction. Like a preview to a movie, a speech preview lets the audience know the highlights of what's to follow. You can accomplish this in just one simple statement listing the main points. Often, speakers use signposts in their previews to show order or sequence, especially with a linear framework (Chapter 7).

> Today I want to share with you the trilogy of closing a sale. First, I'll demonstrate what sales people typically do when closing a deal. Next, I will explain to you why their approach is unreliable, failing them at least 50 percent of the time. Finally, I'll show you how the "principle of threes" works effectively to close a sale for virtually all products and services.

Sometimes, rather than listing a series of main points, the speaker will provide a focus, especially when using a configural framework. In this case, speakers set up the audience in a way that will give them some context to understand what is to come. This may be the location of the story, the critical players involved, or some of the chronology of what to expect. Emelina set up her presentation this way:

> Last January I became an American citizen. What led up to this event began well before I was born. My parents, Jose and Sylvia, came to California from Mexico in the thick of the night crowded among a dozen others in the back of an old van. Working here illegally, one day Jose and Sylvia met a very nice employer named Dolores, who decided to intervene and change their lives. And when she did, my destiny was changed as well. This is their story—and mine as well.

Whether you list main points or provide some kind of focus, the purpose of the preview remains the same: to help the audience contextualize or organize what will follow.

What's the Best Way to End Your Presentation?

Even the best presentations can be spoiled by a bad ending. No doubt you have heard some of these, such as "Well, I guess that's it," "My time's up," or "That's all I have to say." Perhaps you've even seen a speaker who kept the audience's attention throughout, but with nothing left to say, he or she abruptly stopped talking and sat down. Talk about leaving the audience hanging! Like the introduction or beginning to a speech, the conclusion

Kirk Treakle/Alamy

should signal the end of the speech and review the main points and then provide some kind of memorable statement that leaves the audience thoughtful, interested, and aroused.

Signal the End of Your Story and Summarize Your Points

Signal the end of your speech so that your audience knows you are finishing up. This will help your audience mentally prepare to hear your concluding remarks. Transition from your last main point to your conclusion with phrases like these:

- In conclusion
- In overview
- In sum
- In short
- In brief
- To review
- In summary
- And so

You're then ready to provide a summary. A summary is a quick review of the major points of your presentation ("tell 'em what you just told 'em"). Keep the summary brief and to the point, much like your preview. Do not add any new information—that only confuses and annoys an audience.

Compel Your Audience to Remember You and Your Message

An important function of your conclusion is to leave the audience wanting more. You want your speech to be memorable and your closing remarks to be as dramatic as possible. After audience members have gone home or back to work, you want them to

Link Out 8.4:
Plain English

remember you and your message. Use closing lines that hook up with your opening remarks in a clever way, rely on a famous and relevant quotation, or relate a dramatic story.

Whatever device you choose to end your speech, consider carefully *how* to present your conclusion. Memorable speakers use their conclusions to really make a connection with their audiences. To focus on your audience rather than on your speaking notes, memorize your final remarks. Make sure of your audience's attention by pausing for a few seconds and looking carefully around the room. Slow your talking rate, deliver your final story, joke, quotation, or illustration. You need not announce that you have finished—audience members should know it when they hear it. Slowly and deliberately pick up your materials and walk casually back to your chair.

See the end of this chapter for a sample speech that illustrates an effective introduction and conclusion.

What Strategies Will Help Your Audience Understand and Remember?

How you begin and end your presentation is critical to gaining audience members' interest and attention and ensuring that they will remember the essence of your message. At the same time, you can use a number of practical strategies that will help you increase both audience understanding and retention of the body of your speech. Here are six strategies you can use to inform your audiences efficiently and successfully.[12]

Keep It Simple

The fewer the main points in your speech, the more likely your audience will remember them. Excessive details, long lists, lots of statistics, and too many subpoints turn people off. Every aspect of your speech, then, should be brief, focused, and easy to understand. Keep in mind that the audience will hear your presentation only once, with no opportunity to rewind and hear it again. The keep-it-simple principle is particularly important for a presentation of information that is new or totally different from what the audience knows. Unnecessary jargon, technical terms, and acronyms both intimidate and confuse audiences. Keeping it simple requires that you use easy, clear, and concise language to inform.

Keep it simple is also good advice for other forms of business communication. Go to **LINK OUT 8.4: Plain English** to see Alan Siegel, a leading authority on business and legal communication, call for the use of plain English in his presentation on simplifying documents such as credit card statements and IRS letters. How can you apply what he says to a business presentation?

Keep It Concrete

The more concrete and the less abstract your explanations, the more likely your audience will comprehend your message. Suppose, for instance, that you are explaining the difference between good debt and bad debt. You can describe good debt as the debt incurred when the value of the asset increases over time. Bad debt, on the other hand, is debt incurred when you purchase nonessential goods or services that fail to increase your wealth and will likely depreciate in value. And so on. This approach is not wrong, but it might put your audience to sleep.

A much better approach would be to explain these concepts using everyday, concrete illustrations. For example, you might demonstrate the different concepts by asking your audience, "What have you purchased lately that is worth more now than it was when you bought it?" The answers might include a home, home improvements, municipal bonds, or stocks. All these purchases or investments typically appreciate in worth. Even money spent for a college education is good debt, leading to greater job opportunities, higher salaries, and more employment security. Ask your audience next, "What have you purchased lately that is now worth less than it was when you bought it?" Their responses might include a new car, a lawnmower, a vacation, a new pair of jeans—or even a single tall espresso! All these purchases depreciate in value over time and are things you don't need and might not be able to afford. With the concrete approach, you illustrate your idea with examples that audience members can easily relate to or understand.

Making some principles concrete may be easier than others. Consider the informative presentation of Dr. Dean Ornish, a clinical professor at University of California, San Francisco and founder of the Preventive Medicine Research Institute. He makes a very complex issue—the pandemic of cardiovascular disease, diabetes, and hypertension—concrete, visual, real, and at times, entertaining for his audiences. Go to **CHECK THIS OUT 8.2: The World's Killer Diet** to watch one of his speeches. After viewing the video, identify the strategies he employed to make abstract explanations concrete.

Check This Out 8.2:
The World's Killer Diet

Be Repetitive and Redundant

Although the words are often used interchangeably, *repetition* and *redundancy* are two different techniques. The first, repetition, involves referring to something the same way again and again. Redundancy is used to explain something more than once but in a slightly different way each time. The underlined phrases in the following paragraph illustrate repetition:

> Looking for a job is a job. Looking for a job means that you get up every morning and go to work getting a job. Looking for a job means that you keep a log all day long of all the calls you've made and the contacts you've initiated. Looking for a job means that you stick with the plan all day long. Looking for a job means that you continue to work at it every day until you close the deal.

This is the same idea, but it uses redundancy instead of repetition:

> Looking for a job is a job. Begin each day by preparing to look for work. In order to find employment, you may need to keep a log of the calls you've made and the contacts you've initiated. In order to keep your momentum while job hunting, you must stick with the plan all day long. Continue to work at finding a job each and every day until you close the deal.

Both repetition and redundancy are strategies that ensure the audience remembers important points. Each strategy is used for different purposes. Repetition helps people remember simple concepts. For example, to help your audience remember all the names of the new products you're launching, you might repeat their names in order over and over again. Similarly, repeat key definitions, extend explanations, or review main points and connect them to subsequent points.

In contrast, redundancy helps people remember more complex ideas and arguments. Because an audience hears a speech only once, you build in some redundancy with the "tell 'em what you're going to tell 'em, tell 'em, and then tell 'em what you just told 'em" formula. You express similar ideas in the introduction, body, and conclusion, but in a slightly different way in each part.

Without repetition and redundancy, your audience may fail to understand or remember your message.

Elicit Active Responses

Visualize! Practice! 8.4:
Encourage Audience Responses

One way to increase audience understanding and retention is to ask audience members to do something in an open and public way. This ancient technique was used by church leaders and educators for centuries in the form of responsive reading: The teacher or church leader would read aloud a passage from a book or from scriptures, and the students or congregation would read or cite aloud an expected or subsequent passage in unison. Today teachers, pollsters, and marketers use a response system like the i>clicker to elicit active audience responses.

You can use a number of techniques to elicit active responses during your briefings and other informative presentations. Merely asking the audience a question is insufficient, however. In most circumstances the audience will assume that the question is rhetorical and wait politely for you to supply the answer. Instead, ask for a show of hands. For more interaction, you might ask, "People are working harder than ever before. Isn't that true?" Encourage the audience to say yes in unison. Continue with a series of similar questions: "People are working longer hours than ever before. Isn't that true?" By this time, audience members should have the idea and answer, "Yes!" Finally, you might ask, "And people are being paid less than ever before?" You can also invite other responses from your audience: "We demand *more* from our employer. We need *more*. We want *more*. And we *deserve* more. Okay now, what is it that we want?" And with that, you encourage your audience to respond, "More!"

To explore some strategies you might use to encourage reluctant audience members to provide responses during a presentation, check out **VISUALIZE! PRACTICE! 8.4: Encourage Audience Responses**.

PhotoAlto Agency/Jupiter Images

Use Familiar and Relevant Examples

We all rely on methods to help us learn and recall information efficiently and effectively. You store information in your memory, which you tap to recall what you need. These recollections serve as frameworks to help you process new and unfamiliar information. You can help your audience mentally frame your message by providing them with familiar and relevant examples that stimulate their memories.

To illustrate, suppose you had to explain the concept of making a budget. You might first explain that a budget is simply a way of managing your money so that you won't end up eating popcorn or Top Ramen for dinner every day until your next payday. It's also a good way to find out where your money goes every week so that you can make better decisions about how you might really want to spend (or save) it. Perhaps you'd rather have a few dollars left each month to store away for a rainy day or to save for a new car.

By using familiar and relevant examples like these, you help the audience recover from memory a framework to understand your message. With these relevant examples, the audience might want to actually learn how to make a budget. Without linking the new ideas to an established set of familiar ideas, the information might otherwise be ignored, misunderstood, or forgotten. To practice framing topics with familiar and relevant examples, check out **VISUALIZE! PRACTICE! 8.5: Familiar and Relevant Examples**.

Visualize! Practice! 8.5:
Familiar and Relevant Examples

Use Transitions and Signposts

It's always a good idea to use transitions and signposts to let your audience know when you're moving from one point to another or highlighting important information (Chapter 7). Both devices help your audience to think about, organize, and react to your message. They give the audience some direction for how to proceed or how to piece together what you're saying.

Here are some examples of transitions and signposts that are useful for signaling your concluding remarks:

Transitions

so

moreover

therefore

accordingly

consequently

this all boils down to one thing

thus

for instance

unfortunately

along the same lines

on the one hand

Signposts

first, second, third

one, two, three

in conclusion

let's turn our attention to

next

what follows is

to begin with

in sum

first let me begin by

my primary concern

to recapitulate

lastly

Check This Out 8.3:
*Pivot Informative
Presentation*

Check This Out 8.4:
*Headlines Informative
Presentation*

Check This Out 8.5:
*Statistics Informative
Presentation*

How Do the Experts Do It?

Now that you have some idea of what's involved in giving an informative presentation, let's see how the experts do it. Watch and carefully examine the three professional presentations in CHECK THIS OUT 8.3: **Pivot Informative Presentation**, CHECK THIS OUT 8.4: **Headlines Informative Presentation**, and CHECK THIS OUT 8.5: **Statistics Informative Presentation**:

- **Check This Out 8.3:** Dr. Gary Flake, a Technical Fellow at Microsoft and founder and director of Live Labs, talks about how software like Pivot can help us manage large amounts of information in an age where we seem to be drowning in data.

- **Check This Out 8.4:** Rachel Pike, a Ph.D. candidate studying climate change at Cambridge Centre for Atmospheric Science, talks about the laborious, exacting research efforts that are behind the media headlines that most of us take for granted.

- **Check This Out 8.5:** Dr. Peter Donnelly, an expert in probability theory and DNA analysis at Oxford University, discusses how statistics can be used to fool juries. Notice how he elicits active audience involvement in his presentation.

After watching the videos, also refer to the transcript of each presentation—you'll find it on the same webpage that the video appears on. Once you've watched all three presentations, answer these questions about one of them:

1. Write a specific purpose statement for this briefing.
   Specific purpose: _____

2. Write the thesis statement for this briefing.
   Thesis statement: _____

3. What strategy did the speaker use to compel you to listen?

4. How would you summarize this briefing?

5. Identify one strategy the speaker used to keep it simple.

6. Identify one strategy the speaker used to make it concrete.

7. How did the speaker use repetition or redundancy to help you better understand and remember his or her message?

8. Give one example that the speaker used that was familiar or relevant to you.

9. Give one example of a transition or signpost that the speaker used.

10. What did the speaker do to make the conclusion memorable?

Viorika Prikhodko/iStockphoto.com

Check out Speech Studio to see informative speeches delivered by other students. Or record a speech you're working on, upload it to Speech Studio, and ask your peers for their feedback. What feedback could you use to fine-tune your next informative speech before you give it in class?

Sample Student Speech: Informative

In the speech outline shown in Figure 8.1, student Mark Stephenson informed his audience about retail theft. In addition to reading Mark's speech outline here, watch it and read his speech in Student Informative Presentation: Retail Theft. With this link, you can also access several other sample speeches delivered by students. Mark gave this speech in his communication class—he was asked to create and deliver an informative speech about a topic related to his career. As you read through Mark's speech text, note how he builds his credibility in his introduction and previews his main points. What are his main points? Do they seem to be sequenced in some logical order? What does he include in his conclusion that helps the audience "link up" to the introduction? What informative strategies did he use? Are there some others you might suggest that he employ? Which ones?

FIGURE 8.1
Sample informative speech

Retail Theft

Adapted from a speech by Mark Stephenson

General purpose: To inform

Specific purpose: I want to inform my audience about the different types of retail thieves, the methods they use to steal, and how we can be alert to their attempts.

Thesis statement: Retail theft is costly for both consumers and retailers. By recognizing how professional shoplifters, amateur shoplifters, and internal employee thieves steal and conceal merchandise, we can become more alert to their attempts and thus, control this growing problem.

I. **Introduction**
   A. Attention-getter: Ask, "who has ever stolen from a store?" Effects of theft on the economy.
   B. Preview: Different types of people steal from retailers and they use different techniques to do so. In order to prevent retail theft, we need to know the relevant "alert signals."

II. **Body**
   A. Who steals and how do they do it?
      1. Professional Shoplifters
         a. Organized retail crime groups target specific sites
         b. Work in groups separately and together to move, conceal, and distract
         c. Use shopping bags that prevent security detection
         d. Work from the front of the store
      2. Amateur shoplifters
         a. Steal for thrill, not profit
         b. Steal smaller items
         c. Work from the back of the store
      3. Internal employees who steal
         a. Account for 75% of all retail theft
         b. Well planned
         c. Remove sensors, conceal merchandise
   B. What are the preventative or alert signals to look for?
      1. Professionals avoid interacting with staff, spend time on the phone.
      2. Amateurs look nervous and suspicious, eyeing the staff too much.
      3. Internal thieves might have friends come by, carry out trash bags, bring in large purses to carry out the merchandise.

III. **Conclusion**
   A. Summary: Retail theft hurts businesses and consumers, and retailers are banding together to crack down on theft.
   B. Closing remarks: Next time you're in a store, resist your urge to steal candy, CD, or shirt.

Steve Lovegrove/Shutterstock.com

After reading this chapter, it should be clear to you how and why Melvin's presentation on flextime was well received. Following the advice of communication experts, Melvin developed a specific purpose and thesis statement, found ways to compel his audience to listen and appreciate his plan for implementing the new scheduling system, and he employed a variety of strategies to elicit and keep his audience's attention throughout. Effective speakers use informative presentations to teach us something or change the way we think about an issue or topic. In some cases, they communicate new information. In others they extend what we already know; and sometimes they simply update old information about a familiar topic.

Use your Speech Communication CourseMate for *Business & Communication in a Digital Age* for quick access to the electronic resources that accompany this text. These resources include

Study tools that will help you assess your learning and prepare for exams (*digital glossary, key term flash cards, review quizzes*).

Activities and assignments that will help you hone your knowledge and build your communication skills throughout the course (*Visualize! Practice!, Weigh In!, Check This Out, and Link Out activities; modules; review questions*).

Media resources that will help you explore communication concepts online (*Enhanced eBook*), develop your speech outlines (*Speech Builder Express 3.0*), watch and critique videos of sample speeches and communication situations (*interactive video activities*), upload your speech videos for peer reviewing and critique other students' speeches (*Speech Studio online speech review tool*), and download chapter review so you can study when and where you'd like (*Audio Study Tools*).

Key Points

- Informative presentations provide new and unfamiliar information, extend what the audience may already know, update information about a topic, or help the audience view an issue in a different way.
- Begin all presentations by determining not only your general purpose but also your specific purpose and thesis statement.
  - ✔ A specific purpose is a clear, concrete one-statement sentence that identifies what you want your audience to know, believe, or do.
  - ✔ A thesis statement is a concise summary of the central message of your speech, stating your speech's most essential points.
- The basic format of an informative speech is to tell 'em what you're going to tell them, tell 'em, and then tell 'em what you just told them.
- All effective presentations begin with an introduction. The purpose of the introduction is to
  - ✔ Establish and demonstrate your credibility with your topic.
  - ✔ Compel your audience to listen actively by using devices such as personal stories, emotional appeals, humor, repetition, famous quotations, and startling facts and statistics.
  - ✔ Preview your story with one simple statement that lists your main points.
- Effective presentations end with a conclusion. The purpose of the conclusion is to
  - ✔ Signal the end of your story and summarize your points.
  - ✔ Compel your audience to remember you and your message.
- There are several strategies you can use to help your audience understand and remember your main points:
  - ✔ Keep it simple.
  - ✔ Keep it concrete.
  - ✔ Be repetitive and redundant.
  - ✔ Elicit active responses.
  - ✔ Use familiar and relevant examples.
  - ✔ Use transitions and signposts.

Key Terms

informative presentations (170)   **specific purpose** (171)

preview (178)   **thesis statement** (171)

Questions for Critical Thinking and Review

1. Is it ever possible to make a presentation appear too simple or too concrete? How do you know where to draw the line?
2. Can a speech ever be too repetitive or redundant? Where do you draw the line?

3. When do informative speeches become persuasive? For instance, what examples can you provide of college lectures that you think were actually persuasive? How do you know when a speech is really persuasive rather than informative?

4. Can a speech be both informative and persuasive? To what extent were you both informed and persuaded by Flake, Pike, or Donnelly?

5. In this chapter, Flake, Pike, and Donnelly were introduced as effective speakers. And yet you may have found reasons to be critical of their presentations. Assume that you are an expert at giving informative presentations: Provide three recommendations you might give each of these speakers to help them improve their speeches.

6. Organizational communication consultant John Kline argues that managers often make the mistake of assuming that telling equals learning. Why would managers make this assumption? How might you explain to a manager the complexities involved in teaching an employee how to do something?

7. Of the six strategies offered to increase audience understanding and retention, which strategy is most useful or meaningful to you? Why? What other strategies can you think of to add to this list?

Chapter 9

Giving Presentations:
How Can I Best Sell My Ideas at Work?

Jeff Greenberg/PhotoEdit

Chapter Learning Objectives

After completing this chapter, you should be able to
- Differentiate among the three goals of persuasion.
- Analyze your audience's willingness to change or resist.
- Create a coherent story for your presentation using Monroe's motivated sequence.
- Incorporate strategies to make your audience more receptive and less resistant to your persuasive attempts.
- Analyze and evaluate others' persuasive presentations.
- Prepare and deliver an effective presentation to persuade or influence others.

See also **the modules that are relevant to this chapter:**

2: **How Can I Practice Ethical Communication Behavior at Work?**

3: **How Do I Give Specialized Presentations?**

6: **"You Gotta Have Style": Using APA and MLA Styles**

7: **What Methods Can I Use to Analyze My Audience?**

8: **What's the Best Way to Organize and Outline My Presentation?**

Module 2:
How Can I Practice Ethical Communication Behavior at Work?

Module 3:
How Do I Give Specialized Presentations?

Module 6:
"You Gotta Have Style": Using APA and MLA Styles

Module 7:
What Methods Can I Use to Analyze My Audience?

Module 8:
What's the Best Way to Organize and Outline My Presentation?

As CEO of a large manufacturing firm, Alana Alvarez faces a number of difficult decisions as the economy continues to worsen. As it stands now, unless cutbacks are made, her company will likely go under. The most obvious place to cut is employee salaries and benefits. Rather than layoffs, which would jeopardize production, Alana has decided to reduce everyone's salary—including her own. Delivering this bad news and convincing her workforce to accept this drastic reduction in income, Alana must prepare a presentation announcing her plans as soon as possible.

Recognizing the potential for overwhelming resistance to her plan, Alana is unsure how to draft her presentation. She decides, then, just to get it over with and tell her employees what's what. And so she does. She brings them together and announces without much explanation that because of the failing economy, effective immediately, all salaries will be cut by 12 percent. She tells them she is sorry, but she sees no other alternative.

Alana's employees are understandably outraged and angry. They decide to strike and walk out.

The company eventually folds.

What were Alana's alternatives? After all, she wasn't responsible for a bad economy or its impact on the company. She had always been a straight shooter; she laid it on the line and told them the harsh economic realities they must all face. She was even willing to take a pay cut herself. What more could she have said and done?

As it turns out, Alana had a number of options:

- She might have begun by talking about the company's story. She could have described the company's current and projected financial standing, how it got to this point, and what it means to those who work there.

- Because she knew for some time that the financial condition of her company was in jeopardy, she might have solicited input from groups of employees to discuss how to best address the problem as it worsened. She could have encouraged everyone's input in finding ways, both big and small, to save money.

- She might have proposed multiple solutions and urged her employees to work with her in choosing those that made sense.

Proposing a 12 percent pay cut without employee input may have seemed unreasonable, even unwarranted. Proposals to gradually reduce salaries over time, offer fewer benefits, suspend vacation time, or request voluntary furloughs might have been perceived as less draconian.

This chapter discusses ways that you can effectively persuade audiences both within and outside an organization. The principles for persuading generalize across most contexts and are applicable to many types of audiences. You can continue to build your understanding of crafting and delivering business and professional speeches in other chapters: Chapter 7 (preparing to speak), Chapter 8 (informative presentations), and Chapter 10 (sensory aids).

The first section of this chapter considers how you can convey the central idea of your persuasive presentation by identifying how you want to influence your audience and assessing their willingness to change their attitudes, beliefs, or behaviors. We then outline the steps of an organizational pattern that is effective for most persuasive presentations. Next, we offer a variety of proven strategies to help you influence your audience ethically and appropriately. Finally, this chapter concludes with examples of professionals who effectively apply these principles in their efforts to persuade.

What Is Persuasion?

Communication researchers and social psychologists have identified a number of strategies that could have helped Alana better inform and subsequently persuade her workforce. As the example illustrates, preparing and delivering bad news or any kind of formal persuasive presentation to a large group requires careful planning. Strategic planning is particularly important when you need or want to persuade individuals to change the way they think, feel, and act.

Chapter 8 examined informative presentations and ways to best present new ideas or to help others view an issue in a new way. Oftentimes, a persuasive presentation does the same thing, when speakers try to influence others by presenting them with new or more information. How, then, do we differentiate between informing and persuading? Simply put, informing teaches; persuading advocates. A supervisor intends to inform when he clarifies the new parking policy—to persuade employees not to park on Level 3. Similarly, an employee intends to persuade when she argues for a raise or promotion. The same employee describing her work habits, however, may intend to merely inform. Sometimes the distinction is subtle, but the speaker's overriding intent or motive should be clear.

This chapter examines how you can best sell your ideas, products, or proposals to others, whether your goal is to motivate and spread goodwill or to influence others to purchase or adopt products, proposals, or ideas.[1] The common denominator in all of these persuasive speeches is advocacy. In a **persuasive presentation**, a speaker's primary purpose is to advocate some sort of change in attitudes, beliefs, or behaviors.

Errol Rait/Alamy

Where Do You Begin?

One of the most frequent tasks we face daily at work is to try to influence people's ideas, feelings, or actions—either by trying to get others to make a change in their thinking that seems desirable, or by influencing their actions in some way. In addition, we constantly receive other people's messages aimed at modifying our thinking or conduct. Persuasion is something with which all of us are only too familiar. Almost from the moment we get to work until we leave at the end of the day, various kinds of people, groups, and agencies try to get us to attend to messages urging us to support their proposals, change our routine, give our time, donate money to a worthy cause, solve a problem in a particular way, and adopt new ideas and practices.

But the persuasive attempts do not begin and end in the workplace. We can all appreciate how our partner or spouse may try to influence us to go out for dinner, change the baby's diapers, do the laundry, take out the trash, and watch a TV sitcom we do not like. Persuasion also plays a key role in religion, education, and public affairs. In short, persuasion is one of the most ubiquitous communication processes in modern life. It's become so pervasive that many of us have developed "mental calluses" to learn how to ignore and resist most of these efforts. That is, we've decided what we'll allow to influence us and what we won't.

Although ubiquitous, persuading others is no simple process. Precisely because of those mental calluses, it's difficult to persuade others to do anything they don't already want to do. Your challenge in the workplace is to be able to prepare and deliver presentations that have a reasonable chance of influencing others at work. You need to be able to influence others to accept your proposals, adapt to policy changes, adopt new programs, and purchase your products and services. You need to begin by deciding first what it is you want other people to feel, think, or do.

Decide Whether You Want to Influence Attitudes, Beliefs, or Behaviors

To change **attitudes**, the speaker must influence others to feel more positive or negative about an issue. The speaker may want the audience to feel angry, indignant, disgusted, committed, appreciative, or triumphant. Consider these attitudinally based statements:

- Work can be satisfying and enjoyable.

- Writing a technical report is hard work.

- Eating in the office is a disgusting thing to do.

Suppose you want to persuade your audience that no matter how convenient, eating in your office at work is a disgusting behavior. To accomplish this objective, you might help them visualize the negative effects of office eating: "Crumbs accumulate, spillage occurs, and food smells permeate and remain over time." The point is that your goal is to advocate a change in attitudes, to convince your audience to feel negatively about in-office eating.

The speaker can also persuade by changing **beliefs** or what audiences think or believe is true or not true. Consider these belief-based statements:

- As a general rule, employees want to do a full day's work.

- Managers aren't born; they are made.

- How much someone is paid isn't necessarily related to the number of hours he or she puts in.

Efforts to persuade others to change their beliefs is not so different from informative speaking. Providing new information to an audience you want to persuade can often provoke audience members to reexamine what they thought was true or false. The persuasive intent is to advocate that they change their beliefs.

Putting Your Skills to Work

I SEE YOUR VIEWPOINT.

Every day others are trying to persuade you, and you are trying to persuade others. So you already have a lot of experience with persuasion. The trick is to learn how to persuade effectively and ethically. It's one thing to try to persuade your roommate to let him borrow your car. It's another to try to persuade your boss to give you a raise or to persuade a client to use your company's services! The tips and strategies you'll learn about in this chapter will help you hone your persuasive skills.

4x6/istockphoto.com

For instance, assume that audience members believe it's true that wages and hours are positively related—the more you work, the higher your wages. Say you want to convince them that their current belief about wages and hours is false. You will need to demonstrate to them, preferably with data, that many high-wage jobs are actually associated with quality, not quantity, of work. You might further note that many of the lowest-wage jobs in this country are hourly and limited to a minimum wage. So although it's true that if you work more hours, you'll earn more pay, you won't necessarily earn a higher wage.

Throughout your presentation, your goal is to alter audience members' beliefs and to advocate that they reconsider some of their misperceptions. To accomplish this goal, you must first inform audience members (add new information that conflicts with what they thought was true) and then persuade them to accept a new set of beliefs that are true. Changing beliefs, therefore, automatically involves both informing and persuading.

You might also choose to change **behaviors**. In this case, you must motivate your audience to take some kind of action, or at least commit to taking some kind of action. Persuasive speeches that emphasize some kind of behavioral change focus more on explicit behavioral outcomes than do persuasive speeches that emphasize either attitude or belief changes. Consider these behavioral statements:

- Buy American-made cars.
- Switch from IBM to Apple products.
- Join the labor union.

With each of these examples, the speaker's primary purpose is to persuade the audience to behave differently. To accomplish this objective, the speaker might have to first address audience members' current attitudes and beliefs and then lay out the specific observable actions they should engage in. For instance, if you want audience members to join the labor union, you will need to first discover how they feel about unions and what current beliefs they hold. Once you have a handle on this information, you can begin to strategically respond to their objections and encourage them to reconsider and join the union.

Identify Your Specific Purpose and Thesis Statement

Deciding whether you want to influence your audience's attitudes, beliefs, or behaviors is the first step in determining your specific purpose for a presentation whose general purpose is to persuade (Chapter 8). If Alana had prepared a specific purpose for her presentation, it might have looked like this:

> I want to persuade my employees that we all need to take a temporary pay cut in order to stay in business.

And her thesis statement, summarizing the central message of her speech, might read something like this:

> The poor economy is jeopardizing our business, so we must all take a temporary pay cut in order to ensure that we remain in business and avoid layoffs.

Table 9.1 provides more examples of specific purposes and thesis statements for persuasive presentations.

Weigh In! 9.1:
What Kind of Resistor Are You?

> ## TABLE 9.1
> ## Specific Purposes and Thesis Statements for Persuasive Presentations
>
> | Specific purpose | Thesis statement |
> |---|---|
> | I want to persuade my customers that the speech-recognition technology of Google's Android phone is more effective and easier to use than that of their existing phones. | By taking advantage of Google's servers' ability to process speech sounds, the Android phone solves the problems with speech-recognition technology that other phones present: being prone to error, requiring users speak to speak slowly, and using too much of the phone's computing power. |
> | I want to persuade my client's employees to believe that creating more of a work–life balance in their lives will improve their productivity. | You can increase productivity and avoid burnout by taking steps to create more of a work–life balance: set and enforce boundaries between your work and personal life, be realistic about what a balanced life involves when it necessarily includes work, and make small changes in the areas of your life that will make you feel most balanced.[2] |
> | I want to persuade my boss to implement a corporate-giving program in order to assist worthy organizations in our community. | By implementing a corporate-giving program, we can not only assist worthy organizations, but we can also take advantage of tax breaks, increase employee morale, and improve our standing in the community. |

Assess Your Audience's Willingness to Change

All people expect and enjoy the freedom to choose and control how they think, feel, and behave. Open attempts to persuade tend to threaten our personal freedoms. After all, we don't want to be talked into doing something we might not want to do. To reassert or regain our freedom, then, we are strongly motivated to resist any persuasive attempt.

This universal tendency to resist change has been widely documented. Social psychologist Jack Brehm calls this theoretical explanation for people's resistance **psychological reactance**.[3] Psychological reactance occurs when people are motivated to rebel when their established beliefs, attitudes, and behaviors are threatened by persuasion. Consequently, those who *demand* compliance may actually increase others' determination to resist their influence—causing a reaction against the attempt. Before you read on to consider how to overcome others' resistances, consider your own tendency to resist persuasion by taking the self-assessment **WEIGH IN! 9.1: What Kind of Resistor Are You?** Are you a highly active, moderate, or highly passive resistor?

How can you as a persuasive speaker counteract this universal human inclination to resist change? Rather than wait for the resistance to occur, you can rely on a number of preventative strategies. Central to most persuasive efforts is tackling the reasons or motivation for change. Unless the audience becomes convinced that there is something wrong with the status quo (the way things are), they will be resistant to thinking, feeling, or acting differently. Let's examine strategies you can use to influence three different kinds of audiences.

- **The audience agrees with your position.** This is, of course, the best possible audience to influence. They already agree with you; your task is to get them to agree some more. You want them to intensify their position by feeling more passionate about the issue, being more committed than ever to their beliefs, or giving more money than they already do.

✔ Begin by simply reminding them why you and they share attitudes and beliefs about the issue. A brief review of the reasons why you think the way you do is sufficient.

✔ Next, provide them with some motivation to strengthen their attitudes and beliefs. Very often, emotional appeals can be used to energize and motivate.

✔ Finally, you can afford to be direct with supportive audience members and tell them exactly what you want or need.

• **The audience disagrees with your position.** This is the most difficult audience to influence. Any efforts to overtly or directly persuade will stimulate psychological reactance and will cause them to reject your position even further. This boomerang effect is common among people who have invested their egos in an issue that is important to them. Try, for instance, to persuade a parent that his child is "below average" in intelligence or physical attractiveness. Can you imagine how defensively he or she is likely to react?

✔ First, modify your expectations: Do not expect a large amount of change. Influence your audience members to shift their attitudes only slightly. Rather than pushing them to change from complete disagreement to complete agreement, plan to move their attitude from more to less disagreement.

✔ Next, establish common ground with your audience. Communicate your understanding and respect for their point of view. Where there are areas of agreement, say so.

✔ Third, tell them where you disagree, but be careful: The more areas of disagreement you reveal, they more they'll be reminded to resist. Try not to sound disagreeable; only target one or two areas to discuss.

✔ Finally, use a lot of evidence to back up your position.

Radius Images/Jupiter Images

Link Out 9.1:
Motivated Sequence Explained

Visualize! Practice! 9.1:
What Case Can You Build?

- **The audience is neutral or undecided.** This is the case where audience members may not know very much about the issue, or they are sufficiently confused by the facts. As a result, they have no opinion or they can't make up their minds. Although easy to persuade, neutral or undecided audiences are also quite rare.

  ✔ Begin by getting their attention. Make the issue personally or professionally relevant to them. You can do this by providing background information about the issue.

  ✔ Next, explain to them your own beliefs and attitudes, how you think and feel about the issue. Tell them why you believe or feel the way that you do.

  ✔ Finally, back up your position with facts, illustrations, and testimonials. Refrain from inundating them with too much information, which might further confuse or overload them.

You can practice using these strategies with different types of audiences by completing **VISUALIZE! PRACTICE! 9.1: What Case Can You Build?** What arguments can you prepare that would help you convince others to change what they feel, think, or do?

What's the Best Format for a Persuasive Presentation?

If audience members are reluctant to change, then you must give them sufficient reason to change, keeping in mind the effects of psychological reactance. Here is where the format of your presentation really makes difference: The organizational framework must establish *why* audience members must change the way they feel, think, or behave. They must feel that something is wrong with the status quo and that your solution is the best remedy for it.

You can employ a variety of organizational patterns to influence others, including problem–solution and cause and effect (Chapter 7). But the most widely used structure for persuasive speaking is one developed by Purdue University communication professor Alan H. Monroe in the 1930s.[4] Working with business students, Dr. Monroe developed the now-famous **Monroe's motivated sequence**, an organizational pattern used by students, teachers, leaders, marketers, advertisers, and other professionals interested in persuasion and resistance.

Monroe's motivated sequence resembles a problem-solution pattern, but the sequence's approach is a bit more nuanced, taking into consideration potential audience resistance. It can be used for any persuasive presentation, whether the goal is to convince the audience to buy soap or to adopt a proposal for a new product line. Monroe's motivated sequence consists of five steps, rather than the typical three-part framework of introduction, body, and conclusion. For a quick overview of the steps, see Table 9.2.

If you prefer to learn about these five steps from video, watch instructor Krista Price provide an overview of the sequence at **LINK OUT 9.1: Motivated Sequence Explained.** For a sample panel presentation organized by Monroe's motivated sequence, watch "The Dirty Truth about Antibacterial Products" by visiting your CourseMate.

Let's take a look at how one speaker used the motivated sequence to create an entertaining speech that was both informative and entertaining. Gary Lauder, the managing

TABLE 9.2
The Five Steps of Monroe's Motivated Sequence

Step	Function	Ideal audience response
1. **Attention**	To get audience to listen	"I want to hear what you have to say."
2. **Need**	To get audience to feel a need or want	"I agree. I have that need/want."
3. **Satisfaction**	To tell audience how to fill need or want	"I see your solution will work."
4. **Visualization**	To get audience to see benefits of solution	"This is a great idea."
5. **Action**	To get audience to take action	"I want it."

Link Out 9.2:
Lauder's Motivated Sequence Speech

partner in a venture capital firm called Lauder Partners, invests in information technologies. In a recent presentation to the TED conference, held annually in Long Beach, Lauder advocated the elimination of traditional traffic lights and four-way stop signs at intersections and asked audience members to pressure their communities to replace them with more efficient, safer, and less costly roundabouts.[5] For a video and transcript of this presentation, go to **LINK OUT 9.2: Lauder's Motivated Sequence Speech**.

Step 1: Gain the Audience's Attention

As you do in all speeches, begin by grabbing the audience's attention. Make the audience curious about what you're going to say. As you cannot do in other types of speeches, however, skip the preview—in this way, you can avoid the effects of psychological reactance.

What did Lauder do?

In order to gain audience attention, he began by talking about a traffic ticket he received twenty-seven years ago and how it made him think about intersections. Consistent with Monroe's motivated sequence, he did not preview his speech.

What would Monroe advise?

Lauder was able to grab everyone's attention with the traffic violation event. No doubt, everyone in the audience could relate to this topic; who hasn't been ticketed for a traffic violation at one time or another? In order to make the event more compelling, he might have spent a little more time developing a story around that occasion. Why would that be a good idea?

Step 2: Identify Unfulfilled Needs

Probably no step in the sequence is more important than the need step. Critical to persuasion is establishing a clear and urgent, and yet unfulfilled, need. You must show audience members why this issue should concern them and why change is necessary. Do not reveal the solution at this stage. Focus instead on identifying and clarifying the audience's needs. If the solution is communicated too early, the audience may resist.

What did Lauder do?

Lauder noted that "50 percent of crashes happen at intersections." And that's too many. Currently, we use traffic lights at intersections in an effort to reduce the likelihood of accidents. Traffic lights, then, are the status quo. But he noted that traffic lights are problematic. Later in his speech, he also claimed there are too many stop signs and their use in certain intersections is illogical. Within the context of Monroe's motivated sequence, Lauder moved too quickly into the solution by offering roundabouts as a creative alternative. He explained how roundabouts reduce traffic accidents, keep traffic flowing, and reduce the need for braking and acceleration—resulting in less gas, less pollution, and less time wasted driving.

What would Monroe advise?

By offering the solution so soon in his speech, Lauder risked psychological reactance. In order to demonstrate the need for change, he might have spent more time documenting that need. How might he go about doing that?

- He could discuss the amount of gas, pollution, and time involved in stopping and starting at traffic lights.

- He might further cite research that demonstrates what happens when traditional intersections with traffic signals are converted into roundabouts.

- He might also speak from personal experience, sharing with the audience his annoyance at waiting at red lights when the intersection is empty.

In the end, he wants the audience to *anticipate* whatever solution he might have to offer. It is this anticipation that makes the audience willing to listen, visualize, and accept possible alternatives.

Step 3: Propose a Solution That Satisfies Those Needs

Once you have established a problem or need, it is time to present a solution. Describe how your plan will work and how it will satisfy unfulfilled needs. For each of the needs you have described earlier in Step 2, show how your solution will meet those needs. In this step, it's also important to identify and address possible objections to your proposal. Audience members may be concerned about cost, effort, time, or other issues related to your solution. Make an effort, then, to anticipate and address those objections.

What did Lauder do?

Offering roundabouts as a creative alternative to traffic lights and stop signs, Lauder showed how roundabouts meet a variety of needs: increasing safety, optimizing traffic flow, reducing pollution and gas consumption, and so on. He cited evidence that is compelling.

What would Monroe advise?

Unfortunately, Lauder offered the solution early in the presentation, making it less effective. How might he have modified his persuasive message to better utilize this information?

- He could have begun this step by explaining his plan or how roundabouts work in regulating traffic flow. He might have discussed how other countries use roundabouts and why.

- Next, he could have taken the time to reiterate each unfulfilled need and showed how the use of roundabouts would meet each one. For example, one unfulfilled need is safety. Turns out, roundabouts are much safer than traffic lights; they reduce the number of accidents significantly more than do traffic lights.

- Finally, he might have identified and eliminated possible objections by noting the potential upfront costs involved in replacing lights with roundabouts and then refuting that objection by citing evidence of eventual long-term cost savings.

The good news is that all of this information already existed in his speech. Monroe would simply have wanted him to discuss it in this step rather than in Step 2.

Step 4: Visualize What Satisfaction Will Mean

After you propose a solution, you need to intensify audience members' desire for your plan by having them visualize what their lives would be like once they've adopted it. Paint a clear picture of what life would be like with this solution—or what life would be like without it. Use vivid images to illustrate what will happen, as a result.

What did Lauder do?

Lauder argued that if we maintain the status quo, traffic problems will continue, accidents will persist, and long queue lines will form. What he did not explicitly state, however, is what would happen if the audience accepted his solution.

What would Monroe advise?

Monroe would have liked Lauder's demonstration of what would happen if the status quo is maintained, but he would have recommended that Lauder help the audience appreciate or visualize how traffic patterns might change with the use

Michael Newman/PhotoEdit

of roundabouts or T-signs. Lauder might have helped them personalize the solution by illustrating how their own driving habits and safety would be substantially improved.

Step 5: Identify Specific Actions

In this final step, tell your audience what they need to do to implement or adopt the solution. Don't assume that the audience will know how to obtain or carry out your solution. Spell out exactly what they need to do. Keep this step brief and to the point. Don't make it complicated. Close the deal.

What did Lauder do?

Lauder concluded with a little humor by anointing audience members as "Road Scholars" for having an enlightened perspective on how to better manage potential traffic problems. He called for them to take action now. He told them not to wait, to exercise their influence in the community, to encourage their neighborhoods to create more sensible traffic flows.

What would Monroe advise?

Lauder did all the right things with his call for action. We believe that Monroe would have been proud! Can you suggest additional courses of action Lauder might have asked his audience to take? Make sure they are concrete, doable, and easy enough to implement.

Fundamental to Monroe's motivated sequence is this important principle: To persuade, the speaker must focus more on the audience's needs than on the proposed solution. Monroe found that anxious salespeople often begin a sales pitch with a lengthy monologue about product features without first identifying (or learning about) consumers' needs—a highly ineffective sales approach. Like a good sales pitch, effective persuaders need to assess what needs are important to their audience and then respond to those needs. If audience members do not have readily identifiable needs related to the topic, the speaker may need to create needs and wants for them. This is a common strategy for advertisers, who must first convince potential consumers that they have a need or problem and then provide a solution.

What Strategies Will Help You Influence Your Audience?

To successfully influence others, take advantage of the research that examines the dynamics of persuasion and resistance. Here are nine strategies based on this research that you can use to influence and preempt audience resistance.[6]

Conceal Your Intent

Because people resist when speakers try to convince them to do something they don't already do, you must conceal your intent to persuade them to change. Rather than starting by demanding change, focus on addressing the audience's need. Spend sufficient time at Step 2 of the motivated sequence, anticipating and identifying problems with the status quo. By expressing sensitivity to what the audience needs, you can avoid trying to overcome an initial negative response to a pitch or promotion.

Don't Ask for Too Much

Speakers who deliver a message too far afield from what their audiences are willing to accept are doomed. Instead of asking for large-scale change, ask for gradual, minor progress toward the change you want. Otherwise, your message could backfire, causing the audience to disagree with you even more. For a demonstration of how this principle works, complete **VISUALIZE! PRACTICE! 9.2: Asking for Too Much?** Which of the options provided are asking for too much change?

Visualize! Practice! 9.2:
Asking for Too Much?
Visualize! Practice! 9.3:
Bad Words

Avoid Inflammatory Phrases

No doubt, there are certain words and phrases that can make you angry, cringe, or that you find disgusting. These words and phrases act as **semantic barriers** whose connotative or subjective meanings tend to trigger negative feelings or arousals that distract audience members from listening effectively. Carefully choose substitute words that have the same meaning, but are relatively innocuous or even positive. What are some words and phrases that speakers should avoid? Complete **VISUALIZE! PRACTICE! 9.3: Bad Words** to consider alternatives to words that often elicit strong negative reactions.

Use a Two-Sided Message with Refutation

There are three basic ways to present an argument:

- One-sided messages give only the speaker's side while ignoring the opponent's argument.
- Two-sided messages attempt to give both sides a fair hearing.
- Two-sided messages with refutation present both sides and refute the validity of the opposing side.

Which option do you suspect audiences prefer? Audiences are most influenced when the speaker presents both sides and takes the time to argue against the opposition. This is

Putting Your Skills to Work

AND SO, IN CONCLUSION...

Asking for a moderate amount of change is a lot like compromising. When you compromise, you ask for a lot but negotiate to end up getting just some of what you want. The persuasive strategy of not asking for too much skips the negotiation part of the equation. When you're trying to persuade, try to anticipate what your audience would be willing to compromise on and start from there rather than asking for everything all at once.

A-Digit/istockphoto.com;
4x6/istockphoto.com

Visualize! Practice! 9.4:
How Would You Refute It?

the way audience members typically think: When the speaker acknowledges both sides of the argument, the audience perceives the speaker as well-informed, highly credibly, and fair and objective. This two-sided approach opens the audience to potential influence—maybe they'll decide that the opposite side is better. However, when the speaker then refutes the opposing side, the audience learns why it may be a good idea to accept his argument. Just be careful not to denigrate others' points of view when you refute an opposing side—that can cause an audience to perceive you in a negative light. For practice applying this strategy, complete **VISUALIZE! PRACTICE! 9.4: How Would You Refute It?**

Inoculate against Counterarguments

Even if you have an audience that already agrees with your position, it's always a good idea to take the opportunity to "inoculate" the audience against possible counterarguments. For example, if you are preceded or followed by a speaker who advocates a position different from your own, then inoculation by a two-sided message with refutation becomes essential. You may know that the audience already agrees with you, but you want to make sure that they won't be swayed by another speaker. Use counterarguments to inoculate the audience against the other side by systematically dismantling what the speaker is likely to say or has already said. Evidence is key to being able to do this.

Suppose, for instance, that you are giving a presentation advocating the limited use of text messaging for business purposes. Assume your audience already agrees with you. They know that texting is supposed to be brief and informal. They realize that important, sensitive, or controversial information should be communicated by other means, and they recognize that texting during meetings or presentations is rude and inappropriate. Further, assume that they have already been exposed to counterarguments from colleagues: "Only non-texters or digital immigrants ever criticize those of us who are digital natives!"

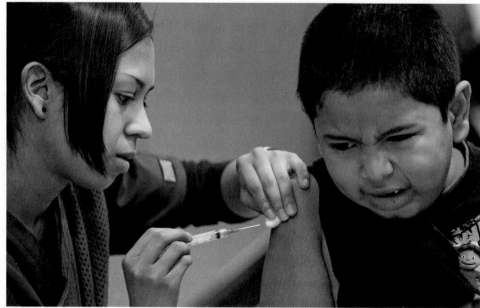

UPI/Roger L. Wollenberg

or "Texting is now; it's immediate; and it's the best way to connect with others." Inoculating your audience from counter-messages like these requires you to briefly identify those arguments and then refute each with solid evidence. In this way, you arm your audience to resist future counterarguments.

Keep Objections to a Minimum

Even though you may be able to identify a whole host of counterarguments and objections to any given argument, don't try to refute them all. Select only the most important or relevant objections and respond to those. At most, discuss only a couple of objections. Spending too much time on objections at the expense of emphasizing the advantages of your own proposed solution will only weaken your position. Moreover, you risk exposing the audience to objections they may never have considered. Once raised, those new objections may sound pretty convincing—to your detriment.

Combine Reason with Emotion

The power to persuade is often based on evidence, including facts, statistics, physical data, expert testimony, and eyewitness accounts. Some topics lend themselves more easily to emotional appeals as well. Emotional appeals often evoke outrage, surprise, anticipation, trust, disappointment, and other feelings.

Obviously, persuasive presentations that address employee layoffs, terminations, cutbacks, pay cuts, furloughs harassment, workplace violence, conflict, workplace stress, and bullying arouse emotions that can be channeled in the direction of change. With the power to manipulate people's emotions, however, comes the responsibility to use it wisely. For example, emotional appeals that reinforce hateful stereotypes, promote greed or jealousy or selfishness, or capitalize on fear and despair are unethical and destructive.

Use Fear Appeals—When Appropriate

Fear is a common way to influence change. **High-fear appeals**, based on threats to one's life or security, are designed to arouse a high level of anxiety. **Low-fear appeals** arouse only a low level of anxiety. Research reveals that high-fear appeals are much more effective at persuading others than low-fear appeals—with two important caveats:

- First, the fear must seem likely or relevant to the target audience.

- Second, the fear must be accompanied by a vehicle for reducing the fear or what researchers call message efficacy.

In other words, when you induce high fear, the fear must appear reasonable and probable ("this could happen to me"), and you must provide the audience with a reasonable means to remove the fear ("I know what to do to make sure it doesn't happen to me"). In the workplace, some issues lend themselves to fear appeals, such as job security, promotions and pay, forced retirements, job relocation, and work safety.

Advertisers often use fear to influence—and it can work. Consider commercials that warn about the dangers of smoking, taking illegal drugs, alcohol abuse, and failing to use seat belts. One very graphic British public service announcement (PSA), for instance, has been used to illustrate the serious ramifications of texting while driving.[7] The PSA demonstrates how likely deadly accidents are for teens who text and drive ("this could happen to me"). What it fails to communicate, however, is a message of efficacy ("I know what to do to make sure it doesn't happen to me"). To be more persuasive, the video should illustrate

a passenger offering to text message for the driver, preserving the safety of all involved. To see the video, watch LINK OUT 9.3: **Texting While Driving**.

So, inducing fear, especially high fear, works. The down side of using fear is the negative association that people might have with you, the company, or the product. For example, take a look at this website LINK OUT 9.4: **Using Fear to Advertise** that illustrates how too much fear can have unwanted, aversive effects.

Repeat Your Message

What's repeated gets remembered (Chapter 8). Even though Monroe's motivated sequence is not set up to either preview or review major points of your speech, it does require the speaker to explain the solution in depth and to have the audience visualize the adopted solution.

Audience members will be more likely to recall the arguments accurately, understand the message more thoroughly, and believe in the solution more fully when you repeat these points several times during your speech.[9] This strategy may be unsuitable for some presentations, but it can be very effective for recorded events. The media often highlight speech segments during political campaigns; major news outlets reprint text or upload it online for consumption; and organizations post newsletters or communiqués for clients and shareholders.

How Do the Experts Do It?

Now that you have some idea of what's involved in giving a persuasive presentation, let's see how the experts do it. Watch and carefully examine the three professional presentations featured in CHECK THIS OUT 9.1: **Sea of Plastic,** CHECK THIS OUT 9.2: **Dangerous Things for Kids**, and CHECK THIS OUT 9.3: **Let's Get Rational**.

- Founder of Algalita Marine Research Foundation, Charles Moore captains the foundation's research vessel to document plastic waste that litters the thousands of miles of the Pacific Ocean. His talk centers on the source of that plastic—you and me.[10]

- Gever Tulley is the co-founder of the Tinker School, a camp where children learn how to build, solve problems, and create. He is interested in helping children become healthy, self-sufficient adults in ways that seem counterintuitive to parents today.[11]

- Dr. Elizabeth Pisani is an epidemiologist with a Ph.D. in infectious disease, an international speaker, and a policy advisor to the World Bank, World Health Organization, U.S. Centers for Disease Control, and many other organizations. Her presentation focuses on the so-called rational decisions that affect the spread of HIV/AIDS.[12]

After watching each video, refer to the transcript of each presentation—you'll find it on the same webpage that the video appears on. Once you've watched all three presentations, select one and answer these questions:

1. What did the speaker want the audience to do as a result of his or her presentation?

2. To what extent do you think the audience was already in agreement with the speaker? What audiences would be more likely to disagree up front with the speaker's intent?

3. Based on Monroe's motivated sequence, what did the speaker use to gain the audience's attention?

4. What needs or problems with the status quo did the speaker identify?

5. What solution did the speaker advocate?

6. How did the speaker get the audience to visualize the solution, if adopted (or if not adopted)?

7. What specific call to action did the speaker ask of the audience?

8. Did the speaker rely on primarily reason, emotion, or both types of appeals?

9. Give an example of at least one of the nine persuasive strategies discussed in this chapter.

10. To what extent were you influenced by this speaker's message? Why or why not?

 Check out Speech Studio to see persuasive speeches delivered by other students. Or record a speech you're working on, upload it to Speech Studio, and ask your peers for their feedback. What feedback could you use to fine-tune your persuasive presentation before you give it in class?

Sample Student Speech: Persuasive

In the speech shown in Figure 9.1, student Kaeli Jones attempts to persuade her audience to eliminate paper banking-transaction slips in favor of going paperless. Kaeli gave this speech in her business and professional communication class—she was asked to create and deliver a persuasive speech about a problem she thought needed solving in her workplace. As you read Kaeli's speech, note how she presents a problem and a solution, how she organizes her speech, and the reasoning she uses. What are some strengths of this speech? What are some aspects of the speech that could be improved?

In addition to reading Kaeli's speech here, watch it and read her speech outline in **Student Persuasive Presentation: Paperless Banking Persuasive Speech**. With this link, you can also access several other sample persuasive speeches delivered by students. To see how to outline a persuasive speech and to see how Kaeli's speech was delivered from a full-content outline, check out **MODULE 8: What's the Best Way to Organize and Outline My Presentation?**

FIGURE 9.1
Sample persuasive speech

Let's Make the Banking Experience Easier
Adapted from a speech by Kaeli Jones, California State University, Long Beach[13]

General purpose: To persuade
Specific purpose: I want to persuade Chase Bank to eliminate paper banking transaction slips in favor of going paperless.
Thesis statement: It would benefit Chase Bank to eliminate paper transaction slips in favor of going paperless, because these slips are costly and environmentally wasteful, and they lower customer satisfaction.

Hi, my name's Kaeli Jones. I'm here to tell you today about how we can make the banking experience easier, not only for our customers, but also for our tellers. *[Kaeli shows a digital slide of various banking transaction slips.]* I'm sure you're all familiar with these banking slips: withdraw, deposit, payment, line of credit, transfer. You probably see them every single time you go into the bank. If you don't fill them out yourself, the teller fills them out for you. I see these dozens of times a day—everyone has to use them, and I need them for every single transaction.

Let me tell you a story really quick: Kelly is a teller for Chase. It's a busy day in the branch, and she just got back from lunch. She sees the line is to the door, so she hurries up and jumps back on the teller line. Customer after customer doesn't have a slip filled out. She knows she's wasting her own time and the time of the people in line by filling them out for each and every customer. Now George comes into the branch. George is not a regular customer of the branch. He's in a hurry, and it's one of those days when he has way too much to do and absolutely no time to do it. So he just gets in line—he doesn't fill out a slip. He doesn't think about it. He waits in line for ten minutes or so. He gets to the front, and Kelly asks him, "Did you fill out your deposit slip?" She probably says it a bit more curtly than she normally would like, but it's a high-stress day. George takes this for rudeness. So now he leaves the branch frustrated because not only did he have to wait for ten minutes, he got rudeness on top of it.

Now, why are transaction slips ineffective? First off, they lower customer satisfaction. Both UPS and Continental Airlines realize that paperless increases customer satisfaction. Mark Bergsrud—he is the senior VP of Marketing Programs and Distribution for Continental Airlines—he says, "We are pleased to take part in this pioneering concept that provides enhanced security and customer service to our passengers." Kurt Kuehn, who is the Senior VP of Worldwide Sales and Marketing for UPS, says: "Returns is a cost-effective way to provide effective customer service around the globe." Both UPS and Continental understand that in this rapidly evolving world, speed and ease are everything to customers. Customers want to get in and out (i.e., boarding passes), and they want things to be simple (i.e., paperless shipping labels).

Second, transaction slips are costly. I do the ordering for my branch, so I understand how much these cost. The average pack is about $2.50. Currently in the branch we have about 70 packages, but that's a little low—you really want about 100 to 150 to fully supply the branch. Now that brings the total cost to supply just my branch to $250 to $375. Multiply that by the 5,100 Chase branches that we have, and you're spending $1.2 million to $1.9 million to supply all the branches. And annually, you're spending $4 to $6 million per year on transaction slips.

Third of all, transaction slips are environmentally wasteful. The paper—we know we have to cut down trees to make them. Every ten slips or so weighs about a gram, so that means there's about 112 thousand pounds of paper used every year to make these transactions slips. That's 51 tons, and that equates to about 280 to 420 trees per year.

So let's get rid of these things. Let's just eliminate transaction slips altogether, so we don't have this issue anymore. We're going to save customers time. Eliminating transaction slips saves customers time because they don't have to fill the slip out, and they don't have to waste the time of the people in line by filling them out at the window. We're obviously going to be saving millions per year by eliminating transaction slips. And thirdly, it's going to save the environment. Not using paper saves trees—it's an easy equation.

I understand that some people are going to say $2 to $3 really isn't that much for a pack. But as I showed before, the cost really does add up. But buying them isn't the only cost. So is storing them the required seven years. We have to keep these transaction slips, and we have to pay for their storage. Obviously that's a lot of transactions slips, so we have to store a lot of pieces of paper.

Less wait time is a happier customer. Let me retell you the story from earlier—this time we're not going to have transaction slips involved. Kelly comes into the branch: still a busy day, the line is still out the door, she still has to hop right back on the teller line. So she comes in, but now she's more able to efficiently help each and every customer get in and out quickly. Also, since the customers aren't distracted by filling out the slip, she can better chat with them to see if there are any referrals she can make for them. So now George comes in. He's still busy, and he still has one of those days when he has no time to do everything in the world. But now he can get right in line, and his time isn't wasted because transaction slips aren't being filled out at the window. George leaves happy because he was in and out in less than ten minutes.

So now how do we get rid of these transaction slips? We need a plan. First, we need to update the teller software. We need to update so that all the banking information can be entered manually or taken from the debit card. (This brings the added bonus of encouraging customers to get debit cards since now they won't be able to write their account number on a slip.) These updates can be incorporated into one of the many software updates that we make every year. Second, we can't do this overnight. According to Jack LaRue in *Accounting Today*, we can't go paperless overnight. While the software update really doesn't take that long, we need to start small. Try getting rid of the account transfer slips first since those don't get scanned into the computer at all. As you find success, then eliminate the rest of the transaction slips. And third, we obviously need teller training. They need to be updated on the new software, and tellers will need to be more proactive in identifying customers since we're not going to have a signature when we go paperless.

So I thank you for your time and attention. I hope you all understand how transaction slips are costly and environmentally wasteful, and that they lower customer satisfaction. Thank you.

Poor Alana. Looking back, you may now have a greater appreciation of both the enormity of her task and the complexities involved in accomplishing her goal. Alana faced an audience of likely resistors who, understandably, would disagree with her proposal. Without a strategic plan to influence them, Alana had no chance of swaying them to accept her solution. Perhaps her biggest challenge was to establish the need for such drastic action, and yet, Alana spent little or no time developing the need or state of affairs. Her audience more than likely perceived her lack of attention to the need as disrespectful, dispassionate, and uncaring. Persuading others to change how they think, feel, or behave is no simple task. Because people tend to resist persuasive attempts, speakers must lay out a careful, effectively organized story that identifies needs, provides a viable solution, and offers a feasible course of action.

Use your Speech Communication CourseMate for *Business & Communication in a Digital Age* for quick access to the electronic resources that accompany this text. These resources include.

Study tools that will help you assess your learning and prepare for exams (*digital glossary, key term flash cards, review quizzes*).

Activities and assignments that will help you hone your knowledge and build your communication skills throughout the course (*Visualize! Practice!, Weigh In!, Check This Out, and Link Out activities; modules; review questions*).

Media resources that will help you explore communication concepts online (*Enhanced eBook*), develop your speech outlines (*Speech Builder Express 3.0*), watch and critique videos of sample speeches and communication situations (*interactive video activities*), upload your speech videos for peer reviewing and critique other students' speeches (*Speech Studio online speech review tool*), and download chapter review so you can study when and where you'd like (*Audio Study Tools*).

Key Points

- In a persuasive presentation, a speaker's primary purpose is to advocate some sort of change in attitudes, beliefs, or behaviors.

- Persuasive presentations often provide new information to help influence others, but persuasive speaking differs from informative speaking in that the purpose of informing is to teach, and the purpose of persuading is to advocate.

- The first step in persuasion is to decide whether you want to influence attitudes, beliefs, or behaviors.

  - ✔ To change attitudes, a speaker must influence others to feel more positive or negative about an issue.

  - ✔ To change beliefs, a speaker must influence others to think or believe something is true or not true.

  - ✔ To change behaviors, a speaker must motivate others to take or commit to some kind of action.

- Deciding whether you want to influence your audience's attitudes, beliefs, or behaviors also helps you determine your specific purpose and thesis statement for your persuasive presentation.

- The next step in persuasion is to assess your audience's willingness to change.

  - ✔ Because all people want the freedom to control how they think, feel, and behave, they may be motivated to rebel when their established beliefs, attitudes, and behaviors are threatened by persuasion. This resistance to change is known as psychological reactance.

  - ✔ Speakers can counteract psychological reactance by using preventative strategies to address three different kinds of audiences: those who agree with your position, those who disagree with your position, and those who are neutral or undecided about your position.

   ✔ The preventative strategies used for each type of audience focus on convincing the audience there is something wrong with the way things are, and change will meet an existing need.

- An effective organizational pattern for persuasive presentations is Monroe's motivated sequence, because it takes into consideration potential audience resistance. The motivated sequence consists of five steps:

  1. Gain the audience's attention.
  2. Identify unfulfilled needs.
  3. Propose a solution that satisfies those needs.
  4. Visualize what satisfaction will mean.
  5. Identify specific actions.

- There are several strategies you can use to influence and address audience resistance:

  ✔ Conceal your intent.
  ✔ Don't ask for too much.
  ✔ Avoid inflammatory phrases.
  ✔ Use a two-sided message with refutation.
  ✔ Inoculate against counterarguments.
  ✔ Keep objections to a minimum.
  ✔ Combine reason with emotion.
  ✔ Use fear appeals when appropriate.
  ✔ Repeat your message.

Key Terms

attitudes (194)

behaviors (195)

beliefs (194)

high-fear appeal (205)

low-fear appeal (205)

Monroe's motivated sequence (198)

persuasive presentation (192)

psychological reactance (196)

semantic barriers (203)

Questions for Critical Thinking and Review

1. From an ethical point of view, does anyone have the right to persuade others to do something they may not want to do? When is persuasion a bad thing? When is it a good thing?

2. This chapter describes combining reason with emotion as a good idea. But are there some speaking situations unsuited to the use of emotional appeals? What are those situations?

3. When is psychological reactance a constructive response to a persuasive attempt? What are some examples of constructive audience resistance in the workplace? When should you resist?

4. In order to be effective, research findings suggest that speakers should conceal their intent to persuade. What ethical problems do you see with this approach?

5. Of the nine strategies offered to increase influence and minimize resistance, which strategy is likely to be most useful or meaningful to you? Why? What other strategies can you add to this list?

6. Research reveals that a two-sided message with refutation is the best way to persuade. Do you think a one-sided message would ever be appropriate? If so, when?

7. Given our propensity to resist persuasive attempts, can you identify a situation in which an audience might actually welcome persuasion?

8. Speaker credibility plays an important role in successfully informing others (Chapter 8). What role do you think credibility plays in effectively influencing or persuading others?

9. Are there certain employers or supervisors that you might be more willing to comply with (or resist) than others? If so, what characteristics about those individuals do you think influence your decision to resist or comply?

10. How resistant to employer demands do you feel you are *in general*? Do you tend to comply, or are you more likely to resist? Why do you think so?

Chapter 10

Sensory Aids:
How Can I Better Engage My Audience?

(Continued on next page)

Chapter Learning Objectives

After completing this chapter, you should be able to

- Define sensory aids and determine their role in various business and professional speaking tasks.
- Evaluate whether to include particular sensory aids into your own presentations.
- Differentiate among the types of sensory aids available for your use.
- Identify the most effective ways to use presentational software, such as Power-Point, in your presentation.
- Identify and apply to your own presentations five guidelines for using sensory aids effectively.

What Are Some General Guidelines for Effectively Using Sensory Aids?

- Don't Overuse Sensory Aids
- Remove Sensory Aids from Sight When You No Longer Need Them
- Never Turn Your Back to Your Audience
- Thoroughly Rehearse with Your Sensory Aids
- Be Prepared for Technical Difficulties

Rob recently graduated with a business degree from a well-respected university. As an

honors student who had successfully completed not one, but two, internships with high-profile financial services firms during college, he had little difficulty securing his first job. His new work involved selling employee health, dental, and disability insurance packages to companies. With all the changes in the healthcare industry, Rob knew that he had his work cut out for him to educate and inform his prospective clients and, at the same time, persuade them that his company's services and products were superior to the competitors'.

Concerned with making highly technical information clear to his prospects, Rob prepared a sales presentation that was accompanied by PowerPoint slides. As he developed his presentation, which was full of material that was new even to him, he put much of the information he needed to communicate on his slides. He reasoned that if his listeners not only heard the information but saw it on the screen and on their handouts (he planned to distribute a copy of his slides), he'd maximize the chances that they would comprehend it and make an informed decision. In the end, Rob had thirty-three slides to accompany a presentation that was to last about twenty minutes.

With his presentation and visual aids developed, Rob set up four visits with prospective clients. His audiences were small groups of decision makers from each client. Each audience was a good prospect; they'd all indicated during screening that their benefits contracts were expiring soon and that they were dissatisfied with their current providers. In other words, Rob had a great chance of landing one or more of these four clients if he took the right approach and made an impression. He had an outstanding set of products and services to offer, and he was armed with all the information his prospects could possibly need or want.

So, imagine Rob's disappointment when none of these four presentations led to any sales. Rather than appearing engaged, his listeners seemed bored by his presentation. Their eyes appeared to glaze over at the thorough and detailed digital slides that he'd worked so hard to develop. He expected questions and interactivity at the conclusion of his presentation, but in all but one case, he just got a polite "Thank you; we'll get back to you."

Where did Rob go wrong? He followed many of the common guidelines for effective business speaking, and he had an important topic that was of interest to his listeners. But his first sales experiences ended in dismal disappointment, and his story provides some clues about why. Like many new (and veteran) professionals, Rob's major mistake revolved around his sensory support for his message. Rob had far too many slides for the length of his presentation, and he attempted to pile far too much detail onto each slide. In his effort to inform his audiences about fairly complex and detailed issues, he inadvertently committed what many call "death by PowerPoint." In other words, he bored his audiences with the excessive number of slides he presented and the heavy amount of text he included on each one.

Additionally, Rob's traditional training in public speaking didn't encourage him to think very far outside the box of visual aids. Graphs, tables, word charts, and yes, bullet points, have long been the standard supporting devices for typical presentations. But when we consider the kinds of visual, aural, and tactile stimuli that we are exposed to every day, the old-school forms of support that Rob used seem rather outdated, outmoded, and, well, *boring.*

Video, hyperlinks, interactive games, color, Flash animation, sound, pictures, and even virtual reality are part of our media- and technology-intensive daily experiences. These kinds of stimuli appeal to many of our senses and, research indicates, engage people of all learning styles, who then become better, more comprehensive listeners.[1] And these exciting new forms of support can be incorporated relatively easily into business presentations. So why should we continue to rely on traditional aids that tend to engage only our visual sense?

In this chapter, we will present the idea of using sensory aids in your business presentations. We will describe the kinds of sensory aids that work well in professional speaking, provide you with criteria for determining when an aid might be useful to your presentational goals, discuss guidelines for using presentational software and other display media effectively, and give you some strategies for evaluating your sensory aids. At the conclusion of this chapter, you will have a contemporary understanding of how to use supporting devices to better engage, inform, and persuade your business audiences—and avoid the costly mistakes that Rob made.

FIGURE 10.1
Digital slide created with presentation software, text only

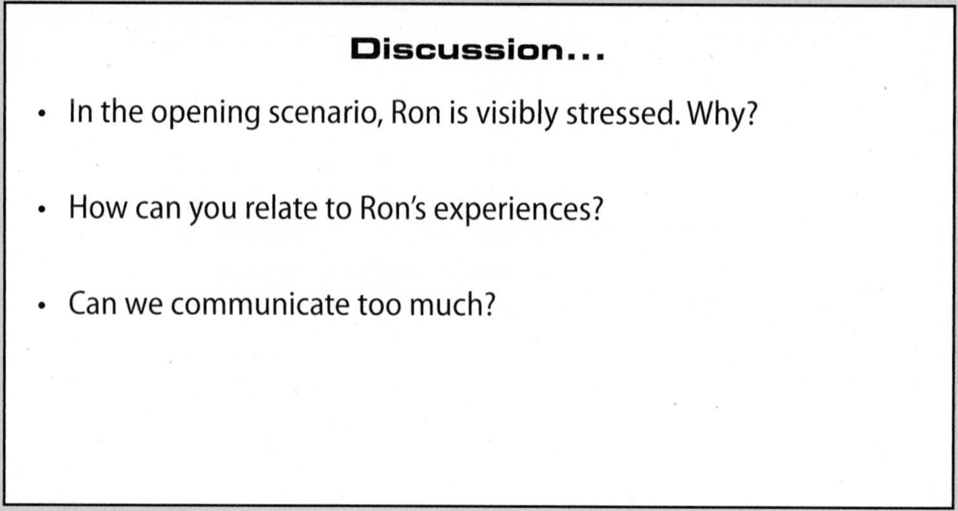

> ## Discussion...
>
> - In the opening scenario, Ron is visibly stressed. Why?
>
> - How can you relate to Ron's experiences?
>
> - Can we communicate too much?

© 2013 Cengage Learning

What Are Sensory Aids?

Traditionally, speakers were taught to support their speeches and presentations with *visual aids,* which are supplemental visible devices that speakers use to clarify their messages. For example, on a recent trip to Spain, one of your authors, Jennifer, found herself lost outside of Barcelona with a rental car. She found a helpful hotel employee whose English was understandable and who took the time to illustrate her message by drawing arrows on a map of the city. Not only did the map make the directions more comprehensible, but it also made the task of remembering the series of turns easier than if she had simply told Jennifer where to go. In other words, it's often much easier to understand and remember something when you *see* it in addition to *hearing* it.

Common visual aids include digital slides generated with software such as PowerPoint or Keynote, charts and graphs, tables, photographs, notes on a flip chart or a whiteboard, and handouts. Figures 10.1 through 10.4 and Table 10.1 provide examples of traditional visual aids. All these visual aids would be useful in a business presentation, but they appeal to only a one sense—sight.

Visual aids can serve the speaker and topic well when they enhance rather than distract from the speaker's message. But traditional forms of visual support require little of audience members other than to passively read and listen. Because contemporary business audiences are sophisticated and expect multisensory engagement, we need to expand our understanding of visual aids.

A new way of thinking about visual support is as sensory support. **Sensory aids** are supporting devices that appeal to one or more of the five senses (sight, hearing, touch, taste, or smell) and highlight or enhance the content of a presentation. Sensory aids

FIGURE 10.2
Pie graph

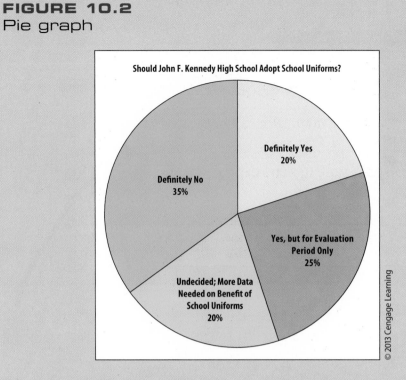

Should John F. Kennedy High School Adopt School Uniforms?

- Definitely Yes 20%
- Yes, but for Evaluation Period Only 25%
- Undecided; More Data Needed on Benefit of School Uniforms 20%
- Definitely No 35%

© 2013 Cengage Learning

FIGURE 10.3
Organizational chart

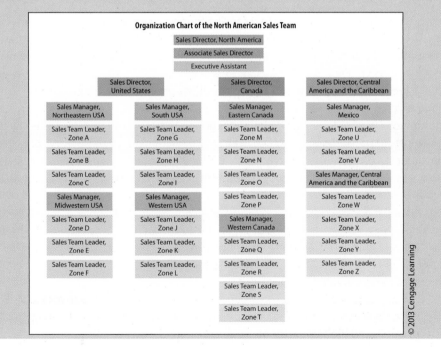

Organization Chart of the North American Sales Team

Sales Director, North America
Associate Sales Director
Executive Assistant

Sales Director, United States
Sales Director, Canada
Sales Director, Central America and the Caribbean

- Sales Manager, Northeastern USA
  - Sales Team Leader, Zone A
  - Sales Team Leader, Zone B
  - Sales Team Leader, Zone C
- Sales Manager, Midwestern USA
  - Sales Team Leader, Zone D
  - Sales Team Leader, Zone E
  - Sales Team Leader, Zone F

- Sales Manager, South USA
  - Sales Team Leader, Zone G
  - Sales Team Leader, Zone H
  - Sales Team Leader, Zone I
- Sales Manager, Western USA
  - Sales Team Leader, Zone J
  - Sales Team Leader, Zone K
  - Sales Team Leader, Zone L

- Sales Manager, Eastern Canada
  - Sales Team Leader, Zone M
  - Sales Team Leader, Zone N
  - Sales Team Leader, Zone O
  - Sales Team Leader, Zone P
- Sales Manager, Western Canada
  - Sales Team Leader, Zone Q
  - Sales Team Leader, Zone R
  - Sales Team Leader, Zone S
  - Sales Team Leader, Zone T

- Sales Manager, Mexico
  - Sales Team Leader, Zone U
  - Sales Team Leader, Zone V
- Sales Manager, Central America and the Caribbean
  - Sales Team Leader, Zone W
  - Sales Team Leader, Zone X
  - Sales Team Leader, Zone Y
  - Sales Team Leader, Zone Z

© 2013 Cengage Learning

FIGURE 10.4
Line graph

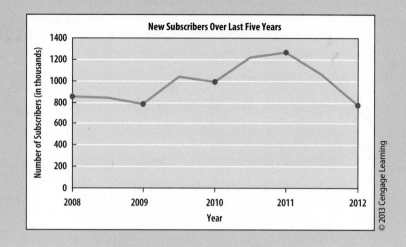

New Subscribers Over Last Five Years

© 2013 Cengage Learning

TABLE 10.1
Attitudes of Community Residents about School Uniforms

Region	Population	Favor	Against	Undecided
Northeast	35,000	45	50	5
Northwest	45,000	55	35	10
North Central	60,000	40	55	5
Central	55,000	35	50	15
South Central	50,000	40	55	5
East	20,000	40	55	5
Southeast	25,000	50	40	10
Southwest	30,000	50	40	10
West	25,000	55	35	10

© 2013 Cengage Learning

mimic the online environments that set the standards against which people evaluate other multisensory experiences. What are the characteristics of the most interesting, memorable, and fun online environments? Overall, they engage your senses, get you actively involved, and get you thinking. For example, they might:

- **Be interactive.** Sensory aids allow you to make choices about: what to explore and when. They may even enable you to customize your experience by filtering out unwanted information on future visits, designing an avatar to represent yourself, leaving feedback for site designers, or communicating with other users through comments and message boards.

- **Include sound, such as music or a voiceover.** People have become used to online experiences that "speak" to them in varied ways. For example, a hit song that relates to the site or an attractive or pleasant person speaking to you about the product or service featured on the site can make the visit compelling.

- **Use colorful and aesthetically pleasing graphics.** Useful online experiences have an appropriate, simple color scheme, quality photography, and meaningful, relevant animation or video that relates to your reason for being there.

It's not just our online activity that makes us crave sensory stimulation. Companies that develop trade show exhibits find that displays which encourage passers-by to actually pick up the product, try it, or physically do something relevant to the item or service being offered are highly effective at engaging prospective customers in crowded, competitive show environments.[2] Retailers have also discovered the power of engaging consumers' senses. For example, Anthropologie has designed its stores to create a sensory experience for visitors. Architect Ron Pompei, responsible for Anthropologie's layout, says,

> We do everything we can to ground the experience in tactile, visual, kinesthetic, sensual elements. From the materials we use to how the space is laid out. There are no aisles—you wander and chart your own course. You always have a sense of anticipation of what's 15 feet in front of you. Consciously or not, your senses are activated. That's fun. Not in the entertainment sense, but in the engaged sense. It's fun because it's stimulating. It's fun because you're seeing things and connections you've never seen before.[3]

Similarly, electronics retailers like Best Buy allow customers to try out cameras, phones, stereos, gaming equipment, and televisions to the point that just visiting one of their stores is a form of entertainment for many people.

In these examples, potential customers aren't simply listening to a sales associate. Rather, they are being given a multisensory, interactive experience designed to help them feel what owning the product would be like. These marketing strategies, deliberately designed to engage consumers' senses, encourage them to experience, through multiple senses, the feeling of owning or using the products and services being offered.[4] The lessons taught by successful retailers and marketing firms apply to business speaking, too—where the goal is to secure some form of commitment to and engagement with an idea, product, or service.

Sensory stimulation isn't just interesting and engaging—scholars believe that it may be changing the way we think, respond to, and process information.[5] Marc Prensky, a researcher interested in how people use technology in the classroom and at work, wrote that "people are not just using technology differently, they are approaching their lives and their daily activities differently because of the technology they use."[6] In other words, we

Visualize! Practice! 10.1:
Best & Worst Sensory Aids

spend so much of our time in a media-rich existence that offers dynamic, attractive, and on-demand content that we no longer have the tolerance for boring PowerPoint presentations that we once did.

Before you read on, take a minute to consider the characteristics of the best and the worst sensory aids you've seen in presentations and why audience members prefer interactive, media-rich presentations. Go to **VISUALIZE! PRACTICE! 10.1:** **Best & Worst Sensory Aids** and discuss it with your classmates.

How Do You Decide Whether to Use Sensory Aids?

It may be tempting to use sensory aids for every presentation you deliver. However, it's important to consider whether sensory aids will limit or enhance your effectiveness as a speaker.

Don't Use Sensory Aids That Limit Speaker Effectiveness
Sensory aids are unnecessary or detrimental when

- The message is simple enough to be understood without a supporting device.
- The sensory aid unnecessarily lengthens a presentation, or it distracts or irritates the audience.
- The sensory aid is used simply to boost the speaker's confidence or is used as a type of crutch.

Rob, whom you met in the introduction to this chapter, violated two of these principles. His sensory aids overwhelmed his audiences, distracting them from his message. In addition, he relied too heavily on his visual aids because he was intimidated by the technical nature of his content. He believed that using presentation software would make his content more digestible, but he didn't consider that sometimes less is more. His visual aids would have been more effective if he had used them only to highlight the most important parts of his message, not to repeat every tiny detail of his message. All in all, he lacked confidence in his own ability to deliver his message simply and without overpowering his audience.

Do Use Sensory Aids That Enhance Speaker Effectiveness
Sensory aids should be used for two primary reasons:

- **To engage the audience in what you have to say.** Often a visual aid, a video, an audio track, a demonstration, or some form of interactivity piques an audience's interest and encourages them to listen more carefully to what you have to say. Let's face it: Not all business topics are that interesting. Sometimes sensory support breaks the monotony of a business presentation.
- **To ensure the accuracy, comprehensiveness, and recall of your message.** Research indicates that people understand and remember information better when they see it in addition to hearing it.[7] This phenomenon is especially relevant when the content of a presentation is technical, detailed, and potentially difficult to recall.

Five Criteria Help You Decide When to Use Sensory Aids
Truly effective and worthwhile sensory aids are time consuming to create, test, and evaluate. They can also be expensive. Before investing your resources into the development of sensory support, ask yourself the following five questions. If you can answer yes to any one of them for a particular presentation, then a sensory aid is a good idea.

khz/Shutterstock.com

1. **Will one or more sensory aids clarify something critical to my presentation?**
   A sensory aid can highlight valuable information, helping audiences remember an important point.

   > **Example:** *Travis works for a major league baseball organization and is responsible for selling season ticket packages and box seats to the team's corporate sponsors. There are various levels of sponsorships, and naturally, the more a sponsor spends on a package, the more luxurious the seats and amenities are for games. As part of his presentation, Travis takes his potential sponsors to a luxury box and gives them the experience of sitting in soft leather seats with a prime view of the field. He could simply tell the sponsors about the perks of a luxury box, and he could show them a picture of a luxury box. However, he goes one step further and gives them a sensory experience, making him one of the team's most successful salespeople.*

2. **Will sensory aids make the presentation more interesting or engaging?**
   The right sensory aid can heighten your audience's interest by emphasizing a point that engages the senses in some striking way. Additionally, effective sensory aids can help you maintain an audience's interest for business presentations that don't have a wow factor, such as routine project updates, budget presentations, and staff briefings.

   > **Example:** *Rhianna works for a university, specializing in outreach to high school students. She makes hundreds of presentations a year at schools with historically low post-graduation college enrollments. In her presentations, she urges students to continue their education, and emphasizes the benefits of a college education. Students become most attentive when she talks about how much more money college graduates earn than people who don't attend college. So she has developed a large graph to visually illustrate the statistical differences in incomes earned by college graduates and non-college graduates. With this graph, she heightens her audience's interest and enthusiasm for what she has to say.*

Visualize! Practice! 10.2:
Sensory Support—Yes or No?

3. **Will sensory aids increase audience retention?** Sensory aids can increase an audience's retention of information by highlighting important points.

   Example: Suppose your boss, the director of Human Resources and Benefits, asked you to give a step-by-step presentation to department managers on what to do in case of an on-the-job injury. Workplace injuries don't happen every day, and when they do, they can cause a lot of emotion and confusion. As a result, the procedure for handling injuries is not easy for managers to remember. If you included a clear, high-quality flowchart highlighting each step in the process, you would increase your audience's recall of how to handle an emergency. If you then gave them a case study and asked them to actually go through the steps on the flowchart during training, you'd significantly improve their retention of this important process. In other words, the more senses you can involve in supporting your message, the better.

4. **Will sensory aids save time?** Some business presentations require a high level of detail. When this is the case, the right sensory aids can quickly convey information that would otherwise require a lengthy, elaborate discussion.

   Example: Mona trains servers at a restaurant with a very large menu. Servers are expected not only to memorize the menu but also to be prepared to answer diners' questions about preparation techniques and ingredients. Preparing new servers to handle the menu requires thorough explanations. To ensure her trainings are efficient and don't wear out her audience, Mona provides high-quality handouts with color photos of menu items and detailed information about each. She gives her trainees time to study the handouts and discuss them with one another. She then asks them to role-play common diner-server conversations about the menu.

5. **Will sensory aids help explain the topic?** The right sensory aid can enhance the organization of your presentation by logically delineating the points being covered.

   Example: Perhaps you need to explain how your company is organized internally. Displaying an organizational chart during your presentation would be an excellent way to help your audience understand. By revealing each part of the chart as you discuss it, you would introduce your listeners to the organization incrementally, giving them time to think about what you are saying and digest the information. This type of sensory aid can help you explain your topic and help your audience follow your logic.

If you'd like to practice determining when sensory support is warranted for a presentation, complete **VISUALIZE! PRACTICE! 10.2: Sensory Support—Yes or No?**

What Are Some Common Types of Sensory Aids?

The ways that speakers can support their ideas by engaging the audience's senses is nearly infinite. Technology offers a host of options that are limited only by your budget or access to the necessary hardware or software. Even when your access to technological resources is lacking, your imagination should give you numerous ways to engage your audience. Once you've decided to use sensory aids, your goal should be to develop aids that will enable your audience to interact with you and your topic by using multiple senses. In this section, we will discuss some of the common types of sensory aids.

Graphs Illustrate Ideas

A **graph** is a pictorial device used to illustrate quantitative relationships.[8] For example, a graph could illustrate the buying habits of your customers over a four-year period or the housing prices in several communities. Graphs can be produced in many different formats and can be two- or three-dimensional in design. Aided by a computer, you can animate graphs or reveal their parts incrementally during your presentation. Primarily a visual aid, graphs are versatile, powerful, and useful.

There are four primary types of graphs:

- The **line graph** is a diagram that shows the relationship between two quantitative concepts. It illustrates how one thing changes with respect to the other. For example, Rita used a line graph to illustrate how unemployment figures relate to her company's gross earnings (see Figure 10.5).

- A **fever graph** is a diagram that shows how the numeric value of something changes over time. For example, Sheila is speaking to a client who is concerned with her company's rising prices. When she investigated his claim that prices had been unfairly and substantially going up every year, she found that over ten years, there had been no price increase at all in some years, and in other years, the increases had been extremely slight. She decided to create a fever graph so that her client could see the very slight increases and even flat lines that characterize her company's prices over the past ten years (see Figure 10.6).

- A **bar graph** displays quantities or values of data in a series of bars that correspond in height or length to the quantities represented. Bar graphs are useful for showing differences in sets of data at one time or over a short period. For example, Brad, a national sales representative for an office supply company, created a bar graph to show his management team the amount of money his clients in each of the four major geographic regions of the country spent with their company in the past year (see Figure 10.7).

FIGURE 10.5
Line graph

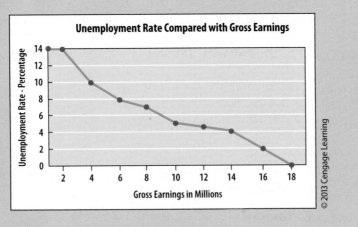

© 2013 Cengage Learning

FIGURE 10.6
Fever graph

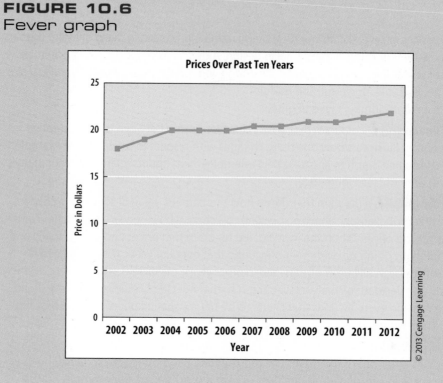

Prices Over Past Ten Years

Price in Dollars

25 — 20 — 15 — 10 — 5 — 0

2002 2003 2004 2005 2006 2007 2008 2009 2010 2011 2012

Year

© 2013 Cengage Learning

FIGURE 10.7
Bar graph

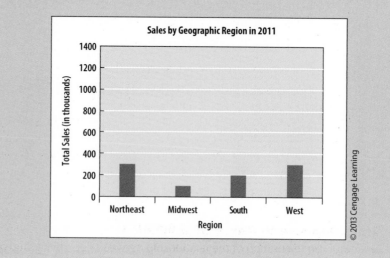

Sales by Geographic Region in 2011

Total Sales (in thousands)

1400 — 1200 — 1000 — 800 — 600 — 400 — 200 — 0

Northeast   Midwest   South   West

Region

© 2013 Cengage Learning

FIGURE 10.8
Pie graph

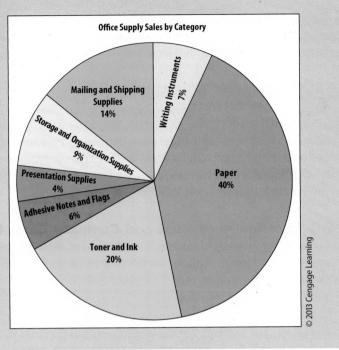

Office Supply Sales by Category

© 2013 Cengage Learning

Link Out 10.1:
Labeling Graphs Clearly
Link Out 10.2:
Images in Graphs
Link Out 10.3:
Diagrams and Proportion

- **Pie graphs** show the division of something into component parts—percentages or proportions of the whole. Pie graphs are presented in the form of a circle divided into wedges that are proportional in angle and area to the relative size of the quantities represented. Pie graphs are most useful for displaying information that can be divided into a small number of categories or parts; too many divisions make a pie graph difficult to read. Damon used a pie graph in his presentation to illustrate the major categories of office supplies that his customers purchased from his company this year (see Figure 10.8).

Although graphs are fairly simple devices, they can become complicated and difficult to understand when not developed carefully. Additionally, since most graphs are presented with presentation software, they sometimes fall victim to the bells and whistles offered by those packages. For example, speakers sometimes use too many colors or attempt to illustrate too many related variables in a graph. For some tips on how to create graphs that illustrate information in digital slides clearly and effectively, check out these podcasts by author and instructor Dave Paradi: **LINK OUT 10.1: Labeling Graphs Clearly**, **LINK OUT 10.2: Images in Graphs**, and **LINK OUT 10.3: Diagrams and Proportion**. These videos show how Dave performed makeovers on awkward graphs.

Charts Help Represent Parts of a Whole

A **chart** is a pictorial representation of the relationship between parts of a group or an object or of the sequence of steps in a process. Many charts take the form of a series of

Link Out 10.4:
*Presenting
Organizational Charts*

Link Out 10.5:
Basics of Flowcharts

Link Out 10.6:
Create a Flowchart

boxes connected by lines or arrows. An **organizational chart**, for example, is an effective way to illustrate the internal organization of a company and is used in many types of business presentations. Go to **LINK OUT 10.4:** **Presenting Organizational Charts** to see a short video that illustrates an effective way to create and present an organizational chart with PowerPoint.

Another effective type of chart is a **flowchart**, which illustrates the steps of a process with various types of boxes that are connected by arrows. This representation can give a step-by-step path to making decisions, solving problems, or taking specific actions. Flowcharts are used in various industries for analyzing, designing, documenting, or managing processes. For a brief introduction to flowcharts and the types of symbols commonly used in them, watch **LINK OUT 10.5:** **Basics of Flowcharts**. And for a brief video that illustrates how to create a flowchart in Microsoft, go to **LINK OUT 10.6:** **Create a Flowchart**.

Tables Help Your Audience View and Compare Data

A **table** is an orderly arrangement of numbers, words, or symbols in rows and columns. A tabular arrangement of information allows for the easy viewing and comparison of large numbers of similar facts. Like graphs, tables are often used to display statistics, but tables use an arrangement of columns and rows rather than a graphic format.

A word of caution about tables: They are very difficult to display properly with PowerPoint and other presentation software because these formats don't allow the speaker to create a large enough table. Slides with a table often look too crowded and cluttered, and they are difficult or impossible to read. Tables are better suited for handouts, or they can be printed in large format, dry mounted, and displayed on an easel. Your organization's art department or any professional printer or copy-services store can help you produce this type of display. Table 10.2 is an example of a table created by a speaker who is advocating zoning limitations on commercial development.

TABLE 10.2
Attitudes of Community Residents about Commercial Zoning

Attitudes	Percentage of females who agree strongly with this statement	Percentage of males who agree strongly with this statement
There is already too much commercial development going on in our community.	57%	41%
Commercial development is bad for small, locally owned businesses.	83%	70%
Commercial development results in traffic problems.	71%	74%
City council should have the right to inspect and approve commercial development plans.	54%	41%

© 2013 Cengage Learning

lev radin/Shutterstock.com

Link Out 10.7:
Sample Flash

Link Out 10.8:
Integrate Flash into PowerPoint

Link Out 10.9:
Integrate Flash into PowerPoint, 2007 Update

Link Out 10.10:
Animation Tutorials

A more sophisticated animated sensory aid involves using a program such as Macromedia Flash. Flash enables you to create relatively small files that can pack a sensory punch. These animations can help bring a still image to life or can help your audience visualize a process by demonstrating something step by step and revealing the steps one at a time. Flash also allows you to integrate video files seamlessly into your presentation without linking to the Internet. In this way, you don't have to leave the PowerPoint environment, wait for the Internet to open, and expose your audience to the unrelated visual clutter of a video hosting site. To see an example of how animation artist Jinho Kang used Flash animation to create a dynamic business card, watch **LINK OUT 10.7: Sample Flash**.

The process for incorporating Flash animation files into a PowerPoint presentation is relatively simple and straightforward. Web designer and marketing communication expert Patrice-Anne Rutledge shows you how at **LINK OUT 10.8: Integrate Flash into Power-Point**. And blogger Wendy Russell updates these instructions for PowerPoint 2007 users at **LINK OUT 10.9: Integrate Flash into PowerPoint, 2007 Update**. If you already have basic animation skills, you may find the tutorials at **LINK OUT 10.10: Animation Tutorials** useful.

Video Illustrates Points and Entertains Your Audience

With the widespread availability of low-cost, user-friendly video cameras and the popularity of video sites like YouTube and Hulu, video has become a popular way to add interest to presentations and clarify content. Video gives you the opportunity to demonstrate action or performance; share the input, ideas, opinions, or expertise of people not in attendance at your presentation; or demonstrate a point from the presentation. For example, George integrated video into his training presentation on job safety for landscape professionals. His video demonstrated proper lifting techniques. Claire, who is in marketing for a liquor and spirits distributor, showed a brief video interview with a vintner responsible for one of her top-selling lines. In his training workshop on effective workplace communication techniques, Mike showed a short clip from the hit show *The Office* to demonstrate what *not* to do when communicating with co-workers.

However, video can easily detract from your message if it is not of professional quality. Important considerations are segment length (amateur video tends to run too long and lack the logical focus of professionally produced video), narration and background music that provides continuity (rather than long, empty, silent transitions), jerky footage, and amateur transitions between shots. An unprofessional, unrelated, or inappropriate video can damage your credibility and make audience members uncomfortable.

Sounds Distinguish Your Presentation

Incorporating audio into your presentation can be a way to stimulate interest, and as business communication blogger Seth Godin wrote, it can "remind your audience that this isn't just any presentation you're running."[10] You can reinforce and clarify your points with music or a sound byte that is relevant, appropriate, and not too loud or distracting. However, don't overuse sound. A general rule is to use no more than two or three sounds or audio clips in a 15- to 20-minute presentation.

Sound can be integrated easily into a PowerPoint file. However, experts advise against using PowerPoint's preloaded sounds. Chances are, your audience has heard these canned noises many times before, so they won't have impact. And those preloaded sounds are not likely to be relevant to your presentation topic. A quick Google search for "presentation sound effects" will take you to many sites offering royalty-free MP3 files, and you just might find one that will work well in your presentation. For advice on embedding mp3 files into a PowerPoint file, go to **LINK OUT 10.11: Integrating MP3 Files into PowerPoint.** **LINK OUT 10.12: MP3 Files as Transition Sounds** offers the steps for using your own mp3 files as transition sounds between slides. **LINK OUT 10.13: Adding Sounds to PowerPoint** addresses a few more audio file types, including .wav and .wma.

Link Out 10.11:
Integrating MP3 Files into PowerPoint

Link Out 10.12:
MP3 Files as Transition Sounds

Link Out 10.13:
Adding Sounds to PowerPoint

Putting Your Skills to Work

If you've ever spent time on YouTube—even just to find that guy talking to his dog about the great food he's missing out on—you've probably run across instructional videos. You may even have created an instructional video yourself, such as one of you teaching others how to play a song on the guitar or how to make jewelry. You can use your skills to search for and create video in the workplace too. Good video is often a useful and welcome sensory aid in business presentations. Just be sure the video you use is appropriate for your audience and is of professional quality.

A-Digit/istockphoto.com

Clickers and Social Networking Get Your Audience Involved

Your instructors may already be using clickers, or **audience response systems**, to encourage student participation and engagement. This technology not only helps a presenter build a visual display of information collected from audience members, but it also provides the speaker with a way to get audience members involved, engaged, and interactive with the topic and one another. Audience response systems have become popular sensory aids for presentations in business and the professions, as well. Research indicates that the use of clickers promotes critical thinking, retention, and audience participation.[11]

If an audience response system isn't available to you, social networking applications may offer an alternative. Meeting and conference experts have written extensively about the use of Twitter and Facebook for getting participants engaged. For example, at one meeting discussed in a blog,[12] the speaker not only displayed digital slides on one screen, but he also projected a live Twitter feed onto another screen. The speaker had created a specialized tag for the meeting on Twitter, and the people sitting in the audience had a running dialogue about the presenter's content. In real time, the audience members were giving the speaker feedback, submitting questions, and requiring the speaker to address their comments. In this way, the audience was not only involved but even served as a type of moderator. Of course, you need to have extensive experience facilitating discussions and thinking on your feet before you allow your audience this type of control. And you will need to become comfortable speaking in front of groups of people who are simultaneously tweeting and listening.

Interactive Engagement Creates a Multisensory Experience

The final category of sensory aids is one that utilizes sophisticated technology to enable your audience to visualize or experience your topic. These forms of sensory support are growing in importance as business presenters are doing fewer in-person presentations and relying instead on podcasts, conference calls, and webinars to train, sell, and connect. There are two primary types of interactive engagement: virtual reality and digital visualization.

Virtual reality (VR) involves computer-generated environments that can simulate places or activities in the real world. These sophisticated forms of sensory support can be visual (displayed on a computer screen), audio (provided through headphones or speakers), and even tactile. For example, high-tech virtual reality has been used in sales presentations for medical devices, giving audience members the sensory experience of seeing, hearing, and feeling what it is like to use the device on a patient. Amazing, isn't it? Virtual reality has been used extensively in training contexts as well, including medical, emergency preparedness, military, and technology training.

Even if you or your organization doesn't have access to expensive and sophisticated VR-creation software, you can use a free site like Second Life to create a virtual environment that simulates a real one. For example, the New Media Consortium has created a virtual learning community in Second Life, and individual presenters can use the community to deploy simulations of specific communication behavior and activities. Other companies and institutions of higher education use Second Life in their training and development activities to help participants visualize spatial layout and flow, make connections among people and business units, and even develop virtual relationships with others that may lead to productive real-time connections. Whatever

Link Out 10.14:
Wii & Second Life Training Simulator

Link Out 10.15:
Improving Meetings through Visualization

Link Out 10.16:
Sample Visual Digitalization

platform you are able to use, if it is used effectively, virtual reality is a way to engage people's senses so that they may better understand behaviors, activities, and processes important to their professional development. To read a *Wired* article on how VR and Second Life can engage the "Wii Generation," check out **LINK OUT 10.14: Wii & Second Life Training Simulator**.

A second type of technology-aided interactive engagement is **digital visualization**. Digital visualization software, such as Let's Focus,[13] enables presenters, moderators, trainers, and facilitators to visually depict and document the knowledge, ideas, and contributions of individual session participants. For more on the uses of digital visualization software in business, go to **LINK OUT 10.15: Improving Meetings through Visualization**. In this fascinating video, Dr. Martin Eppler, a leading researcher from Switzerland, describes how visualization can be used in meetings and training. As you watch, think about applications for visualization in other business speaking situations. If you'd like to learn more about how digital visualization can work in a business setting, go to **LINK OUT 10.16: Sample Visual Digitalization** to see a product demonstration of software that uses visual tools to help illustrate workplace information.

What Do You Need to Know about Presentation Software?

The first thing you need to know about presentation software is that most people (your textbook authors included) use it totally wrong. Instead of enhancing a speaker's message and engaging the audience, presentation software used incorrectly makes a speech

sellingpix/Shutterstock.com

boring, monotonous, predictable, and longer than it needs to be. What are some common mistakes that business speakers make when using digital slides?

- Speakers puts their entire message in the slideshow.
- The content of the slides is disorganized and does not flow logically.
- Individual slides focus on more than one idea.
- Slides contain too much text and lack other forms of visual or sensory stimulation.
- Slide content is in a typeface that is too small for audience members to read.
- Slides contain grammatical and spelling errors.
- Slides are cluttered with competing colors, fonts, and not-very-special effects.
- Speakers use presentation software just because it exists or because everybody else uses it. Sometimes, an experienced and skilled speaker can be more effective and influential *without* using digital slides.

To watch an amusing video that captures many of the mistakes PowerPoint users make, go to **LINK OUT 10.17: PowerPoint—What Not to Do!** How many of these mistakes have you seen in presentations? How many have you made? Although the video is meant to by funny, it conveys more truth than fiction. Your authors have collectively spent thousands of hours in meetings and workshops plagued by all of the problems captured in this short clip. Our goal is to get you, the new professional, out of the death-by-PowerPoint trap that we and so many of our colleagues have fallen into.

Although a Google search for "disadvantages of PowerPoint" turns up far more results than a search for "advantages of PowerPoint," there are several advantages to using presentation software. If there weren't, people wouldn't use it so much! Let's take a look at some of these advantages.

The Advantages of Using Presentation Software

Interestingly, research indicates that some of the primary benefits of using presentation software may occur even before you deliver a presentation—using the software effectively can help you design and package a more logical story than if you were to simply write notes on cards or a legal pad.[14] When you use the product effectively, presentation software has the functionality to allow you to do a number of things well:

- Remain organized and focused on a central set of key ideas in both the creation and delivery of your presentation.
- Create clean, professional charts, graphs, and tables easily.
- Organize a set of speaker's notes for yourself.
- Display a sensory experience for your audience that can include smooth transitions between slides, animations, and timed reveals of important points.
- Save, update, reuse, and edit material as needed for different audiences. PowerPoint files are portable and load easily on any computer that has the software. (Keynote files open only on Apple computers, so before using a non-Microsoft program, be sure to find out what type of computer is available for your presentation if you don't plan to bring your own).

Link Out 10.17:
PowerPoint—What Not to Do!

Link Out 10.18:
Using the Slide Sorter View

- Launch the presentation file along with audio of your presentation on a website for live streaming or later access by people who did not attend your presentation.

If you understand what presentation software can do well, you will avoid falling into the trap of allowing your slideshows to control your presentations.

Steps for Creating Effective Digital Slides

Let's take a look at some guidelines for creating digital slides that will enable you to take back your power from computer software and dazzle your audiences for all the right reasons.

1. **Prepare your presentation outline first.** Focus on the content of your speech before you select any design elements for your slides. Begin by creating an outline that organizes the introduction, main points, and conclusion of your speech (Chapter 7, Module 8). Just use a simple sheet of paper or a Word document to prepare your outline, and then work from the outline to build your slides.

2. **Create a headline for each slide.** Determine what the headline of each of your slides should be, and create a slide for each headline.

   - **Headlines should correspond to your main points.** However, you do not necessarily need a slide and headline for every main point and subpoint. Be selective and consider which of your points would be best highlighted with a slide.

   - **Headlines should take the form of a complete sentence or a question.** Listeners cognitively process complete sentence headlines more quickly and accurately than they do short phrases. Alternatively, pose a question in a headline that you will answer during your presentation.

     Examples:
     - ✔ The best slide headlines are complete sentences.
     - ✔ How can I dazzle my audience with better PowerPoint?

   - **Headlines should be brief and simple.** Avoid overly complex headlines. Each headline and slide should present a single idea.
     - ✔ *Poor:* U.S. jobs are moving overseas, and local economies are suffering.
     - ✔ *Better, Slide A:* U.S. jobs are moving overseas.
     - ✔ *Better, Slide B:* Many local U.S. economies are suffering as a result of job outsourcing.

3. **Create a storyboard from your outline.** Originally used by filmmakers for visualizing the flow of motion picture or animation scenes, a storyboard is a series of visual images designed to help develop and spot flaws in the flow of a presentation.

   - **Use PowerPoint's Slide Sorter feature to periodically evaluate the logical flow of your ideas.** Working from the View menu and switching from the Normal view to the Slide Sorter view enables you to see how the ideas in your headlines relate to one another (See Figure 10.9). From this view, you can move slides and delete them. To continue editing a slide, simply double click on any slide to return to the Normal view. For a short demonstration of how to use Slide Sorter and its usefulness in organizing a presentation, watch **LINK OUT 10.18: Using the Slide Sorter View**.

   - **Evaluate whether your series of headlines, tells a cohesive story.**

FIGURE 10.9
PowerPoint's slide sorter view

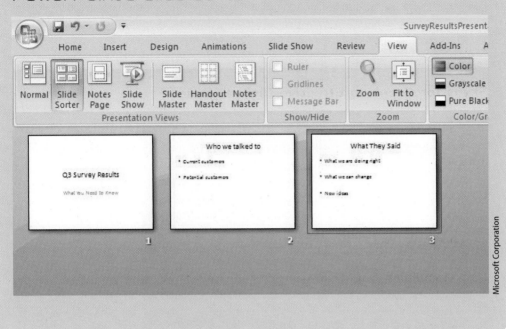

Microsoft Corporation

4. **Once your headlines are in place, develop the content for each slide.** Remember that bullet points, lists, and other text are not the only way to present information on a digital slide. Would a picture or image work well? How about a video? A simple quote or a statistic?

   - **Your slides should *not* tell your entire story.** *You* are telling your story, and your slides are supporting it. Think of each slide as an opportunity to *enhance* a particular point in your presentation, not convey it.

   - **A slide should *never* contain everything you need to communicate about its headline.** That's your job—otherwise, you could prepare a written report and hand it out to your audience to read themselves. Sometimes, a headline alone is a sufficiently engaging supporting aid for what you have to say about a particular point. Some experts even advise that you include no more than six words on a single slide![15]

Guidelines for Formatting Digital Slides
Once you settle on the basic content for each of your slides, you're ready to format them. There are several guidelines you can follow that will help you create slides that are easy to read and pleasant to look at.

Slides Should Have Plenty of White (Unfilled) Space Don't feel compelled to fill every empty space with graphics, logos, or worse yet—more text. Allow plenty of space around text and images so that your content is easy to see and read.

Limit Your Use of Animations Use only the most subtle and professional slide transitions and text reveals, similar to what you might see on the evening news. A simple

FIGURE 10.10
Which slide reflects a better choice of artwork? Why?

"wipe left-to-right" (from the Animations menu) is good for a bullet point, but a "move" or "fly" is too slow and distracting. Your audience will get bored or even annoyed if you use too many animations. When selecting transitions between slides, use no more than two types of transition effects, and do not provide transition effects after every slide.

Use High-Quality Graphics   Avoid cartoonish clip art and most preloaded clip art. Your audience has seen anything preloaded in the software package far too many times to have impact (see Figure 10.10).

FIGURE 10.11
Preloaded PowerPoint template

Link Out 10.19:
PowerPoint Templates

Link Out 10.20:
Creating PowerPoint Templates

Use a Visual Theme for Your File, But Avoid Preloaded Templates How many times have you seen the slide template in Figure 10.11? Chances are, quite a few. And your business audience will have seen it even more frequently. As a result, its impact will be very limited.

Your audience expects a unique presentation, and anything that suggests they are being fed a cookie-cutter speech will be off-putting. Check to see if your organization has a library of proprietary or custom slide templates. Or better yet, if your company employs a graphic designer, find out if he or she can help you develop a customized template for to your specific presentation and audience. If these resources aren't available, consider one of the many online sources of PowerPoint templates that haven't been overused. Some are even available free of charge. Most are a better choice than preloaded templates. You can find one good resource of templates at **LINK OUT 10.19: PowerPoint Templates**. You can also create your own templates—check out **LINK OUT 10.20: Creating PowerPoint Templates** for clear instructions.

As always, be careful that your finished product is polished and professional, not amateurish and sloppy. If in doubt, rely on a professionally created background template.

Be Selective in Your Use of Fonts Use no more than two complementary fonts (such as Arial and Arial Bold). In addition, use only very basic fonts, and avoid fonts that are difficult to read (such as Mistral or Brush Script). Generally, use sans-serif fonts (Helvetica, Arial) rather than serif fonts (Times New Roman, Bookman). Serif fonts have little lines stemming from the ends of the strokes of letters. These fonts were designed to be used in documents with a lot of text because they are easier to read in small sizes. But for on-screen presentations, the serifs tend to get lost due to the relatively low resolution of projectors. Sans-serif fonts are generally best for PowerPoint presentations. Regardless of what font you choose, make sure the text is large enough to be read from the back of the room.

Link Out 10.21:
Learning from the Design around You

Link Out 10.22:
PowerPoint Community

A serif font
A serif font
Times plain and bold

A sans serif font
A sans serif font
Arial plain and bold

Think Outside the Box When Creating Your Layout Don't feel confined to the predesigned boxes and frames provided in most slide templates. For example, you don't have to put every headline at the top of the slide. And you don't have to frame every slide with margins. In fact, some research suggests that allowing text or images to run right to the visible edge of the slide (or "bleed") can have meaningful impact. PowerPoint expert Garr Reynolds noted that working outside of predefined frames can make images seem larger, "while at the same time leaving more empty space on the canvas, giving more clarity to the overall visual and plenty of breathing room for another element."[16]

For more on this idea and other ways to achieve sensory impact using PowerPoint, check out **LINK OUT 10.21: Learning from the Design around You**. This page from Reynolds's blog, "Presentation Zen," demonstrates that your best resource for design tips and strategies is not necessarily a book like this one. Examples of good design are everywhere, and it's quite possible that you can find creative and innovative ways to design your PowerPoint slides in your everyday environment. You might also consider joining an online networking community of PowerPoint users, like the one at **LINK OUT 10.22: PowerPoint Community**. (You will need a LinkedIn account to join this community.) Their discussions and ideas about how to use PowerPoint effectively are useful and thought-provoking.

Now that you have a good sense of what a good digital slide should look like, see Figures 10.12 and 10.13 for examples of ineffective and effective formats.

What Are Some General Guidelines for Effectively Using Sensory Aids?

Even when speakers elect to use sensory aids for the right reasons and design them carefully, the aids lose their impact if speakers don't use them properly during a presentation. Here are some final words of advice for using sensory aids, regardless of type.

Don't Overuse Sensory Aids
Remember that the primary objectives of sensory aids are to clarify, add interest, increase information retention, save time, and help explain the topic more effectively. You will not accomplish these goals if you have so many sensory aids that your audience spends more time attending to them than they do to you and your presentation.

Remove Sensory Aids from Sight When You No Longer Need Them
Present each sensory aid at the appropriate time. When its usefulness is over, remove it. When your listeners linger over an object, look at a digital slide, or play around with a clicker, they are spending less of their energy paying attention to you and your message.

Never Turn Your Back to Your Audience
As communication instructors, one of our most common complaints is students who talk to the projection screen at the front of the room instead of the people sitting in the room

FIGURE 10.12

This slide is an example of an ineffective but common use of presentation software. The slide has a vague headline, far too much text, and a graphic image that bears no relationship to the headline.

Gender Equality in Japan

•According to the latest reports from the Japanese Ministry of Labor, 72% of part-time workers in Japan are women. This is the highest rate reported yet. The number of part-time workers has been increasing for years. For many women, full-time employment is not available, or their family obligations make it impossible for them to keep fulltime hours. Below are some comments from some prominent politicians:

"Japanese work office environment is not yet conducive for promoting gender equality."
Shoji Nishimoto
UNDP

"The conservatives... want to keep Japanese society traditional."
Keiko Higuchi
Tokyo Kasei University

John T Takai/Shutterstock.com

FIGURE 10.13

This slide is a good example of how presentation software can highlight and illuminate a critical point. Note that the speaker chose a relevant graphic image, a simple background, and made a straightforward statement by relying on the slide's headline to carry the point. The speaker, then, did the rest.

72% of part-time workers in Japan are women

Phil Date/Shutterstock.com

during a presentation. First of all, you should never, ever read from a digital slide (or from notes in front of you, for that matter)! Second, regardless of the type of sensory aid you are using, you should maintain eye contact with your audience at all times. Do not allow yourself to be distracted by your aids.

Thoroughly Rehearse with Your Sensory Aids

Practicing how you will introduce and handle your sensory aids is very important. Even the best-researched presentation and the highest-quality sensory aids will be wasted if you do not spend time rehearsing how you will introduce, explain, and remove your sensory aids during your presentation. Be sure to time when you present your aids so that you can introduce them without awkward pauses or fidgeting. In addition, working out your timing will help ensure that you don't run out of time to use all your aids. Take care to ensure that you are comfortable with the specific equipment you will be using to project or display your sensory aids. Recognize that the computer or the projector in the room where you plan to give your presentation may differ from the one you're accustomed to using.

Be Prepared for Technical Difficulties

Always bring a copy of your aids on a flash drive, in case the computer you plan to use malfunctions. As an additional emergency preparedness measure, bring color transparencies of your slides. In the worst-case scenario, be prepared to deliver your presentation without any sensory aids. If you've implemented the strategies we've shared in the last four chapters of this book, you will be ready to engage and excite your audience regardless of what technology is available.

However you tell your story and whatever sensory devices you select to enhance and clarify that story for your audience, your goal should remain the same. Your style and your approach as well as the sensory support you use should help build your audience's affinity for you and your message. When that happens, you increase the chances of securing your audience's commitment to the ideas, concepts, products, or services you are advocating—a hugely successful business communication outcome.

Use your Speech Communication CourseMate for *Business & Communication in a Digital Age* for quick access to the electronic resources that accompany this text. These resources include

Study tools that help you assess your learning and prepare for exams (*digital glossary, key term flash cards, review quizzes*).

Activities and assignments that help you hone your knowledge and build your communication skills throughout the course (*Visualize! Practice!, Weigh In!, Check This Out, and Link Out activities; modules; review questions*).

Media resources that help you explore communication concepts online (*Enhanced eBook*), develop your speech outlines (*Speech Builder Express 3.0*), watch and critique videos of sample speeches and communication situations (*interactive video activities*), upload your speech videos for peer reviewing and critique other students' speeches (*Speech Studio online speech review tool*), and download chapter review so you can study when and where you'd like (*Audio Study Tools*).

Key Points

- In the past, visual aids were the gold standard for business presentations, but contemporary business audiences demand an expanded repertoire of sounds, images, objects, and experiences that appeal to multiple senses.

- A new way of thinking of visual support is as sensory support. Sensory aids are supporting devices that appeal to one or more of the five senses and highlight or enhance the content of a presentation.

- Used improperly, sensory aids can limit speaker effectiveness. Answering five questions about your presentation can help you decide when it would be helpful to use sensory aids:
  - ✔ Will one or more sensory aids clarify something critical to my presentation?
  - ✔ Will sensory aids make the presentation more interesting or engaging?
  - ✔ Will sensory aids increase audience retention?
  - ✔ Will sensory aids save time?
  - ✔ Will sensory aids help explain the topic?

- There are several types of sensory aids commonly used in business presentations:
  - ✔ Graphs illustrate ideas.
  - ✔ Charts help represent parts of a whole.
  - ✔ Tables help your audience view and compare data.
  - ✔ Visual representations heighten audience comprehension.
  - ✔ Digital slides help focus and interest your audience.
  - ✔ Physical representations take visual aids a step further.
  - ✔ Animated images depict processes and steps.
  - ✔ Video illustrates points and entertains your audience.
  - ✔ Sounds distinguish your presentation.
  - ✔ Clickers and social networking get your audience involved.
  - ✔ Interactive engagement creates a multisensory experience.

- As presentation software like PowerPoint and Keynote have become more widely used, they've become more widely abused. But there are steps you can take to create effective digital slides:
  1. Start by preparing your presentation outline so that you can organize the introduction, main points, and conclusion of your speech.
  2. Create brief, simple headlines for your slides that correspond with your main points.
  3. Create a storyboard from your outline to evaluate the flow of your ideas and to determine whether your story is cohesive.
  4. Once your headlines are in place, develop the content for each slide, making sure that your slideshow doesn't simply repeat everything in your presentation.

- Several guidelines help you format slides that are easy to read and pleasant to look at.
  - ✔ Allow plenty of white (unfilled) space.
  - ✔ Limit your use of animations.

✔ Use high-quality graphics.

✔ Use a visual theme for your file, but avoid preloaded templates.

✔ Use sans-serif fonts that are easy to read and see from a distance.

✔ Think outside the box when creating your layout.

- There are several guidelines speakers can follow to use sensory aids properly for maximum impact:

    ✔ Don't overuse sensory aids. Use them only to enhance your presentation by high-lighting and clarifying important points, adding interest, and increasing information retention, and the like.

    ✔ Remove sensory aids from sight when you no longer need them.

    ✔ Never turn your back to your audience; always maintain eye contact. Don't read your speech from your sensory aids.

    ✔ Thoroughly rehearse with your sensory aids.

    ✔ Be prepared for technical difficulties.

Key Terms

audience response system (231)

bar graph (223)

chart (225)

digital visualization (232)

fever graph (223)

flowchart (226)

graph (222)

line graph (223)

model (228)

organizational chart (226)

pie graph (225)

sensory aids (216)

table (226)

virtual reality (231)

Questions for Critical Thinking and Review

1. Select one of your presentation assignments in this course. Given the topic that you've either chosen or been assigned, do you believe that sensory aids would be a good choice for enhancing your talk? Why or why not?

2. Sometimes people learn better and remember more when they are able to see an idea in addition to hearing about it. What are some examples of topics that are well-suited for visual aids like charts, graphs, and tables? Explain your response.

3. Why do you think it is important for business communicators to think beyond visual aids to the more comprehensive idea of sensory aids? Why do contemporary business audiences expect multisensory, as opposed to only visual, support?

4. This chapter has alerted you to current trends about using social networking, virtual reality, and visualization to involve audiences during presentations. In the past, public speaking instructors always cautioned speakers not to give their audiences anything to do that might distract them from listening. These new forms of sensory support seem to contradict that advice. Are contemporary audiences better at

multitasking (such as tweeting and listening to a presentation at the same time) than audiences of the past? Explain your answer.

5. Do some basic web research on the topic "resolving conflict in the workplace." Based on your research, outline a 5- to 7-minute presentation and create the headlines that you would use on digital slides. Be sure to follow the guidelines for using presentation software discussed in this chapter. Why did you make the choices that you did in developing this outline and the corresponding headlines? How easy or difficult was the process of sticking to the guidelines?

6. A common problem associated with presentation software is including too many ideas in a single presentation and ending up with a file of disjointed slides that have no logical structure binding them together. Why do you think so many speakers have trouble staying focused and organized when developing a PowerPoint presentation? How might using the Slide Sorter view, as recommended in this chapter, alleviate this problem? What other strategies might you employ in order to stay focused on a core set of central ideas?

7. Are there certain audience characteristics that should prevent you from using some forms of sensory support? For example, what audience characteristics would lead you to avoid incorporating interactive engagement, or perhaps digital slides? Explain.

8. What are your biggest pet peeves about how people use sensory aids during a presentation? For example, perhaps you get annoyed when speakers attempt to show video but don't have the clip cued to the right spot. How do these particular actions affect your overall evaluation of the speakers who commit them?

9. Given what you have studied and discussed in this course so far about contemporary business communication, summarize your own list of the "Top Five Issues to Keep in Mind as You Develop Sensory Support." Why did you select those five issues? Explain.

10. Overall, why is sensory support important for business presentations? We're all adults—shouldn't we be able to simply listen to a speaker? Why do we need to be entertained and spoon fed important points? Explain your answers.

Chapter 11

Making Meetings Matter:
How Can I Do That?

Chapter Outline

When Do Meetings Matter?
- Why a Meeting?
- Why Not a Meeting?

How Should You Plan a Meeting?
- Identify Your Objectives
- Choose the Participants
- Set an Agenda
- Schedule the Meeting
- Send a Reminder
- Prepare to Take Minutes
- Arrange for Catering and AV Equipment

How Should You Conduct the Meeting?
- Begin the Meeting
- Conduct the Meeting
- Conclude the Meeting

How Should You Follow Up after the Meeting?
- Provide the Minutes
- Monitor Progress
- Evaluate Outcomes
- Prepare the Next Agenda

What Are the Responsibilities of Participants?

Yuri Arcurs/Shutterstock.com

Chapter Learning Objectives

After completing this module, you should be able to

- Appreciate what meetings can and cannot do for an organization.
- Determine when and why a meeting might be inappropriate.
- Plan a meeting.
- Conduct a meeting.
- Follow up after a meeting.
- Appreciate participants' roles and responsibilities.

See also the modules that are relevant to this chapter:

4: **What Do I Need to Know about Business Etiquette?**
10: **What Parliamentary Procedures Do I Really Need to Know?**

Module 4:
*What Do I Need to
Know about Business
Etiquette?*

Module 10:
*What Parliamentary
Procedures Do I Really
Need to Know?*

Joanne works for an Internet-based sportswear and athletic company, a much smaller version of Nike.
She manages a department of designers responsible for creating athletic shoes to compete with Nike's customized fit-and-feel running shoe. Her most immediate task is to call a creative product development meeting to begin to discuss product innovation that offers her company a creative advantage.

Where and how to begin? Important to her success is bringing together the right group of people. Whoever she brings to the meeting will have a powerful impact on what happens in the meeting. Each individual brings different resources, ideas, biases, attitudes, and agendas. For instance, she knows that her team is creative and resourceful, but she also recognizes their idiosyncrasies, which influence how they interact with each other. For instance, Edie is opinionated and forceful, Daniel is ambitious and aggressive, Praveen can be intense and annoying, and Darlene becomes easily distracted. Because Joanne wants the energy of the meeting to be constructive and contagious, she must be selective about who should (and should not) attend this first meeting.

Once she decides who to include, she begins to plan her agenda. She needs to identify what she wants to accomplish in the meeting and how she will lead the group there. One of the things Joanne has learned about meetings is that work rarely gets done during the meeting itself. More often, meetings create work for participants to do afterward. How can she use this meeting to her advantage? What should happen during the meeting that will help participants move toward her goal of product innovation? Joanne quickly determines that a single meeting cannot accomplish her overriding goal. She sits down and writes out a series of developmental milestones that the team can meet about and manage over time.

Joanne decides to give her participants some "homework" to do before the initial meeting to get them up to speed and to encourage

(continued)

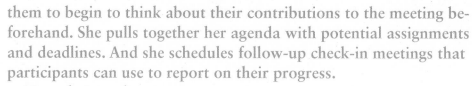

them to begin to think about their contributions to the meeting beforehand. She pulls together her agenda with potential assignments and deadlines. And she schedules follow-up check-in meetings that participants can use to report on their progress.

Now she's ready to meet.

Apparently, Joanne has a great deal of experience planning and conducting business meetings like these. Her approach parallels the advice of a number of experts who recommend strategies for making meetings work. For example, with thirty-eight years of experience teaching, coaching, leading, consulting, and training in leadership, teams, and organizational effectiveness, Dr. David Hartl could easily have been Joanne's coach. When people are planning a meeting, Hartl contends that they should ask three essential questions:[1]

1. Who will participate?

2. What purposes will you and the other participants want to have achieved when the meeting is over?

3. What do you want to have happen after the meeting that will be helped by having the meeting?

Joanne wisely considered each of these questions as she pulled together her meeting plan.

In this chapter, you will learn how to plan meetings as effectively as Joanne does. In addition, you'll learn to conduct meetings that are meaningful and functional, to facilitate interactions that ensure each participant's contribution, and to follow up on meetings effectively, monitor progress on delegated tasks, and evaluate outcomes. Finally, you'll learn how meeting participants can best take responsibility for making meetings matter. Let's start by considering when meetings are necessary and, as important, when they're not.

When Do Meetings Matter?

Meetings are ubiquitous in the workplace. In the United States, workers spend about 5.5 hours each week in meetings. That amount of time might seem perfectly reasonable until you consider that 71 percent of these workers complain that their meeting time is unproductive.[2] *Meetings in America*, a study commissioned by Verizon,[3] examined how some of America's busiest professionals feel about attending meetings. On average, they attend sixty meetings per month. Nearly all (91%) admit to daydreaming, and quite a large number (39%) admit to dozing off during meetings. Over 70 percent bring other work with them to do during meetings. And because they often must travel to attend meetings, professionals contend that technology like videoconferencing will make meetings easier and less expensive in the future. Even so, they most prefer to meet in person.[4]

How do you feel about meetings? Before you read on, complete **VISUALIZE! PRACTICE! 11.1: Worst Meeting Ever** to consider the worst meeting you ever attended and how it could have been better.

Why a Meeting?

If meetings are so common and yet so often seem to be unproductive, why meet? It's true that when meetings are unplanned, they can be tedious, counter productive, and a distraction from individual work time. However, *well-planned* meetings can serve important and well-meaning functions:

Visualize! Practice! 11.1:
Worst Meeting Ever

- They can provide a forum to disseminate and explain complex, high-level information about important topics, giving participants ample opportunity to ask questions and seek clarification.

- They encourage brainstorming and problem solving.

- They help employees coordinate the activities and efforts of a large organization.

- Although primarily task oriented, meetings stimulate relationship development, alleviate boredom, boost individual morale, and provide an excuse for people to socialize.

- Perhaps most important, meetings promote increased commitment or "buy-in" to decisions that emerge from active participant involvement.

The term **meeting** generally refers to two or more people who get together either in person or in virtual space to communicate in such a way as to achieve some common goal or objective. Businesses use a number of different types of meetings to accomplish their objectives, such as staff meetings, management team meetings, interdepartmental meetings, status meetings, board meetings, and ad hoc meetings. Conferences and seminars are also meeting types, but they are larger and more public than the typical business meetings discussed in this chapter. Almost all workplace meetings are held to achieve one of three objectives: information sharing, problem solving, and collaboration. Although these objectives often overlap, one objective will likely dominate the particular situation or circumstance.

People Meet to Share Information People organize and participate in meetings fairly regularly to simply share or exchange information. For example,

- Organizational leaders use the meeting format to update others on policy changes, announce plans for new facilities or equipment, brief employees or team leaders on budget allowances, and so on.

- Regular staff meetings occur in virtually every company and serve to check the status of ongoing projects, generate new ideas and identify new proposals, recount the events of the week, resolve conflicts, and discuss action items.

- Business meetings with clients and customers generally include some kind of presentation describing the product, service, or initiative followed by Q & A. They can also serve to develop trust and strengthen existing relationships.

- Project team meetings provide opportunities for participants to share progress reports, assign responsibilities, re-establish project goals, and schedule timelines.

- Conferences, seminars, workshops, and retreats are designed to share expert information on specific topics or issues, set long-range goals, discuss plans, strategies, and tactics, and work in smaller subgroups.

Vladimir Wrangel, 2009/Used under license from Shutterstock.com

People Meet to Solve Problems People also meet to identify and solve problems or make decisions important to the organization. For example,

- Management team meetings normally occur to set policy, define problems, and find solutions or identify better ways of doing business.
- Ad hoc or emergency meetings convene to address very specific and often unexpected issues or problems that emerge.

Problems that demand immediate attention, thorough analysis, and feasible solutions necessitate pulling together a group of individuals to take quick action. For instance, what action needs to be taken to replace a recent and unexpected resignation? How will budget cuts affect our delivery service? How will recent federal legislation on health care influence our ability to provide coverage for our employees? What are the anticipated consequences of moving in-person meetings to virtual ones?

People Meet to Collaborate Much of the work in both large and small organizations requires employees to collaborate with others. Putting together people with shared interests and concerns often leads to the sense that "we are all in this together." Talking about a project as *ours*, rather than *mine*, often leads to greater buy-in or commitment to the solution or results that evolve. Involving others or working collaboratively requires people to cooperate in ways so that they might work together long term. Effective, productive organizations cannot exist without people being able to work together to build consensus, make decisions, and solve problems.[5]

When people coordinate meetings, they often bring together meeting participants who can address the political nature or sensitivities of the issue involved. For example, a vice president of a large organization can choose to rely on the advice of expert financial advisors when putting together a budget, but she could also choose to include individuals who have a stake in how the budget is defined and implemented. Similarly, boards of directors often include community leaders who share an interest in the decisions that affect their community. Their input in board meetings is often vital to the decisions that are made and the policies that result.

By collaborating in meetings, all the **stakeholders**, or people who have a vested interest in the issue, share a consensus-based outcome. This results in a decision or recommendation that may be more acceptable to everyone. Commitment to a decision, solution, policy, or set of recommendations is highest when stakeholders are involved in the deliberative process.

Check out **LINK OUT 11.1: The Value of Meetings** for more reasons why well-planned meetings with specific goals are important to any organization. (Click on the "Value of Meetings" link in the left-hand menu.) The organization that sponsors this website focuses on conferences, but the information it offers can pertain to any type of business meeting.

Link Out 11.1:
The Value of Meetings

Why Not a Meeting?

Organizational psychologists Alexandra Luong and Steven Rogelberg proposed "that despite the fact that meetings may help achieve work-related goals, having too many meetings and spending too much time in meetings per day may have negative effects on the individual."[6] They reasoned that a full **meeting load**, the frequency and length of meetings an employee attends, pulls people away from their work, creating disruptive interruptions in their days.

In addition, they argued that increased meeting load can deplete employees' resources and reduce their rate of work progress or completion, resulting in fatigue and a negative mood. Sure enough, their research found that the number of meetings employees attended each day adversely affected feelings of fatigue and perceptions of their workload. Employees complained that meetings caused them to leave their work unfinished, requiring further effort to do the job. However, meeting length did not similarly influence those perceptions. Apparently, it's the frequency of interruption, not the time consumed during the meeting, that makes all the difference. Bottom line: Only meet when you must, and when you do meet, take the time necessary to ensure that frequent, subsequent interruptions are minimized.

When, then, should a meeting *not* be called?

- **When there is no reason to meet.** Determine first if the meeting is really necessary. Not every meeting should be held just because it's scheduled. People tend to attend standing meetings—meetings that that are regularly scheduled for a certain time during the day, week, or month—even when agenda items are few and could be easily folded into the agenda of a subsequent meeting. Before deciding to pull people away from their work, then, determine if the meeting is essential.

- **When the objectives can be better accomplished in another way.** The decision to call a meeting should depend primarily on the objective that needs to be addressed. Might your objectives be accomplished more efficiently by using email, phone, memo, or brief report? Some decisions, especially minor ones, might best be handled by a single decision maker who has expertise in the relevant area. And some information might be better disseminated in a formal, public presentation that addresses many people at once, with follow-up information posted online or sent to stakeholders through email.

- **When decisions aren't likely to be converted into action.** Sometimes decisions are made in a meeting, but then there's no follow-through. This can happen with issues that aren't high priorities, especially in busy workplaces where employees are

Link Out 11.2:
Put Mustard on It!

Check This Out 11.1:
Deadly Meetings

overstretched. Or a decision is made that doesn't require follow-through until a much later date, and meeting participants feel that they've wasted their time. In these situations, participants may learn that even when decisions are made, the outcomes are never actualized. This can lead to employees coming to feel that nothing gets accomplished in meetings.

- **When two heads aren't better than one.** Meetings are a must for high-level issues, such as making policy or setting organizational priorities. The outcomes of meetings for these issues empower administrators to make subsequent decisions of significant magnitude that wouldn't be wise to make without a collective effort. But other decisions are not so significant and don't warrant a committee. Instead, a single expert can make a decision that would be acceptable to all stakeholders. For example, deciding what kind of stapler to purchase might best be delegated to a single person. Not everyone in an organization wants or needs to be involved in solving every problem or making every decision.

- **When a decision must be made now.** Inviting collaboration may be impossible in emergency or crisis situations. For example, evacuating bank employees during an earthquake or a terrorist attack should depend on the quick actions of one person in charge. In these types of situations, convening a meeting—inviting "paralysis by analysis"—would likely be disastrous. For a quick laugh, go to **LINK OUT 11.2: Put Mustard on It!** to watch an *Saturday Night Live* short about group efforts to avert a catastrophe when an immediate decision should have been made.

For more on how you can avoid being responsible for bad meetings, complete **CHECK THIS OUT 11.1: Deadly Meetings**. How could you prevent the seven worst mistakes meeting planners and participants make?

How Should You Plan a Meeting?

Why are some meetings productive, and why do others fail? It's all about preparation. Winging it with meetings is simply not an option in the business community! How substantive a meeting is for all participants is directly related to the amount of time spent planning it. To plan for a successful meeting, identify your objectives, choose your participants, set an agenda, schedule the meeting, send reminders, prepare to take minutes, and arrange for catering and AV equipment.

Identify Your Objectives

Determine what you want to accomplish with the meeting. At the conclusion of the meeting, what are the specific things you want to know or achieve? Be clear about your immediate and long-term objectives, and consider whether you might need subsequent meetings to achieve your goals. Try not to be overly ambitious or optimistic—keep your objectives doable and realistic. For example, most large organizations, like Boeing or Kaiser Permanente, hold regular meetings to define ways to give back to communities where they reside and operate. Although their overall objective is improved community relations, every meeting will be targeted toward very specific, well-defined objectives. They may meet to set and standardize criteria for evaluating community outreach grant proposals. And a series of subsequent meetings may refine the criteria, evaluate actual proposals, and make decisions about financial awards.

Choose Your Participants

In our opening scenario, Joanne chose to be very thoughtful about who she wanted to include in her product development meeting. She considered meeting participants carefully, recognizing that whoever came to the meeting would have a powerful impact on what happened in the meeting. You must do the same. Every employee brings different resources, ideas, biases, attitudes, and agendas with them to meetings. Consider how those predispositions and points of view will affect how the group interacts and the eventual decisions that are made.

Not every person should be included in every meeting. Sometimes employees' time is better spent doing their work than attending yet another meeting. Keep in mind that pulling people away from their primary work costs the company money. For example, if you ask eight people to attend a one-hour meeting, you're allocating a full day's work to a meeting. Be resourceful and mindful of others' value when determining who should attend your meeting.

LINK OUT 11.3: Who Should Come to a Meeting? provides a helpful checklist to determine who should (or should not) be invited to a meeting.[7]

Set an Agenda

An **agenda** is a plan of action that specifies what you intend to do at a meeting and how discussion items will be prioritized. Agendas both structure and regulate what should happen during the meeting, in what order, and in some cases, in what time frame. Agendas help participants stay on task and allow the meeting to be conducted efficiently and effectively.

To set an agenda, decide what topics need to be covered and how much time you need to devote to each topic. If special presentations are warranted, determine who to invite, how much time presenters will need, and whether they are available. Prioritize the topics in a way that will help meeting participants achieve the meeting's objectives.

Link Out 11.3:
Who Should Come to a Meeting?

Augusto Cabral/Shutterstock.com

FIGURE 11.1
Sample meeting agenda template

[Company/Department Name]

Meeting Agenda
[Date]
[Time]

Type of meeting: **[Description of meeting]**

Meeting facilitator: **[Name of meeting facilitator]**

Invitees: **[List of invitees]**

I. Call to order

II. Roll call

III. Approval of minutes from last meeting

IV. Open issues
   A. **[Description of open issue]**
   B. **[Description of open issue]**
   C. **[Description of open issue]**

V. New business
   A. **[Description of new business]**
   B. **[Description of new business]**
   C. **[Description of new business]**

VI. Adjournment

The format for an agenda can be found in a number of software programs, including Microsoft Word (see Figure 11.1). You can use a template to ensure that all the necessary information is provided in your agenda—including the time, date, location, and name of your meeting. Once you've drafted your agenda, check it for errors. A few days before the meeting, make the agenda available to all meeting participants and presenters. Because people often forget to bring the agenda to the meeting, make copies of it and bring them with you to the meeting for distribution. Better yet, if you prepare a presentation slideshow for the meeting, include the agenda in one of your digital slides.

Schedule the Meeting

Once the agenda is set, you are ready to schedule the meeting. How hard can that be? Very. Coordinating everyone's schedules can be challenging. Participants may not keep their own calendars and may reroute you to their assistants who do. Others may commit, only later to cancel. Consider also the organization's hierarchy; some higher-ranked participants are likely to require others to accommodate their schedules.

Perhaps the best way to get a group of five or more together is to use an online meeting wizard such as doodle.com or scheduleonce.com Participants can log on to these sites and indicate their availability—and see when other participants can and cannot attend. Once participants see others' availability, they may make more of an effort to accommodate. You may discover that some participants are never available; you will have to adjust and find substitutes.

Book the time and *the place*. Find the appropriate context for your meeting. Consider the size of the room, the potential distractions (outside noises), comfort level (ventilation, temperature, type of chairs), table configuration, smart-room capabilities, and location accessibility. For meetings of importance, be sure to utilize a conference room that's intended for that purpose. Once you identify the location, schedule it immediately—conference rooms are often in constant demand and can be hard to reserve. For reoccurring meetings, schedule the room for the duration of the meeting sequence. And don't forget to let all the participants know where the meeting is scheduled. Some may even require directions or a map.

Link Out 11.4:
How to Prepare Meeting Minutes

Link Out 11.5:
Sample Board Meeting Minutes 1

Link Out 11.6:
Sample Board Meeting Minutes 2

Send a Reminder

Once the meeting is scheduled and each of the participants knows when and where to meet, do not assume that they will remember to attend. Remind them of the date, time, and location two to five business days before the meeting. If you expect them to bring a copy of the agenda, minutes, or other materials, remind them to bring those things, too. Let them know that you are looking forward to their participation.

Prepare to Take Minutes

Minutes are a written record of what happens during a meeting, including all the important motions, announcements, decisions, and discussions. Minutes serve as a "memory" of all that happened for later access, retrieval, and reference. Typically, minutes are created while the meeting takes place, with a secretary or meeting participant taking notes or recording the discussion. They are then cleaned up, and a draft is written soon after the conclusion of the meeting. Once the draft of the minutes is completed, it is posted online or distributed to meeting participants. Often meeting participants are asked to read, offer corrections (if any), and vote for their approval of the minutes to verify their accuracy.

The format for minutes can be highly structured, depending on the meeting's purpose and the organization's culture. Minutes usually include the name or purpose of the meeting; the meeting's date, time, and place; the time the meeting commenced; the names of all those present; and discussion summaries or highlights. For detailed instructions on how to take minutes, see **LINK OUT 11.4: How to Prepare Meeting Minutes**. And for samples of minutes, see **LINK OUT 11.5: Sample Board Meeting Minutes 1** and **LINK OUT 11.6: Sample Board Meeting Minutes 2**.

Arrange for Catering and AV Equipment

For long meetings or meetings held during breakfast or lunch, participants need food and drink. Having food and drink available for participants makes them a whole lot

Link Out 11.7:
Arrive on Time

easier to facilitate and collaborate with—hungry or thirsty people can be irritable and disagreeable. At minimum, provide water, tea, and coffee. For meetings that will last at least half a day, supplement drinks with cookies, yogurt, or fresh fruit and vegetables. Working lunch meetings may require sandwiches and fruit, soft drinks, and juice. Catered hot lunches and dinners are also common for high-level business meetings. Whatever your plan, consider the context: Where will the food and drink be set up? Where will participants eat? Consider also individuals' dietary needs: Include vegetarian options, for instance.

Check with participants and presenters well ahead of time to determine what AV equipment they may require. For instance, you may need to provide a laptop, digital projector, and screen for PowerPoint presentations. Anticipate the need for extension cords, back-up equipment, and even replacement light bulbs for projectors. Once you have the essential equipment, check it out before hand to ensure that everything is in working order—plan to come early for set up and calibration. Perhaps nothing is more unnerving to a well-planned meeting than failed equipment. Don't let it happen to you. Become technologically adept to assist presenters—or ask an AV technician to be available.

How Should You Conduct the Meeting?

When you lead a meeting yourself, you are the meeting's *facilitator,* or *chair*. Leading a meeting is not as easy as it looks. Ensuring that the participants leave the meeting feeling that their time was well spent requires that you facilitate the interactions constructively and efficiently.

Begin the Meeting

Arrive early and make sure all the equipment is in order. Project your digital slide of the agenda or distribute hard copies at each of the empty seats. Review the agenda silently, take a deep breath, and relax. As the meeting facilitator, be the first to arrive—and the last to leave. As soon as participants begin to arrive, stand up, acknowledge each of them by name, and exchange small talk. Your immediate objective is to make each participant feel welcome and comfortable.

Start on time. Even though some people often assume that "on time" means being ten minutes late, don't let that influence your own timetable. Once participants realize that you start your meetings on time, they will make an effort to arrive on time for subsequent meetings. Business consultant Alexander Kerjulf offers some ideas on how to encourage participants to arrive to your meetings on time, at **LINK OUT 11.7: Arrive on Time**.[8]

Conduct the Meeting

To conduct is to orchestrate, to coordinate, execute or carry out some kind of activity. When you conduct a meeting, you execute the agenda by facilitating interactions among the participants. Here's where a well-planned agenda really works for you. In addition, effective communication skills make all the difference when you're facilitating a meeting. A competent communicator can elicit the kinds of interactions essential to making the meeting productive. Active participation must be encouraged; at the same time, discussions must remain focused, and momentum maintained. Follow these guidelines.

Set the Tone As the meeting facilitator, the tone you set will likely influence everyone's willingness to participate. Important to eliciting lively discussion is ensuring that people feel safe and comfortable asking questions, making comments, and offering contrary points of view. At the same time, you want them to take the discussion seriously. You might begin by expressing your concern that everyone feels comfortable participating and that the goals and objectives of this meeting have important implications for others. Look professional and act professionally, and bring a sense of formality and seriousness to the occasion. From time to time during the meeting, remind them that they are doing important work, and that this a serious endeavor.

Rely on Rules for Interaction Follow some rule-governed system for conducting meetings, such as parliamentary procedure. Rules for interaction bring a sense of importance and seriousness to a meeting. Moreover, they help facilitators conduct meetings efficiently, which leaves all participants feeling that their voices are heard and opinions respected, even if they are in the minority. Common rules for interaction include keeping discussion centered on one issue at a time, ensuring that each discussion has a specific, well-defined purpose, and insisting on proper decorum to avoid ineffective or destructive communication and to ensure that exchanges stay on track.

    MODULE 10: **What Parliamentary Procedures Do I Really Need to Know?** provides you with some of the essential rules for governing discussion and decision making in meetings.

Manage the Time Every meeting has a specified time frame, and as the facilitator, you are responsible for managing the time so that critical agenda items are covered. When you've asked an expert to present a briefing during a meeting, schedule a specific time for that person to come, and make sure you're ready for him when he arrives. Guests simply cannot be left waiting, particularly high-ranking executives who have other pressing commitments.

    For agenda items where closure seems unlikely, you may need to **table** the discussion and move on to the next item on the agenda. When you table an agenda item, you postpone discussing it until another time. Seek input on this decision from the group. At times, the group may decide to sustain discussion on a particular item and table later items for discussion at subsequent meetings.

Edyta Pawlowska/Shutterstock.com

Link Out 11.8:
Closed versus Open Questions

Visualize! Practice! 11.2:
Closed to Open

Perhaps most important to time management is ending the meeting on time. People have other commitments, appointments, and obligations. Good meeting facilitators begin and end meetings on time.

Ask the Right Kind of Questions The right kinds of questions stimulate participation. Closed questions, for instance, do little to encourage lengthy responses. Avoid questions that can be answered with a simple yes, no, or other single-word answer. Open questions elicit elaboration and discussion. Importantly, asking open questions during a meeting moves control of the discussion from the facilitator to the participant. Begin your questions with *what*, *why*, or *how*, and you might be surprised at how much dialogue you will stimulate. When asking questions, make sure participants know you care about their responses. Be engaged and sincere. Make eye contact, lean forward, face the participant. If warranted, ask follow-up questions to stimulate even further discussion.[9]

For practice rephrasing closed questions as open questions, go to **VISUALIZE! PRACTICE! 11.2: Closed to Open**. And for an overview of closed versus open questions, check out **LINK OUT 11.8: Closed versus Open Questions**.[10]

Be Impartial, Assertive, and Tactful Your role as meeting chair is to govern the process, not control the content. Remain impartial or neutral on issues, encouraging others to voice their points of view. At the same time, be assertive, controlling the flow, ensuring that everyone participates, and managing the time. Tact will help you come across as understanding, open, caring, and diplomatic. Even if you disagree with the group or believe others are dead wrong, your role is to guide and encourage others to engage. If you come across as opinionated or disagreeable, you will likely alienate others and shut down the discussion. Either keep your opinions to yourself or ask questions that redirect or point out alternatives. In this way, others will be encouraged to rethink and remain engaged.

Reinforce Participation When individuals contribute to the discussion, reinforce them for it. Acknowledge a good point, a critical question, or an astute observation. At times throughout the meeting, you can also reinforce the entire group by reminding them that the discussion is meaningful and moving in the right direction. Try out these reinforcing statements:

"Good point!"

"I couldn't agree with you more."

"What a good idea!"

"I appreciate you saying that."

"I hadn't thought of that before."

"Good insight!"

"And then what happened?"

"I like the way you think."

"Thank you for bringing that up."

What are some other verbal reinforcing statements that might work? What nonverbal strategies could you use to encourage others to participate further?

When people are reinforced publicly for their participation, they feel good about themselves, about you, and about the entire group. They will likely look forward to the next meeting. On occasion, however, you might run into those who overtalk or try to dominate the discussion at the expense of others' contributions. With these people, try withholding reinforcement. When "talkaholics" dominate, do not follow up with comments or questions. Avoid eye contact, and ask for others' input.

Link Out 11.9:
The Idea

Maintain Momentum Maintain the momentum of the meeting by keeping its objectives front and center. Continue to remind participants why they were chosen for this group and how important they are to reaching the objectives. Once solutions are offered and decisions are reached, consider how and when they will be implemented. Participants need to believe that what they are doing will lead to or produce something meaningful.[11]

Seek Consensus Well-managed discussions generally result in some kind of consensus or partial consensus. Reasonable people will likely agree at some point during a discussion. Compromises are made, and individual agendas are left behind or redefined. Recognizing that buy-in or commitment to a decision is an important by-product of group participation, try to achieve as close to total agreement as possible. At times, however, you may need to fall back on decision by vote. In order to move along, you can call the question and take a vote.

For a humorous look at a facilitator who is *not* going for buy-in, watch **LINK OUT 11.9: The Idea**.[12]

Conclude the Meeting

Important to managing meetings effectively, conclude the meeting when the scheduled time is up. Participants like meetings to begin and end on time so that they can get on to the rest of their day. Take a few minutes to summarize where agreement has occurred. Note agenda items that were not discussed and that need to be revisited or new items that need to be addressed in subsequent meetings. Review what tasks need to be accomplished by the next meeting. Then schedule the next meeting, making sure that all participants are available to attend and that their follow-up tasks can be reasonably accomplished by that date. Finally, conclude the meeting with heartfelt thanks for their contributions.

How Should You Follow Up After the Meeting?

What happens *after* the meeting is perhaps even more important than what happens *during* the meeting. Once meeting participants have deliberated as a group, the bulk of the work must be done—they must follow through on their delegated tasks and commitments. Thus, meeting follow-up is critical to the overall effectiveness of the group's work.

Provide the Minutes

Even if a secretary recorded the minutes, it's the meeting facilitator's responsibility to see to it that the minutes are accurate and complete. Moreover, the facilitator must ensure that the minutes are posted or distributed within three or four working days of the meeting. Participants and relevant stakeholders must have the minutes to read and reference as soon as possible.

FIGURE 11.2
Meeting evaluation checklist

Meeting Plan
- [ ] The agenda included a manageable number of items for the time allotted.
- [ ] Agenda items were comprehensive.
- [ ] Members were notified well in advance.
- [ ] The meeting started on time.
- [ ] Presenters were ready to report.
- [ ] Guests were introduced and welcomed.
- [ ] The purpose of the meeting was clear to everyone.
- [ ] The meeting moved along at a workable pace.
- [ ] All that was planned for the meeting was covered sufficiently.
- [ ] Work tasks were delegated for future meetings.
- [ ] The meeting ended on time.

Meeting Participation
- [ ] Attendance was good.
- [ ] Everyone arrived on time.
- [ ] All members participated in the discussions.
- [ ] The facilitator made good use of questions.
- [ ] The pros and cons of all issues were considered.
- [ ] All members were actively involved.
- [ ] One topic was discussed at a time.
- [ ] One person had the floor at a time.
- [ ] Discussion stayed on track and was relevant to each topic.
- [ ] Participants seemed to enjoy the experience.

Monitor Progress
Work is often delegated to participants during the meeting. Follow up with each individual to ensure that they understand their assignments and their completion dates. Oftentimes, participants may discover that they are unsure about their assignment, find that they need additional resources, or require more direction. As meeting chair, your responsibility is to help them in any way you can to ensure project completion or implementation. Encourage them to continue their work, reinforce meaningful progress, and, if needed, remind them again of the importance of the activity.

Evaluate Outcomes
Take the time to reflect on what you and the participants accomplished at the last meeting. Most chairs engage in this activity almost immediately after the meeting. Others ask for input from the participants themselves. Where can improvements be made? What went right and what went wrong? The checklist in Figure 11.2 might be helpful for making

a comprehensive, yet detailed assessment of the overall meeting experience.[13] The first part examines how well the meeting was planned. The second part assesses the level and type of participant interaction during the meeting.

Evaluating the meeting provides you with important feedback for learning how to become even more effective in the future. Once you identify problems, you might decide, for instance, to reduce (or expand) the number of agenda items, increase meeting duration, send more frequent reminders to ensure attendance, provide greater guidance to presenters, introduce some humor into difficult discussions, and other remedies important to the planning and facilitation of future meetings.

Prepare the Next Agenda

We began our discussion of meetings by talking about the importance of a well-planned meeting agenda. Now we end our discussion with the same message: Plan your agenda for the next meeting. Determine right away what you intend to do at the next meeting and how items will be prioritized. Think of agendas as dynamic, working documents. List items, add to and delete items as needed, and revisit priorities in the days that follow and precede each meeting. Agendas are your friend; they will help you and guide you as you prepare for and conduct your next meeting.

What Are the Responsibilities of Participants?

Just as meeting planners and facilitators are responsible for making meetings matter, so are participants. If you are in the role of participant, take it seriously. There is much you can do to make meetings work—at the same time, there is much you can do to undermine their effectiveness. What do effective participants look and act like?

You might have read or heard Woody Allen's often-cited quotation on life: "Eighty percent of success is showing up." The success of any meeting begins with this simple responsibility. After all, you have been invited to attend for a very specific reason or purpose. Beyond simply showing up to the meeting, what are other participant responsibilities?

- Be on time.
- Be prepared.
- Actively participate.
- Listen to others' contributions.
- Acknowledge others' ideas and opinions.
- Stay on topic.
- Be positive and solution-oriented.
- Be respectful.
- Take turns. Try not to monopolize the discussion.
- Be engaged and enthusiastic. Make eye contact, smile encouragingly, and lean forward.
- Look and act interested.
- Ask relevant questions.

Visualize! Practice! 11.3:
How Do I Rate as a Participant?

Check This Out 11.2:
You Are Where You Sit

Diego Cervo/Shutterstock.com

- Be friendly.
- Disagree with ideas, not people.
- Be open to compromise.
- Leave your personal or political agendas at the door.
- Stay until the meeting is over. Don't leave early.

Finally, make every effort to enjoy the experience. Serious discussion aside, sometimes it's a good idea to interject a little humor into the process. Have some fun. You might even try changing where you sit in meetings to see how others respond differently to you. **CHECK THIS OUT 11.2: You Are Where You Sit** looks at where people choose to sit in business meetings and what that might suggest about who they are in the organization. How accurate do you think these observations or profiles are? Does seating choice really make a difference?

For a checklist that allows you to rate yourself as a meeting participant, go to **VISUALIZE! PRACTICE! 11.3: How Do I Rate as a Participant?** Are you the type of participant who makes meaningful contributions to the meeting, or could you be more effective?

Business meetings can be good or bad, effective or ineffective, productive or unproductive. What makes the difference? How do we make meetings matter? How do we ensure their effectiveness? After reading this chapter, you should have a pretty good idea how to answer those questions. Meetings aren't inherently boring or a waste of time. They just end up that way when people approach meetings as if they simply happen on their own. Meetings done well rely on well-established principles and on all participants making their interactions meaningful, substantive, and enjoyable.

Use your Speech Communication CourseMate for *Business & Communication in a Digital Age* for quick access to the electronic resources that accompany this text. These resources include

Study tools that help you assess your learning and prepare for exams (*digital glossary, key term flash cards, review quizzes*).

Activities and assignments that help you hone your knowledge and build your communication skills throughout the course (*Visualize! Practice!, Weigh In!, Check This Out, and Link Out activities; modules; review questions*).

Media resources that help you explore communication concepts online (*Enhanced eBook*), develop your speech outlines (*Speech Builder Express 3.0*), watch and critique videos of sample speeches and communication situations (*interactive video activities*), upload your speech videos for peer reviewing and critique other students' speeches (*Speech Studio online speech review tool*), and download chapter review so you can study when and where you'd like (*Audio Study Tools*).

Key Points

- A meeting is two or more people who get together either in person or in virtual space to communicate in such a way as to achieve some common goal or objective.
- Almost all workplace meetings are held to achieve one of three objectives:
  ✔ information sharing
  ✔ problem solving
  ✔ collaboration
- Holding a meeting is not always necessary and can be counter productive when it takes employees away from their work unnecessarily. Do *not* call a meeting when
  ✔ There is no reason to meet.
  ✔ The objectives can be better accomplished in another way.
  ✔ Decisions aren't likely to be converted into action.
  ✔ Two heads aren't better than one.
  ✔ A decision must be made now.
- The effectiveness and success of a meeting for all participants is directly related to the amount of time spent planning it. To plan for a successful meeting,
  ✔ Identify your objectives.
  ✔ Choose your participants.
  ✔ Set an agenda.
  ✔ Schedule the meeting.
  ✔ Send reminders.
  ✔ Prepare to take minutes.
  ✔ Arrange for catering and AV equipment.

- A meeting's facilitator, or chair, leads a meeting. To ensure that participants leave a meeting feeling that their time was well spent, begin, conduct, and end a meeting according to these guidelines:

  ✔ Arrive early to set up the room, begin on time, and make participants feel welcome and comfortable.

  ✔ Set a professional tone; follow some established rules of order; manage the time so that critical agenda items are covered; ask the right kind of questions to stimulate participation; be impartial, assertive, and tactful, and reinforce participation; maintain momentum; and try to seek consensus.

  ✔ Conclude the meeting when the scheduled time is up, summarize important points, note items that need to be discussed another time, and review follow-up tasks.

- After a meeting, follow up by providing the meeting minutes, monitoring the progress of follow-up tasks, evaluating the outcomes of the meeting, and preparing the next agenda as needed.

- If you are a meeting participant, do what you can to make the meeting as effective as possible.

  ✔ Be on time, be prepared, stay on topic, and stay until the meeting is over.

  ✔ Actively participate. Listen to others' contributions, acknowledge others' ideas and opinions, and ask relevant questions.

  ✔ Be respectful. Take turns and try not to monopolize the discussion, disagree with ideas rather than with people, leave your personal or political agendas at the door, and be open to compromise.

  ✔ Be friendly, positive, and solution-oriented.

  ✔ Be engaged and enthusiastic. Look and act interested—make eye contact, smile encouragingly, and lean forward.

Key Terms

agenda (251)

meeting (247)

meeting load (249)

minutes (253)

stakeholder (249)

table (255)

Questions for Critical Thinking and Review

1. We have provided a number of reasons why people in organizations need meetings. We have also noted a surge in the number of meetings that employees must attend. Are there too many meetings in the workplace? Do you believe that you are involved in too many meetings that take you away from school or work time? Why or why not?

2. One of the major reasons people meet is to collaborate. Why do you suppose that people who make collaborative decisions are more likely to commit to those decisions? How does this work? What do you suppose happens during collaboration that secures such buy-in?

3. Suppose you are facilitating a meeting and you notice that it's time to move on to the next agenda item. Without alienating participants, what communication strategies might you employ to redirect the discussion? Why might this be difficult to do? Are there times when it's a good idea to quit the agenda and stay with the current discussion topic? When are those times?

4. How might you manage difficult participants during a meeting? For example, how would you manage the person who talks too much, the woman in the corner who never participates, or the guy who insists on his own position, refusing to compromise or relent?

5. What if you held a meeting and almost no one who was supposed to be there attended? What would you do? How might you anticipate and prevent that from happening in the first place?

6. How much reinforcement is appropriate for a meeting? When does reinforcement become insincere and manipulative? How and when do you draw the line?

7. Meeting leaders are advised to remain impartial during meetings and to concentrate instead on facilitating discussions. Does that seem equitable to you? Are there times when a facilitator has the right or the obligation to argue for a position, cause, or solution? Under what circumstances might that be appropriate and acceptable?

8. After a meeting, it's useful to evaluate the meeting process and outcomes, and to obtain feedback from meeting participants. As the facilitator, how do you reconcile these two different evaluations if you, for instance, perceived the meeting as successful, but the participants complained about the pace and momentum of the discussion? Whose perceptions are likely to be more accurate? Yours or theirs? Why?

9. Although consensus is highly desirable in group discussions, it's not always possible. When you facilitate a meeting held to make some decisions, at what point do you decide to take a vote to bring the discussion to a close? What if the vote was fairly evenly split and the decision was made by only a simple majority? How might that affect future deliberations among the participants? Is it ever a good idea to simply table the deliberations and begin again at another date and time? When might that be a preferable way to go?

10. To what extent might day of week or time of day influence how well a meeting goes? What days are bad days to get a group together to meet? What days are good days? Why is that? What times during the day do you think meetings should be avoided? What times are good? Why?

Ivan Cholakov Gostock-dot-net

Chapter Learning Objectives

After completing this chapter, you should be able to

- Explain why teams are essential in the workplace.
- Identify what makes a group of individuals a team.
- Describe what makes teams work.
- Explain why some teams fail.
- Lead or facilitate a team.
- Participate more effectively as a team member.

See also **the modules that are relevant to this chapter:**

1: How Do I "Get In and Fit In" to My Organization's Unique Culture?
9: How Do I Navigate Office Politics?

Module 1:
*How Do I "Get In and Fit
In" to My Organization's
Unique Culture?*

Module 9:
*How Do I Navigate
Office Politics?*

Ted Ross, founder and president of Ross-Campbell, Inc. of Sacramento, operates a successful marketing and advertising organization.

His firm specializes in social and political cause-related campaigns. Ted is an Emmy-award-winning director and producer of television documentaries targeting health care, education, and environmental issues. Ted is an unusual guy. His core staff is small, but he knows how to put together successful teams of highly technical and specialized players to do research, design campaigns, produce video, package training and instruction, and much, much more. Not only is Ted well respected for his own talents and skills, but he's also well recognized for his ability to assemble the right resources, people, and subcontractors into a team to do just about anything.

That's where the authors of your book come in. Before Ted built his own company, he studied communication with Dr. Plax and Dr. Kearney. After graduation, Ted wanted to run his own business, so he did. One day (years later) he called us at home, reminded us who he was, and asked us if we would consider joining his team of experts to work on one of his projects. We said sure, not knowing what he really wanted. Much to our surprise, he wanted us to work on California's first recycling campaign. This was back in the mid-1980s. What did we know about recycling? Not much. Back then, recycling issues were just beginning to gain momentum.

Ted told us not to worry. He assured us that we were being brought into the team not as experts on recycling or on marketing or advertising. Instead, he wanted to utilize our expertise in communication, survey research, and focus-group interviewing. He found others to join the team who knew quite a bit about recycling. Others were good at graphic design. He relied on the client to provide us with some background on waste management. And Ted knew all about how to market a service or product.

The first thing he did was to get us all together at a retreat. There we identified goals, delegated tasks, collaborated on strategy, produced a timeline, and developed an identity as Ted's recycling project team. Everyone knew who was responsible for what. We learned to work together, to depend on each other, and to value each other's

(continued)

Check This Out 12.1:
The Power of Teams

contributions. That particular team's project lasted about a year. The team was disbanded once its contract was fulfilled. Even so, today Ted's company continues to do contract work that evolved from that original project.

Over the last twenty years or so, we have collaborated with Ted and other members of his team on numerous other projects, including college student loans and financial literacy campaigns, alternative vehicle technologies (such as hydrogen, hybrid, and electric cars), re-refined oil, hazardous waste, and, of all things, California truckers' oil and filter disposal!

As new projects were contracted, the members of Ted's work teams necessarily changed. Some members remained, but new members were added based on project need and member specialization. Some of Ted's project teams have been short term, lasting only weeks or months. Others have been ongoing, consuming as many as five years of working with the same team members.

Unlike many large employers who pull together teams from their existing pool of employees, Ted's small company relies on external contractors (like your authors) to supply essential players and resources to fill out a team. A group of people becomes a **team** when they share a common purpose or goal. Unlike most group members, team members are carefully chosen for the particular and complementary skills that allow the team to achieve or complete complex goals and tasks. Whether the team is a product of internal or external specialists, the process of building a team is pretty much the same. The need to assemble work teams has become increasingly more important as product or project design and development have become more complicated. Some projects simply cannot be accomplished by a single individual working alone. Even though Ted is a really capable guy, he would be the first to admit that he couldn't tackle these projects alone. That's why his ability to put together project teams is an essential part of his business plan—and ultimate financial success. Ted also knows that in order for teams to be effective, he must be very careful how to go about assembling team members and facilitating their work.

What Ted seems to be able to do so well is something we can all learn to do. In this chapter, we examine how and why teams exist—and why certain tasks are better managed in teams. Even though teams are common in the workplace, some teams are clearly more effective than others. What then, makes a group of employees an effective team? By identifying the features that characterize a team, you can begin to appreciate how teams are built, developed, and managed, and what makes teams work or fail. Appreciating how teams function can help you better lead or facilitate a team. Your understanding of teams should also help you to become an effective team player on the job.

The U.S. Navy's flight exhibition team, the Blue Angels, is the ultimate example of effective teamwork. Discover the principles that make their precise coordination possible in **CHECK THIS OUT 12.1: The Power of Teams**.

Why Work in Teams?

Recent theoretical thinking on the nature of work today suggests that jobs are defined much differently than they used to be:

- Many people telecommute to work instead of coming into the office every day.

- They may work on a variety of activities, none of which comprises their major job responsibility.

- Employees may work in several different work teams in any given day as the demands of their workplace change.

- Manufacturing jobs have been relocated to other countries, altering how we work and what we work on.

- Instead of being permanent employees of a single company, many people now operate as independent contractors or subcontractors for multifaceted organizations like Ted's.

- There may be no single boss, no "home" organization, and no job security.

In short, the word *job* means something entirely different than it did in previous generations, requiring us to rethink and redefine ourselves as workers.[1]

Given the changing nature of our jobs, the use of teams has become even more prevalent. More than ever before, organizations are turning to teams to deal with the new requirements of the job. Over half of all U.S. organizations rely on work teams in one form or another.[2] This is standard business protocol. About 80 percent of *Fortune* 500 companies report using long-term teams, with 77 percent also relying on temporary or ad hoc teams to do core work.[3] Much has been written about the importance of teams, how to build teams, how to manage them, and how to make them work. The collective perception of organizations today is that teams are good and necessary. However, not all tasks or projects are suited to teamwork. Some tasks can be better accomplished by individuals working alone. Moreover, not all teams are functional—some teams simply can't get the job done for one reason or another. Let's take a look at when it's best to use teams and when it's not.

Teams That Make Sense

Teams can offer great benefits to an organization. First of all, teams make complex tasks doable. Some projects and tasks are simply too big or too complex for one or two individuals to tackle. Consider how difficult it would be to build a highway, plan a housing development, or perform an entire symphony alone! These sorts of projects are too labor intensive and require a variety of specialized skills and talents that go far beyond what a single person can do.

Second, teams allow a large workforce to complete a variety of parallel activities by dividing employees into specialized and more manageable groups. For instance, in a large software company, multiple teams of software engineers and programmers produce a variety of computer games. Other teams design business software. Still other teams work on home and educational software applications.

Third, teams offer organizations greater workforce flexibility and focus:

- The team concept allows managers to flexibly select which employees should belong to any given team at any given time.

- Workers are selected to focus on projects that benefit from their unique skills and talents.

- Worker specialization and expertise drive work assignments, not job description or job parameters.

- Such teams can be assembled quickly, directed to focus on a particular project or task, and then easily disbanded.

For example, consider a regional environmental agency that is in the business of bidding on and acquiring contracts that address managing wastewater runoff into the ocean. The manager regularly selects individuals across departments and divisions to generate proposals. Some projects might require an environmental statistician, several marine biologists who specialize in water contamination, waste management and/or oceanography, and perhaps an in-house grant writer. Other projects might require bringing in outside consultants, other specialized biologists, and sampling experts. For each project, individuals are selected to lend a particular expertise to the table. Once the project is completed, the team members move to other teams or resume their individual assignments.

Finally, one of the by-products of work teams may be one of the best reasons for using them: People who work in teams generally feel a greater sense of commitment or ownership of the project and outcome. For example, a team assembled to generate a workable furlough plan for the company that affects their own employment, salary, and benefits has a vested interest in the outcome. And that results in greater buy-in to a very difficult yet personally relevant project.

These and other benefits of teams typically lead managers to utilize teams whenever possible, often leading to what researchers call a "group frenzy"[4] within the business community. Before you make the leap that teams are unilaterally useful, however, read on.

Teams That Don't Make Sense

Not all teams are unilaterally useful. People mistakenly believe that groups of people working together make higher-quality decisions and products than individuals working alone. For decades, the adage "two heads are better than one" prevailed.[5] But contemporary thinking and research suggests that for the same task, teams are "better than the average individual but seldom better than the best."[6] So, even the process of brainstorming generates creative ideas or solutions that are no better than ideas produced by highly talented individuals on their own.[7]

Some tasks just don't work very well with teams. Creative tasks, like writing a song or painting a picture, don't often lend themselves to teamwork. Highly specialized, sophisticated tasks, like watch repair or electrical work, are better completed by highly trained individuals—not teams. Work should not be delegated to teams unless the task itself is amenable to teamwork.[8]

Sometimes controversial issues are assigned to teams in an effort to diffuse individual responsibility or blame. For example, juried decisions, employee terminations, and tuition increases are issues sufficiently controversial or sensitive to warrant a team or group decision.[9] No single individual, then, becomes singularly accountable for making the wrong decision or for coming up with an unpopular solution. Although politically correct, using teams solely to relinquish responsibility or to escape blame can be questionable at best.

Other potentially negative uses of teams derive from the deliberative process itself.[10] Pressure for members to prematurely conform to a solution or decision is common in groups—particularly if the members value or prioritize getting along over conflict. The well-documented phenomenon **groupthink** is team members' overwhelming drive to reach consensus, disregarding any critical analysis of the problem and ignoring alternative solutions.[11] Prioritizing agreement or consensus over reasoned argument and conflict leads to flawed decision making and failed policy. **CHECK THIS OUT 12.2: Groupthink** uses a classic movie to show how this phenomenon can result in a life or death situation.

Finally, team participants may be guilty of **social loafing**, exerting little or no effort to contribute to the team goal. Researchers have found that compared to working with others, individuals working alone put forth more effort to accomplish a task. Several factors might account for the social loafing effect. Team members may feel like they can hide in the crowd, avoiding effortful contributions, or get lost in the crowd, despairing in their ability to receive individual recognition. Alternatively, an effort-matching interpretation suggests that some team members may assume that because others on the team are likely loafing, they might as well, too.[12]

What Makes a Group a Team?

Many collections of individuals might appear, on the surface, to be a team. However, the mere fact that they occupy the same space or share some common characteristic is not a sufficient basis for calling them a team. People who congregate at a street corner to view the results of a car accident or who gather around a water cooler to exchange small talk might be called a group in the loosest sense of the word, but they are certainly not a team. What, then, are the precise criteria or conditions that you can use to decide whether a set of people actually makes up a team?

For a humorous but revealing example of teamwork, take a look at the video in **CHECK THIS OUT 12.3: It Takes a Team to Harmonize** and consider how different the result would be if each person was just singing his own song.

Teams Are Goal-Oriented
The first important consideration is whether the people are collectively pursuing a common objective.[13] People in teams do not come together for no reason and behave in some

Check This Out 12.2:
Groupthink
Check This Out 12.3:
It Takes a Team to Harmonize

random way. Instead, they seek some goal by collective action that could not be achieved by each member acting alone as an individual. For example, teams are organized around a particular task with the goal of completing the project or product.

A second important criterion is that members share responsibility for the team's outcome. For example, one production team member might manufacture ink cartridges and pass along her component part to another team member who produces the plastic casing for the printer (and so on), with these and other members of the team sharing responsibility for the quality of the final outcome produced.[14]

A third important criterion is whether the people have worked out a set of rules and expectations that define how they interact with one another and regulate their behavior to reach the team's goal. In other words, participants learn how to coordinate their actions based on what is expected of each member, what will (or will not) be tolerated, and what will be rewarded by the other members of the team. In this way, individuals identify who is to do what, who will have more (or less) power or authority, and what will happen to those who do not do what others on the team expect and want.

Somewhat like the larger organizational structure that we discussed at length in Chapter 5, teams develop a pattern of social organization. Every team consists of **norms** that all members of that team are expected to follow; **roles**, or specialized functions that each member of the team plays; **ranks**, or the hierarchy that prescribes levels of authority; and **controls** that members use to reward desired contributions and punish negative deviations.

For example, a team might have norms of arriving on time for meetings, coming prepared, and leaving all personal agendas behind. But some teams also have norms that can be detrimental to group outcomes, such as multitasking or checking phone and text messages during meetings. Individuals within a team might take on the role of note-taker, social facilitator, or conflict moderator. Others might become isolators or obstructionists, disrupting team morale and momentum. Team leaders often assume higher ranking in the group; new members share lower ranks or status. When a team member distracts

Vitaliy Hrabar/Shutterstock.com

others or draws focus away from the goal, other members may control the deviation by encouraging the individual to get back on track. Consistent and extreme deviations may even result in a member's expulsion from the team. These norms, roles, ranks, and controls are the four common regularities that shape team culture.

Teams Are Specialized Groups

All teams are groups, but not all groups are teams. Groups can exist for personal, social, professional, and relational reasons, with members sharing goals of personal fulfillment, connection or affiliation, status, enjoyment, or companionship. Teams, however, consist of individuals who come together for a very specific purpose: "to provide an organizational product, plan, decision, or service."[15] Teams, like groups, are more than an aggregate of individuals. They are a specialized work group. These teams are manifested in a number of different forms or types in the workplace.

Project versus Production Teams[16] Teams can be differentiated by the type of their task or product. Project teams focus on processing information, such as planning, deliberating, creating, making decisions, and solving problems. Production teams—such as manufacturing, construction, or assembly teams—are groups that engage in some kind of hands-on physical activity to accomplish behavioral tasks. Of the two types, project teams are more common.

Project-team members usually sort through copious amounts of information important to the task and interact extensively with each other. Members critically analyze and evaluate data, deliberating over possible solutions. As you can see, communication skills are key to the effectiveness of project teams. Production teams consist of highly skilled members who can execute particular behaviors in coordination with other team members, given the task requirements of sequenced or synchronized activity. Production teams that assemble a new car require that each specialist coordinate with others on the team to provide and install a particular part or unit in the proper sequence. Frames are built first, engines are installed subsequently, and tires are last.

Ad hoc versus Ongoing Teams Teams can also be differentiated on the basis of duration, or how long they tend to exist. Ad hoc teams are those that are short lived. They typically exist to tackle one single issue, policy, or problem; once it is solved, members are disbanded. Team members are brought together to address an emergency, a specific problem, or a special purpose. Ad hoc teams might be called to develop an emergency plan to clean an oil spill, write a grant proposal, draft a job description, develop performance-appraisal criteria, or prioritize the allocation of onetime funds from some charitable organization.

Ongoing teams canexist indefinitely. These teams may focus on the same task over and over again or they may be continually assigned new tasks. For example, the budget advisory team at California State University, Long Beach consists of faculty, staff, and administrators who come together to set priorities and to propose and recommend an annual budget to the president. With each new budget cycle, the team resumes membership roles and the process begins again. Large organizations often employ training teams to design and implement a variety of technical and nontechnical workshops as the needs of the organization evolve.

Ongoing teams are more common in organizations than ad hoc teams are. Moreover, ad hoc teams some times morph into more permanent ongoing teams. Ted Ross in our opening vignette began with ad hoc teams of graphic designers; as contracts came into the company, he eventually hired a permanent design team. Obviously, team duration might influence members' sustained motivation, satisfaction with the team, rules for resolving conflict, and more. How these teams are managed, then, becomes critical to their ongoing effectiveness and utility within the organization.

Face-to-face versus Virtual Teams[17] Teams are further defined by member proximity. Members of face-to-face teams are co-located in the same work environment and physically meet to deliberate and coordinate activities. They work together in real time. Virtual teams (also referred to as distributed teams) are not co-located, and they do not necessarily interact with each other in real time. As digital natives, virtual team members rely on new media to communicate, including instant messaging, email, VoIP or Skype, videoconferencing, audioconferencing, and webconferencing. Such technologies allow members to work interdependently with one another, often at times of their own choosing. As Chapter 6 explains, the features of new media have removed most of the barriers of time and space that made virtual teams so difficult in the past. New media technologies have made virtual teams not only possible but also increasingly popular and, for many organizations, cost effective. In spite of its popularity, recent research suggests that the degree of virtuality affects team members' satisfaction and perceptions of team effectiveness. The greater the real and perceived distance among members of the team, the less satisfied they become and the less productive they feel.[18]

What Makes Teams Work?

Effective teams don't just happen. They need to be planned, built, maintained, and sustained. In order for teams to work, to progress toward some meaningful goal or objective, certain conditions must be met. The popular trade literature is full of recommendations for making teams work. Much of these recommendations are supported by academic research. As we review these recommendations, keep in mind that such advice is targeted primarily toward project rather than production teams. Consolidating the research and thinking across both academic and applied communities reveals a number of important considerations.

First Determine If You Need a Team

Teams may be fashionable, but they are not always appropriate, as we discussed earlier in this chapter. Carefully consider the task: Can it be handled by a highly skilled individual working alone or does the task require the input of a variety of individuals who can bring different skill sets and experiences to the table? Teams work when the task can be better accomplished by a group than by an individual working alone.

Provide Organizational Support

Teams work best when the organization provides the team with all the necessary resources to meet their objectives. These resources typically include access to information, desirable meeting places and times, administrative and technical support, capital, allocated work time, and external support and expertise as needed. Rewards and recognition for group efforts and outcomes are additional forms of organizational support. The degree of **team potency**, defined as members' collective perceptions that their team will be successful, is determined in large part by these external factors of organizational support.[19]

Managers who give authority to teams, who let them know that their collective decisions will be implemented also add to perceptions of team potency. In other words, team members have to believe that their actions will be taken seriously and that their decisions will not be shelved. These forms of organizational support lead to better team enthusiasm, satisfaction, energy, and commitment. Teams simply perform better as perceptions of potency increase.[20]

Define Team Objectives

Critical to any team's effectiveness is knowing what the team intends to accomplish. Results-driven goals or objectives provide the basis for any action the team takes. A clear statement of the team's objectives becomes the basis for identifying the particular skills and expertise needed for team membership.

Once defined (and team members identified), the objectives must be clearly communicated to the team. Members must be able to articulate and openly commit to those objectives. Moreover, the team needs to be reminded of those objectives throughout deliberations. Objectives, by definition, give clear direction to deliberations and team activities. Too often, teams are given only vague direction of what to do or how to do it. Teams should always begin by asking and answering these questions:

- Why are we here?
- What do we want to accomplish; what's our target?
- How will we know when we get there; how will we measure or assess outcome?

Create the Team

Like any good sports team, selecting the players requires careful, thoughtful planning so that they can develop and grow into a cohesive, winning team. First, determine what skills and capabilities are required to accomplish the team's objectives. Next, identify key individuals who have those particular talents and expertise. At some point, tasks will need to be assigned or aligned with those members' special strengths. Consider also individual personalities; some people simply do not get along well with others—however competent they may be. In other words, some of the "best" people are not always the "right" people. Optimal team size ranges from five to twelve, depending on what article you read. Size is key; smaller teams accomplish more than do larger teams, and fewer participants are easier to facilitate and coordinate. Finally, not all members are available to meet at the times and dates when others can. Managing schedules can be challenging; moreover, some people are less accommodating than others.

Once the team is created, you may find that some members simply do not belong. For instance, team members who cannot be genuinely open to others about their own mistakes and weaknesses undermine perceptions of trust. The lack of trust often leads to "veiled discussions and guarded comments" which further destroy essential and constructive conflict.[21] Other members may lack commitment to the team's goals. When members undermine teamwork, they must either be counseled and rehabilitated—or removed.

Establish Ground Rules

Members need to know why they have been chosen for the team. Explain their specialized roles. Tell Jack, for instance, that he's been brought in to serve as a technical expert; Mary Elizabeth knows the client; Harry offers managerial experience; and Charles is the best sales rep on staff. Explain their responsibilities to the team, emphasizing the team's goals, team ownership of the outcome, and team identity. Set agendas, assign tasks, and provide team training, as needed. Identifying roles and responsibilities up front minimizes subsequent ambiguities and role conflict. Individuals should know what they are supposed to do and who will be held accountable for what.

Members also need to know how they are supposed to behave in the team. In a recent team experience with department heads who came together to do strategic planning for their organization, Dr. Plax explored and established with the team a number of ground rules. Before the team's deliberations commenced, they agreed on this set:

- Keep expectations high.
- What we do here matters.
- There are no bad ideas.
- We listen to others, even with their views are extreme or wrong.
- Consensus is desirable, but not essential. We may not all agree.
- Leave personal agendas at the door. The team agenda is all that's important here.
- Strategic planning is a good thing: Believe it.
- Let's not worry about costs for our plans at this point; when funds are limited is exactly when establishing priorities is essential.
- We share ownership of whatever results we generate. This is no longer "their" plan; it's "our" plan.
- We all arrive on time, and we all leave together.
- Cell phones, texting, and email are suspended during deliberations.

Notice that these rules are both general and specific. The best rules are those that emanate from the team members themselves. Participants are more likely to adopt and adhere to rules they helped to generate—rather than those that are assigned from above.

Facilitate Collaboration, Disagreement, and Trust

Working well together is fundamental to the success of any team. At first glance, you might suspect that working well together means always getting along, easily agreeing, achieving consensus most if not all of the time, and thinking and acting alike. But your

Greg Epperson/Shutterstock.com

suspicions would be wrong. Working well together is often messy, complicated, and tiring. (Your "team" authors speak from experience!)

Effective team members trust one another. They show their trust in a number of important ways. First, they say what they think and they mean what they say. Second, they listen to what others in the team say and they fully respond. Third, they treat others with dignity and respect at all times. (It's okay to disagree, but it's not okay to be disagreeable.) Fourth, they come across as consistent, predictable, and dependable. They hold themselves and others in the group accountable. They also know that it's safe to voice minority views or controversial ideas. Finally, if individual members stumble momentarily, others will compensate by stepping in and ensuring the job gets done for the sake of the team.[22] **MODULE 1: How Do I "Get In and Fit In" to My Organization's Unique Culture?**

Define Standards for Performance

Teams that work have clearly defined standards or expectations for performance. Successful teams establish high standards of performance, and unsuccessful teams have either ill defined or very low standards for performance. Moreover, teams determine how they want to meet those standards; sometimes the means to achieve may be dishonest, coercive, or manipulative. Other teams may choose to excel by performing with integrity, true grit, and individual skill and perseverance.[23]

For instance, a college basketball team may set standards to compete as one of the Final Four in the NCAA March Madness competition; another team may set their standards much lower by settling for winning one more game than they lose during the season. In order to achieve, team members might shove, purposely trip, or foul out opponents' players; others might work together to pass the ball around quickly, set up a sophisticated defense, and rebound more effectively.

Organizational teams that work effectively share a concern for excellence and high-quality outcomes. The members coordinate their activities in such a way that meeting these standards for performance makes them feel good about being members of the team.

Push for Commitment

Commitment to the team is often cited as crucial for team success. Members must feel some enthusiasm and excitement about working with one another. They must be galvanized to pursue the team's common goal, sublimating their own personal agendas. Committed team members will do just about anything to assure that the team succeeds. They will shift and assume one another's responsibilities as the job requires. Moreover, members share an identity with the team, subsuming their individual identities for that of the group.[24]

Although much as been written about the importance of team commitment, often overlooked is the role of organizational commitment. Both types of commitment are essential for team success. Consider this scenario: Team members of Organization X are intensely committed to one another but at the expense of the organization. They work hard to find ways to undermine the organization, to ignore institutional goals, and to justify their dissatisfaction and dissension. Do they have team commitment? Sure, but they lack organizational commitment. By developing norms counter to the organizational culture, they lack an identity with Organization X.

Teams committed to the organization view their contributions as supporting the organization as a whole. To make this happen, team members must understand the goals and objectives of the organization more generally and perceive some sense of connection with those goals. Moreover, they need to appreciate how their work within the team supports those goals. When teams see their outcomes as part of the bigger picture, they take pride in the organization and believe that what they do is for some greater good of the company.[25]

Pause and Reflect

To ensure continued focus among team members, it's a good idea to regularly review the team's objectives. Check in with team members; go over the reasons for their existence as a team:

- Why are we here?

- What do we want to accomplish; what's our target?

- How will we know when we get there; how will we measure or assess outcome?

While taking the time to review objectives, revisit as well standards of performance. Members should collectively evaluate their current levels of performance and what compromises they may have made. Most importantly, use the time to reflect on how well the team is doing. Give recognition for both individual and team accomplishments along the way. Remember that sometimes the process is even more meaningful than the immediate outcome. Teams that work spend the time reflecting on their group identity and ensuring that everyone feels valued for his or her contributions.

You'll find an intriguing team-building exercise in **CHECK THIS OUT 12.4: The Marshmallow Challenge** that shows the importance of process for team productivity.

What Makes Teams Fail?

In spite of the popularity of teams and all the advice about how to make them work, the truth is that organizations spend millions of dollars and thousands of hours on teams that eventually fail. For example, year after year the data on failure rates for information technology (IT) team projects demonstrate that "20% of IT projects are canceled before completion and less than a third are finished on time and within budget."[26] A study of an apparel manufacturing company with 122 sewing teams revealed that team output varied by as much as 100 percent between highly productive teams and those struggling to meet performance goals.[27] Clearly, not all teams are successful.

We might argue that team failure is the absence or obverse of all the reasons why teams work that were discussed above: insufficient organizational support, ill-conceived team objectives, personality conflicts, undifferentiated roles and responsibilities, lack of trust, too much or too little consensus, low standards for performance, and little or no team synergy. And all those reasons for failure would be true. Let's look at six common obstacles that make teams fail.

Team Members Don't Know What to Do[28]

Members are chosen for their individual expertise; they provide a particular kind of resource. It's not skills or experience they lack; rather, it's direction. As we discussed earlier, team members need clear objectives that they can articulate and commit to. Objectives,

Check This Out 12.4:
The Marshmallow Challenge

by definition, tell people what must be done. Without specific objectives defined and conspicuous, members flounder and drift from the target.

In addition, team members may not know how to play as a team. They do not know how to work together; neither do they understand the dynamics of teamwork. Constructive conflict, collaborative decision making, open communication, shared responsibility, and trust are lacking. They do not appreciate what it means to relinquish or put aside individual identity and become identified with the team. As a result, personal agendas prevail, often at the expense of group goals.

Students often complain to your authors that they hate semester-long group work. They argue that some members bail from their responsibilities, forcing others in the group to take on even more of the load. Frustrated and discouraged, students contend that loafers are not held accountable. Quality or output, then, suffers. Clearly, students come to the group fully capable of completing the task, but they may neither recognize nor assume their roles and responsibilities as team players. Sometimes these student groups fail because they lack the necessary direction. They do not know what to do or how to do it.

We find the same kinds of complaints from individuals in the workforce. They find themselves on a project team only to discover that they are unsure about what they are supposed to do. As a result, they spend a lot of time talking about their uncertainties, anxieties, and dislike for the team experience.

Employees and Managers Mistrust Teams[29]

For a variety of reasons, an anti-team culture prevails in many organizations. This sentiment holds true for both employees and management. Employees are often resistant to teamwork, claiming that they work better alone, preferring social isolation to the communication demands of a group, or in the case of high performers, they may not want to sublimate personal successes and individual recognition. Some employees enjoy competition and eschew group dynamics of cooperation and collaboration. Politically driven or ambitious employees may be reluctant to work in teams, fearing that team outcomes will quell opportunities for upward mobility.

Management may mistrust and resist teams for similar reasons and more. Some managers find teams difficult to manage, requiring new kinds of collaborative leadership skills. Those locked into a traditional, hierarchical, functional management system may fear losing some of their authority or control of teams. Successful teams need the authority to act and make decisions. Requiring less supervision, then, managers may feel threatened about their own job security. Finally, some managers may resist acknowledging the efforts or successes of a team, preferring instead to take full credit themselves. **MODULE 9: How Do I Navigate Office Politics?**

Team Training Is Expensive, Time Consuming, and Effortful[30]

Remember that making teams work requires careful planning. Added to that, team members and leaders or facilitators require extensive training to operate effectively in teams. Establishing and maintaining good working interpersonal relationships can be difficult, and yet team work demands that members find ways to interact and get along. Developing relationships in the workplace is the topic of Chapter 5.

All too often, management and employees underestimate the time involved in learning complex communication skills requisite to building and maintaining teams. Consider, for instance, the importance of developing these basic skills:

Giving feedback.

Responding to criticism.

Asking open-ended questions.

Providing reinforcement.

Asking for help.

Admitting mistakes and failures.

Admitting when you don't know.

Demonstrating trust.

Negotiating to a compromise.

Disagreeing with others.

Asking for clarification.

Advocating a position.

Showing concern or empathy.

Listening actively.

Facilitating others' participation.

Taking turns.

Giving deference to others.

Showing respect.

Maintaining eye contact.

Demonstrating interest.

Spending time in the team developing and testing out these person-centered skills, although essential, is often perceived as taking time away from real work. Moreover, team members may complain that these kinds of softskills are both intuitive and obvious and don't require training. These same people look at team training seminars as a waste of time, intrusive, and unhelpful. Yet, putting people into teams without the essential skills predisposes teams to fail. People have to know how to work together as a team, how to comfortably interact and disagree—or they can't and won't be effective. Not surprisingly, the more people fail in teams, the more likely they will criticize teamwork activity as unproductive and useless.

The Team Lacks Urgency

Sometimes teams fail because there is no sense of urgency to win, to do well, or to complete a project on time. When teams do not perceive that their objective is important or urgent, they find little or no reason to maintain momentum and focus. When a car bomb was left in New York's Time Square in May 2010, the urgency of locating an unknown terrorist led a team of investigators to find Faisal Shahzad within forty-eight hours, pulling him off a plane headed for Dubai. The risk or fear of failing to apprehend the terrorist suspect incentivized investigators to succeed—and succeed now.

In most workplaces, target completion times provide teams with a sense of urgency as well. Urgency becomes time certain. Contractual deadlines often drive team members to complete projects. Failure to meet deadlines costs the organization money (and

karam Miri/Shutterstock.com

Weigh In 12.1:
*Which Would You
Rather Do?*

potentially clients as well). Without some kind of deadline, teams will lose their sense of urgency and purpose.

Team Members Have Other Priorities[31]

Work places a lot of demands on employees. Many workers today find that they simply can't do everything on their lists. Thus, they must prioritize or rank order their individual and team tasks. Although deadlines often dictate priorities, individuals find all kinds of reasons to avoid some tasks and spend more time on others. For instance, if a team member's individual projects are inherently more interesting than the team tasks, that individual may focus on those at the expense of the team's. Sometimes, the people on the team make all the difference in the amount of pleasure or satisfaction derived from the task. Individuals may be reluctant to work on more difficult tasks, preferring instead to focus their energies on something easier. Finally, some tasks provide greater rewards than others, like money, promotions, and other forms of recognition.

Use **WEIGH IN 12.1: Which Would You Rather Do?** to come up with a "bucket list" of your work priorities.

One Bad Apple Can Spoil the Team

Some teams thrive, but enough of them fail to warrant a look at the members themselves. Most of the research on teams looks at group or organizational factors that make teams work or fail. One group of researchers argued that "in some cases, a single, toxic team member may be the catalyst for group-level dysfunction,"[32] resulting in the **bad apple effect**. Sure enough, their findings revealed that one team member can sufficiently disrupt a team to have a profoundly negative impact on group functioning. Toxic team members typically withhold effort, communicate negative affect toward the group, task, and process, and engage in socially inappropriate behaviors (such as bullying or refusing to cooperate). Wetlaufer calls these bad apples "team destroyers."[33] Andrews talks about how these "hard-core offenders" can "cripple employee morale."[34]

Link Out 12.1:
Lencioni Talks Teams

Check This Out 12.5:
What Makes Teams Work or Fail?

The sequence of events in response to bad apples in groups goes like this:[35] First, when the bad apple emerges, other team members try to change the person's negative behavior. When that fails, members assume that the individual is either resistant or unwilling to change. They conclude that the bad apple's behavior is probably personality-based and intractable. Next, members decide to exclude or reject the bad apple, but that's almost impossible to do in a team. Bad apples within a group are hard for people to ignore, demand a lot of attention, and consume a lot of the group's time and effort. As you might expect, bad is stronger than good in these team contexts, causing an insidious spillover effect of negativity and frustration, alienation and helplessness. In the end, team members are likely to feel sufficiently discouraged to give up or give in. The good news is that such toxic team members are not all that common; the bad news is that their impact on teams is substantial.[36]

Executive-team development consultant and author Patrick Lencioni approaches team failure from another perspective in his book *The Five Dysfunctions of a Team*.[37] He tells the fable of a new CEO who must face and unite a dysfunctional team of players—or fail. Using story telling to illustrate his model, Lencioni draws upon many of the same reasons for team failure and success discussed in this chapter and more. For an online interview with Lencioni, go to LINK OUT 12.1: **Lencioni Talks Teams**.

For thoughts about team success from other experts—from the space shuttle's launch director to a coach of U.S. women's World Cup soccer team to the founder of Habitat for Humanity as well as many business executives—see CHECK THIS OUT 12.5: **What Makes Teams Work or Fail?**

What Influence Can You Have on the Team?

In most team situations, the level of effectiveness is determined in large part by the team leader. However, the transactional nature of the communication exchanges in teams means that both team leaders and members are important. In Chapter 1 we explained how sources and receivers simultaneously exchange messages, verbally and nonverbally. They assess each others' messages, modify their own, and continually adapt to each

fstockfoto/Shutterstock.com

other's feedback. What happens during team exchanges, then, is the responsibility of both team leaders and members. Even so, what the leader says and does sets the stage for how all other members of the team will react and participate. As a team member, your influence on the team can be substantial, but it's even more so if you are the leader.

Leaders Who Make a Difference

Do a Google search for "effective team leaders" on the Internet and you'll find about 7,320,000 postings, each identifying characteristics of good and bad team leaders. Apparently, we don't lack for recommendations on how to be effective as a team leader. An examination of the academic literature[38] reveals a number of theoretical perspectives (not millions, however) that speak to leaders' personality traits (self-confidence, integrity, and sensitivity), leadership styles (such as authoritarian or democratic), situational or contingency leaders (whose leadership strategies depend on the task or situation), functional leaders (such as information-giver, gatekeeper, and energizer), and leaders' use of power (such as coercive, reward, and expert power).

Perhaps the most viable of all the perspectives advanced is what researchers call transformational leadership theory. This theory rests on the assumption that what leaders say and do can arouse or stimulate others to a higher level of thinking and doing.[39] Whereas traditional leaders operate from a "tell" orientation, **transformational leaders** "sell" their vision and ideas to others. The evidence overwhelmingly supports the idea that leaders are most effective when they persuade their constituents to get on board with their goals and objectives. Transformational leaders communicate to inspire team members, to build trust, and to unleash members' talents. In essence, they lead the charge!

A substantial body of literature over the last twenty-five years documents the validity and benefits of transformational leaders.[40] For instance, transformational leaders are able to energize or motivate others and keep them engaged in their work. As a result, workers report greater job satisfaction and higher levels of commitment to their organization. Both creativity and quality of job performance are enhanced under the direction of transformational leaders. Transformational leaders seem to create some kind of contagion or multiplier effect, whereby followers become inspired to do their best—and enjoy doing it. These findings seem to hold true across different kinds of groups (even virtual groups),[41] teams, and tasks. So, how do they do it? Researchers uncovered four dimensions or ways that transformational leaders make a difference with their teams.

- **They communicate a vision.** Visionary leaders, like Barack Obama, Ronald Reagan, and Eleanor Roosevelt, are able to articulate a desirable future that others might also want and appreciate. They visualize for people what the future will look like with (and without) the particular solution or cause that they advance. Similarly, transformational team leaders, compel others to share in their vision and goal for the team, and in some cases, for the whole organization. A vision is a simple statement of the direction that the team is headed or should be headed. Good or effective visions provide members with a sense of purpose and commitment to the team's goal.[42] Transformational team leaders communicate optimism and give meaning to projects.

- **They stimulate and challenge others.** Transformational leaders challenge conventions, take risks, and encourage others to think outside the box. They motivate team members to be creative, to ask questions, and to challenge or disagree with one another. They like messy team interactions that produce higher-quality outcomes.

- **They provide support.** Like any good mentor or coach, transformational leaders step in when needed, providing emotional, social, and intellectual support or guidance. These leaders are good listeners who know how to empathize with participants' problems or frustrations as they progress toward task completion. They pay attention to individual needs and concerns, respecting and acknowledging each member's unique contributions to the group. In each of these ways, transformational leaders boost participants' self-esteem and self-efficacy.

- **They model good behaviors.** Often charismatic, these leaders know how to be both charming and interpersonally attractive. People seem to genuinely like these leaders, and they want to spend time with them. At the same time, transformational leaders have convictions, take stands when others cannot or do not, and encourage others to do the same. Team members both admire and respect this kind of leader; they are inspired to want to be just like this individual.

It's no wonder, then, that teams led by transformational leaders flourish. Members enjoy working with them, are inspired to do their best work, and feel rewarded for a job well done.

Team Members Who Make a Difference

As inspirational as transformational leaders might be, team members cannot expect to find too many of them hanging around at work. These exceptional leaders are just that—an exception to the rule. Your team leader may not exhibit all the behaviors and qualities of the transformational leader; your team leader may be very good, average, or poor. Regardless of what kind of leader you have, you can make a difference in how the team works. What can you do?

Unlike the theoretical basis for team leadership, no corresponding framework defines what effective team members do. Researchers funded by the National Science Foundation developed an instrument to assess team members' effectiveness.[43] In so doing, the researchers combed the literature on teamwork and peer evaluation. They came up with "an initial pool of 392 items that reflected the broad array of behaviors and characteristics that describe individual team members' contributions to teams." After administering the items to almost three thousand college students university-wide, they uncovered five underlying factors or dimensions that reflect what it means to be an effective team member. So, what do effective team members do to make a difference?

1. **They contribute to the team's work.** Effective team members are perceived to do their fair share, fulfilling their work responsibilities to the team. They come to team meetings prepared, complete their work on time, and make important contributions to the team's final product. These individuals don't give up; they keep trying even when the task or situation becomes difficult. Importantly, these people pitch in and help others on the team when it's needed.

2. **They communicate effectively with teammates.** Effective team members encourage others on the team, facilitate interaction, and express enthusiasm about working on the team. They're also active listeners; they hear, acknowledge, and respond to what others have to say. They solicit team input as needed, take criticism well, and use others' feedback to improve their own performance. They also ask for and take help from others when they need it.

3. **They keep the team on track.** These members hold not only themselves but others accountable for their work progress. They monitor and evaluate what others do, and they provide constructive feedback. They stay on top of any external distractions that may prevent the team from progressing. These individuals motivate others to do a good job. They make sure that members have the necessary resources to complete their tasks.

4. **They expect quality.** Effective team members believe in the team. They expect the team to succeed and to do high-quality work. They care not only about team members but also about the performance standards of their task. Emphasizing a strong work ethic, these team members both expect and want their team to excel.

5. **They have relevant knowledge, skills, and abilities.** As might be expected, effective team members possess the essential skills and expertise to do a good job for the team. They know just enough about other team members' responsibilities to fill in when needed. They have special talents important to the team's outcome that others on the team do not have.

Weigh In 12.2:
What Kind of Team Member Are You?

A close examination of these team-member characteristics reveals an uncanny resemblance to the transformational qualities exhibited by effective team leaders. In essence, effective team leaders and effective team members literally transform others on the team to be the best that they can possibly be. Recall that both leaders and members have mutual responsibilities to fulfill in order for a team to be successful. Perhaps, then, it comes as no surprise that leaders and members coordinate their actions and interactions in ways that inspire, demand, demonstrate, and achieve team goals. To see how you stack up as a team member in terms of these five factors, answer the questions in **WEIGH IN 12.2: What Kind of Team Member Are You?**

As the nature of jobs change, teams become an inevitable part of contemporary work life. Teams are a special type of work group, and like all groups, team members collectively pursue some kind of common objective, sharing in the responsibility for the group's outcome. Teams are essential to managing complex tasks that require the specialized skills of a group of people. Work teams can be project or production types, ad hoc or ongoing, and face-to-face or virtual. Regardless of team type, what makes teams work follows a particular set of principles that direct team fate.

Teams need to be planned, built, nurtured, and sustained. In spite of all we know about how to make teams effective, far too many of them fail. As a result, both management and employees share reservations about the use of teams in the workplace. Recognizing the reasons why teams fail sets the stage for anticipating and confronting obstacles as they occur. Perhaps most critical to team success (and failure) is you. Whether your role is to lead or to participate as a member of the team, what you say and do can make all the difference in how the team functions and what outcomes might result. Given the transactional nature of communication that occurs in team deliberations, both sources and receivers, both leaders and followers, are mutually responsible for the processes and results.

This chapter overviews the research that underscores both the utility and hazards of using teams. We have shown you what makes teams work and what makes teams fail. We have provided you with some guidelines on what to do and what not to do as leaders and members of work teams. Finally, we have identified specific strategies you can use and a theoretical frame from which to use them.

Use your Speech Communication CourseMate for *Business & Communication in a Digital Age* for quick access to the electronic resources that accompany this text. These resources include

Study tools that will help you assess your learning and prepare for exams (*digital glossary, key term flash cards, review quizzes*).

Activities and assignments that will help you hone your knowledge and build your communication skills throughout the course (*Visualize! Practice!, Weigh In!, Check This Out, and Link Out activities; modules; review questions*).

Media resources that will help you explore communication concepts online (*Enhanced eBook*), develop your speech outlines (*Speech Builder Express 3.0*), watch and critique videos of sample speeches and communication situations (*interactive video activities*), upload your speech videos for peer reviewing and critique other students' speeches (*Speech Studio online speech review tool*), and download chapter review so you can study when and where you'd like (*Audio Study Tools*).

Key Points

- Organizations use teams to make complex tasks more doable and a large workforce more manageable. Teams also offer greater workforce flexibility and focus, and a sense of commitment and ownership.

- But teams don't always make sense, especially when a particular task can be better accomplished by one individual, among other factors.

- A group of people becomes a team when they share a common purpose or goal. Unlike groups, team members are carefully chosen for the particular and complementary skills that allow the team to achieve or complete complex goals and tasks.

- Effective teams don't just happen; they need to be planned, built, maintained, and sustained. We provide several important considerations to facilitate this process.

- Too often teams fail. Several obstacles to making them work include
  - ✔ Team members don't know what to do.
  - ✔ Employees and managers mistrust teams.
  - ✔ Team training is expensive, time consuming, and takes effort.
  - ✔ The team lacks urgency.
  - ✔ Team members have other priorities.
  - ✔ One bad apple can spoil the team.

- Team leaders can make a difference by communicating a vision, stimulating and challenging members, providing support, and modeling good behaviors.

- Team members can make a difference by contributing to the team's work, communicating effectively with teammates, keeping the team on track, demanding quality, and bringing with them special talents and skills important to the task.

Key Terms

team (266)

groupthink (269)

social loafing (269)

norms (270)

roles (270)

ranks (270)

controls (270)

team potency (272)

bad apple effect (279)

transformational leaders (281)

Questions for Critical Thinking and Review

1. Some teams make sense; some teams don't. What teams have you participated in that ended up not making much sense to you? Why was that the case?

2. Most of us would prefer to work with people who we like as opposed to people who we don't. Why might "friends" among team members be problematic? What implications might that have for constructive conflict or group think?

3. What makes the use of teams so cost effective to an organization?

4. Research reveals that the degree of virtuality negatively affects team members' satisfaction and perceptions of team effectiveness. Might these effects change with people who happen to be "digital natives"?

5. What does *team potency* mean, and why does it matter to the overall functioning of the team? Research suggests that managers who give authority to teams increase perceptions of potency. How do managers do that?

6. Team members typically come together and then spend an inordinate amount of time figuring out what they are supposed to do. How might a lack of direction influence members' perceptions of the team experience?

7. How might team members hold social loafers accountable for their behavior in groups? If the loafer is a friend of yours, how will that influence your response to him or her?

8. What kind of person doesn't like a team? In other words, what kind of people aren't all that well suited to be team players?

9. Some very interesting research on "bad apples" suggests that bad outweighs good when it comes to team members. That is, it only seems to take one toxic member to spoil an entire team experience. As a team member, how would you handle a toxic member? As a team leader, how would you manage a toxic member?

10. Have you ever worked with a transformational leader? What qualities did this person display? What impact did this leader have on you personally and professionally?

Chapter 13

Business and Professional Writing:
How Do I Best Present Myself in Writing?

Chapter Outline

What Are the Most Common Types of Business Documents?

- Letters: Formal Written Communication with a Person or an Organization
- Memos: Brief and Concise Written Internal Communication
- Proposals: A Written Means to Obtain Business
- Brief Reports: Updates on Organizational Issues
- Formal Reports: In-Depth Accounts of Business Issues
- Blogs and Social Media: Quick and Wide Dissemination of Information

What Are the Steps to Creating a Business Document?

- Step 1: Determine Your Objectives and Audience
- Step 2: Compile Facts, Supporting Data, and Other Research Materials
- Step 3: Develop a Logical Organizational Structure
- Step 4: Write a Draft of the Document
- Step 5: Revise the Document until It Is Clear and Concise

Ilja Mašík/Shutterstock.com

Chapter Learning Objectives

After completing this chapter, you should be able to

- Distinguish among the most common types of business documents.
- Employ a five-step process for successful business writing.
- Create documents that successfully engage and persuade your readers.
- Appreciate the value of a visually appealing document.
- Avoid common business writing problems which may detract from your credibility.

See also the modules that are relevant to this chapter:

   6: "You Gotta Have Style": Using APA and MLA Styles
   8: What's the Best Way to Organize and Outline My Presentation?

Module 6:
"You Gotta Have Style": Using APA and MLA Styles

Module 8:
What's the Best Way to Organize and Outline My Presentation?

Steve recently left his position as an advertising salesman

for a large metropolitan newspaper to pursue full-time what had been his part-time business and passion for the past few years: selling a vitamin supplement for horses that he and a group of nutritionists had developed and patented. His plan was to sell the supplements at horse shows and to continue to build his nationwide network of distributors.

Not long after taking the leap, Steve discovered how difficult the life of an entrepreneur really is. Many of the business tasks that he'd had support in accomplishing at the newspaper were now his sole responsibility. Steve was the bookkeeper, salesman, delivery man, and 24/7 customer service provider. He communicated with his product suppliers and distributors, answered the phones, and responded to incoming email. Additionally, a friend told him that many start-up ventures benefit by having a presence on Facebook and in the blogosphere. So now he was the chief social networker and blogger.

Not only was Steve overwhelmed with the sheer amount of work it was going to take to get his new venture off the ground, but he also worried that he lacked some of the skills to make it a success. Steve felt very confident in his product. He loved meeting people and talking with them about the supplement. Making sales at horse shows and feed stores, or even over the phone? No problem. However, Steve had very little confidence in his ability to write persuasively about his product either in print or online. College composition classes had long come and gone, and his previous job had required very little writing. When important documents like proposals or reports had to go out, Steve had relied on an entire department at the newspaper dedicated to writing business documents. And a blog? Forget about it! Every time he sat down at the computer to send an email, write a letter, or post something online, he struggled. But he knew that if his new business was going to succeed, he was going to have to brush up on his old writing skills—and learn some new ones.

Steve's story is common not only for entrepreneurs like him but for many new professionals. So you're getting an engineering degree? Going to be a doctor? Perhaps become a professional athlete? Think you won't need to write? Think again. The ability to express oneself well in writing is critical for all professionals in all business sectors. In fact, the significance of writing to the business enterprise is growing as people spend less time communicating on the phone and in person and conduct more business by email and over the Internet. Furthermore, as most organizations downsize and streamline their operations, writing departments like the one that helped Steve at the newspaper are mostly a bygone luxury.

This chapter will introduce you to the most common types of business documents, with special attention to preparing these documents for electronic transmittal. Additionally, we will cover some foundation principles for writing effective blog posts and comments as well as how to write persuasively and succinctly on social networking sites. We will give you five steps for preparing a winning document and cover how to proofread perfectly and format your documents so that they will be read and understood. Additionally, we will focus on some skills that will enhance your credibility and help you overcome limiting, mediocre writing.

Let's begin by discussing the importance and purpose of effective business writing. **Business writing** is defined as the preparation of any print or online document which supports or helps a business enterprise grow. For example, some business writing supports and facilitates work within an organization. This internal written communication includes project reports; written performance appraisals; internal memos or emails about issues like staffing, benefits, and project management; and written correspondence among colleagues. On the other hand, external written communication, such as proposals, business letters, blogs, and social networking posts, helps a business grow. In **LINK OUT 13.1: Writers on Business Writing**, a number of experienced writers talk to students about the importance of their business writing skills.

Effective business writing not only allows you to present yourself well, but it also gives you a powerful tool for doing whatever you do successfully. An internal study conducted by IBM compared the interactivity and engagement metrics for a series of edited and unedited webpages from IBM's site, and the results are startling: The edited pages received 30 percent more clicks on embedded links than the unedited pages did.[1] In other words, readers were far more responsive to pages that had been carefully written and edited for spelling, grammar, format, expression, and organization. If you could do something that would help you achieve 30 percent more success in your career, wouldn't you be interested in perfecting that skill? This chapter will help you do that.

What Are the Most Common Types of Business Documents?

In this section, we will overview a range of traditional business documents, such as memos and letters, and more contemporary forms of expression, such as blog posts. All the forms of written communication that we highlight here are more likely to be executed in digital form than in hard copy. Therefore, throughout this section, we will point out ways to effectively present the digital versions of these documents.

pavila/Shutterstock.com

Link Out 13.2:
Business Letter Scripts

Letters: Formal Written Communication with a Person or an Organization

Letters, whether printed and sent in an envelope via the postal service or transmitted digitally online, are an important form of external business communication. Letters can be used for many different business objectives, and each type of letter has unique characteristics. Examples include letters of application, reference letters, complaint letters, letters of acceptance, letters of inquiry, rejection letters, and acknowledgement letters. **LINK OUT 13.2:** **Business Letter Scripts** provides samples and templates for many different kinds of business letters.

Common to all types of business letters is the need for clarity and brevity. Business letters are not an opportunity for you to demonstrate your creative writing skills; they are an opportunity for you to communicate a specific point to a specific person. To do so effectively, you will need to be mindful of the appropriate *tone* and *style* as well as the visual *layout* of the letter.

When you engage someone outside your organization through a letter, whatever the reason, your primary objective is to convey a positive impression of yourself and your company. The best way to accomplish this objective is to carefully consider who will be reading your letter and why. Even if you don't know the recipient of your letter, you should know enough about him or her to write a reader-centered document. When you write a letter with your reader in mind, you are apt to use appropriate language and stay focused on the purpose of your letter, because you have an understanding of why the reader is taking the time to read it. For example, compare two versions of a rejection letter (Figures 13.1 and 13.2). Which letter conveys a more positive image of the writer and the organization she represents? In what ways is Letter B more reader-focused than Letter A?

Your writing style in a letter may range from informal (when writing to a close associate) to formal and restrained (when addressing a new client, writing a "cold" sales letter,

FIGURE 13.1
Letter A

Midtown Orthodontic Office
7745 Main Street
Surf City, FL 55555

July 31, 2011

Terry Smith
East Coast Orthodontic Supply Co.
157 Beach Rd.
Atlantic Beach, SC 44444

Dear Mr. Smith:

We received the sample supplies that you sent last week. We are not interested in your company's products; we have located a vendor more qualified than you.

Sincerely,

Sue McFarland
Office Manager

FIGURE 13.2
Letter B

Midtown Orthodontic Office
7745 Main Street
Surf City, FL 55555

July 31, 2011

Terry Smith
East Coast Orthodontic Supply Co.
157 Beach Rd.
Atlantic Beach, SC 44444

Dear Mr. Smith:

Thank you for taking the time and effort to provide our office with samples of your supplies. We evaluated your products and pricing with that of our current supplier, and determined that our existing arrangement is working well for us.

We will keep your company information as well as your contact data on file and contact you should our supply needs change.

Sincerely,

Sue McFarland
Office Manager

or writing to someone you don't know). Here is a brief example of the difference between informal and formal:

> **Informal:** Our decision to adopt your software was the best we've made in a long time. Thanks so much for all your help!

> **Formal:** You will be pleased to know that using your firm's software package has resulted in positive changes for our department. We appreciate your assistance with our purchase.

Link Out 13.3:
*Business Letter
Formats*
Link Out 13.4:
*Business Letter
Basics*

Because letters are a fairly formal type of business communication, you will more often than not need to adopt a fairly formal writing approach. However, your letters should not be so formal and stylized that the reader feels as if he or she is reading a legal document. As in business speaking, you should strive simultaneously for professionalism and interpersonal connection with your audience. For example,

> **Inappropriate in most cases:** In response to your query, be advised that we will not be renewing our agreement with you. You may address any further questions with regard to this matter to my office.

> **Better:** I received the annual agreement renewal form from your office. However, we have decided not to renew this year. If you would like to discuss this further, please let me know.

The inappropriate version of this statement is outdated and sounds rather pretentious. Effective contemporary business writing is more personal and down to earth, as illustrated by the "better" choice.

Using a standard format for a business letter can enhance its visual appeal as well as your credibility. Standard formats include the *block style* (every line begins at the left margin, including the date, salutation, closing, and signature); the *modified block style* (the date, close, and signature all begin at the center of the page; paragraphs are left justified); and the *modified block style with indent* (paragraphs are indented five spaces; the date, closing, and signature appear to the right of center). **LINK OUT 13.3: Business Letter Formats** summarizes these three styles.

Purdue University's online writing lab (OWL) provides an excellent overview of the basic elements of a business letter: **LINK OUT 13.4: Business Letter Basics**.

The format you select is not particularly important. What is important, however, is that you use one of the standard formats and use it consistently throughout the letter.

When formatting a letter to be read digitally (on a computer screen, iPad, or mobile phone), you should keep in mind some special formatting considerations. Research indicates that people read the same amount of text more slowly on a computer screen or tablet than in hard-copy print.[2] Therefore, when writing a digital letter, write succinctly and keep the message as brief as possible to avoid losing your reader. Embed the letter within the email field, but attach it as a PDF file, as well. Doing so will preserve the fonts and spacing that you used in case the reader prints the letter.

Additionally, when you send a digital letter, take advantage of the medium to make your message user-friendly. For example, embed links to sites or documents that may offer support for your letter's points. The reader can choose to visit those sites, or not. Be sure to include the http:// at the beginning of any website address in a digital letter so that the reader can easily click on the link and head to the site. Finally, use the Urgent flag on email sparingly, and create a brief and highly descriptive subject line for emailed letters. Meaningful subject lines will call attention to your message in a crowded inbox, as well as help the recipient file the message appropriately.

For some things to avoid in your subject lines, read **LINK OUT 13.5: Six Subject Line Mistakes**. For a list of words never to use in your subject lines because they can trigger spam flags and push your message into the trash before it's read, go to **LINK OUT 13.6: Spam Triggers**. And here is some advice for writing persuasive subject lines: **LINK OUT 13.7: Subject Lines That Get Clicked**.

After you check out these pieces of advice, see if you can tell the difference between good and bad subject lines in **VISUALIZE! PRACTICE! 13.1: Subject Lines That Work**.

In summary, business letters are used to communicate on a relatively formal level with individuals outside your organization. There are many reasons for writing a letter, but your overarching goal should be to create a positive impression of you and your company for the reader. Be professional yet conversational; write with an understanding of your reader. Use a standard business letter format. If you plan to send your letter digitally, keep in mind that it should be shorter and more concise than a letter you mail in hard-copy form. Additionally, digital letters give you the opportunity to offer your readers additional information without overwhelming them with paper materials.

Luna Vandoorne/Shutterstock.com

LINK OUT 13.8: Job Search Letters provides advice for letters at all stages of job searches, from requesting a reference to accepting a job offer and replying to a rejection.

Checklist for a Business Letter

✔ Business letters should be single-spaced with double spaces between paragraphs.

✔ Margins should be uniform.

✔ Hard-copy letters should be centered on the page between the top and bottom.

✔ The letter should include the date it was written.

✔ The letter should be addressed to a person or persons by name, never "to whom it may concern." Using no name at all is even better than this trite phrase.

✔ Each paragraph of a letter should have at least two sentences.

✔ Paragraphs of a letter should start with different words.

FIGURE 13.3
Email Memo

To: Orange County Campus Team
From: Russell Parker
Date: July 27, 2011
Subject: Mandatory Staff Retreat

Good Morning OC Team,

Please arrange your schedules to attend the upcoming staff retreat on August 23, 2011 from 8:30 to 3:30 in Building C, Room 117 at our OC Campus.

I know that you all are busy working on important projects. However, this retreat is a critical day for strategic planning and setting priorities for the rest of the year. Therefore, all team members are expected to attend. Discussion items for the day include the following:

- Remaining 2011 projects
- 2011 goals
- Temporary and permanent staffing needs
- Facility improvements

A continental brunch and lunch will be provided. Please confirm your attendance with an email to mcmurray@campus.biz. I look forward to seeing you all on August 23.

Russ

✔ Most paragraphs of a letter should start with a word other than *I* or *we*.

✔ Letters sent digitally should have an appropriately descriptive subject line.

✔ Complimentary closings should be simple and sincere. Limit yourself to "Sincerely" or "Cordially" unless your industry has other norms. (For example, the legal profession uses "Very Truly Yours" more often than other closings).

✔ Hard copies of letters should be signed.

Memos: Brief and Concise Written Internal Communication

Memos may be the most widely used type of written business communication. They tend to be informal, brief, and in almost all contemporary cases, digital. Memos are used to request information or action, promote goodwill (such as congratulations), convey routine information such as a meeting time or procedure, summarize oral conversations, and deliver short reports about organizational activities.[3] Memos are popular forms of written business communication because they are convenient (quick to prepare and to read), they can reach large numbers of readers, and they provide a written record for senders and receivers that may prevent misunderstandings.

There is a single, simple format for memos, which is shown in Figure 13.3. They are headed by four basic elements: *to, from, date,* and *subject.* (When you create a digital memo, your email program takes care of preparing this heading for you.) The *body* of the memo,

Visualize!
Practice! 13.2:
Writing a Memo

then, contains the information that you need to communicate. You should state the objective of your memo in the first sentence and then provide the content that your readers need. Here are some guidelines for the presentation of content in memo form:

Checklist for a Memo

✔ Memos should be used for communicating about a limited number of topics.

✔ Memos should be organized in such a way that avoids confusion or oversight. Use signposts to make your points noticeable:

- Use numbers or headings to differentiate the issues in the memo.
- Develop paragraphs deductively, so that the main point appears in the first sentence and each subsequent sentence in the paragraph is related to the first.
- Use bullet points to summarize lists and make them visually eye-catching. For example, instead of "In tomorrow's meeting we will discuss contract negotiations, summer casual dress code, the new travel reimbursement policy, and the performance appraisal schedule," create a bullet list to present these items.

Be sure to create all lists using parallel structure; they should be similarly constructed sentences that start with a similarly constructed phrase.

Lack of Parallel Structure for Bullet Points
We should reconsider our agreement with XYZ Inc. because

- Job requires equipment we don't have.
- Possible revenue loss.
- Must hire new staff to complete job.

Correct Parallel Structure for Bullet Points
We should reconsider our agreement with XYZ Inc. because it

- Requires purchase of new equipment, the costs of which won't be recouped.
- Might result in revenue loss.
- Requires additional staff.

- Memos should be single-spaced, with double spaces between paragraphs.
- Emailed memos should conclude with the author's name (even though it appears in the header).
- Although memos are concise, you should use a courteous and professional tone. Avoid being so brief that your memo could be perceived as curt or rude.

Use this checklist to write your own memo about a business magazine article in **VISUALIZE! PRACTICE! 13.2: Writing a Memo**.

Proposals: A Written Means to Obtain Business

Proposals are important business documents, because through them, organizations and independent contractors (such as consultants or freelance designers) obtain new business. *Solicited* proposals are prepared in response to a Request for Proposal (RFP) issued by a prospective customer. The RFP is an invitation to qualified organizations or individuals to bid for specific work. In it, the prospective client indicates the nature of the goods or services required. The RFP indicates what information the bidder should provide and may include a format or structure for responding.

When preparing a proposal, you should read the RFP very carefully and follow its instructions precisely. A well-written RFP contains a great deal of explicit and implicit information that will help you understand exactly what the prospect requires. In his contribution to the Harvard Business School publication *Written Communications That Inform and Influence*, consultant Nick Wreden observed that well-written proposals are based on a careful reading of the RFP and that proposal readers are generally looking for the "the start of a relationship—a partner who recognizes [the customer's] needs and speaks to them clearly."[4] For more details on how RFPs are created and how to read them, visit **LINK OUT 13.9: RFP How-Tos**.

Link Out 13.9:
RFP How-Tos

An *unsolicited* proposal is also an attempt to get new business, but it originates with the organization or individual hoping to interest a prospect in a contract for goods or services.[5]

Many people usually contribute to a proposal because proposals address numerous organizational functions. For example, most proposals will address your company's *technical ability* to provide goods or services competently and efficiently, so a great deal of information needs to come from the units of your organization that will provide the technical aspects of the project. Additionally, proposals address issues of *project management*. Who will serve as key personnel; how will the various aspects of the project be coordinated; and what kind of oversight, performed by whom, will occur? Finally, proposals must address *cost*. If you are responsible for preparing a proposal, you will need to obtain accurate information from the appropriate person or unit in your organization about the specific costs for delivering the work requested.

Because proposals are so critical to organizational development, your company will probably have a streamlined process in place for preparing them. If you are involved in preparing a proposal, you should have (or should seek) guidance and participation from others in the organization. (Chapter 14 provides strategies and suggestions for preparing a proposal for communication consulting work.)

Here are some guidelines for the preparation of a proposal:

✔ **Follow to the letter the instructions in the RFP. If the RFP suggests or requires a structure, use it.** If you deviate from the prospective customer's wishes at this stage in your relationship, you are demonstrating that you won't listen later either. Failing to provide the customer with what is requested in the RFP, in the requested format, will diminish your credibility and the chances that your proposal will be seriously considered.

✔ **Be clear in addressing the prospect's needs, as stated in the RFP.** Exactly how you can solve the prospect's problems or meet its needs should drive your proposal. Consultant Nick Wreden says that "proposals should never be about what you can do, but what you can do for your prospect."[6] If you are submitting an unsolicited proposal or if the RFP is vague, do some research to better determine the company's needs and the best way for you to approach them in your written proposal.

✔ **Follow your organization's established process for developing the proposal.** Necessary research, allocation of responsibilities, a timeline for completion, and the actual writing of the proposal should be carried out in a systematic, organized fashion. If your organization does not have a process in place, suggest that one be created prior to responding to any RFP. Any help that you can offer in creating this process will significantly enhance your value to the organization as well.

✔ **Customize the proposal to the prospect.** Avoid boilerplate proposals. **Boilerplates** are standardized business text that can be recycled for different purposes without being changed much, if at all. The only acceptable boilerplates are standard contract language, rate sheets, and proprietary and nondisclosure statements.[7]

✔ **Be concise.** Some RFPs will specify page limits, but these should be thought of as maximum limits, not your goal. Short proposals are easier to read, usually read first, and may have a greater impact on readers than long, wordy, detailed proposals.[8] Address all issues required by the RFP in as brief and compact a format as possible.

The online RFP Database contains Requests for Proposals about a wide variety of projects from website redesign to lawn-mowing services to house demolitions and street repair. Take a close look at one of them with **VISUALIZE! PRACTICE! 13.3: Taking Apart an RFP**.

Brief Reports: Updates on Organizational Issues

Brief reports are documents designed to provide information about day-to-day operations to internal and external business stakeholders. Organizations cannot function without a consistent, systematic flow of accurate information, and written reports are one of the primary sources of that information. Business communicators write brief reports to keep interested parties on the same page with regard to a project, to document progress on a project, to guide decision making, and to justify expenditure of money or other resources.

A **progress report** is a type of brief report designed to inform someone, usually your manager, of your progress on a specific project. Progress reports typically have four short sections: background, work completed, evaluation of work completed, and a summary.[9] A well-organized progress report begins with a brief background of the assignment . After that introduction, summarize the work completed so far. Place greatest emphasis on the work you've completed since your last progress report. Next, evaluate the work you've completed so far. What challenges or problems have you encountered, and how did you overcome or solve them? If you believe that you need additional, unplanned resources to finish the assignment, state your needs here and provide justification for them. Finally, conclude the progress report with a summary of the work that remains and a projected time frame for completion of the project. For more guidance on writing a progress report especially when working with a team see the website at **LINK OUT 13.10: Progress Report How-Tos**.

Try your hand at your own progress report about this class or another class with **VISUALIZE! PRACTICE! 13.4: DIY Progress Report**.

A **periodic report** is a document designed to communicate specific information on a routine (periodic) basis to concerned stakeholders.[10] For example, periodic reports might provide sales-volume data, market research results, customer service statistics, or safety data for the week, month, or quarter. Because periodic reports tend to be data-rich, you need not spend much time on writing text. Begin the periodic report with a brief, direct summary of the activities for the period covered and then follow with the actual data. If you are requesting that some or all of your readers take specific actions based on the data in your periodic report, be specific and directive about who should do what and when.

You may be required to write a brief report on virtually any topic; the uses of the brief report are almost unlimited in organizational settings. Because the most common or useful types of reports vary by organization and business sector and may be highly technical, we cannot introduce you to all of the types of reports you might need to prepare.

Regardless of the type of brief report you need to generate, you should keep in mind the following guidelines:

✔ **Determine the scope of your report and its objectives before you begin to write.** A brief report should focus on a limited number of issues and objectives; more complex issues should be formatted in a longer, more formal report (explained in the next section of this chapter).

✔ **Consider the nature of your readers and why they will be reading your report.** When writing a brief to a manager, for example, be even more concise and brief than you would be with other readers. The higher up in the organizational food chain an individual is, the more reports and information they are required to read. You want to give them a report they will read with enthusiasm, not irritation.

✔ **Use the report as an opportunity to let your readers know what you are doing and why it's valuable.** The report is not an advertisement, but when written professionally and persuasively, it will enhance others' perceptions of your credibility. As a result, additional resources and accolades could come your way.

✔ **Write objectively, accurately, and concretely.** Readers want to see both sides of a problem or a situation. Be thorough and exact in presenting facts, and support your claims with evidence. Although you are writing objectively, you will also use your influence skills to build a persuasive case.

✔ **Use a consistent scheme of lists and italicized, boldfaced, and underlined text to emphasize important information.** In other words, choose one scheme. Position the text and data attractively; do not crowd information.

✔ **Find out if your organization or department has a style guide or standard template for reports.** If it does, use it. If there is no official guide, keep a file of reports written by others that you think are especially well written and organized. Model your own style after these samples, and create a template that works for you.

Stephen Derr/Getty Images

Formal Reports: In-Depth Accounts of Business Issues

Formal reports in business settings report the status of a complex problem or business issue and approach the solution of the issue in a logical fashion. They are lengthier than a brief report. Often, formal business reports rely on original research data collected by the author or someone else in the organization.[11]

For example, Susan wrote a formal report for her employer in which she exposed a growing problem in their organization: the lack of employee time for participation in training and continuing education. She reported on the effect this problem was having on the organization's productivity and employee innovation and supported her claims with data she collected in a questionnaire designed to assess the state of employee training and development. She then proposed self-paced Web-based learning as an alternative to traditional classroom learning. In support of her suggestion, she included secondary research data collected by other companies that had successfully implemented Web-based learning. Additionally, she included primary research data indicating that her company's employees were favorable about participating in Web-based learning. She ended the report with her recommendations for developing and deploying a series of Web-based training courses over the next twelve months.

Because formal reports are longer and potentially more challenging to read than are briefs, letters, or memos, they require special attention to organization and format. Your organization may have a standard template for formal reports. If one is available, be sure to use it. Formal reports are typically structured using the following elements:

- ✔ **Title page:** Identifies the name of the report, authors' names and titles, date of submission, and sometimes the person or entity who will receive the document.

- ✔ **Transmittal letter:** Overviews the contents of the report and transfers the report to its readers.

- ✔ **Table of contents:** Lists the major headings and subsections within the body of the report, along with the page numbers where they can be found.

- ✔ **Executive summary or abstract or synopsis:** Delivers a business case efficiently and briefly by establishing the need or problem, recommending a valuable solution, and providing substantiation for the solution.[12] If the report is delivered electronically, use the linking functions in Microsoft Word so that readers can click and move quickly to relevant areas of the report when reading the executive summary.

- ✔ **Introduction:** Provides background of the problem, primary objectives of the report, sources and methods of data collection, and preview of the report's structure and contents.

- ✔ **Body:** Delivers a logical presentation of your findings. Serves as a rationale for your conclusions and recommendations in the next section.

- ✔ **Conclusion and recommendations:** Provides a summary of your findings, and recommendations based on the findings. No new data or findings appear in this section.

- ✔ **Appendices:** Contain information that supplements or supports the content of your report but that would be unnecessarily distracting to the reader if presented in the body of your report. Examples of material typically presented as appendices include questionnaires, interview forms, and other exhibits.

- ✔ **Bibliography:** Lists, alphabetically, the sources cited in your text. Rely on a style guide for attributing sources and preparing your bibliography. For more information

APA — American Psychological Association
MLA — Modern Language Association for writers of research papers

on the two most widely used style guides, the *Publication Manual of the American Psychological Association* (APA) and the Modern Language Association's *MLA Handbook for Writers of Research Papers*, consult **MODULE 6: "You Gotta Have Style": Using APA and MLA Styles** or check out these links: **LINK OUT 13.11: Modern Language Association (MLA)** and **LINK OUT 13.12: American Psychological Association (APA)**.

Module 6:
"You Gotta Have Style": Using APA and MLA Styles

Link Out 13.11:
Modern Language Association (MLA)

Link Out 13.12:
American Psychological Association (APA)

These major sections as well as their subsections should be presented using headings that divide the material into readable sections. You should consult the style guide that you are using for advice on what system of headings to use, and how to indicate visually sections of the report for your readers. Here are some additional guidelines for preparing a readable, effective formal report:

✔ **Use logical paragraphs to keep your report organized.** When writing a business report, structure your paragraphs deductively. In other words, create a topic or thesis statement that begins the paragraph, and then be sure that the sentences that follow are related directly to your thesis statement. Be sure that the paragraph is coherent, and that it flows together smoothly.

✔ **Use internal previews, summaries, and signposts.** In addition to using headings to keep your reader oriented, use transitions between sections of your report to illustrate how ideas and sections are related. Include internal summaries and previews of material you have covered and plan to cover. Use signpost language to keep your reader focused.

- **Example of a preview statement:** "Employees in the production division have three primary concerns about job safety."

- **Example of signpost language:** "*First*, workers worry that equipment is aging. *Second*, they are concerned that shifts are too long and that many employees are too tired to work safely by the end of their shifts. *Third*, they complain that they have not received enough safety training."

- **Example of an internal summary and preview:** "Overall, employees are satisfied with their jobs but, as illustrated here, have some concerns related to safety and benefits. In the next section, we will suggest ways to address these issues."

✔ **Use graphic illustrations where appropriate.** Tables, figures, graphs, and illustrations can enhance the visual appeal and readability of your data. Consult Chapter 10 of this book for guidance on the preparation of these graphic aids.

Blogs and Social Media: Quick and Wide Dissemination of Information

In the digital age, almost all traditional business documents, like the ones we've discussed so far, will be transmitted via computers. Most are read on a screen and filed digitally without ever being printed. But advanced digital and information technology has also enabled the creation of new forms of business writing: blogs and social networking site communication. (Chapter 6 discusses social media in depth.)

Blogs are shared, public online journals where people can post entries about their experiences related to work, hobbies, or other interests in chronological order.[13] The authors of blogs, known as bloggers, can include pictures, video, and other graphics; readers of blogs can post comments about and reactions to the blog posts. In recent

Link Out 13.13:
Blog Builds Cookie Company

Link Out 13.14:
Data Privacy Law Blog Fills a Need

Link Out 13.15:
Bad Blogs

Visualize! Practice! 13.5:
The Secrets of a Successful Blog

years, blogs have become effective tools for communicating with customers and marketing to prospective customers. Blogs offer low-cost, real-time connectivity with readers. You could use a blog to:

- Promote your products, services, and ideas.
- Obtain consumer feedback.
- Showcase your ideas and products visually.
- Develop communication relationships with your customers and prospective customers.
- Engage in off-task communication with your readers.
- Publicize events.
- Provide links to tools, resources, or other content that might be of interest to your readers.
- Journal an event (such as a meeting, conference, or trade show).

Take a look at these examples of how blogs have helped real businesspeople connect with existing customers or clients and attract new ones: **LINK OUT 13.13: Blog Builds Cookie Company** and **LINK OUT 13.14: Data Privacy Law Blog Fills a Need**.

Now, take a close look at a blog from a favorite store or brand with **VISUALIZE! PRACTICE! 13.5: The Secrets of a Successful Blog**.

Blogging requires a different writing style from most other forms of business documents. Blogs are like an extended conversation between the author and readers—many of whom contribute to the conversation through their comments added to the blog. In this way, blogging is a very interactive form of business writing. Therefore, although business-related blog entries should be written in a professional manner, your blog must also reflect a tone that encourages response and interaction from its followers. Read one blogger's take on the problem with most business-related blogs: **LINK OUT 13.15: Bad Blogs**.

Your objective should be to employ a writing style and deliver content in your blog that will attract readers and give them a positive impression of you and your business. Here are some strategies for blogging:

- **Express an opinion.** Blogs differ from formal reports and other objectively written, dispassionate forms of business writing. People read blogs because they represent the ideas and viewpoints of a person—not a corporation, marketing department, or lawyer. Your own opinion will stimulate comments and online conversation among your readers, and that's a good thing.[14]

- **Write with your readers in mind.** Throughout this book, we have stressed that business communication is really all about the receiver. Every business message needs to target its intended audience in a meaningful way. Readers will be examining your blog for an answer to the question, "What's in it for me?" Make sure you give them one.

- **Provide useful links.** Within your blog, embed links to other Web-based material that supports your post and that readers may find interesting. Anything your readers find interesting or useful will enhance the value of your blog to them and, as a result, enhance their loyalty to you and your products or services.

- **Use a headline that attracts attention.** Your blog post's headline should be clear, interesting, and relevant to its content. Here are some good resources for how to write headines: LINK OUT 13.16: **Sure-Fire Headline Formulas** and LINK OUT 13.17: **How to Write Attention Grabbing Headlines**.

- **Pay attention to keywords.** Think about the kinds of keywords that potential customers use when thinking about you and your products or services. Use those liberally throughout your blog to increase the likelihood that readers will find your blog when they use search engines.

- **Develop an upbeat, conversational writing style.** Remember, blogs are about developing "friends" for your products, services, and ideas. So, while paying attention to grammar and spelling, write much like you'd write to a friend.

- **Keep it simple and brief.** Contemporary business audiences are busy and easily distracted. Many people follow two hundred or more blogs! So you have a very short amount of space and time to capture your readers' attention. Most bloggers recommend that posts should be 250 words or less. Sentences should be short and concise so that readers don't have to spend time determining what they mean.

- **Write like you talk.** Yes, despite what your English composition instructor taught you, when you're blogging, it's fine to use expressions like "Go figure," "Gotta love it," and "Seriously?!" In fact, this informal and friendly conversational style will make your blog more enjoyable to readers. However, keep in mind the demographics (such as age and gender) of your target readership as you decide the appropriate tone of your language.

For links to many articles that will provide guidance on determining if a blog is appropriate for your business, how to start a blog, and strategies for making your blog successful, visit LINK OUT 13.18: **Is a Blog for You?**

Finally, blogs can be used for internal communication with colleagues, training, and idea exchange as well. For more on this growing trend, see LINK OUT 13.19: **How to Make an Internal Blog Work**.

Link Out 13.16:
Sure-Fire Headline Formulas

Link Out 13.17:
How to Write Attention Grabbing Headlines

Link Out 13.18:
Is a Blog for You?

Link Out 13.19:
How to Make an Internal Blog Work

Michael Woodruff/Shutterstock.com

Link Out 13.20:
Lunchtime Tweets

Link Out 13.21:
Twitter Outreach

Link Out 13.22:
Fashion Fans Speak Up

Link Out 13.23:
Social Media Rules

Link Out 13.24:
What Social Media Newbies Need to Know

Link Out 13.25:
Social Media Etiquette

Visualize! Practice! 13.6:
Tell Me More— or Don't Tell Me

Visualize! Practice! 13. 7:
Pull Them In

Social media sites like Facebook and Twitter have also become popular ways to communicate about business ideas and connect with consumers. **LINK OUT 13.20: Lunchtime Tweets** showcases how social media has turned the food truck industry into a cultural phenomenon. **LINK OUT 13.21: Twitter Outreach** highlights ways Twitter has been used to find work, hire new employees, and sell products. And **LINK OUT 13.22: Fashion Fans Speak Up** describes how one retailer is using Facebook to promote conversation with customers and to collect valuable market feedback. (The comments on this blog post provide some interesting insight into how social media enhance business communication, too.)

Like blogging, social media writing is different from other forms of business writing. Status updates and tweets express a thought and need to excite or interest readers in as few as 140 characters. That's right: characters, not words. Here are some tips for reaching your readers through social media:

- **Make sure your status updates and tweets have a clear point.** You have just a sentence or two to say something meaningful to your readers. Make them count.

- **Balance self-promoting messages with ones your readers will find useful or entertaining.** Don't use social media sites solely as personal billboards.

- **Consider a creative strategy such as "recurring status updates."** By building a narrative, telling an ongoing story, and referring back to previous updates, you can build interest and buzz for something new.

- **Be careful to not overdisclose.** Although social media offer a way for you to create relationships with professional colleagues and clients, make sure that you maintain professional boundaries in your online writing.

- **Keep your online friends and followers wanting more.** Don't post too often. Provide your readers with something they can use or think about.

- **Post a question to start a conversation.** This strategy, when effective, fulfills all the promises of using social media for business purposes.

- **Follow the rules.** Social media communities have unwritten cultural rules that you must follow in order to be successful on those sites. **LINK OUT 13.23: Social Media Rules LINK OUT 13.24: What Social Media Newbies Need to Know**, and **LINK OUT 13.25: Social Media Etiquette** are useful articles about the social norms of Facebook and Twitter.

Armed with this information about social media messaging, take a second look at the updates from your Facebook friends with **VISUALIZE! PRACTICE! 13.6: Tell Me More—or Don't Tell Me**. Then try your hand at writing social media messages for a variety of business scenarios in **VISUALIZE! PRACTICE! 13.7: Pull Them In**.

What Are the Steps to Creating a Business Document?

Many of our students complain that they have difficulty writing because they don't know how or where to begin. They become frustrated when they sit down at the computer and the blank screen doesn't simply fill itself. We suspect that this common tendency, which exists among professionals as well, is a result of lacking a systematic, focused approach to the writing process.

With the exception of blogging, successful business writing is typically not a matter of inspiration or creativity. Successful business writing involves knowing how to approach a writing task logically, assemble relevant information, and structure ideas and premises through the use of words, phrases, sentences, and paragraphs. If you recognize that any writing project can be tackled in five steps and you practice those steps consistently, writing will become easier for you, and the results of your efforts more satisfying. The five steps of creating a business document are these:

1. Determining your objectives and audience.
2. Compiling facts, supporting data, and other research materials.
3. Developing a logical organizational structure.
4. Writing a draft of the document.
5. Revising the document until it is clear and concise.

Step 1: Determine Your Objectives and Audience

Preparing to write a business document is as important as the actual execution of the document. Preparation requires identifying two factors critical to the success of your document: your objectives and your readership.

Establishing one or more objectives for a business document involves identifying what you want your readers to know or do when they have finished reading your document. Once you have your goal in mind, everything you write should be directed toward accomplishing it. Objectives, whether they be for memos, letters, proposals, briefs, or formal reports, should be specific, realistic, and stated in writing:

✔ **Objectives must be specific.** Key to successfully writing the document is knowing *exactly* what you want to happen as a result of people reading your document. Be very clear about what you want people to think about or do after having read your report, letter, or memo. Take a look at the following objectives for a formal report, each stated two different ways. Why is the more specific objective going to be more helpful to the writer than the nonspecific objective?

- **Specific objective A:** To compare the relative advantages of the two prospective sites for future plant construction.
- **Nonspecific objective A:** To discuss future plant construction.
- **Specific objective B:** To present evidence that supports our department's funding request for future plant construction.
- **Nonspecific objective B:** To ask for funding.

✔ **Objectives should be stated in writing.** Once you have identified one or more specific, relevant objectives, write them down in a file or on a piece of paper where you can refer to them while writing your document. This will help you to stay focused and organized as you write. For example, in writing this textbook, your authors always had a printed copy next to their computers of the learning objectives for the particular chapter they were writing.

✔ **Objectives should be realistic and achievable in the length and type of document you intend to prepare.** The type of document you choose to write should be based on the objectives you have identified. For example, you would not use a lengthy, formal report to announce a new vacation policy to employees.

Sometimes, however, the nature of your audience will dictate that you write a certain type of document. For instance, if your manager has asked you for a brief report although you believe the information you need to convey is too complex for a brief report format, you will need to construct a set of objectives appropriate for a brief report and give your manager what she or he requested. Perhaps you will need to deliver two different reports in order to communicate all of the relevant material or offer to provide an oral briefing in addition to the short written report. When you are asked for a particular type of document, you must determine a way to deliver that document and not exceed its capabilities with too many or unrealistic objectives.

After you establish your objectives, you must identify who will be reading this document, and why. Once you determine your intended audience, you need to ask yourself some questions about your readers before you begin to write. This list is adapted from Brusaw, Alred, and Oliu's *Business Writer's Handbook:*[15]

- What are my readers' needs relative to the objective or topic of my document?
- If my audience is diverse (for example, if your proposal will be evaluated by the CEO, a purchasing manager, and an accounting official), what are each individual stakeholder's concerns? How can I address each unique perspective without alienating anyone?
- What do my readers already know about my subject?
- Do I need to define basic vocabulary, jargon, or acronyms related to this subject for my audience?
- What are my readers' expectations for this document, if any? How long or how detailed do they expect it to be? How much supporting evidence and what types will they require?

Step 2: Compile Facts, Supporting Data, and Other Research Materials

For any type of business document, you cannot write it effectively if you do not have a strong grasp of the content you need to communicate. In addition to understanding and being able to write fluently about your topic, you need to have an understanding of what others think, know, or believe about your topic. This external support can enhance your writing in important ways. Therefore, you will need to engage in some form of *research* before you begin to write your document.

Research may involve collecting **secondary research materials** (such as articles, blogs, websites, books, case studies, whitepapers, archival/historical data, or published interviews), conducting **primary**, or original, **research** (through the use of surveys, observations, or interviews), and drawing on your own experiences and knowledge. The amount of research you need to conduct will depend on the nature of your project and the requirements of your readers, but you should be aware that many forms of research exist. For a routine email, for example, you may simply rely on your own experience and knowledge about the subject. For a formal report, you may need to conduct original research. For a brief report, such as a periodic sales report, you may choose to consult historical sales figures in order to present comparisons. When you conduct either primary or secondary research, be thorough and accurate in keeping track of sources that you consult and methods that you use for collecting your own data.

Step 3: Develop a Logical Organizational Structure

Of all the mistakes you can commit in writing a business document, being disorganized or lacking logical structure may be the most irritating to your readers. Without a sound logical structure, your business documents will be unreadable. The longer and more complex your document, the more critical it is that you select an appropriate sequence for your ideas.

We have offered you some suggested formats for several of the most common business documents in the section prior to this one. Some documents, such as memos, brief reports, and letters, are better structured according to your objectives and needs rather than a predetermined template. Here are some common logical structures for business documents, adapted from Ringwood's useful paper on the preparation of technical reports[16] and Blake and Bly's book on business writing:[17]

- **Topical and prioritized:** Present issues by topic, and rank them by their overall priority. You may choose to begin with the most important item, or end with the most important. There are benefits to both strategies, and you should weigh them both in determining how to order your message.[18]

- **Chronological:** Discuss issues in the order they occurred or will occur. This sequence is useful when reviewing an event or describing a process.

- **Comparison and contrast:** Describe similarities (comparisons) and differences (contrasts) of two ideas for purposes of evaluation. These sequences work well when asking your readers to decide among two or more courses of action, decisions, or things.

- **Spatial:** Discuss important points according to their physical relationship to one another (such as left to right, top to bottom). This structure is effective when describing, for example, a piece of equipment or the layout of a physical location. Documents using a spatial structure should be accompanied by one or more graphics that correspond to the text. (See Chapter 10 for more information on preparing graphic aids.)

Whether you use a template, one of the four logical structures suggested above, or some other method for organizing and sequencing your content, always remember these important guidelines:

- **Follow the principle of chunking.** Present ideas in small, digestible units that will be easy for your reader to comprehend and remember. Research suggests that readers may be able to cognitively process only between five and nine units of information at a time.[19] This means that even a long, formal report should contain no more than nine major sections or points, and lists should contain no more than nine bulleted points.

- **Always consider your reader when organizing.** In our chapter on organizing business presentations, we discussed that different people have different preferences for logic; those varied responses to organization extend to business writing, as well. Consider what you know about your reader, and structure your document for him or her. As you prioritize content, for example, be concerned with what your reader will find most important—not what you believe is most important.

- **Construct an outline for most business documents.** Outlining makes large amounts of complex information easier for you to write about in a logical, organized way. Module 8 describes the best way to create an outline. Even when you are writing a simple memo, email, or brief letter, you will be aided by creating an informal outline. When you do so, you will be sure not to leave out an important point and can take a look at how your ideas flow before drafting the document.

Weigh In 13.1:
Can You Improve Your Writing Habits?

Step 4: Write a Draft of the Document

At this point in the process, you will develop your own personal habits for writing. Some writers prefer the method suggested by Brusaw, Alred, and Oliu,[20] which involves writing a fast rough draft with little concern for writing style or polished presentation. This strategy results in quick development of a full draft but requires the writer to spend more time on proofreading, editing, and revising. The authors of your textbook tend to spend more time on creating a strong first draft, resulting in a shorter proofreading and revision cycle. We like to complete a section of a document and then read it closely, make changes, and revise as we work through the full draft. When you employ this strategy, the first draft will take a bit longer, but you will spend less time revising later.

Whatever strategy you employ for writing a first draft, our best advice is this: Write. Getting started with a writing project, especially a long or challenging one, can be the most difficult aspect of creating business documents. Create a disciplined schedule for completing the phases of the writing process and spend part of every work day writing, from the day you begin the project and your deadline. That may mean ten minutes per day of writing or five hours. But when you have a writing project, you need to write. Do not become overly involved in thinking about or researching your writing project beyond that which is minimally necessary for getting started. The goal of a writing project is a finished document. So write! And then write some more.

Take a moment to assess your approach to writing with **WEIGH IN 13.1: Can You Improve Your Writing Habits?**

Step 5: Revise the Document until It Is Clear and Concise

Even experienced writers spend a significant amount of time reading and revising their work. The easier a report is to read, the more time the author probably put into revision. As you read your draft, evaluate it from the reader's perspective. Sometimes,

Will Hughes/Shutterstock.com

a second proofreader can be helpful and important to ensuring an objective set of revision recommendations. In some cases, a professional proofreading service can be the best investment you can make in an important writing project. One that we like is Proofread*NOW*.com. The service assigns three proofreaders to your project and allows you to specify the types of proofreading you would like: stylistic changes, spelling and grammar editing, or application of a particular style (APA or MLA, for example). The service may be expensive for a simple project, but can make a big difference in the quality of your proposals, grant applications, contracts, and competitively evaluated work.

Here are some questions to consider as you revise:

- Is the tone correct for your audience?
- Are the sentences a readable length?
- Are your sentences clear?
- Are there any unnecessary words or phrases you can eliminate to make your sentences more precise?
- Are the paragraphs structured deductively, and do all of the sentences in each paragraph relate to the thesis?
- Do all of the paragraphs in the document relate to your initial objectives?
- Have you employed transition statements between paragraphs and sections?
- Have you double-checked numbers, citations, and direct quotes for accuracy?
- Have you provided attributions for all external sources you utilized in preparing the document?
- Is your coverage of your subject complete and thorough, without taxing the reader with too much information?
- Is your writing free of spelling, punctuation, and grammatical errors?
- Is your document formatted with a consistent set of headlines, fonts, and typefaces?
- Have you used active voice throughout the document?

When you write with the active voice, you make the subject of your sentence perform the action. Your writing will be less wordy and more powerful when you write actively. For example:

Passive: The report was delivered by Mr. Schmidt.

Active: Mr. Schmidt delivered the report.

Passive: These procedures were established by the board of directors.

Active: The board of directors established these procedures.

Use **VISUALIZE! PRACTICE! 13.8: Get Active!** to be sure you understand how to change the passive voice in your writing.

This five-step process provides you with a system for writing business documents that are informative, credible, and readable. As you acquire business writing experience, you will probably find ways to modify these five steps that make sense for you and your preferences.

Visualize!
Practice! 13.8:
Get Active!

Although business writing tends to be more formulaic and technical than creative writing, it is still part art and part science. In this chapter, we have provided you with some of the science—strategies for creating clear documents that are reader-focused and objective-centered. Additionally, we have shared with you some of the art that we have practiced and perfected over the years—strategies for being disciplined writers, making logical choices that will make sense to a particular reader, and revising documents.

How well you are able to prepare, draft, and revise written material is likely to be central to your success as a professional. Additionally, how well you write will have a great effect on others' perceptions of your credibility, regardless of the profession or industry you enter and whether writing is one of your key responsibilities. Hollywood celebrities, professional athletes, chefs, and reality TV stars, for example, have found themselves unwitting writers thanks to Facebook, blogs, and Twitter—and some are better at it than others! If you choose a more traditional career path, memos, letters, and reports will be part of your daily life. If you have an understanding of the mechanics of writing and the ability to adapt your writing style for a particular readership and medium, you will enhance your professional credibility through whatever documents you produce. If you ever find yourself in the same position as Steve, whom we met in this chapter's opening scenario, you will have the knowledge and experience to tackle a wide variety of writing tasks and succeed.

As authors ourselves, we know that in order to be a successful writer, you still need one more ingredient: confidence. When you have a solid grasp of the mechanics of writing, have developed a discipline of personal writing habits, understand the steps of the writing process, and have something interesting or valuable to say, you need to be confident in your ability to do so. That sense of confidence will distinguish your writing from others' and ensure that your ideas are noticed for all the right reasons.

Use your Speech Communication CourseMate for *Business & Communication in a Digital Age* for quick access to the electronic resources that accompany this text. These resources include

Study tools that will help you assess your learning and prepare for exams (*digital glossary, key term flash cards, review quizzes*).

Activities and assignments that will help you hone your knowledge and build your communication skills throughout the course (*Visualize! Practice!, Weigh In!, Check This Out, and Link Out activities; modules; review questions*).

Media resources that will help you explore communication concepts online (*Enhanced eBook*), develop your speech outlines (*Speech Builder Express 3.0*), watch and critique videos of sample speeches and communication situations (*interactive video activities*), upload your speech videos for peer reviewing and critique other students' speeches (*Speech Studio online speech review tool*), and download chapter review so you can study when and where you'd like (*Audio Study Tools*).

Key Points

- Business writing is the preparation of any print or online document designed to support a business enterprise or help it grow. These may be written for internal or external readers. Examples include memos, letters, brief reports, proposals, and blogs.

- Business letters should be clear and brief, and written with the intended reader(s) in mind.
  - ✔ Tone, style, and visual layout are important considerations when writing business letters.
  - ✔ Business letters are written on a continuum from informal to formal. Writers should, in most cases, avoid an overly formal or contrived style.
  - ✔ Writers should select a format and use it consistently thoughout the letter.
  - ✔ When transmitting a letter using email or other digital media, construct an appropriate subject line.

- Memos are brief, informal, and usually digital forms of written communication. Memos are the most common kind of document in business and professional settings.

- Proposals are a written means to obtain business.
  - ✔ Solicited proposals are written in response to a Request for Proposal (RFP).
  - ✔ Some proposals are unsolicited.
  - ✔ Proposals often require input from various people and/or departments.
  - ✔ Business writers should find out if their organizations have a standardized process in place for writing proposals, and follow it.
  - ✔ Proposals must address the recipient's specific business needs.

- Brief reports are designed to provide up-to-date information on day-to-day organizational activities. Examples include progress and periodic reports.

- Formal research reports identify the status of a complex business issue and approach the solution in a logical fashion. They are longer than brief reports.
  - ✔ Formal reports may rely on original research, historical/archived data, or a combination of both.
  - ✔ Organization and format are very important due to the length of formal reports.

- Blogs are online, public, shared journals where writers can document their experiences in a chronological format using text, images, audio and/or video.
  - ✔ Readers can comment on blog entries.
  - ✔ Blogs are used in business to develop relationships with customers; and to promote products, services, or ideas.
  - ✔ Blogs are written in a conversational, familiar tone and style.

- Social media like Twitter and Facebook are additional media for connecting with customers and colleagues.

- There are five steps to creating successful business documents:
  - ✔ Determine your audience and objectives.
  - ✔ Compile facts, supporting data, and other research materials.
  - ✔ Develop a logical organizational structure.
  - ✔ Write a draft of the document.
  - ✔ Revise the document until it is clear and concise.

Key Terms

blog (299)

boilerplate (296)

brief report (296)

business writing (288)

chunking (305)

formal report (298)

memo (293)

periodic report (296)

primary research material (304)

progress report (296)

proposal (294)

secondary research material (304)

Questions for Critical Thinking and Review

1. What are the most important characteristics of good business writing?

2. Why are strong business writing skills perhaps even more critical in the digital age than they were before?

3. Imagine your supervisor has asked you to prepare a formal report on the state of an organizational problem about which you know very little. In fact, you aren't even sure if this "problem" really exists or affects the functioning of the organization. How would you approach the task? What would you do in the preparation and research phases of the task?

4. Consider each of the following types of readers. What are two things you know about each group that might be helpful in planning and writing a document for them?

   a. Managers

   b. Company executives

   c. Prospective customers who have solicited your proposal

   d. Prospective customers who know little or nothing about your company

5. How might you utilize a blog to encourage the exchange of ideas and to build motivation among colleagues at work?

6. In what ways do social media sites like Twitter help foster personal connections between companies and their clients?

7. What are some benefits of digital media that enhance the usefulness traditional paper documents? In other words, how can creating a report for viewing in a digital format improve on a document in a traditional hard-copy format?

8. One of the principles mentioned in this chapter was chunking—presenting written material in readable, understandable chunks. Do you think that different readers and audiences might require different chunking strategies? What guidelines or criteria might you use to decide how to best chunk your material?

9. In your experience, what are some of the differences between reading a paper document and reading one on a digital screen?

10. From your perspective, are there any limitations or drawbacks to writing business documents for digital consumption and use? Are there times when we should deal with traditional paper documents?

Chapter 14

Communication Consulting:
What Skills Do I Need?

Gunnar Pippel/Shutterstock.com

Chapter Learning Objectives

After completing this chapter, you should be able to
- Determine what services consultants provide in the workplace.
- Identify what communication consultants need to know to be effective.
- Make client contacts.
- Cost out your work.
- Prepare a consulting plan.
- Implement the plan.
- Evaluate plan effectiveness.

See also the modules that are relevant to this chapter:

   4: What Do I Need to Know About Business Etiquette?
9: How Do I Navigate Office Politics?
11: How Do I Use Social Media for Professional Networking?

Prologue: All three of us, as authors of your book, engage in quite a few consulting activities. We talk about what we do in our classes, and students often ask us, "What do communication consultants do?" and after we tell them, they ask us next, "How can I become a consultant, too?" Books used in courses like this one generally omit discussions about consulting and training in organizations, but our experiences as teachers illustrate to us that communication and business students want to know how to do both types of activities. So we approach Chapters 14 and 15 with real-life examples of some of our own consulting and training experiences.

A consulting contract with the California Air Resources Board (ARB) led the Ross-Campbell, Inc. team to a project examining how California drivers' and fleet managers' attitudes about Clean Vehicle Technologies influenced their own energy choices when it came to purchasing vehicles.[1] Eager to reduce toxins and emissions as well as our dependence on foreign oil, California's ARB posted a call for proposals to conduct a statewide research project. Because of our research skills and experiences doing environmental research for California agencies statewide, Ted Ross asked us to join his team and operate as principal investigators for the project.

As consultants, we spent some time talking with the client, ARB, identifying goals and specifying a series of research questions. With these questions or objectives in mind, we developed and implemented a research plan providing us with data from archival resources (namely, the library and Internet data bases), focus-group interviews, and supplemental surveys with California drivers and fleet managers. We collected these data in four major cities across the state. What we learned from this research surprised our clients and influenced their thinking about how to better reach, inform, and influence California drivers.

Briefly, we learned that California consumers are largely unfamiliar with new vehicle technologies, like hybrids, electric cars, and hydrogen vehicles—and they are not particularly motivated to purchase such nontraditional cars and trucks. Concerns about the environment do not appear to influence their personal purchase decisions either. Consumers are unwilling or uninterested in becoming early adopters of the new vehicle technologies. Preferring instead to wait and see, they are reluctant to try anything too new that may be unreliable, unsafe, or costly.

With this profile in mind, the ARB subsequently launched a statewide communication campaign urging consumers to consider nontraditional vehicles as their next purchase choice. The strategies they employed in their campaign followed from our findings, beginning with media messages illustrating how the new technologies worked to making the link between personal vehicle choice and air quality, climate change, and dependence on foreign oil. You can read the complete report online at **LINK OUT 14.1: ARB Report**.[2]

Link Out 14.1:
ARB Report

This project with California's Air Resources Board represents one of thousands of consulting contracts awarded each year by a variety of both public and private organizations. Companies rely on **consultants**, or professional experts with specialized skills, to advise or help them accomplish a variety of services and tasks. Technical consultants are hired to train people how to use or integrate technology; financial consultants help individuals invest and manage money; and **communication consultants** help organizations solve managerial or employee problems and teach people skills.

Sometimes consultants, like your authors, offer research skills important to identifying, understanding, and solving problems. They might design programs, recommend campaigns, offer coaching and guidance, improve work performance, increase employee morale, identify strategic goals, audit agencies, evaluate programs and systems, and more. Most companies cannot afford to maintain a staff of highly specialized consultants that they can draw upon as needed. Moreover, they may be reluctant to utilize internal staff as consultants because employees might be too closely associated with sensitive or political issues in the organization, or they may be unable to pull them away from other assignments. As a result, businesses often contract with consultants outside their organization.

This chapter examines what communication consultants do and how they do it. Becoming a consultant requires a special set of skills, skills that you can begin to develop now as a student studying business and communication. Getting started as a consultant necessitates a client base to keep you employed and a schedule of fees based on what your services are really worth. Once you have a client, you must deliver some sort of service. Working closely with the client, consultants generally put together a plan of action that they implement and evaluate. Whereas this chapter focuses on how consultants solve problems, the next chapter, Chapter 15, addresses the role of one particular type of consulting activity that is widely used across all industries—training or teaching individuals particular skills or knowledge to enhance their performance.[3]

What Do Communication Consultants Do?

Organizations are challenged with numerous and persistent human and technological communication problems. The larger the organization, the more ubiquitous these sorts of problems seem to be. Managers may have problems conducting performance appraisals,

giving briefings, or negotiating contracts. Workers may face personality conflicts among coworkers, suffer from job burnout, or experience family issues that interfere with their performance at work. In some cases, these sorts of problems can be managed internally, but in many instances, an expert will be brought into the organization to help sort things out, give advice, implement solutions, and evaluate outcomes.

To give you some idea of what consultants do, we developed this list from our own experiences working individually and in teams with expert others:

- Train or teach others special skills.
- Design training or instructional packages.
- Evaluate systems.
- Write reports.
- Define problems.
- Offer solutions.
- Interview.
- Develop and administer surveys.
- Facilitate group discussions.
- Do focus-group research.
- Analyze quantitative data.
- Analyze qualitative data.
- Gather and interpret archival research.
- Interpret information for others.
- Write and present speeches.
- Prepare and give briefings.
- Give advice to management.
- Design media blueprints.
- Develop marketing plans.
- Direct and produce videos.
- Write research and grant proposals.
- Conduct human resource audits.
- Develop instructional curricula.

Another way to describe what consultants do is to look at four key processes of consulting work. The entry point into an organization for all consultants is some kind of problem or issue that needs to be addressed.

Consultants Diagnose Problems

By the time the consultant enters the organization, the client has already decided a problem exists and usually believes that the problem is fully understood and that the solution warrants the expertise and expense of a consultant. In our experience, we have learned that clients typically believe they already know what the problem is and all they want us to do is to come in and quickly solve it for them. However, the reality is that organizational

Dmitriy Shironosov/Shutterstock.com

problems are complex and best diagnosed, identified, and understood in collaborations with the client. The first task for the consultant is to determine the nature and extent of the problem.

For example, a client we'll call Alex came to us about a problem he was having with his management team. Alex told us that his management team was plagued by one problem member who was disruptive, overbearing, and obstinate. We'll call her Michelle. Alex explained that Michelle did not get along with other members of the team; as a result, much of the work had stalled, deadlines had been missed, and anxieties were intensifying. Alex asked us to come up with an approach to better integrate Michelle into the group's culture so that the team could work effectively again. In our deliberations with Alex and in interviews with Michelle and the other team members, we learned that the problem was more complicated and extended beyond issues associated with Michelle. As it turns out, other members felt similarly alienated and discouraged, but they failed to be as outspoken (or obvious) as Michelle. We learned that a number of managers on the team resented their lack of authority to make decisions, perceived leader favoritism toward some members over others, and felt that resources were not readily available to them all. In other words, "fixing Michelle" wasn't going to solve the problems with this team.

In conversations with all the key players, we were able to more accurately diagnose the source, nature, and scope of the problem. Only then could we begin to recommend solutions. Spending the time necessary to fully understand the problem may be the most meaningful aspect of what consultants do. A problem clearly defined is a problem on its way to being solved.

Consultants Recommend Solutions

Once the problem has been made clear, the consultant's next step is to give advice or propose courses of action. Given the earlier limited understanding of the problem, removing Michelle or teaching her key communication skills might have seemed the right thing to do. In the broader context of the problem, however, we offered several

alternative solutions for the client to consider. The client's options included (1) moving away from a team-based, transformational approach to a traditional, hierarchical decision-making process; (2) creating a new team of employees to manage the task; (3) implementing team-building techniques and skills; (4) increasing team potency by empowering members with greater authority; and (5) appointing or allowing the emergence of a new team leader. Selecting the best solution would depend on a number of factors, including but not limited to expense, time, context, task importance or urgency, long-term implications, and the political climate of the organization. Although the consultant might recommend a preferred solution, the client always makes the final decision.

Consultants Facilitate Interventions

Interventions are, by definition, some action taken to change, alter, or solve a problem. Once the organization decides how to approach a problem, consultants might be used to intervene or implement a course of action. If so, consultants might take on additional assignments, extending an initial short-term contract for problem diagnosis to a contract for long-term intervention. In the case of Michelle, the client told us that she was here to stay, as were the other members of the team. In addition, the client preferred maintaining a team decision-making environment and agreed to provide members with greater decision-making power. Eager to promote this approach, Alex opted to hire us to work with the team to facilitate trust, collaboration, and constructive disagreement.

Sometimes interventions are short-term and involve skills training via workshops or training seminars. Such interventions, although immediate, are typically short-lived. Individuals might be trained to listen actively or to acknowledge one another, but without scrutiny or continued reinforcement, these new behaviors are not likely to be maintained. Other interventions are protracted over longer periods of time, occurring incrementally but consistently, typically resulting in greater utilization and internalization. Working with Alex's team to increase their sense of potency or empowerment required both initial and multiple opportunities for them to make decisions that really mattered to them and to others in the organization.

Consultants Evaluate Outcomes

At times consultants are asked not only to evaluate an intervention they had proposed and facilitated but also to assess the effectiveness of another system or program already in place. Evaluating interventions or preexisting programs involves assessing what worked and what did not. Naturally, such **assessment** requires criteria from which to evaluate. Working in collaboration with the client, the consultant typically crafts the evaluation measures around the outcomes that the client expects or desires. Unfortunately, most of the clients we have worked with over the years had given little or no thought to the specific criteria they might use to evaluate their programs, or the criteria were limited only to bottom-line, cost-based efficiencies.

Our task as communication consultants is to help the client determine a set of suitable criteria and to design measures based on those criteria. We spend time asking clients what they hope to gain from a particular program, practice, or campaign, with questions such as these:

- Who is the target audience for this program? Might gender, ethnicity, or work experience make a difference in the outcome?

- Who might or should be affected by this intervention or program?

- What attitudes or behaviors should change?
- What do or did you expect to happen as a result of this program?
- What changes do or did you expect to see?
- What indices or indicators would illustrate your program's success or failure?

At times the evaluation consists of simple survey items measuring employee satisfaction, commitment, or knowledge base. At other times we rely on trained observers to record and evaluate. Still other consulting contracts require telephone interviews asking targeted questions about what individuals actually do or don't do.

An examination of these common consulting practices should give you some idea of what communication consultants do. It should also provide you with some insight into the skills and perspectives that consultants bring to an organization. **CHECK THIS OUT 14.1: Why Consider Outsider Opinions When Planning Strategy?** is a window on the life of one business consultant. In the next section we describe what competencies and skills are important to operating a successful consulting business.

Check This Out 14.1:
Why Consider Outsider Opinions When Planning Strategy?

What Credentials Does a Communication Consultant Need?

You must be perceived as an expert in something before you are recognized as someone worth hiring to consult. Acquiring the credentials to be a highly paid (and consistently employed) consultant begins with your education. At minimum, a bachelor's degree is required; however, a graduate or professional degree further solidifies your academic credentials. The higher the degree, the more credibility you carry. Even though people will tell you that "everyone has a degree" these days, not having the degree will likely eliminate you from consideration.

In most cases, your major will determine the kinds of consulting jobs you can do. That said, some majors more than others focus on skill proficiencies important for business and industrial environments. Obviously, a business degree is easily recognized by clients or customers who have a business to run. (Of course, the down side of this degree is that many of your clients and customers, having the same or similar degree, will perceive they already know what you know—even when they might not.) Other highly useful majors include English (writing skills, in particular) and many from the social sciences, such as psychology, sociology, anthropology, archaeology, economics, and communication studies. Other majors might also offer unique or specialized sets of skills important to businesses. The first step in establishing your credentials as a consultant, then, is to finish your degree and, if possible, pursue advanced study.

In order to be a communication consultant, the most appropriate educational background is a degree in communication or business and organizational communication. Essential to your study in the major are specialized communication skills, a working knowledge of the scientific method, the ability to interpret and translate relevant theory and research, and client-building relational skills.

Consultants Need Specialized Communication Skills
Others expect graduates with a communication degree to have a particular repertoire or skill set of communication proficiencies. Every degree has its own unique set of skills;

communication majors are recognized as having specific abilities that can be generalized across any environment. When making decisions about what courses to take in your program of study, focus on building this basic but important set of communication skills:

- presentational speaking skills
- conversational skills
- interviewing skills
- facilitation skills
- conflict management skills
- leadership skills
- small group communication skills
- argumentation skills
- persuasive skills
- nonverbal communication skills
- bargaining and negotiation skills
- intercultural communication skills

Proficiencies in these skills will go a long way toward developing perceptions of your expertise as a communication consultant. Clients will want you to be able to practice what you preach. If you are to be considered seriously to offer presentational skills training, for instance, the client will want to perceive you as an expert, skilled public speaker.

Consultants Need a Working Knowledge of the Scientific Method

At first glance, this particular credential may not seem all that obvious. When we began consulting part time, we learned very quickly how useful our knowledge of science was.

R. Gino Santa Maria/Shutterstock.com

We discovered that most organizations work from a scientific perspective. They rely on science to design products, assess market needs and trends, determine performance standards (such as safety and environmental), defend product quality, promote products and services, monitor morale, and so on. It's virtually impossible for businesses to survive without the benefits of science.

Science is something that clients both understand and appreciate. Because we were well versed in the language of the social sciences, we were able to talk to them in ways they valued. When we mentioned recent research and theory on a particular issue, like financial literacy or attitudes toward recycling or business planning, clients became eager to know more. They clearly wanted to learn what others already knew. Moreover, they appreciated any defensible, objective, and well-documented case we could make when defining and solving problems. Clients also recognized and understood scientific language in our discussions with them. They were able to hypothesize about what might occur and develop theories or explanations about why it would. They also appreciated the rigor and thinking involved in planning for interventions or designing evaluation measures.

Most consulting contracts require a working knowledge of research or the scientific method. In planning your academic program of study, then, aim for a working knowledge of the scientific method. Develop competencies in these important skills:

- deriving testable hypotheses
- research design
- measurement
- assessment and evaluation methods
- basic descriptive statistics (and preferably inferential statistics, too)
- archival data retrieval
- interviewing—individual and group

Science in business and industry is no abstract, ivory tower concept. Instead, science is an integral part of what business leaders do every day. With an economy driven by profit-loss ratios, companies are preoccupied with objectively predicting, quantifying, and calibrating acquisitions, operations, and sales or services. In today's market, consultants need to be able to frame or reframe all that they do within a scientific model. The process of diagnosing problems, predicting to solutions, implementing and testing those interventions, and evaluating outcomes is what academics have long termed the scientific approach.

Consultants Must Be Able to Draw upon Theory and Research

Corollary to the scientific method is the utilization of theory and research. As you already know, the function of science is to develop, test, revise, and extend theory. Theories provide us with logical explanations of causal relationships. Theories ask and answer the questions, "What happens?" and "Why is this so?" Kurt Lewin, the founder of modern social psychology, was right when he said that "there's nothing more practical than a good theory."[4] Theories begin with the study of practical problems. Someone identifies a problem, posits potential explanations of how and why the problem exists, proposes hypotheses or predictions to test out that presumed relationship, designs and conducts a study to test those predictions, and then makes inferences from the data which either support or fail to support the theoretical explanation of the problem. As you can see, then, theories offer consultants and businesses explanations and insights that can be used to manage problems.

A variety of theories currently exist that can assist consultants in defining and solving problems in the workplace. Because these theories are constantly being tested, modified, revised, and extended, consultants must be current in their understanding of theories relevant to their business activities. Effective consultants belong to professional organizations in their area of expertise, keep up to date by subscribing and reading relevant research, and stay actively involved in sharing what they know and do with researchers and other consultants.

Not all theories and research articles are written for direct application to the real world. Consultants must be able to read, understand, and translate such theory and research into working principles that can be easily applied to problems in the organizational context. It is consultants' responsibility to translate and adapt relevant theories and research findings when working within the organizational setting. This is no easy skill. Only with experience and practice can practitioners effectively apply theoretical principles to applied contexts. The ability to use theory in consulting activities begins with your familiarity with the relevant theories and research. Communication consultants should have a working knowledge of theory and research in these areas:

- instructional theories and pedagogical design
- instructional communication theories
- organizational communication theories
- conflict theories
- group communication theories
- interpersonal communication theories
- social influence theories
- bargaining and negotiation theories
- team-building theories
- leadership theories

Assuming a working knowledge of these and related theories, communication consultants are at a distinct advantage when meeting with clients, diagnosing problems, and proposing workable solutions or interventions. Theory and research provides consultants with a firm justification for what they do and why they do it.

Consultants Must Be Able to Work with Clients

Communication students are uniquely positioned to initiate, develop, and sustain good working relationships with clients. This is what makes people with an academic background in communication different from those who don't. Communication students are often drawn to the major because they like working with people. The degree helps them refine their relational skills to make that process systematic, strategic, and, ultimately, effective. They learn how to get along with people, assert themselves, listen actively and empathetically, adjust to difficult exchanges, manage conflict, confirm others, initiate new relationships, develop trust, engage in relational repair, self-disclose appropriately, and adapt to intercultural, international, and intergenerational relationships. All of these skills can be used to initiate client relationships, handle difficult clients, bring closure to important contract negotiations, sustain long-term relationships with customers, listen to client concerns, and so on. Chapter 5, "Relationships in the Workplace," offers a good overview of the skills and principles required to get along with people at work.

Module 4:
What Do I Need to Know About Business Etiquette?
Module 9:
How Do I Navigate Office Politics?

As it turns out, some clients are more difficult to work with than others. Even so, you may want to make the best of the situation if you want to obtain and sustain lucrative contracts. Some years ago we were facilitating focus groups in Memphis, Tennessee. Normally, we encourage the client to unobtrusively observe the focus-group discussions behind a two-way mirror along with others in the focus-group suite. We ask that the client be as quiet as possible during the videotaped facilitation to make sure that the focus-group participants stay focused on the discussion rather than on the mirror—and what's behind it. One particular observer, who we'll call Dianne, proved to be challenging. She continually made comments, asked questions, criticized the interview protocols, and demanded changes for subsequent interviews. Adding to the problem, Dianne ordered in and ate massive amounts of food, drank an entire bottle of wine, and laughed much too loudly. On two occasions, the researcher politely asked her to be quiet. Rather than comply, Dianne only behaved worse, and she eventually complained to her boss that the researcher was insubordinate and rude to her. Given the magnitude of the contract in terms of both money and longevity, our options for handling the situation with the client were limited. On one hand, we could have terminated the contract and moved on. On the other, we could have sucked it up and apologized. What would you have done?

Problems like this are not unique or uncommon. Part of being an effective consultant is learning how to manage and adjust to all kinds of people. Anticipating problems, remaining calm, making thoughtful decisions, and monitoring your reactions are all part of the business of working with clients. **MODULE 4: What Do I Need to Know About Business Etiquette? MODULE 9: How Do I Navigate Office Politics?**

How Do I Develop a Client List?

You can starve if you try to start out consulting full time. Most people do not have the financial luxury of moving directly into the consulting business. Instead, people typically freelance or moonlight as consultants on the side for a while. Begin your consulting business part time, and gradually transition your business into a full-time operation. Getting started as a consultant is a slow process. Accumulating experience will make you more marketable as a consultant over time.

In order to do this, we recommend that you get a full-time job in an area where you can eventually operate as a consultant. We began and continue to be consultants part time while we maintain full-time careers as professors. Having a secure, full-time position puts us at an advantage over those whose primary or sole source of revenue comes from consulting contracts. It also allows us to be highly selective in our choice of agencies and types of consulting jobs we want to do. Teaching full- or part-time offers you an opportunity to flexibly manage your time. Working in human resources in large organizations is another way to start. Find an employer who will allow you some flexibility in your

Module 11:
How Do I Use Social Media for Professional Networking?

Link Out 14.2:
Leading Communication Consultants

Link Out 14.3:
Finding Clients

Check This Out 14.2:
What Kinds of Clients Should I Target?

schedule and hours, even if it means a pay cut, so that you can pursue your career plans as a consultant.

Once you have a "home" from which to operate, you need to develop a client base. Developing a client base is a lot like finding a job; you may have something to offer, but you must find someone who needs your skills and is willing to pay you for those skills.

Appreciate first what you have to offer your clients. What skills, proficiencies, and expertise do you possess that others might want to pay you to do? Keep in mind those specialized skills we discussed earlier, including communication and public speaking, research, theory and application, and relational skills. Look at other communication consultants' websites. Examine several that promote the kinds of skills you want to market. Our perusal of the web led us to these websites of leading communication consultants: **LINK OUT 14.2: Leading Communication Consultants**.

Check out the Link Out activity above to see what other consultants are doing, how they market themselves, and what kinds of clients pay them. Once you design your webpage, be sure to get your own domain name (clients aren't too keen on hotmail.com or aol.com), and then submit your website to important search engines.

There is a variety of other ways to get out the word about what you have to offer and that you are available for hire. **MODULE 11: How Do I Use Social Media for Professional Networking?** For instance,

- Print business cards.
- Frequent places where potential clients might go (such as trade shows or sports clubs)
- Join professional networking services such as www.LinkedIn.com
- Network with friends and acquaintances; talk to people who can put you in touch with clients.
- Attend community events.
- Join community organizations.
- Volunteer within the community.
- Get involved in professional organizations.
- Join training and consulting professional organizations, like ASTD (American Society for Training and Development), APCC (Association of Professional Communication Consultants), and IMC (Institute of Management Consultants).
- Give presentations or workshops at professional trade shows.
- Write articles and editorials for newspapers, magazines, or trade journals.
- Develop relationships with contracting companies.
- Examine RFP databases, such as www.rfpdb.com/ and www.findrfp.com.
- Look for community service grant offerings online.

Take a look at **LINK OUT 14.3: Finding Clients** to see how other freelance consultants reach out to obtain clients.

For an example of just how wide the range of consulting possibilities is, see **CHECK THIS OUT 14.2: What Kinds of Clients Should I Target?**

How Much Am I Worth as a Consultant?

The question we're asked most frequently by colleagues and students is, "How much should we charge for consulting services?"[5] The question seems simple enough, but the answer is complex and worth addressing in this chapter. Most clients want to know up front how much your work is going to cost them. They typically prefer a detailed estimate or proposal of what the consultant is going to do and how we cost out each activity. Examples of activities include background research, identifying objectives, designing messages, editing, interviewing, developing or designing surveys, designing interview or focus-group protocols, data collection and analysis, writing the report, revising the report, and providing briefings or updates. Other clients might be satisfied with a daily rate or an overall project completion rate.

Cost Out Your Time for Services

Both clients and inexperienced consultants typically underestimate the amount of time required to do a job well. An apparently simple two-day training contract, for instance, consumes many more hours than sixteen. As a consultant, you would need to consider three kinds of work time:

- **Preparation time** could involve assessing the audience, identifying the objectives, researching the content, designing the message delivery, preparing and editing instructional materials, generating evaluation forms, and rehearsal.

- **Delivery time** would include the actual two-day training session, setting up the environment, arranging for food, beverage, and parking, and commuting to and from the facility.

- **Debriefing time** would consist of analyzing feedback forms, writing, revising, and editing the report, and briefing the client.

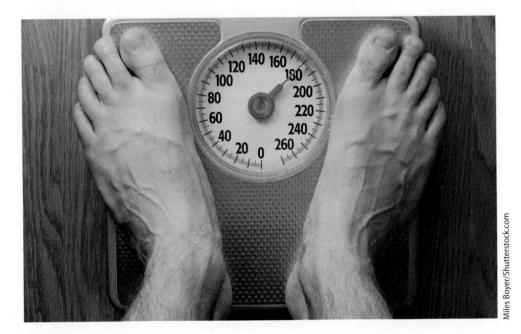

Miles Boyer/Shutterstock.com

Link Out 14.4: *Salary Calculators*

Remember that costing out time for the contract—whether it's an hourly, daily, or project rate—does not include the time you spent finding the work, writing the proposal, talking with the client beforehand, or negotiating the terms of the contract.

Estimating time can help you compute the total number of hours involved in doing the workshop. Having conducted a number of these over the years, we estimate, on average, forty hours of preparation time for *each* day of actual training—sometimes more or less, depending on the number of participants, their level of expertise, and the training content. Adding a second trainer to a two-day training contract adds substantially to the costs. Other overhead costs include reproducing and assembling materials for distribution, providing food and beverage throughout the day, and other miscellaneous expenditures.

Determine How Much Your Time Is Worth

Few consultants start out making a lot of money. The more experience you have, the more money you can charge for any given job. If you are just beginning to seek contracts, take any and all offers that come your way. That's how you gain experience. With experience, the types of work you can do broadens, your marketability increases, and your client base grows. When that happens, you can become more discriminating in the kinds of work you are willing to do, the clients you are willing to take, and the amount of money you are willing to accept for services.

Many factors enter into the decision to charge more or less, including your work history with the client, the size and complexity of the job, the client's budget, the importance of the job to the company, the size of the company or institution, and the funding source. The first rule is to overestimate your time. Every contract seems to take more time than you originally estimated. Moreover, clients always ask for more work than what you originally committed to do.

Once you project the amount of time it will take to complete the project, you must calculate an hourly rate. One benchmark is how much the average individual with your educational background and work experience makes per hour; align your fee accordingly. A number of websites provide salary calculators and median or salary ranges that should give you some idea of what employers are willing to pay. Select a job category, like human resources specialist, and follow the online instructions: **LINK OUT 14.4: Salary Calculators**.

The gross annual salary of human-resource professionals living in Chicago ranges from a low of $52,362 to a high of $78,037; the typical median salary, according to payscale.com's calculator, is $64,132, or $1,233.31 per week, or $30.83 per hour. Estimating forty hours of work for a one-day training session, a new consultant could reasonably ask for $1,200; for a two-day session, $2,500. (More experienced consultants will likely charge a great deal more.) Before moving too quickly to accept this job offer, realize that this sum does not include medical benefits, accrued vacation time, retirement or pension plans, or any of the other perks normally associated with permanent employment. Moreover, the $2,500 is pre-taxed money. Unless it is specified in the contract, this amount will also have to cover expenses incurred for this work. Finally, this fee is a one-time payment for services rendered; future or continued work with this client is not guaranteed. It costs money and time to cultivate more clients. Build in time in your estimate for finding more work. Given this picture, you might reasonably add another forty hours into your initial estimate and charge $3,700 for the two-day seminar.

Keep in mind that costing out a budget for a project, particularly a large, long-term project, is not a pure science. For projects lasting as long as six months or a year, it is more difficult to project expenses, time-on-task, travel, and other unexpected expenses. With experience, you will get better at estimating with greater accuracy and more profit. For additional online help with estimating fees for services, go to **LINK OUT 14.5:** **Consulting Fee Rates**.

Link Out 14.5:
Consulting Fee Rates

Relationships with Clients Influence How Much You Can Charge

One of the talents of organizational or business communication graduates that makes them so marketable is their ability to develop good relationships with all kinds of people. Communication majors know how to make people like them and trust them. Developing a client base, particularly one that is long term, depends on your ability to initiate and sustain relationships with those who will pay you for your work. You may not be able to ask for as much money as you would like with newer, more tentative client relationships, but with established, well-developed client relationships, you can ask for more, and you are likely to get it.

One way to develop long-term relationships is to begin by helping new clients with smaller, low-profit jobs that lead to additional work with greater profit. This incremental approach allows the client to learn what you can do for them and how well you can do it. As consultants, we have spent a lot of unpaid hours doing work for people with expectations of future returns on investment. This **client mining** process involves doing initial work for little or no money in order to cultivate lucrative work over time.

Self-Efficacy Is Worth Money

Perhaps the single most important quality of a seasoned and successful consultant is the ability to project a sense of self-confidence or **self-efficacy**. No one wants to hire or pay someone who doesn't exude the self-confidence to do the work. Some years ago, a client asked us for a referral for a focus-group facilitator after we had indicated that we were currently unavailable. Our response was a simple no. "We're the best. No one else can provide you with what you want." Sure, the client laughed, but he deferred and decided to wait

Yuri Arcurs/Shutterstock.com

Link Out 14.6:
USA Funds Life Skills

Weigh In 14.1:
*Assess Your Level of
Self-Efficacy*

until we were free to do the job. Projected self-confidence is worth money. Individuals who come across as experts, confident in what they know and what they can do, are also those the client is likely to hire and be willing to pay the most. Do you have the self-confidence to be a successful consultant? **WEIGH IN 14.1: Assess Your Level of Self-Efficacy** will help you answer that question.[6]

Setting your fee schedule is only one important phase in the consulting process. Part of developing your proposal for contracted services is outlining your work plan. In the next section, we sketch out the basic principles involved in preparing, implementing and evaluating a consulting plan.

How Should I Prepare, Enact, and Evaluate a Consulting Plan?

In order to make this section consumable and relevant to you as a potential consultant, we have organized the material around an actual case study of a consulting contract we had for a number of years. This project is a good illustration of how proposals and contracts evolve. We use this case to demonstrate the basic principles for preparing, implementing, and evaluating a consulting intervention or plan. We begin each *principle* with a definition or explanation, use our project to demonstrate how that principle can be utilized *in practice*, and conclude with a brief *analysis*.

To give you some background on the consulting project, some years ago our consulting team contracted with a client who we'll call VP Ralph. Ralph worked for USA Funds, a nonprofit organization and the nation's leading guarantor of student loans. In addition to guaranteeing student loans, the company develops initiatives, products, and services that educate and inform college students about the importance of and responsibilities associated with repayment of federally insured student loans. Although our initial contract with USA Funds was for a series of focus groups with college students, their parents, and financial aid officers, subsequent contracts with the client resulted in the development of an entire curriculum designed to help students better manage their finances and complete their degree programs on time. This nationwide financial literacy program, called Life Skills, is offered via webcasts and workshops at over five hundred universities across the country since its implementation in 2002. Perhaps you've experienced workshops in Life Skills on your campus or online. For an overview of this product, go to **LINK OUT 14.6: USA Funds Life Skills**.

As you might guess, our work with this agency consumed about four or five years of consulting work. What began as basic research about the reasons for increasing student loan debt and default rates evolved into the design and implementation of a modular curriculum to assist students with debt management. We rely on this "story" as we overview how a consulting plan is developed over time.[7]

Principle 1: Meet Frequently with the Client

A consulting plan is a product of frequent interactions with the client. We cannot emphasize enough the importance of meeting frequently with the client so that every step of the work process is coordinated, understood, and approved. Checking in is essential when developing the proposal, defining the problem, specifying objectives, designing interventions, and evaluating outcomes. Even with clients who are reluctant or too busy to interact frequently, the consultant must continually encourage them to stay closely connected to the project. The greater the client involvement in the consulting process, the more likely the client will be satisfied with the outcome. Clients who remain aloof or separate and apart from the process will likely be more critical of the work, lack an appreciation or understanding of the process and product, and fail to benefit fully from the contract.

In Practice Meeting early and often with our client, Ralph, was easy enough to do. He welcomed our discussions and made an effort to participate in all of the planning and implementation. We shared even small details with Ralph. In some respects, Ralph became a member of our consulting team. For example, when we were developing protocols for the focus groups, Ralph wanted to see drafts of our questions, distributed them for review to other members of his organization, and asked us to incorporate feedback. Although such involvement was time-consuming and a bit tedious, the overall result made each phase of our consulting work better. Moreover, the client perceived a greater sense of ownership or commitment to both our team and to the project as it developed.

Analysis Some clients really want to be involved; others do not. We were fortunate that Ralph was a client who wanted to be involved. Because of his involvement, we produced a higher-quality product, additional contracts, and a long-term relationship with the company. Frequent phone calls, face-to-face meetings, and online discussions are all vehicles for making this happen. Build time into your plan for these important exchanges.

Principle 2: Develop the Proposal Strategically

Project proposals must be thoughtfully prepared, consumable, and targeted. They must also be virtually perfect, both substantively and grammatically. For this reason, proposals often go through several drafts and revisions before a decision is made. The larger the project or the bigger the funding organization, the more challenging and time-consuming is the process of drafting and developing an acceptable proposal.

In Practice Given the success of initial contracts with the client, Ralph contacted us to discuss some ideas he had about student loan debt management. After several early discussions with Ralph about the possibility of doing research with students on student loan debt and repayment, he asked us to meet with his Default Prevention Council consisting of twenty-two financial aid professionals from colleges, universities, and proprietary schools across the country. This council assists USA Funds in its efforts to enhance student loan repayment and to minimize default rates nationally.

Meetings with the council revealed that neither Ralph nor the council had a clear understanding of what they wanted us to do. Our discussions with the council helped both them and us unravel and outline their research agenda. We began to identify a number of projects, each one building upon the results of the previous one. With each draft of the proposal, council members weighed in on the details. Everyone involved in the decision was given an opportunity to provide input, and we were advised to address all of their concerns. Six months and several iterations of the project proposal later, we all agreed on what needed to be done. At that point, the formal proposal was submitted, and the contract was officially funded and awarded to our team.

Analysis As you might guess, our team invested a lot of time and effort in developing what would eventually be a fundable contract, and yet, no money was exchanged until the contract was ultimately awarded. Whereas this contract was funded, other contracts may

Check This Out 14.3:
How to Write a Consulting Proposal

not be similarly obtained. The costs associated with developing proposals for contracts that are not awarded are simply out of pocket. In spite of the inherent risks, proposals that take time, careful thought, and a lot of energy are more frequently funded, produce better products, and typically result in greater profit. Consultant William Frank offers advice about successful proposals in CHECK THIS OUT 14.3: **How to Write a Consulting Proposal**.

Principle 3: Define the Nature and Extent of the Problem

Without a clear understanding of the problem, no viable solution can be formulated. Imposing a premature solution on a problem either ill-defined or undefined wastes company time, effort, and money. Yet, premature solutions and interventions are imposed all the time.[8] A **needs assessment** is the most common way to identify or diagnose the nature and extent of a problem. A needs assessment identifies the gap between current conditions, or what is, and what should or ought to be. One trainer commented that the needs assessment she conducted with a client organization "transformed an original plan of gut feeling to one of documented client need."[9] By spending the time to fully understand the status quo, you can begin to consider how things might be improved or what needs to be changed.

In Practice Once the contract was signed, our task was to assist USA Funds in defining the problem. After multiple sessions with the Default Prevention Council, the client wisely decided to do a needs assessment utilizing focus-group interviews. Council members wanted us to identify the problems and challenges involved throughout the student loan and repayment process. Working closely with the client and the council, we decided to solicit information from students themselves, their parents, and financial aid officers. We further planned to use surveys to supplement the interviews.

We conducted thirty-nine focus groups with 312 participants (students, parents, and financial aid professionals), recruited from four geographic regions and twelve different cities. What did we learn? First, college students evidenced little or no ability to manage their money, live within their means, and progress through school in a timely fashion. (Sound familiar?) Second, the data showed that even though all kinds of information were available to students, borrowers failed to process, comprehend, and retain information relevant to loans and their repayment. (Why would they? Loan documents are confusing!) Third, products and services that had been created to inform borrowers about loans were, for the most part, ineffective. (Why would they assume that a brochure or a sticker was sufficient?) Taken together, these results clearly substantiated the need for borrower life-skills instruction focusing on what it means to be a responsible consumer of student loans. Thus, the problem was clearly defined for the client.

Analysis Most needs assessments are not as extensive (or nationwide) as the one in this project. Assessments can be formal, consisting of focus-group interviews, surveys, and analysis of archival documents. Other assessments can be more informal, consisting of one-on-one discussions with a sample of the target group or systematic observations of people at work. Whatever method you choose, be sure to ask and answer these questions:[10]

- What do you know?

- What do you think you know?

- What do you still want to know?

Visualize! Practice! 14.1:
How to Write Objectives

Answers to these questions will help you determine what you need to measure and how you should go about measuring it.

Our client felt that the costs of conducting such an extensive, nationwide needs assessment had been a good investment. Unfortunately, this is not always the case. Too many clients skip the needs assessment, presuming they already understand the problem and know what needs to be done.[11] Moreover, clients are reluctant to spend money up front defining a problem when they perceive greater value in targeting funds toward the solution or the intervention. Your task, then, as a consultant, is to educate the client about the importance of establishing the need or defining the nature and extent of the problem before any real remedy is considered. It's always a better value to come up with the right solution the first time than to suggest a number of possible solutions and hope that one works.

Principle 4: Specify Objectives That Need to Be Targeted

Once the problem is defined, one or more possible solutions can be considered, planned, and implemented. Before doing so, however, the consultant should ask the client, "What outcomes would you like to see as a result of the solution?" Other ways of asking the question are, "What changes would you like to see?" and "How would you like people to behave differently as a result of the intervention?" With greater specificity, the consultant is in a better position to develop a solution that meets the client's expectations. Try your hand at describing specific behavioral objectives with VISUALIZE! PRACTICE! 14.1: **How to Write Objectives**.

In Practice The client and council focused on two overriding goals: (a) to help students better manage their debt while in school and (b) to help students repay their loans after they graduate. Although these general goals were important, they obviously weren't specific or tangible enough for us to propose ways to make them happen.

We urged the client to look again at the findings. The focus groups and surveys suggested a number of particular factors that influence students' ability to reach those goals, including time management, managing credit card debt, selecting a program of study early in their college career, and generating and living within a budget. The more we talked with the client and the council, the more we realized that these and related issues were essential "life skills" important to developing a well-rounded, fiscally responsible adult. What specific life skills did we need to target in order to make that happen?

Together with the council, we worked to develop a set of sequentially defined **behavioral objectives** that targeted specific outcomes or life skills that students needed to master in order to become financially literate and to complete school on time. For example, we wanted to ensure that students prioritized their education and successfully graduated within a reasonable amount of time. Whatever solution we designed and implemented then, we wanted students to be able to

- Develop a plan for finishing school on time.
- Identify strategies for making satisfactory progress toward their degree.
- Develop coping strategies for the demands of student life.

Eventually, we isolated enough objectives or learning outcomes that would consume an entire curriculum. Specifying the objectives served as a basis, then, for crafting and implementing a solution or intervention.

Analysis We spent an inordinate amount of time talking with the client and council members about the specific outcomes students should be able to do in order to demonstrate and internalize these life skills important to managing their debt and repaying their loans. In other words, we worked with the client to specify and to make sure we had identified all the relevant objectives that would lead to the development of the curricular intervention that we called Life Skills. Moreover, we grouped and prioritized objectives to make sure that essential skills were identified and included in the intervention. With this list of fifteen to twenty objectives defined as essential to the solution, we could begin to craft a meaningful intervention. Absent these objectives, we might have assumed a very different priority list and proposed a solution inconsistent or unaligned with client and council members' perceptions.

Principle 5: Craft a Workable Intervention

Once the problem is clearly defined and objectives are specified, the real work begins on the design and development of the solution or intervention. Solutions come in all shapes and sizes depending on the nature of the consulting project. Sometimes the solution is a training program, a written report, a briefing, a video, a website, a brochure, a communication campaign, more research and development, an evaluation of some kind, or a one-shot workshop. In short, the solution or intervention includes some kind of product, service, or some other deliverable.

In Practice In the process of specifying objectives with the client and the council, we discovered that what we had was the basis for an entire curriculum that USA Funds could promote and deliver to their customers nationally. Because our team had background and experience in instructional design, technology, and training, we were asked to develop a second proposal to design the Life Skills curricular packages. As with other proposals, this one required several iterations. Recognizing the need for an additional expert in instructional design, we added to our team another member, Dr. Terre Allen, and we employed an online proofreading service, www.proofreadnow.com, that could help us transform our documents into the style preferred by the client.

Over the course of many months, we crafted five independent, yet interrelated instructional modules, each designed as a one-hour workshop to be delivered to undergraduate student borrowers by financial aid professionals. For example, one module titled "Get a Grip on Your Finances: Smart Spending for Students" was designed to teach four specific objectives:

- Make smart choices about spending and saving.
- Develop a financial game plan.
- Make a budget and stick to it.
- Borrow only what you need for school.

Other modules targeted other objectives related to financial literacy, borrowing money, loan repayment, and developing an academic plan to finish school. Important to the success of this new Life Skills product, we had to make the information easily consumable and student friendly. Beyond merely informing, then, we designed the modules to be highly involving, interactive, motivating, and edu-taining.

Analysis In continued discussions with the client and council, we were able to facilitate a solution, one that was well beyond a simple workshop or a new brochure. We started with one module, demonstrated it to the council, revised it, and pilot-tested it with students and financial aid professionals. Soon we were contracted to do four more. Later on, we were asked to develop an entire curriculum of eleven modules and ten mini-modules for an audience that included graduate and professional students as well. What began as a research project of focus group interviews and surveys evolved into a multistage, curriculum-based solution. Our eventual product was rolled out to students and financial aid professionals over a period of several years.

Notice how we added an additional member to our team and we employed a proofreading service. We did so even though we fully recognized that additional overhead expenses would be incurred. Adding the design specialist allowed us to meet what appeared at the time to be unreasonable deadlines that were nonnegotiable with the client. Employing the proofreading service helped us avoid problems with an antagonistic employee of the client organization who demanded that we convert our documents to an unknown and unfamiliar style manual. Sometimes you simply have to spend more in order to assuage or appease client demands.

Principle 6: Evaluate the Intervention

Assessing the effectiveness of any intervention should be built into your plan. The goal of any evaluation is to provide useful feedback to all the interested parties. Evaluating the results of the interventions provides clients with justification for having invested time and money in the program, gives the consultant feedback on what worked and what did not, and speaks to meeting the specific objectives of the project. Without evaluation data, clients have no basis upon which to argue for the program's continuation and additional funding; the consultant cannot know what to revise, remove, or add to continuing interventions; and the client can only guess at the worth or merit of the program.

The success or failure of any intervention or program can be assessed in a variety of different ways. The dominant evaluation approach used by consultants today relies on the scientific method. The principles of this method allow for evaluation data that are essentially objective, reliable, valid, and impartial. Evaluation methods can be either formative or summative.

Formative evaluations access feedback about the delivery or the product or service as it unfolds during implementation. Consultants rely on frequent formative evaluations to help them revise or refine the intervention as it is occurring. Consultants may develop simple feedback forms or surveys for participants to evaluate targeted aspects of the intervention, such as the content, the delivery system, the product's consumability, the trainer or facilitator, and overall evaluation of the program so far. Other indices might include participant attendance, level of participant interaction or attentiveness, and unsolicited feedback or testimonials.

Summative evaluations are obtained after the intervention has been implemented. Typically more formal in design, summative evaluations measure the outcomes of the intervention and are tied specifically to the objectives.[12] Consultants might utilize instruments that reliably assess attainment of each of the objectives, including anonymous surveys, exit interviews, and short-term and long-term outcome indicators that measure impacts, benefits, or changes as a result of the intervention.

In Practice Both types of evaluation played a prominent role in our intervention with USA Funds. Throughout the process of curriculum development, we solicited feedback from the client and council members that helped to form and shape the final product. Moreover, we pilot-tested each of the modules with sample students and financial aid officers before the final product went into production. Upon completion of the contract, we relied on a variety of summative indices to determine project effectiveness. Perhaps the most credible index of the program's quality was program adoption among colleges, universities, proprietary schools, and professional and graduate schools across the country. In addition, users of the product evaluated the delivery and content of each module they completed. We also provided summary quizzes tied to each of the objectives designed to assess student learning. Other milestone indicators were long term and focused on student borrowing or graduation rates at particular institutions.

Analysis The feedback gleaned from formative and summative evaluations brought substance and credibility to the intervention. Building into the consulting plan multiple vehicles for evaluating what we were doing along the way and how effectively we accomplished our objectives at the end allowed us to make claims about the program's value to the client. Such evaluation efforts produce meaningful and consequential data that the client can use to justify existing and future projects. That's exactly what happened. No sooner were we done with that contract than the client asked us to do another project.

Our experience working with USA Funds on this project was unusually positive. One reason was our good working relationships with the client, Ralph, his staff, and all the members of the Default Prevention Council. Everyone went out of their way to help us develop and roll out the Life Skills modules. They were easily accessible by phone, email, and face-to-face interactions when needed. The Life Skills project not only yielded a successful product for the client, but it also gave our consulting team the opportunity to try out many of our academic skills, like research and course design, for a corporate client.

The six principles discussed in this section played a critical role in our efforts to define and satisfy the expectations of our client. We relied heavily on these principles to guide our decisions and operations. Although consulting contracts vary in size and magnitude and in breadth and depth, the principles remain the same. Additional principles might also emerge with different kinds of consulting projects, such "remain flexible," "adapt to unintended circumstances," "negotiate project completion dates," "be sensitive to politics of the organization," and "recognize client misconceptions about what can be reasonably accomplished."

Companies rely on consultants to help them accomplish a variety of services and tasks. Communication consultants in particular help organizations identify and solve managerial or employee problems and train employees in relevant people skills. In this chapter we have made the case for the acquisition of a variety of specialized academic and relational skills important to developing credentials necessary for a consultant that people will want to hire. Making contacts and developing a client list is a lot like looking for a job; it takes time, effort, and persistence. One of the more delicate but important aspects of what consultants do is determining how much their work is worth and, therefore, how much to charge their clients.

Preparing, implementing and evaluating consulting projects is at the core of what consultants do for a living. Successful consultants operate from a set of basic principles that they use to guide their work. They meet frequently with the client to gain feedback and ensure understanding. They make a point of communicating with the client regularly throughout the duration of the contract. Preparing a marketable proposal is an important part of getting work. Proposals normally go through a variety of phases of development and revision prior to being funded. Even though clients may be reluctant to spend time and money up front defining a problem, good consultants establish and document the nature and extent of the problem before considering or recommending any real remedy. Once the need has been clearly identified, specific objectives are articulated, a workable intervention is developed and implemented, and both formative and summative forms of evaluation are executed. Overall, the consulting process is systematic, relying on basic principles to guide the activity. Perhaps most important to effective consulting is the ability to initiate and sustain good working relationships with clients.

Use your Speech Communication CourseMate for *Business & Communication in a Digital Age* for quick access to the electronic resources that accompany this text. These resources include

Study tools that will help you assess your learning and prepare for exams (*digital glossary, key term flash cards, review quizzes*).

Activities and assignments that will help you hone your knowledge and build your communication skills throughout the course (*Visualize! Practice!, Weigh In!, Check This Out, and Link Out activities; modules; review questions*).

Media resources that will help you explore communication concepts online (*Enhanced eBook*), develop your speech outlines (*Speech Builder Express 3.0*), watch and critique videos of sample speeches and communication situations (*interactive video activities*), upload your speech videos for peer reviewing and critique other students' speeches (*Speech Studio online speech review tool*), and download chapter review so you can study when and where you'd like (*Audio Study Tools*).

Key Points

- Communication consultants are hired by organizations to diagnose problems, recommend solutions or courses of action, facilitate interventions, and evaluate outcomes associated with those interventions.

- In order to be a successful communication consultant, you need special skills and knowledge, including
  - ✔ Specialized communication skills
  - ✔ A working knowledge of the scientific method
  - ✔ The ability to draw upon relevant theory and research
  - ✔ The ability to work well with clients.

- Getting started as a consultant is a slow process, requiring you to "get the word out" about what you have to offer and that you are available for hire.

- The most frequently asked question about being a consultant is, "How much should I charge for my services?"
  - ✔ When costing out your time for services, you need to consider preparation time, delivery time, and debriefing time.
  - ✔ Determining how much your time is worth depends on many factors, including your prior work history with the client, the size and complexity of the job, the client's budget, the importance of the job to the company, the size the organization, and the amount of funding available.
  - ✔ The nature and longevity of your relationship with the client affects how much you can charge; with well-developed, established client relationships, you can ask for more.
  - ✔ Perhaps the single most important quality that will make you money is your ability to project a sense of self-confidence or self-efficacy to do the work.

- Six basic principles for preparing, enacting, and evaluating a consulting plan are
  - ✔ Meet frequently with the client. Checking in is essential when developing the proposal, defining the problem, specifying objectives, designing interventions, and evaluating outcomes.
  - ✔ Develop the proposal strategically. Proposals must be thoughtfully prepared, consumable, and targeted.
  - ✔ Define the nature and extent of the problem. Viable solutions can only be formulated with a clear understanding of the problem. A needs assessment, then, is essential.
  - ✔ Specify objectives that need to be targeted. Identify ahead of time the changes the client wants to see as a result of the intervention.
  - ✔ Craft a workable solution. Once the problem is defined and objectives are specified, a solution or intervention (such as a training program, report, video, or website) can be developed or implemented.
  - ✔ Evaluate the intervention. Evaluating the results of the intervention gives both the consultant and the client feedback on what worked (and what did not). All evaluations should be tied directly to objectives.

Key Terms

consultant (313)

communication consultant (313)

intervention (316)

assessment (316)

needs assessment (328)

client mining (325)

self-efficacy (325)

behavioral objective (330)

formative evaluation (332)

summative evaluation (332)

Questions for Critical Thinking and Review

1. What kinds of communication problems typically occur in the workplace that might require consulting services?

2. How would you go about determining if a problem really exists in the organization? What would you do? Why are some clients so reluctant to spend the money for a needs assessment? How might you convince them to do so? What arguments would you use?

3. Why would anyone want to be a consultant full time? What are the advantages of being a consultant? What are some of the disadvantages?

4. A number of factors influence how a consultant might cost out a job. How would you estimate the costs for any given project? How much is your time worth?

5. Consultants work with all kinds of clients, some of whom might be difficult or challenging. How difficult would a potential client have to be for you to walk away from a contract? Explain why.

6. What sorts of consulting projects might require you to develop a consulting team? What special skills would you require for a well-rounded team of communication consultants? What people do you currently know who might make valuable members of your consulting team?

7. All organizations are political. How much should you let politics influence the design, implementation, and evaluation of your intervention?

8. What academic theories have you learned that might be helpful to you as a communication consultant? Why do some theories seem more applicable or practical than others?

9. Of all the communication skills you have mastered in your academic career, which ones are likely to serve you the best as a consultant? In addition, what communication skills do you think organizations value the most?

10. What is meant by *self-efficacy*? Why do your authors claim that self-efficacy as a consultant is worth money?

Chapter 15

Communication Training:
What Skills Do I Need?

StockLite/Shutterstock.com

Chapter Learning Objectives

After completing this chapter, you should be able to
- Identify credentials important to being an effective trainer.
- Assess client training needs.
- Specify training objectives.
- Develop the training content.
- Rely on a variety of instructional tools to train.
- Evaluate the training process, learning outcomes, and the trainer.

See also the modules that are relevant to this chapter:

 7: What Methods Can I Use to Analyze My Audience?

Darlene's problem is her medical insurance company.

The company keeps denying her claims and refuses to pay. She has called on numerous occasions to argue her case, but the company representative continues to tell her no. It's not the refusal alone that concerns Darlene—it's the cavalier attitude that the representative projects. She's convinced that the company is intentionally ignoring her claims. After repeated attempts to get a representative to understand her case, Darlene is frustrated, angry, and dejected.

Jack's problem is stage fright. As a new supervisor in his company, he assumes the responsibility for preparing and delivering weekly briefings to a group of twenty or more employees. He has no idea where to begin. Even thinking about giving a speech makes him feel panicky.

Arleen's problem is hostile clients. She works in an online service department for a large computer company. Her job is to respond to customers who are having difficulty with their newly purchased computer equipment. Because her department is understaffed, clients typically must wait on average fifteen minutes for her to respond. By the time she makes contact, clients are hopping mad and downright rude. Their complaints are beginning to wear her down.

Gerry's problem is evaluating his employees. By law, Gerry is required to write and provide an oral performance appraisal annually for each of his ten employees. He hates doing it and puts it off as long as he can. He's discovered that no matter what kind of evaluation he gives, good and bad, employees come into the interview angry and indignant. They simply don't want him to question anything they do, right or wrong. Moreover, they aren't interested in recommendations that might help them improve.

What's common to all of these scenarios? In each case someone needs to be trained to do their job more effectively. Darlene's insurance company representative needs to be trained to provide greater clarity, understanding, and compassion. Jack needs to learn how to manage his stage fright, prepare a briefing, and deliver it with confidence. Arleen needs training in managing hostile customers. Gerry needs to learn how to conduct an employee appraisal that invites employee input, problem-solving, and mutual discussion.

Link Out 15.1:
*What's a Training
Specialist Worth?*

U.S. corporations spend quite a bit of money on training. Recent estimates of just how much reveal that for formal training, such as workshops and seminars, expenditures exceed $50 billion a year, averaging about $1,200 per employee.[1] Why would companies be willing to spend that kind of money? Organizations offer training programs in virtually every conceivable area of work, both technical and nontechnical. Employees learn new skills, acquire new or updated information, and practice new managerial or coping strategies every day. The whole idea behind training is to improve worker productivity, employee morale, and product or service quality. In these ways, training is an investment that is directly or indirectly tied to profit.

Corporate training is only expected to increase in the coming years, with the U.S. Bureau of Labor statistics projecting greater and greater demand for training specialists.[2] As baby boomers retire, as new technologies appear, and as new skills are required, corporate trainers become more integral to the successful running of a business. The demand seems to be supported in the wages trainers can expect. For instance, the median annual salary for corporate training specialists who design and conduct training programs in and around Long Beach, California, is about $85,000, with most specialists having a bachelor's degree (36 percent) or higher (51 percent).[3] In Peoria, Illinois, the median salary is $80,000, and in Baton Rouge, Louisiana, training specialists can expect to earn about $75,000. Apparently, choosing a career in industrial or corporate training is worth considering. To find out the wages for training specialists in your local area, try out this salary wizard: **LINK OUT 15.1: What's a Training Specialist Worth?**

Organizational training is a particular type of consulting activity where individuals are trained or taught particular skills or knowledge to enhance their work performance.[4] Companies make decisions to train employees for several reasons. Most common to organizations is the institutionalized training offered to new hires who may have skill deficits requiring specialized training unique to the company or who may need to be socialized into the organization. Training may also become necessary when innovations or new regulations are introduced into the company, especially if they demand formal certification, special expertise, or employee sensitivity training. A third reason for training typically results from the work and advice of consultants who may recommend training as a solution to a newly identified problem in the organization.

This chapter examines the basics of training, beginning with the credentials typically required to become a trainer who organizations will hire. Getting started as a trainer, like getting started as a consultant, requires a well-developed client list. Chapter 14, on communication consulting, provides you with detailed direction on how to identify and acquire clients. Once you have a client, you will need to work from a plan of action that always begins with meeting with the client, identifying the target audience, and determining what the employees already know and what they still need to learn. By specifying explicit and specific training objectives, you and the client will have a road map from which to operate. Those objectives become the basis for everything else the trainer does, including the content of the training, the strategies important to teaching the content, and the evaluation measures used to assess the extent to which the training worked.

What Credentials Does a Communication Trainer Need?

Corporate trainers plan and implement a wide range of instructional activities. They provide programs to orient new employees, upgrade employee job skills, improve managers' and employees' interpersonal skills, and teach executive and leadership skills.

Communication trainers typically provide workshops and seminars in the following basic how-to skills:[5]

- Listen actively.
- Become more assertive.
- Avoid issues of sexual harassment.
- Use and interpret customers' nonverbal messages.
- Manage conflict.
- Deal with angry customers.
- Develop collaborative teams.
- Solve problems and make decisions in groups and teams.
- Lead and participate in meetings.
- Deliver sales presentations.
- Use computer graphics in business presentations.
- Persuade a customer to purchase a product.
- Manage time and be more productive.
- Present briefings, reports, and presentations.
- Improve the quality of employee communication.
- Communicate the leadership vision of an organization.
- Communicate with people from a culture different from their own.
- Lead others by being collaborative.
- Develop a cooperative management style.
- Train trainers to prepare and deliver a successful training program.
- Conduct employee appraisal interviews.

Communication trainers, then, must be able to teach others to do all of these and similar communication skills. What credentials should communication trainers bring to the table?

Trainers Need Credible Background in Communication Theory and Skills

Obtaining a communication degree is minimum for successfully building a client list for training opportunities. Trainers typically have a B.A. or higher degree with relevant coursework in interpersonal communication, organizational communication, nonverbal communication, conflict management, small group communication, leadership and team building, public speaking, persuasion, and more. (The coursework for consultants described in Chapter 14 is also applicable to trainers.) The degree matters; it represents systematic study of human communication. Paid or unpaid internships in human resources where training is most likely to occur can also provide important and marketable experiences. Most recently, corporate training certification programs have become available online or at selected universities. Being certified as a trainer adds to your credibility with potential clients.

auremar/shutterstock.com

Trainers Need to Be Able to Translate What They Know

It's one thing to know about a subject academically and quite another to be able to translate that information for workplace consumption. Good trainers can do that. They learn how to make theory and research both relevant and consumable to their target audiences. Even though many college students can prepare and deliver a speech for a communication class, few have the ability to teach a group of engineers how to do the same thing. Appreciating and adapting to the context within which engineers work makes the material meaningful to what they do. Talking the client's talk is an important skill that trainers must learn. Sometimes trainers learn the context by talking to those who work in that area. Others study the context by researching and reading about it. Still others have spent time working in the environment. The more the trainer knows and understands the client's workplace, the more effectively he or she can translate the material into a consumable and usable form. **MODULE 7:** **What Methods Can I Use to Analyze My Audience?**

Trainers Must Be Able to Work with Clients

Trainers, like good consultants (as discussed in Chapter 14), must be able to initiate and sustain long-term relationships with clients. Effective trainers know how to get along with people, assert themselves, listen actively and empathetically, adjust to difficult exchanges, manage conflict, develop trust, engage in relational repair, self-disclose appropriately, and adapt to intercultural, international, and intergenerational relationships. All these skills can be used to initiate client relationships, handle difficult clients, bring closure to important contract negotiations, sustain long-term relationships with customers, and listen to client concerns.

Trainers Need a Working Knowledge of Andragogy and Instructional Design

Knowing how adults learn is critical to teaching them new skills and principles that they will adopt, practice, and utilize. Much has been written about the differences between teaching children, typically referred to as pedagogy, and teaching adults, now called **andragogy**. For instance, whatever trainers teach must be perceived as *relevant* and *practical*. Having a great deal of life *experiences and knowledge*, adult learners prefer trainers to recognize and build upon what they bring to the training environment. Because adults are *goal oriented*, they appreciate being involved in the planning of instruction; they know what they know and what they still need to know. As *autonomous, self-directed* adults, these learners are intrinsically motivated if they believe the training will give them some sense of satisfaction and accomplishment. Perhaps most critical to working with adult learners is to treat them with *respect*.[6] **LINK OUT 15.2:** **Adult Learners 101**[7]

Instructional design is the systematic development of an instructional plan, beginning with needs assessment, defining objectives, specifying content, identifying relevant and varied teaching strategies (including multimedia aids), and evaluating learning outcomes. This plan is informed by a variety of tested learning theories, principles, and research. Teaching and learning from this perspective is not trial and error. With a systematic instructional plan, science guides what is taught, how it's taught, and how outcomes are assessed. All effective training follows this plan of action. Prospective trainers are strongly encouraged to take course work in how adults learn and how instruction is systematically organized and implemented. **CHECK THIS OUT 15.1:** **Working with Adult Learners**[8]

Link Out 15.2:
Adult Learners 101
Link Out 15.3:
Checklist for Hiring a Trainer

Check This Out 15.1:
Working with Adult Learners

Trainers Must Be Able to Draw upon Theory and Research

Theories and research findings offer trainers explanations and insights that can be used in training workshops and seminars. Staying current in the discipline ensures that you will always have something new to add to your instruction. People working in business and industry want and need to know the latest information, trends, research findings, and solutions. From our own experiences with training in organizations over the years, we've discovered that managers and employees alike appreciate our ability to support what we say and do with relevant theory and research. They find research results that we've translated for them to the workplace interesting, informative, and applicable to what they do. Trainers need to be able to offer them all this—and more. Trainers should stay abreast of the current technologies to assist them in training; they need to stay on top of the most recent thinking and research on how adults process information, stay on task, and retain what they hear and learn. Like consultants, trainers should rely on theory and research to inform and direct everything they do.

Trainers Must Be Perceived as Experts

In addition to all of the credentials cited so far, the single most important characteristic of a successful trainer is the ability to communicate a sense of self-confidence in what she or he is able to do. Developing and projecting a sense of **self-efficacy** is requisite to conveying expertise as a trainer (and as a consultant). No one wants to hire or pay someone who does not exude the self-confidence to do the work.

Projecting a deep understanding of the subject matter and demonstrating a clear appreciation of the needs of adult learners adds to perceptions of trainer competencies. Examine **LINK OUT 15.3:** **Checklist for Hiring a Trainer** to get an idea of what clients look for when hiring an expert to come into their organization.[9]

Trainers who come across as experts, confident in what they know and comfortable with what they do, are also those the client is likely to hire and be willing to pay the most. The more expert qualifications you have, including experience and educational

background, the more you can justify your fees.[10] Once you've established your credentials as a trainer, you must be able to produce or perform. The rest of this chapter is devoted to making sure that you will know how to develop and implement your training plan.

Where Do I Begin?

Once you have your training contract in hand, the next step is to meet with the client to discuss the training plan. All of this upfront work with the client is critical to your success and the success of the training program. Preparing a training plan is a product of frequent interactions with the client, a well-designed needs assessment, and a well-defined list of training objectives.

Meet with the Client

Like all consulting projects, the greater the client involvement in the training process, the more likely the client will be satisfied with the outcome. Ask the client a series of questions. Try these:

- What do you want to achieve?
- Who is the target audience?
- What do they already know?
- What do they still need to know?
- How does the work environment influence their performance?
- What financial restrictions do employees operate under?
- What's the general level of work stress that your employees experience?
- How seriously will the employees commit to the training?
- What incentives are employees given for attending?
- How much time are you willing to devote to training?
- What previous training have they experienced?
- How did they respond to previous training?
- Where will the training occur?
- Are there special employee problems or issues that I need to know?
- Would it help for me to meet with the group before training?
- What will you tell them about the training?
- What expectations do you have about the training?
- What expectations might they have about the training?
- Is there anyone else I should meet with to discuss the training?
- Will management be present during the training sessions?

Answers to these and similar questions will influence the development of the training plan. Spending time talking with the client about these issues can only make your job easier. The more informed you are about the environment, the audience, the organization, and expectations, the more strategic you can be in targeting and achieving outcomes.

Discover Training Needs

A **needs assessment** provides a systematic way to acquire an accurate accounting or portrayal of the strengths and weaknesses of the employees to be trained. Often referred to as a **gap analysis**, a needs assessment identifies current skills or knowledge and then compares them to the desired skills and information yet to be acquired. Identifying the gap helps the trainer understand and appreciate what kind of training needs to occur. In addition, the trainer is better able to set priorities and identify solutions.

Information or data about the employees can be gathered in a variety of ways. Informally, your initial meetings with the client should provide you with a general understanding of the targeted group of employees. Asking the client to describe the employees individually and as a group is a good place to start. Ask the client what they already know—and what they still need to know. Determine through conversations the reasons for the training and why particular individuals were chosen to participate. The client might direct you to others who have more direct experiences with the employees. Consult with key individuals who have regular contact with the group.

A second strategy is to talk with some of the employees themselves. Ask them what they hope or need to learn. Recall that adult learners often like to participate in the instructional process. Rely on them for input about what they know and what they still need to know. Interview them for suggestions to make the training program consumable, practical, and relevant to their work.

A third strategy is more formal and relies on focus groups, surveys, or questionnaires to assess learner needs and wants. With client input, you can develop a series of questions or items that tap into employee beliefs or knowledge bases, attitudes or emotions, and behaviors or skills important to your training topic. Needs-assessment questionnaires can be designed as a checklist of skills and beliefs that respondents can identify as strengths or weaknesses. You might ask the respondents to rank order skills in order of importance to doing their job effectively. You can provide a series of open-ended questions, inviting them to respond with their reactions and opinions; this can be done with questionnaires or with focus-group interviews.

A number of needs-assessment instruments are available online. For examples of training needs assessments, take a look at these webpages: **LINK OUT 15.4: Training Needs Assessments**.

Link Out 15.4:
Training Needs Assessments

Specify Objectives

What do the following four situations have in common?

- Training participants find it difficult to take notes or do the activities because they don't know what is important and what is not.

- After the activity, some of the participants are disappointed because they focused on the wrong thing.

- While observing participants during workshop activity, the trainer notes that the group is having a lot of fun but seems to be learning little of value.

- Performance evaluations following the training are unacceptably low, and yet the trainer feels she did all she could by covering the important content. The trainer concludes that this group of employees either didn't take the workshops seriously or they are simply stupid.

haveseen/Shutterstock.com

Each of these situations is characterized by a lack of objectives. **Objectives** specify for learners what they are expected to learn; at the same time, they specify for the trainer what needs to be taught. A clear statement of objectives further helps to determine or evaluate how effective the training was. Knowing where you want to go or what you want to accomplish substantially increases the chances that everyone will get there and that they'll know when they've arrived. In these ways, objectives serve as a kind of path or road map for instruction.

Specifying objectives, or what the learner needs to be able to do, is no simple matter. Objectives are specific statements that identify the desired goals or outcomes that the learners should achieve as a result of the training experience. The needs assessment will give you a sound basis from which to formulate those objectives. For example, if your needs assessment determined that employees lack motivation to meet project deadlines, you might write a training objective to reflect a change in their motivation:

> At the end of this training workshop, participants should be able to negotiate and commit to project deadlines.

If your needs assessment determined that managers seem to be spending far too much time in their offices and not on the floor interacting with employees, your training objectives might read like these two:

> At the end of this workshop, management participants should be able articulate two reasons why spending time interacting with employees is important.

> At the end of this workshop, managers will spend one hour each day walking around the workplace and interacting with employees.

Writing and specifying good training objectives takes a great deal of thought and time. Good objectives must be observable, measurable, attainable, and specific.[11] Most of all, training objectives must be preapproved by the client. Once the objectives have been solidified and approved, you can turn your attention to what is taught and how to teach it.

Suppose you are hired to train new managers some basic managerial skills. After discussions with the client and as a result of a needs assessment, you discover that one of your goals is to teach them how to delegate tasks to others that they might normally do themselves. Here are two different ways you might specify your training objectives:

Example 1: As a result of this training session, you will be able to

- Manage others better.
- Delegate tasks to your employees.

Example 2: As a result of this training session, you will be able to[12]

- Identify key individuals who can handle special tasks.
- Explain to those individuals exactly what needs to be done.
- Communicate the quality of the work that you expect.
- Set deadlines for task completion.
- Check for progress on the delegated task at frequent intervals.
- Verify task completion and quality when the deadline arrives.

Of the two examples, which provides greater specificity? Which example gives the trainer greater direction on what to teach? Which example gives the trainer some idea of how to go about teaching particular content or skills? Which example lets the learner know exactly what he or she is expected to do following training?

What should be apparent from these two examples is that writing objectives well is requisite to your success as a trainer. With the benefits of the objectives in Example 2, you would have a much better idea of what to train and how to go about doing it. How to write objectives for training workshops is beyond the scope of this book, so we urge you to examine professors Beebe, Mottet, and Roach's seminal textbook on training and development.[13] For online instruction on how to write objectives, see LINK OUT 15.5: **Writing Learning Objectives**.

What Do I Teach?

The content of a training workshop or seminar is directly tied to the objectives that have already been defined and approved by the client. What you teach in the training workshop should be guided by those the objectives. All you have to do is research or locate the relevant information and organize the materials in some meaningful way that will make sense to the participants. Finding information is a lot like researching a paper for a class. The assistance of the Internet and online libraries simplifies your task. Within seconds or minutes, you should be able to locate and retrieve a wealth of information about virtually any topic. Much of the research for this book, for instance, was gathered from online databases, including university libraries, the Bureau of Labor Statistics and other governmental agencies, commercial websites, and more.

Link Out 15.5:
Writing Learning Objectives

Visualize!
Practice! 15.1:
Training Session Openers

Once you have accessed a number of sources, you will need to rely on criteria to evaluate the materials' suitability, relevance, and accuracy. When evaluating the quality of the materials, consider these questions:[14]

1. Is the material relevant to your training purpose?
2. Is the material relevant to your trainees in their context?
3. Is the material from a credible source?
4. Is the material documentable?
5. Is the material useful?
6. Is the material understandable to your audience?
7. Is the material in useable form?
8. Is the material relevant to the training objectives?
9. Is the material relevant to the needs of the trainees?

Once you have determined that the information is suitable, relevant, and accurate, you can begin to organize or structure the materials into some kind of sequence or priority. Again, rely on the objectives. What needs to be taught first, second, and third? What skills need to be learned first so that subsequent skills can be learned? What materials are more important than other materials?

Now you are ready to do a more formal outline. Determine what sections of the outline might have too much or not enough material. You may find that you need to do additional research or eliminate unnecessary or duplicative materials. Look over the objectives again, making sure that no objective is overlooked or shortchanged in the outline. Once you know exactly what information you need to provide participants in order to meet each objective, you can turn your attention to how you might want to do that.

How Do I Teach It?

Selecting the best ways to teach objectives in order to maximize learning success requires a great deal of strategy, forethought, and preparation. Training doesn't just happen. Trainers don't just walk into a workshop armed with materials and start to talk. Everything that happens during a training workshop or seminar is planned and deliberate. No detail, no matter how small, goes unnoticed. Every activity has been carefully chosen, timed, and tied to particular outcomes or objectives. For instance, a good trainer knows that participants will be tired following the lunch break and will strategically select activities that reinvigorate them. The trainer might spend hours beforehand reviewing dozens of online videos and find that only one truly fits. The layout of the physical environment is often modified to elicit just the right amount of participation. Even restroom breaks are predetermined so as to minimize disruptions in the learning process. Recognizing that adult learners appreciate active participation in the learning process, lecture time is minimized. What participants often miss during the actual training session is just how much time and thought is involved in preparing for the instructional event. To experience this kind of careful preparation, try out **VISUALIZE! PRACTICE! 15.1: Training Session Openers.**[15]

A variety of methods can be used to train. Educational psychologists and other experts in pedagogy and andragogy have researched the advantages and disadvantages of each instructional approach. What you need to know is that sometimes an approach works,

Visualize!
Practice! 15.2:
Method Matters

auremar/Shutterstock.com

and sometimes it doesn't. Sometimes a particular method will work in one situation with one group of trainees, but on another occasion with a different group, the same method won't work at all. Some material lends itself better to one method than another. A way to view the different methods available is to consider each one as a tool; the more tools in your toolbox, the better equipped you'll be to select and use just the right one at any given time. To see just how important the right method is, try **VISUALIZE! PRACTICE! 15.2: Method Matters.**[16]

Effective trainers are those with the largest toolbox. They rely on a combination of approaches to reach their objectives. Variety is critical to instruction. If you have ever sat through a course where the teacher only lectured or relied only on small-group work or on peer-teaching, you will likely recall a great deal of frustration with both the teacher and the course. Good trainers, like good teachers, use a mix of teaching methods to sustain momentum and to ensure active participation. Because seasoned trainers know that not all people learn in the same way, they recognize the importance of using multiple methods for a diverse group. What follows is a list of possible teaching methods:

Lecture	Small groups
Role-playing	Self-paced instruction
Peer teaching	Simulations and games
Case study	Panel discussion
Presentations	Collaborative team work
Worksheets	Drills
Textbooks	E-learning
Films and videos	Papers or short essays
Homework	Demonstration

Link Out 15.6:
*Books about
Training Techniques*

Check This Out 15.2:
*Role-Playing as a
Training Technique*

A variety of trade books and texts are available on training methods. See **LINK OUT 15.6: Books about Training Techniques** for an initial reading list.

Which method or combination of methods you utilize will depend primarily on your list of objectives. Whatever outcome is expected should give you some direction into how you plan to teach it:

- If the outcome is a particular skill, you will want participants to actively try out, practice, or role-play the behavior.

- If the outcome is more or new information, you may want to lecture or encourage e-learning.

- If the objective involves changes in attitude or motivation, you might use simulations, games, or videos.

- If the outcome requires problem-solving skills, you will find case studies, collaborative group work, and panel discussions particularly suitable.

Communication consultants and authors Beebe, Mottet, and Roach offer additional factors that you might consider when selecting the best training method or methods to employ.[17] For instance, some trainers are more comfortable with some methods than with others. They may enjoy lecturing to large groups but are uncomfortable or unfamiliar with computer-mediated resources. Others might appreciate facilitating small group discussions but dislike role-playing activities. Your comfort level with the methods you use is an important consideration, but don't be afraid to try out something new.

Another consideration is the trainees themselves. An examination of the demographic and psychographic characteristics of the participants can provide important clues for selecting particular teaching methods. Who are the participants? How old are they? How many in the group are men, and how many are women? What is their cultural background? How long have they been with the company? What are their work histories? Why were they selected for training? If it turns out that participants aren't all that familiar with one another, you might consider selecting activities that encourage them to get to know each other. If the participants have a history of working together in teams, you might rely on teamwork or groupwork for instruction. Evaluate the training approach used in the video in **CHECK THIS OUT 15.2: Role-Playing as a Training Technique.**[18]

Finally, these communication consultants encourage trainers to consider the pros and cons of using any particular training method. Although lecturing can be stimulating and informative, too much of this approach can put people to sleep. Group work may be an excellent way to encourage participation, but left unmonitored, groups can easily move off task. Experienced trainers have learned to operate in and around the strengths and weaknesses of each method. In this way, they maximize the utilization of each approach, while avoiding potential pitfalls.

How Will I Know if the Training Worked?

Clients are preoccupied with ROI, or their return on investment, in virtually every decision they make. The task of the trainer is to demonstrate that the training was useful and can be tied to the bottom line. Clients want the trainer to provide them with data that illustrate that their investment in the training program was worth the money, time, and inconvenience. In other words, they want and need to see some results. How do trainers provide clients with these data? Data come in many forms, but the more systematic or scientifically derived the information is, the more defensible it is to most corporate clients. Providing clients with evidence that the training made a difference can be accomplished in multiple ways: by (a) evaluating the process, (b) evaluating the short- and long-term impact, and (c) evaluating the trainer's performance.

Evaluate the Process

For training programs that extend beyond a few hours or an afternoon, clients typically want to know how things are going so far. They may be excited or nervous about their investment; they may have received some initial observations from one or two participants; and they may want to provide advice and recommend revisions for the remainder of the training. At the same time, adult participants want to be involved in the process of learning and are eager to provide the trainer with feedback on what is working and what is not. Anticipating all of these concerns, then, an effective trainer will provide regular and systematic opportunities for input as the training unfolds.

Such **formative evaluation**, which was discussed in Chapter 14, accesses feedback about the delivery or the product or service as it occurs during implementation. Trainers rely on frequent formative evaluations to help them revise or refine their instruction or intervention as it evolves. In order to do this, trainers may develop simple feedback forms or questionnaires for participants to evaluate targeted aspects of the workshop, including the training methods employed; the consumability of the information provided; the trainer's appearance, rapport, and responsiveness; and the overall evaluation of the program so far. Other more directly observable evidence might include participant attendance, level of participant interaction or attentiveness, and unsolicited feedback or testimonials. Trainers might also want to "test" participants on what they have learned so far with a short recall test targeting important principles taught during the session or asking them to demonstrate new skills that they had practiced earlier.

During one of our own training workshops, we developed and employed a simple evaluation form to assess how the workshop was faring so far (see Figure 15.1). We were able to utilize the findings to revise our plans for the second day of training. We learned, for instance, that a number of participants disliked the group work, preferring instead more direct interactions with the trainers and peers at large. So, for Day 2, we relied on more individual work and eliminated small-group activities. In subsequent evaluations, we discovered that our trainees appreciated the change and perhaps more importantly, indicated mild but pleased surprise at our willingness to listen and adapt to their feedback.

Evaluate the Outcomes

If the trainer has done the necessary work in writing meaningful, specific, observable, and measurable objectives, then the task of evaluating outcomes should be easy enough to do. Unlike formative evaluations that inform the trainer about the process of instruction, **summative evaluations** inform the trainer about the overall impact of the training on participants' knowledge acquisition and skill development. As a result, they are normally obtained after the intervention or training has been implemented. As discussed in Chapter 14, summative evaluations are typically more formal or systematic in design than formative evaluations. They measure the outcomes of the intervention and are tied specifically to the objectives.[19]

FIGURE 15.1
Daily formative evaluation form

Directions. Please take the time now to provide your trainers with feedback about today's session. Your responses will be anonymous, and the information will be useful in making any changes in subsequent sessions with you and others at work. We value your input, and we want you to be involved in the planning of your own training.

1. List the three most important things you learned today.

   a. _____

   b. _____

   c. _____

2. What did you find most useful about what you learned today?

3. What information or activities did you find it most difficult to relate to?

4. What recommendations would you make to the trainers to revise today's session?

5. What trainer characteristics or behaviors did you find most helpful?

6. What trainer characteristics or behaviors did you find distracting or unhelpful?

7. Overall, how would you evaluate today's session? Use a 1–10 scale with 1 = Useless and 10 = Useful. _____.

8. How enjoyable did you find today's session? Use a 1–10 scale with 1 = Boring and 10 = Fascinating. _____.

Additional comments:

_____

_____

_____

_____

Each test item, survey question, or interview protocol should be written by targeting a particular objective. If you'll recall our earlier example about training new managers to delegate responsibilities to their employees, we specified these six specific objectives:

As a result of this training session, you will be able to

1. Identify key individuals who can handle special tasks.
2. Explain to those individuals exactly what needs to be done.
3. Communicate the quality of the work that you expect.
4. Set deadlines for task completion.
5. Check for progress on the delegated task at frequent intervals.
6. Verify task completion and quality when the deadline arrives.

Because these objectives are specific, observable, and measurable, we can easily construct a test to determine if participants learned these skills following training. For

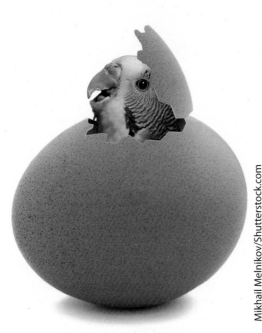

Mikhail Melnikov/Shutterstock.com

Visualize!
Practice! 15.3:
Measuring Objectives

objective 1, we might ask participants to list specific tasks that can be delegated and then assign names of those employees who they believe are good matches for those tasks. For objective 2, we might ask them to write or record instructions they would give to those individuals to make sure that they understand exactly what needs to be done. Perhaps they could role-play exchanges, digitally record those interactions, and then review and critique what they did well and what they still needed to do differently. For objective 3, we could ask participants to list the criteria they will use to evaluate the quality of the work they expect from those employees for each of those tasks. Perhaps they could identify what would be acceptable work and then add criteria for what they perceive as highly acceptable work. The group of trainees might even devise standardized criteria they could all use. You get the idea? For each objective, you should be able to generate one or more ways to assess participants' attainment. **VISUALIZE! PRACTICE! 15.3: Measuring Objectives** is your chance to figure out how to assess objectives 4 through 6.

When constructing evaluation instruments, trainers might utilize a number of different kinds of measures that reliably assess attainment of each of the objectives. Anonymous surveys, observations, role-playing, tests, and exit interviews that measure impacts, benefits, or changes as a result of the training are all common indicators. More general end-of-workshop evaluations are common to most training. These summative evaluations, also referred to as reactionnaires, assess participants' overall reactions to the content, the training activities, and the trainers themselves. Such reactions give both the trainer and the client feedback about participants' self-perceptions of their experiences. Figure 15.2 provides an example of a summative reactionnaire that we used in our own training.

What is not all that common is follow-up or long-term assessments of training impacts. Businesses often want to know if the effects obtained from training continue to be evident six months or two years later. In our example with new managers, a client will want to know if their managers have internalized their newly learned skills of delegating responsibilities. Although the managers may have adopted the new skills during and immediately following training, they may need additional follow-up instruction to sustain

FIGURE 15.2
Summative reactionnaire evaluation form

Directions. Now that the workshop is completed, we'd like for you to take a few minutes to evaluate your experiences over the last two days. Below are a number of statements for you to use to evaluate the instruction and materials presented during your workshop. Rate each item on a scale of 1 (Strongly Disagree) to 5 (Strongly Agree). Thank you for your input and active participation during our time together.

CONTENT

SD   SA

1—2—3—4—5   I learned a lot from this workshop.
1—2—3—4—5   What I learned from this workshop is important to me.
1—2—3—4—5   The information provided in this workshop is useful to me.
1—2—3—4—5   What I learned in this workshop is helpful and beneficial to me.
1—2—3—4—5   The material presented in this workshop was easy for me to understand.

TRAINERS

SD   SA

1—2—3—4—5   The trainers were knowledgeable and well prepared.
1—2—3—4—5   The trainers were effective in facilitating workshop participation.
1—2—3—4—5   The trainers were clear and articulate when presenting the material.
1—2—3—4—5   The trainers were highly approachable and made it easy for me to ask questions.
1—2—3—4—5   Overall, I would rate these trainers as highly effective facili-tainers.

ACTIVITIES

SD   SA

1—2—3—4—5   I enjoyed the activities and discussions included in this workshop.
1—2—3—4—5   The activities included in this workshop were useful for learning the information.
1—2—3—4—5   It was easy for me to participate in many of the activities presented in this workshop.
1—2—3—4—5   I found the activities (and discussions) relevant to what I need.
1—2—3—4—5   These activities will help to make my job easier.

Additional Comments:

_____

_____

_____

_____

permanent change. The trainer might gather feedback a few weeks (or months) after training by asking participants to complete an online survey assessing what they remember and how they are utilizing their new skills. Upper-level management might include in performance reviews criteria for evaluating the outcomes of previous training workshops. Trainers might conduct post-training interviews with participants or their employees to determine long-term training effects.

Evaluate the Trainer

Because successful training depends so heavily on trainer preparedness, personality characteristics, instructional style, and other personal and professional attributes, it's a good idea to evaluate the trainer—in addition to formative and summative measures of learning outcomes. Such evaluations can be one of two types: self and other assessments. The trainer may want to work from a checklist of effective training behaviors to do a **self-assessment**, including presentational or facilitation skills, relational effectiveness, instructional, coaching, and mentoring skills, content competencies, technology use, self-efficacy, cultural sensitivity, and overall preparation. Such a checklist can be useful both before and after the training session.

In addition to a self-assessment, the trainer can obtain participant observations and reactions, or what is referred to as an **other assessment**. In order to measure others' evaluations, trainers rely almost exclusively on anonymous feedback forms with items asking questions about specific trainer behaviors during the sessions and other relevant characteristics and attributes. If you'll notice in our example summative evaluation form in Figure 15.2, specific items were written to target participants' reactions to trainer behaviors that we thought were important to what we wanted to accomplish during our training with them, including perceptions of trainer content competence, facilitation skills, clarity in instruction, approachability, and ability to "facili-tain" or edu-tain (make learning fun). CHECK THIS OUT 15.3: **Evaluate the Trainer**[20] asks for your feedback about the trainer in a training session on presentational skills.

Evaluating training offers much-needed feedback to the client, the participants, and the trainers themselves. Finding multiple ways to assess process, outcomes, and trainer effectiveness provides everyone with important information about how learning occurs, what is learned and what is not, and what changes need to be made or sustained. A good online source of sample evaluation forms that measure all these outcomes (and then some) is available at LINK OUT 15.7: **Training Toolkit's Evaluation Forms**.

This chapter provides you with some idea of what's involved in preparing for a career in communication training, beginning with the credentials you will need. Developing a training plan involves repeated discussions with the client, working with him or her to identify training needs and concerns, and to specify objectives or outcomes that should occur as a result of the training program. Once objectives are well defined and agreed upon, the trainer's next tasks are to research the content and strategize approaches to teach the material. Both during and after the training is completed, assessments need to be taken to determine if the training process is successful, what revisions needs to be made, and to what extent the objectives have been met.

Our own experiences as trainers over the last twenty to thirty years have been mostly successful, but not all of our workshops have gone as planned. The best

Link Out 15.7:
Training Toolkit's Evaluation Forms

Check This Out 15.3:
Evaluate the Trainer

workshops were those where all the participants wanted to be there, where participants believed they had something to learn, and where the client fully supported our efforts to train. Those workshops that we remember as problematic or frustrating were fraught with both large and small problems. We recall one where participants insisted on doing business as usual during the session, texting, taking calls, and coming and going at will. We discovered that the client wasn't all that respected by the group, which made our own credibility suspect and made it impossible for us to enforce participation rules and norms important to training success. Our early efforts at training were real learning experiences for us. We discovered that we "lectured" far too much, misjudged time allocations for activities, and assumed erroneously that as adults, our trainees would not require motivational prompts and positive reinforcement for work well done. Despite these challenges, over the years of training we have met some wonderful and interesting people, made and sustained friendships, and learned as much from them as we hope they learned from us.

Use your Speech Communication CourseMate for *Business & Communication in a Digital Age* for quick access to the electronic resources that accompany this text. These resources include

Study tools that will help you assess your learning and prepare for exams (*digital glossary, key term flash cards, review quizzes*).

Activities and assignments that will help you hone your knowledge and build your communication skills throughout the course (*Visualize! Practice!, Weigh In!, Check This Out, and Link Out activities; modules; review questions*).

Media resources that will help you explore communication concepts online (*Enhanced eBook*), develop your speech outlines (*Speech Builder Express 3.0*), watch and critique videos of sample speeches and communication situations (*interactive video activities*), upload your speech videos for peer reviewing and critique other students' speeches (*Speech Studio online speech review tool*), and download chapter review so you can study when and where you'd like (*Audio Study Tools*).

Key Points

- Organizational training is a particular type of consulting activity where individuals are trained or taught particular skills or knowledge to enhance their work performance.
- Communication trainers must be able to teach a variety of communication skills, ranging from active listening and managing conflict to delivering a sales presentation and conducting an employee appraisal interview.
- In order to be able to teach others to do so many different communication skills, communication trainers need the following credentials or skills:
  - ✔ Credible background in communication theory and skills.
  - ✔ The ability to "translate" what they know academically for workplace consumption.

- ✔ The ability to work with clients by initiating and sustaining long-term relationships.
- ✔ A working knowledge of andragogy and instructional design.
- ✔ The ability to draw upon current theory and research findings that can be used in training workshops and seminars.
- ✔ A sense of self-efficacy or expertise; the self-confidence that they can successfully do the work.

- Developing a well-designed training plan requires repeated meetings with the client, discovering the organization's unique training needs, and specifying detailed, written objectives.

- The content of any training workshop or seminar is tied directly to the objectives that have already been defined and approved by the client. What is taught should be guided by those objectives.

- How a trainer teaches requires careful consideration of a variety of instructional methods available. A combination of methods should be used with a preference for active learner participation, such as role-playing, presentations, demonstrations, simulations, and small group activities.

- Because clients are preoccupied with their return on investment, the trainer must demonstrate in some overt way that the training itself was useful. Three types of data can help to illustrate that the training program was warranted and successful:
  - ✔ Evaluate the process through some kind of formative review.
  - ✔ Evaluate the outcomes; assess or demonstrate the extent to which each participant met each and every objective.
  - ✔ Evaluate the trainer's performance through self- and participant assessments.

Key Terms

andragogy (341)

instructional design (341)

self-efficacy (341)

needs assessment (343)

gap analysis (343)

objectives (344)

formative evaluation (349)

summative evaluation (349)

self-assessment (353)

other assessment (353)

Questions for Critical Thinking and Review

1. What kinds of communication problems typically occur in the workplace that might require training services?

2. Why would anyone want to be a communication trainer full time? What are the advantages of being an independent contract trainer as opposed to working as a trainer for human resources in an organization? What are some of the disadvantages?

3. What academic theories have you learned that might be helpful to you as a communication trainer? Why do some theories seem more applicable or practical than others?

4. What communication skills have you learned that would be helpful to you as a communication trainer?

5. Some experts in instruction maintain that adults learn differently than children. One difference they cite is that adults prefer to learn only what is relevant to their needs and wants. In other words, the information or skills must be directly relevant to what they do. How does this preference differ from what children want to learn? Is this difference only perceived, or is it real? Why or why not?

6. Suppose you have a client who doesn't believe that a needs assessment is required for your training intervention. What three arguments would you use to convince or persuade your client to have you do the assessment anyway?

7. Being prepared is essential to your effectiveness as a trainer. What kinds of things could go wrong if you failed to test out your technological aids prior to delivering your training?

8. Why might you want to include one or more objectives in your training plan that target participants' attitudes or feelings about learning something new?

9. Give two reasons why you should do formative evaluations during training. Give two reasons why summative evaluations might be useful.

10. What communication skills in the workplace might not require training or retraining? Make a list. Then justify each item on your list. (Hint: It should be a very short list!)

Glossary

A

2/3 vote* Vote requirement to pass a previous question motion.

abstention* When a motion comes to a vote and a member chooses not to vote on the question.

accommodation Adjusting your style of communicating to match the communication style of the person you are interacting with.

acronyms Words or abbreviations formed from the first letter of each word in a name or phrase, such as NASDAQ or CEO.

active listening Making a conscious effort to pay full attention to and comprehend the message being communicated.

adaptors Unintentional hand, arm, leg, or other body movements used to reduce stress or relieve boredom.

affect displays Facial expressions that communicate emotions, such as disgust, hostility, or joy.

agenda A plan of action that specifies what you intend to do at a meeting and how discussion items will be prioritized.

amendments* A change made to a pending motion to make it clearer, more complete, or more acceptable to the group as a whole.

andragogy Teaching or learning strategies that focus on adult, rather than child, learners.

assessment A criterion-based means of evaluating existing programs, interventions, and outcomes.

asynchronous media Media that enable communication and collaboration outside the constraints of time and place.

attending Using our senses to respond to communication stimuli.

attitude A predisposed way of feeling positively or negatively about someone or something. Statements of attitudes often begin with "I feel that . . ."

audience analysis The systematic gathering of information about your audience and the stake they hold in the topic of your speech.

audience response system "Clicker" technology that enables audience members to give feedback to the speaker and interact with the topic and one another. Also helps the presenter build a visual display of information from the audience.

B

bad apple effect Team disruptions that occur as a result of a toxic team member who withholds effort, communicates negative affect toward the group, task, and process, and engages in socially inappropriate behaviors.

bar graph A visual display in which a series of bars of different heights or lengths represents different quantities or values of data.

behavior Action in response to a particular stimulus or situation.

behavioral objective A statement of measurable outcomes specifying what an individual should be able to do as a result of a particular intervention.

belief A statement of truth that an individual accepts about some object, situation, or event. Statements of belief typically begin with "I believe that . . ."

bias-free language Words and phrases that communicate respect for and the dignity of others.

blog A shared, public online journal where the author (known as a blogger) can post entries in chronological order about his or her experiences related to work, hobbies, or other interests.

body* Part of a formal report that delivers a logical presentation of your findings. Serves as a rationale for your conclusions and recommendations in the next section.

boilerplate A standardized text that can be reused for different purposes without being changed much, if at all.

bona fide occupational qualifications (BFOQs) Requirements directly related to the job, such as educational background, work experience, work qualifications, special skills and pertinent physical abilities, and relevant personality characteristics.

border crossers People who frequently cross back and forth across the border between work and personal life.

brief report A document designed to provide information about day-to-day operations to internal and external business stakeholders.

briefing A short, structured informative overview of specific or technical information, packaged appropriately for the intended audience.

business writing The preparation of any print or online document that supports or helps a business enterprise grow.

C

channel The medium that carries a message from sender to receiver.

chart A pictorial representation of the relationship between part of a group or object or of the sequence of steps in a process.

chronemics The study of what time means to people and how they schedule what they do.

chronological* Discuss issues in the order they occurred or will occur. This sequence is useful when reviewing an event or describing a process.

chunking The principle that written ideas should be presented in small, digestible units (chunks) that will be easy for an audience to remember.

client mining A way for consultants to obtain clients by doing unpaid or underpaid work in order to cultivate more lucrative work over time.

closed-ended questions Questions that can be answered by choosing one of two or more alternatives or a simple yes or no.

communication competence The ability to effectively use a variety of communicative behaviors to achieve a goal.

communication consultant A professional expert with specialized skills in communication hired to help organizations solve managerial or employee problems and teach critical people skills.

comparison/contrast* Describe similarities (comparisons) and differences (contrasts) of two ideas for purposes of evaluation. These sequences work well when asking your readers to decide among two or more courses of action, decisions, or things.

configural framework An approach to organizing a speech that is relatively indirect, relies on speaker self-disclosure, allows audiences to engage with the speaker, and asks audience members to impose their own structure and meaning onto a presentation.

confirming messages Praise and other messages that reinforce the receiver's value.

consultant A professional expert with specialized skills hired to advise or help organizations accomplish a variety of services and tasks.

controls Rules, expectations, and strategies that organizational members use to reward desired contributions and punish negative deviations.

credible evidence Information about a topic that is consistent with other facts and comes from expert sources that are impartial and fair.

D

decoding Translating a message's symbols into thoughts and feelings in an effort to understand the message.

demographic data* Consists of information based on social, economic, and geographic categories.

digital immigrant A person who had to learn how to use computers, the Internet, and other digital technologies as an adult.

digital media Electronic media that operate on digital codes.

digital native A person who grew up with digital technologies like computers, the Internet, mobile phones, and MP3 players.

digital visualization A type of technology-aided interactive engagement that enables presenters to depict and visually document the knowledge, ideas, and contributions of individual audience members.

disconfirming messages Messages that undermine or attack the receiver's self-worth.

E

emblems Nonverbal actions that have a specific, widely understood meaning, such as blowing a kiss or cupping an ear and leaning forward.

employment interview A face-to-face encounter designed to evaluate whether an applicant is suitable for a particular position in an organization.

encoding Translating thoughts and feelings into specific symbols that can be used to accomplish a goal.

ethics* Criteria or guidelines for what is right and what is wrong.

ethnocentric Using your cultural background to judge other groups of people.

evidence Facts or opinions attested to or endorsed by experts.

experts People who, through education, training, and experience, have special knowledge about a particular subject.

F

feedback The verbal or nonverbal message returned to the sender as the receiver is perceiving and interpreting the sender's message.

fever graph A diagram that shows how the numeric value of something changes over time.

flowchart A series of boxes connected by arrows that illustrates the steps of a process.

formal report A document that reports the status of a complex problem or business issue and approaches the solution to the issue in a logical fashion.

focus group method* Small groups of people who are interviewed by a trained facilitator to discuss a particular topic or issue. This method can be used to analyze an audience's psychographic responses to a speech topic.

formative evaluation A method of measuring or assessing feedback about the delivery of the product or service as it unfolds during implementation.

G

gap analysis Another name for needs assessment; identifies current skills or knowledge and then compares them to the desired skills and information yet to be acquired, thus locating the gap between what is and what ought to be.

general purpose The broad goal of a presentation: to inform, to persuade, or to commemorate or accept.

grapevine* Rumor mill that can sometimes produce valuable information but which should be filed away in your memory and not repeated.

graph A pictorial device that illustrates quantitative relationships.

groupthink Team members' overwhelming drive to reach consensus, disregarding critical analysis of the problem and ignoring alternative solutions.

H

haptics The study of how touch is interpreted and understood in relation to factors such as gender, culture, status, personality, and context.

high-fear appeal An emotional strategy designed to arouse in the audience feelings of intense fear or anxiety in order to induce change.

I

illustrators Hand and arm movements that enhance or reinforce a verbal message, such as putting a finger to the lips while saying "Be quiet."

imagery Language that appeals to the senses of touch, taste, sound, sight, and smell.

impression management Deliberately designing verbal and nonverbal messages to create a particular set of impressions.

in order * The action or statement is correct from a procedural standpoint.

informative presentations Briefings, reports, lectures, training presentations, and demonstrations that provide new information, add to what the audience already knows, or update information about a topic or issue.

instructional design The systematic development of an instructional plan, beginning with needs assessment, defining objectives, specifying content, identifying relevant and varied teaching strategies (including multimedia aids), and evaluating learning outcomes.

intercultural communication Communication between and among individuals and groups across national and ethnic boundaries.

intervention Some action taken to change, alter, or solve a problem. Once the organization decides how to approach a problem, consultants might be used to intervene or implement a course of action.

interview protocol The list of questions prepared for the interview that have been designed to ensure that the interview process is equally reliable and valid for all candidates.

J

jargon Technical terms used in a particular work group or profession.

job profile* The information you gather through your research and the interview process.

K

kinesics The study of body language used to communicate meaning.

L

leading questions* Questions that suggest the answer the individual should give.

lean media Media that are least capable of carrying information and facilitating understanding among communicators.

line graph A diagram that shows the relationship between two quantitative concepts and shows how one thing changes with respect to the other.

linear framework A clear and fact-based approach to organizing a speech that follows a straightforward pattern: preview main points, discuss one point at a time, and summarize each point.

linear model of communication A model that characterizes communication as a simple exchange in which a sender transmits a message to a receiver.

low-fear appeal An emotional strategy designed to arouse in the audience minimal or low levels of fear or anxiety in order to induce change.

M

main motions* Motions that begin discussion or propose action.

making a decision* In parliamentary procedures, once discussion has ended, the Chair should restate the motion, including any passed amendments, to ensure members are clear on what is being voted upon before they vote.

Monroe's motivated sequence A problem-solution organizational pattern that anticipates audience resistance. Its five steps are attention, need, satisfaction, visualization, and action.

meaning Subjective responses to objects, events, and ideas based on our experience.

mediated communication The use of various media to facilitate communication between senders and receivers.

medium A device that moves information over distance or through time and thus enables people to communicate.

meeting Two or more people who get together in person or in virtual space to communicate in order to achieve some common goal or objective.

meeting load The frequency and length of meetings an employee attends.

memo A brief, informal, and often digital document used frequently within business organizations to request information, promote goodwill, convey routine information, and deliver short reports.

message Verbal, written, or nonverbal information transmitted from a sender to a receiver.

minutes A written record of what happens during a meeting, including all the important motions, announcements, decisions, and discussions.

misemployment Working at a job that does not match one's skills or interests.

model Copy of an object, usually built to scale, that represents the object in detail.

motion* When you are formally proposing that the group do something, such as take an action or officially express an opinion.

motion to limit debate* Motion which restricts the number and length of each member's opportunities to speak, particularly when there are many participants or a large volume of business to conduct.

motion to refer or **commit*** A motion which can be made to refer to a committee for more study. This motion should identify the committee to which the original motion will be referred, and when the committee will report back to the group.

N

needs assessment A specialized type of assessment used to identify the gap between current conditions or status quo and what should or ought to be.

networking The interconnectivity of digital devices.

networking* Creating a group of contacts that could benefit you.

new media Digital and networked information and communication technologies that began emerging in the later part of the twentieth century. Examples include the Internet, computer games, CD-ROMs, DVDs, email, instant messaging, mobile phone and smartphone technology, and computer multimedia such as video, animation, and audio.

norms Expectations about how people in an organization should communicate and behave.

O

objectives Specific statements that identify the desired goals or outcomes that the learners should achieve as a result of the training or instructional experience.

open-ended questions Questions that can be answered with as much information as the candidate wants to provide.

organizational chart A series of boxes connected by lines or arrows representing the internal structure of company or organization.

organizational culture* What life is like in a particular company or position.

other assessment An assessment that relies on participants' observations and reactions to determine the effectiveness of both the trainer and the training intervention.

out of order* In the context of parliamentary procedure, "out of order" means the action or statement is not correct from a procedural standpoint.

P

panel discussion A team presentation in which a moderator manages spontaneous interactions among panel participants.

parallel labels Equivalent names for comparable people or groups, such as *men* and *women* instead of *men* and *girls*.

parliamentary procedure* Defined by the National Association of Parliamentarians as "... the *rules of democracy*—that is, the commonly accepted way in which a group of people come together, present and discuss possible courses of action, and make decisions" (National Association of Parliamentarians, 2010).

passive listening Receiving a message without bothering to exert much effort to comprehend it.

pending* The status once a motion has been made, seconded, and restated by the Chair.

perceiving Identifying and classifying communication stimuli based on our knowledge, experience, and culture.

periodic report A document designed to communicate specific information on a routine (periodic) basis to concerned stakeholders.

personal profile An inventory of your personal strengths and weaknesses so that you can explain to an interviewer why you are suited to a particular job and what you could add to the organization.

personal space The zone around you in your interactions with other people. It contracts and expands depending on the nature of your relationship, what you are doing, and your gender, age, and cultural background.

persuasive presentation A speech whose primary purpose is to change audience attitudes, beliefs, or behaviors.

pie graph A circular diagram that is divided into components to show them as percentages or proportions of the whole.

point of order (orders of the day)* The procedure to point out and object to the departure from proper procedure.

politics* The use of power (legitimate or imagined) to obtain resources at work.

postponing a decision* There are several procedural options for this action if the group feels more information or further review is needed to properly vote on the motion, that the meeting has already run too long, or that absent members should have the opportunity to vote.

power language Direct, unqualified speech that conveys expertise, confidence, and conviction.

presentation of self Creating and sending verbal and nonverbal messages that tell others about the kind of person you are.

preview In a speech introduction, telling your audience briefly what you're going to tell them in the body of the speech.

previous question motion* A motion made to end discussion of a main motion or a motion to amend, particularly if debate seems to be dragging on unproductively. Previous question does require a second, though the motion is not itself debatable.

primary research material Information that an individual collects directly from sources through surveys, observational strategies, or interviews to use in a document or presentation that he or she is preparing.

professional profile An inventory of your professional qualifications, experiences, and assets, including any special skills and talents.

progress report A type of brief report designed to inform someone, usually a manager, of progress on a specific project.

proposal A description of an idea or product to motivate action and commitment by members of your organization. A document written to offer services or goods to another organization. A *solicited proposal* is written in response to a *Request for Proposal (RFP)*.

proxemics The study of meanings associated with the use of space and distance.

psychographic data* Describes the attitudes, beliefs, and opinions of audience members.

psychological reactance People's inherent tendency to resist attempts to persuade them.

Q

questionnaire method* An audience analysis method in which a group of audience members is given a list of questions to answer, either via phone interview, in person, or in writing.

quorum* The number of members who must be present to legally conduct business. It is generally specified in the organization's by-laws and, in a committee or small board, is usually a simple majority of the members.

R

ranks Hierarchy or levels of authority in an organization. Hierarchy that prescribes levels of authority in a team.

receiver The intended recipient of a message.

recent evidence Relevant information about your topic that is not outdated. Information in different fields changes at different rates, so you must just judge what is "recent" for your topic.

relevant evidence Information directly associated with your presentation topic and understandable by your audience.

reliable questions Standardized questions asked of every candidate for a given job, allowing the interviewer to fairly compare the candidates.

rich media Media that are most capable of carrying information and facilitating understanding among communicators.

roles Specialized functions of organization or team members.

S

sales presentation An attempt to persuade an audience to purchase a product or service; one of the most common types of business presentations.

secondary research material Archived or historical data reported on a topic of interest by someone else in the form of an interview, article, case study, website, book, or monograph. Writers and speakers assemble secondary research material as they prepare their presentations and documents.

seconded* A main motion must be supported with this action by at least one additional member of the group in attendance in order to be considered and discussed by the group.

self-assessment An assessment that relies on a checklist or other criteria to examine and evaluate one's own behaviors. Trainers often rely on both self- and other assessments to determine their preparedness before and effectiveness after training.

self-awareness Conscious knowledge of your character, feelings, and motivations.

self-concept The set of relatively stable perceptions you hold about yourself.

self-efficacy An individual's belief or perception that he or she is capable of succeeding in specific situations.

self-esteem Your evaluation of your intelligence, capabilities, appearance, accomplishments, and everything else that defines who you are.

self-talk Your internal dialogue about everything you do and experience.

semantic barriers Words and phrases whose connotative meanings often trigger negative feelings that distract audience members from listening effectively.

sender The source of a message.

sender-receiver reciprocity Constantly sending and receiving messages and feedback and adapting to each other in a communication encounter.

sensory aids Devices supporting a presentation that appeal to one or more of the five senses (sight, hearing, touch, taste, or smell), highlighting or enhancing the content.

signpost A word or phrase that signals the organization of ideas, indicating where a speaker is in a speech or highlighting an important idea.

simultaneous transactions model of communication A model that characterizes communication not only as the sender transmitting a message to a receiver but also as the sender receiving feedback from the receiver. In this model, communication is a transaction that mutually influences each person involved.

social loafing Exerting little or no effort to contribute to team goals.

social media New media that promote interaction, such as social network sites, social news sites, and blogs.

spatial* Discuss important points according to their physical relationship to one another (e.g., left to right, top to bottom). This structure is effective when describing, for example, a piece of equipment or the layout of a physical location. Documents formatted using a spatial structure should be accompanied by one or more graphics which correspond to the text.

speaking environment The physical setting, time of day, and length of your presentation; the size of the audience and the room's seating capacity and physical arrangement; the sound and lighting; and other aspects of the site where you will give your speech.

special occasion speech A speech at an informal or a formal business event for a purpose such as presenting an award to a colleague, accepting an award, introducing a guest, or giving a toast or a roast.

specific purpose What you want your audience to know, believe, or do as a result of your presentation.

stakeholder A person with a vested interest in an issue.

stereotype To assign attributes to people because of their age, gender, or other social or demographic group.

summative evaluation An assessment obtained after the intervention has been implemented. Typically more formal in design, summative evaluations measure the outcomes of the intervention and are tied specifically to the objectives.

symbols Words, sounds, and gestures that represent ideas and feelings.

symposium A type of team presentation in which each member delivers a short, planned speech about the same topic from a slightly different perspective; common at academic, business, and professional meetings and conferences.

synchronous media Media that allow for an instantaneous reply from another communicator.

T

table An orderly arrangement of numbers, words, or symbols in rows and columns.

table In a meeting, to postpone discussing an agenda item until another time.

team A group of people who share a common purpose or goal. Unlike group members, team members are carefully chosen for the particular and complementary skills that allow the team to achieve or complete complex goals and tasks.

team potency Team members' collective perception that their team will be productive, effective, and successful.

team presentation A persuasive or informative presentation by a group of people about a specific product or idea.

territoriality The space and objects in it that you claim as yours, such as your favorite parking spot or your desk chair.

thesis statement A concise summary of the essential points of your presentation.

topical/prioritized* To present issues by topic and rank them by their overall priority.

transformational leaders Team leaders who provide a vision and inspire their members to do their best work and to enjoy the process.

transition A phrase that links one main point of a speech to another.

V

valid questions Interview questions that appropriately relate to the skills and qualities required for the position.

verbal immediacy Words, phrases, and nonverbal behaviors that reduce the perceived physical and psychological distance between communicators.

virtual reality (VR) Computer-generated environments that can simulate places or activities in the real world.

vocalics The study of nonverbal uses of the voice, including how pitch, tone, rate, volume, and accent affect interpretation of meaning.

W

whistleblowing* Raising concern about specific wrongdoing in an organization.

work–life balance* Your efforts to deal with both *career* and *non-work related pursuits* such as pleasure, leisure, family, and spiritual development.

*These terms are from the online modules.

Notes

Chapter 1

1   Crippen, A. (2009, July). Warren Buffett and Bill Gates share their "optimism" with eager Columbia Business School students. CNBC.com. Retrieved from http://www.cnbc.com/id/33888348/Warren_Buffett_and_Bill_Gates_Share_Their_Optimism_With_Eager_Columbia_Business_Students

2   Quoted in Locke, M. (2007, December 10). Engineering students learn people skills. *Orange County Register*, p. A9.

3   Kristoff, K. M. (2008, May 4). New graduates have plenty to learn about work etiquette. *Los Angeles Times*. Retrieved from http://www.latimes.com/business/la-fi-perfin4-2008may04,0,4799164,full.column; Alexander, S. (2008, February 22). Communication for managers 101. Retrieved from http://www.managesmarter.com/msg/content_display/presentations/e3i09b57ed04d93841932a0efba1fb98c7e; Morreale, S. P., & Pearson, J. C. (2008). Why communication education is important: The centrality of the discipline in the 21st century. *Communication Education, 57*, 224–240; Winsor, J. L., Curtis, D. B., & Stephens, R. D. (1997). National preferences in business and communication education: A survey update. *Journal of Applied Communication Research, 3*, 170–179.

4   Watson Wyatt Worldwide. (2007). Secrets of top performers: How companies with effective communication differentiate themselves. Retrieved from http://www.watsonwyatt.com/research/resrender.asp?id=2007-US-0214&page=1

5   Kleinbaum, A. M., Stuart, T. E., & Tushman, M. L. (2008, July 31). Communication (and coordination?) in a modern, complex organization. *Harvard Business School Working Knowledge*. Retrieved from http://hbswk.hbs.edu/item/5991.html

6   Gravett, L. (2009). Diversity efforts can help support business imperatives. Retrieved from http://www.multiculturaladvantage.com/recruit/metrics/diversity-efforts-can-support-business-imperatives.asp.

7   Richmond, V. P., & Roach, K. D. (1992). Willingness to communicate and employee success in U.S. organizations. *Journal of Applied Communication Research, 20*, 95–116.

8   Modaff, D. P., DeWine, S., & Butler, J. (2008). *Organizational communication: Foundations, challenges, and misunderstandings* (2nd ed.). Boston, MA: Pearson.

9   The definition of information as "physical events that permit a message to conquer long or short distances, such as sound and light waves" was developed by Claude Shannon and Warren Weaver in *The mathematical theory of communication* (1949). Urbana: University of Illinois Press.

10 Weiner, N. (1954). *The human use of human beings: Cybernetics and society*. Boston, MA: Houghton Mifflin.

11 Weimann, J. M. (1977). Explication and test of a model of communicative competence. *Human Communication Research, 3*, 195–213.

12 Spitzberg, B. H., & Cupach, W. R. (1984). *Interpersonal communication competence*. Beverly Hills, CA: Sage.

13 Jablin, F. M., Cude, R. L., House, A., Lee, J. & Roth, N. L. (1994). Communication competence in organizations: Conceptualization and comparison across multiple levels of analysis. In L. Thayer & G. Barnett (Eds.), *Organization-communication: Emerging perspectives* (Vol. 4, pp. 114–140). Norwood, NJ: Ablex.

14 Zorn, T. E. (1993). Motivation to communicate: A critical review with suggested alternatives. In S. A. Deetz (Ed.), *Communication yearbook 16* (pp. 515–549). Newbury Park, CA: Sage.

15 Fulk, J., Schmitz, J., & Steinfield, C. W. (1990). A social influence model of technology use. In J. Fulk & C. Steinfield (Eds.), *Organizations and communication technology*. Thousand Oaks, CA: Sage.

16 Trevino, L. K., Daft, R. L., & Lengel, R. H. (1990). Understanding managers' media choices: A symbolic interactionist perspective. In J. Fulk & C. Steinfield (Eds.), *Organizations and communication technology*. Thousand Oaks, CA: Sage.

17 Fulk, Schmitz, & Steinfield. A social influence model.

18 Hall, E. T. (1976). *Beyond culture*. New York: Doubleday.

19 Lustig, M. W., & Koester, J. (1993). *Intercultural competence: Interpersonal communication across cultures*. New York: HarperCollins; Hofstede, G. (1984). *Cultural consequences: International differences in work-related values*. Beverly Hills, CA: Sage. http://www.geerthofstede.nl/

20 Workers suffering from e-mail stress. (2007, August 13). *The London Evening Standard*. Retrieved from http://www.thisislondon.co.uk/news/article-23408089-workers-suffering-from-email-stress.do

Chapter 2

1   Goffman, E. (1956). *The presentation of self in everyday life*. Edinburgh, Scotland: Social Sciences Research Centre.

2   Moore, C. D. (2007). Impression formation. In G. Ritzer (Ed.), *Blackwell encyclopedia of sociology* (pp. 310–311). Hoboken, NJ: Wiley-Blackwell.

3   DeFleur, M. H., Kearney, P., Plax, T. G., & DeFleur, M. L. (2005). *Fundamentals of human communication* (3rd ed.). New York, NY: McGraw-Hill.

4   DeFleur et al. *Fundamentals*.

5   Honeycutt, J. M. (2010). *Imagine that: Studies in imagined interaction*. Cresskill, NJ: Hampton Press.

6   Kearney, P., & Plax, T. G. (2006). *Public speaking in a diverse society* (3rd ed.). Mason, OH: Thomson; DeFleur et al. *Fundamentals*.

7   Snell, D. (2009, March 31). Media interviews: Avoiding the evasive answer. *Articlesbase*. Retrieved from http://www.articlesbase.com/training-articles/media-interviews-avoiding-the-evasive-answer-843892.html

8   Kearney & Plax. *Public speaking*; DeFleur et al. *Fundamentals*.

9   Obama, B. (2009). Obama health care speech: Full video and text. *Huffington Post*. Retrieved from http://www.huffingtonpost.com/2009/09/09/obama-health-care-speech_n_281265.html

10 Kearney & Plax. *Public speaking*; DeFleur et al. *Fundamentals*.

11 Gorham, J. (1988). The relationship between verbal teacher immediacy behaviors and student learning. *Communication Education, 37*, 40–53.

12 Witt, P., Wheeless, L., & Allen, M. (2004). A meta-analytical review of the relationship between teacher immediacy and student learning. *Communication Monographs, 71*, 184–207; Witt, P., Wheeless, L., & Allen, M. (2006). The relationship between teacher immediacy and student learning: A meta-analysis. In *Classroom communication and instructional processes: Advances through meta-analysis* (pp. 149–168). Mahwah, NJ: Erlbaum; Witt, P. L. (2004). An initial examination of observed verbal immediacy and participants' opinions of communication effectiveness in online group interaction. *Journal of Online Behavior, 2*(1). Retrieved from http://www.behavior.net/JOB/v2n1/witt.html

13 Turner-Bowkar, D. M. (2001). How can you pull yourself up by your bootstraps, if you don't have boots? Work-related clothing for poor women. *The Journal of Social Issues, 57*, 311–322.

14 Dress for success: Suits for self-sufficiency. (n.d.) Dress for Success. Retrieved from http://204.13.109.252/whatwedo.aspx

15 Andersen, P. (2008). *Nonverbal communication: Forms and functions* (2nd ed.). Long Grove, IL: Waveland Press; Richmond, V. P., Hickson, M., & McCroskey, J. C. (2007). *Nonverbal behavior in interpersonal relations* (6th ed.). Boston: Allyn & Bacon.

16 Briñol, P., Petty, R., & Wagner, B. (2009). Body posture effects on self-evaluation: A self-validation approach. *European Journal of Social Psychology, 39*, 1053–1064.

17 DeFleur et al. *Fundamentals*.

18 Hall, E. T. (1966). *The hidden dimension*. Garden City, NJ: Doubleday; Richmond, Hickson, & McCroskey. *Nonverbal behavior*.

19 Andersen, P. *Nonverbal communication*.

20 Goll, D. (2002, March 3). Workplace touching can be a touchy issue. *San Francisco Business Times*. Retrieved from http://www.bizjournals.com/eastbay/stories/2002/03/04/smallb3.html

21 Andersen, P., & Liebowitz, K. (1978). The development and nature of the construct touch avoidance. *Environmental Psychology and Nonverbal Behavior, 3*, 89–106.

22 Knapp, M. L., & Hall, J. A. (2001). *Nonverbal communication in human interaction*. Belmont, CA: Wadsworth.

23 Andersen, P. A. (2007). *Nonverbal communication: Forms and functions* (2nd ed.) Long Grove, IL: Waveland Press.

24 Andersen, *Nonverbal communication*; Richmond, Hickson, & McCroskey. *Nonverbal behavior*.

Chapter 3

1   Cooper, L., & Buchanan, T. (2003). Taking aim at good targets: Inter-rater agreement of listening competency. *International Journal of Listening, 17*, 88–114.

2   Cooper & Buchanan, Taking aim, p. 97.

3   Smeltzer, L. R. (1993). Emerging questions and research paradigms in business communication research. *Journal of Business Communication, 33*, 29–37.

4   Janusik, L. A., & Wolvin, A. D. (2002). Listening treatment in the basic communication course text. In D. Sellnow (Ed.), *Basic Communication Course Annual, 14*, 164–210. Boston, MA: American Press.

5   Wolvin, A., & Coakley, C. (2000). Listening education in the 21st century. *International Journal of Listening, 14*,143–152.

6   Haas, J. W., & Arnold, C. L. (1995). An examination of the role of listening in judgment of communication competence in co-workers. *Journal of Business Communication, 32*, 123–139.

7   Maes, J. D., Weldy, T. G., & Icenogle, M. L. (1997). A managerial perspective: Oral communication competency is most important for business students in the workplace. *Journal of Business Communication, 34,* 67–80.

8   Janusik, L. (2002). Listening facts. Retrieved from http://www.paragonresources.com/library/listen.pdf; see also Listening facts. International Listening Association. Retrieved from http://www.listen.org/index.php?option=com_content&view=category&layout=blog&id=43&Itemid=74

9   Wanzer, M. B., Booth-Butterfield, M., & Gruber, M. K. (2004). Perceptions of health care providers' communication: Relationships between patient-centered communication and satisfaction. *Health Communication, 16,* 363–384; Brown, R. F., Butow, P. N., Henman, M., Dunn, S. M., Boyloe, F., & Tattersall, M. H. N. (2002). Responding to the active and passive patient: Flexibility is key. *Health Expectations, 5,* 236–245; du Pre, A. (2002). Accomplishing the impossible. Talking about body and soul and mind during a medical visit. *Health Communication, 14,* 1–21; Hickson, G. B., Clayton, P. B., Giethen, P. E., & Sloan, F. A. (1992). Factors that prompted families to file medical malpractice claims following perinatal injuries. *Journal of American Medical Association, 268,* 1413–1414.

10 Worobey, J. L., & Cummings, H. W. (1984). Communication effectiveness of nurses in four relational settings. *Journal of Applied Communication Research, 12,* 128–142.

11 Lee, J. (2000). 10 ways to communicate better with patients. *Review of Ophthalmology, 7,* 38–42.

12 Hickson et al. Factors that prompted families.

13 Hamilton, C., & Parker, C. (1987). *Communicating for results* (2nd ed.). Belmont, CA: Wadsworth.

14 Vander Houwen, B. A. (1997). Less talking, more listening. *HR Magazine, 42,* 8, 53.

15 Listening skills: Why listening is important. Exforsys. Retrieved from http://www.exforsys.com/career-center/listening-skills/why-listening-is-important.html

16 Mehrabian, A. (1967). Orientation behaviors and nonverbal attitude communication. *Journal of Communication, 16,* 324–332.

17 DeFleur, M. H., Kearney, P., Plax, T. G., & DeFleur, M. L. (2005). *Fundamentals of human communication* (3rd ed.). New York, NY: McGraw-Hill.

18 West, R., & Turner, L. H. (2009). *Understanding interpersonal communication: Making choices in changing times.* Boston, MA: Cengage Learning.

19 Wood, J. V., Perunovic, W. Q. E., & Lee, J. W. (2009). Positive self-statements: Power for some, peril for others. *Psychological Science, 20,* 860–866.

20 DeFleur et al., *Fundamentals.*

Chapter 4

1   DeFleur, M. H., Kearney, P., Plax, T. G., & DeFleur, M. L. (2005). *Fundamentals of human communication* (3rd ed.). New York, NY: McGraw-Hill.

2   GuideStar. (2008, January). Communicating your organization's culture to job candidates. Retrieved from http://www2.guidestar.org/rxa/news/articles/2008/communicating-your-organizations-culture-to-job-candidates.aspx?articleId=1177

3   Taleo Research. (2003). Strategic talent management: Calculating the high cost of employee turnover. Retrieved from http://www.taleo.com/research/articles/strategic/calculating-the-high-cost-employee-turnover-15.html

4   The Rain Maker Group. The real costs of employee turnover. (2005). Retrieved from http://www.therainmakergroupinc.com/add.asp?ID=94

5   Macan, T. (2009). The employment interview: A review of current studies and directions for future research. *Human Resource Management Review, 19*(3), 203–218. doi:10.1016/j.hrmr.2009.03.006; McDaniel, M. A., Whetzel, D. L., Schmidt, F. L., & Maurer, S. (1994). The validity of employment interviews: A comprehensive review and meta-analysis, *Journal of Applied Psychology, 79,* 599–616; Hoffcutt, A. I., & Arthur, W. (1994). Hunter and Hunter (1984) revisited: Interview validity for entry-level jobs. *Journal of Applied Psychology, 79,* 184–190.

6   van der Zee, K. I., Bakker, A. B., & Bakker, P. (2002). Why are structured interviews so rarely used in personnel selection? *Journal of Applied Psychology, 87,* 176–184; Lievens, F., & De Paepe, A. (2004). An empirical investigation of interviewer-related factors that discourage the use of high structure interviews, *Journal of Organizational Behavior, 25,* 29–46.

7   Arvey, R. D., & Campion, J. E. (1982). The employment interview: A summary and review of recent research. *Personnel Psychology, 35,* 281–321.

8   Stewart, C. J., & Cash, W. B. (2003). *Interviewing: Principles and practices* (10th ed.). New York, NY: McGraw-Hill; Arvey & Campion, The employment interview.

9   Stewart & Cash. *Interviewing.*

10 Stewart & Cash. *Interviewing,* p. 196.

11 In the development of this section, we discovered some parallels with Stewart & Cash's "stages for the applicant in the selection interview." We would like to acknowledge their thinking and their pioneering work in this area (*Interviewing,* pp. 227–261).

12 Career Builder for Employers. Top interview questions. (n.d.). CareerBuilder.com. Retrieved from http://www.careerbuilder.com/jobposter/small-business/article.aspx?articleid=atl_0082interviewquestions&cbRecursionCnt=1&cbsid=9089102dc6fc443fa0acb477d60d26ad-321031703-x7-6

13 Stewart & Cash. *Interviewing,* p. 256.

14 Martin, C. (2008, September 29). Sell your skills in an interview. Military.com. Retrieved from http://www.military.com/opinion/0,15202,176362,00.html

15 Green, E. (2009). 5 signs you took the wrong job. *Pittsburgh Post-Gazette.* Retrieved from http://www.abc15.com/content/financialsurvival/yourjob/story/5-signs-you-took-the-wrong-job/sLFM4-X_nUGroCBwUpvpVQ.cspx

16 Career Builder for Employers. Top interview questions; Doyle, A. (2010). Interview questions and answers. About.com: Job Searching. Retrieved from http://jobsearch.about.com/od/interviewquestionsanswers/a/interviewquest.htm

17 College Grad.com. (2010). How to handle illegal interview questions. Retrieved from http://www.collegegrad.com/ezine/23illega.shtml; Stewart & Cash. *Interviewing,* pp. 254–256.

18 Krajnik, M. (2007, July 30). Tips for answering those tricky interview questions. CNN.com/Living. Retrieved from http://www.cnn.com/2007/LIVING/worklife/07/27/cb.interviews/index.html; Answering interview questions. (n.d.). Job-application-and-interview-advice.com. Retrieved from http://www.job-application-and-interview-advice.com/answering-interview-questions.html

Chapter 5

1   American Time Use Survey Summary—2008 Results (2009, June 24). Bureau of Labor Statistics. Retrieved from http://www.bls.gov/news.release/atus.nr0.htm

2   Klemmer, E. T., & Snyder, F. W. (1972). Measurement of time spent communicating. *Journal of Communication, 22,* 142–158.

3   Muzio, E. G., Fisher, D. J., & Thomas, E. (2008). *Four secrets to liking your work: You may not need to quit to get the job you want.* Upper Saddle River, NJ: Financial Times Press. Retrieved from http://www.ftpress.com/store/product.aspx?isbn=0132344459

4   Omdahl, B. L., & Fritz, J. M. H. (2006). Stress, burnout, and impaired mental health consequences of problematic work relationships. In J. M. H. Fritz & B. L. Omdahl (Eds.), *Problematic relationships in the workplace* (pp. 109–130). New York: Peter Lang.

5   Strauss, D. (2002). *How to make collaboration work.* San Francisco, CA: Berrett-Koehler.

6   Rath, T. (2006). *Vital friends: The people you can't afford to live without.* New York, NY: Gallup Press.

7   Hannon, K. (2006, August 13). People with pals at work more satisfied, productive. *USA Today.* Retrieved from http://www.usatoday.com/money/books/reviews/2006-08-13-vital-friends_x.htm

8   Gibbons, D., & Olk, P. M. (2003). Individual and structural origins of friendship and social position among professionals. *Journal of Personality and Social Psychology, 84,* 340–351.

9   Gibbons & Olk, Individual and structural origins.

10 DeFleur, M. H., Kearney, P., Plax, T. G., & DeFleur, M. L. (2005). *Fundamentals of human communication* (3rd ed.). New York, NY: McGraw-Hill.

11 Bell, R. A., & Daly, J. A. (1984). The affinity-seeking function of communication. *Communication Monographs, 51,* 91–115.

12 Heathfield, S. M. (n.d.). How to demonstrate respect at work. Retrieved from http://humanresources.about.com/od/workrelationships/a/demo_respect.htm

13 Defleur et al., *Fundamentals.*

14 Zupek, R. (2009). 13 things not to share with your co-workers. Retrieved from http://msn.careerbuilder.com/Article/MSN-1219-Workplace-Issues-13-Things-Not-to-Share-with-Your-Co-workers/?sc_extcmp=JS_1219_advice&SiteId=cbmsn41219

15 Watzlawick, P., Bavelas, J. B., & Jackson, D. D. (1967). *Pragmatics of human communication: A study of interactional patterns, pathologies, and paradoxes.* New York: Norton. See also Schrodt, P., Ledbetter, A. M., & Ohrt, J. K. (2007). Parental confirmation and affection as mediators of family communication patterns and children's mental well-being. *Journal of Family Communication, 7,* 23–46; Schrodt, P., Turman, P. D., & Soliz, J. (2006). Perceived understanding as a mediator of perceived teacher confirmation and students' ratings of instruction. *Communication Education, 55,* 370–388.

16 Britto, C. (2010). Five ways to give praise: Small efforts with a huge return. *Leadership in Action.* Retrieved from http://www.cmoe.com/blog/5-ways-to-give-praise-small-efforts-with-a-huge-return.htm

17 Accountemps. (2004). Career counselor: How to accept criticism at work. Retrieved from http://accounting.smartpros.com/x44765.xml; Heathfield, S. M. (n.d.). How to receive feedback with grace and dignity. Retrieved from http://humanresources.about.com/cs/communication/ht/receivefeedback.htm

18 Dana, D. (2006). *Managing differences: How to build better relationships at work and home* (4th ed.). Archer, FL: MTI Publishing.

19 Wayne, E. K. (2005, May 6). It pays to find the hidden, but high, costs of conflict. *Washington Business Journal.* Retrieved from http://washington.bizjournals.com/washington/stories/2005/05/09/smallb6.html

20 Scimia Consulting Group. (n.d.). Statistics: Domestic violence, workplace violence, and workplace conflict. Retrieved from http://www.scimiaconsulting.com/stats.pdf

21 Gallois, C., Ogay, T., & Giles, H. (2005). Communication accommodation theory. *Theorizing about intercultural communication* (pp. 121–148). Thousand Oaks, CA: Sage.

22 Giles, H., & Wiemann, J. M. (1987). Language, social comparison and power. In C. R. Berger and S. H. Chaffee (Eds.), *The handbook of communication science* (pp. 350–384). Newbury Park, CA: Sage.

23 Long, M. (2010, January 20). Survey finds children's media use jumps in five years. *Top Tech News*. Retrieved from http://www.toptechnews.com/story.xhtml?story_id=11000CHGZ8SE&page=2

24 Twenge, J., & Campbell, S. (2010). Generation me and the changing world of work. *Oxford handbook of positive psychology and work* (pp. 25–35). New York, NY: Oxford University Press. Retrieved from PsycINFO database.

25 Giles, H. (2008). Accommodating translational research. *Journal of Applied Communication Research, 36*(2), 121–127. doi:10.1080/00909880801922870

26 Giles, Accommodating translational research.

27 Cennamo, L. ,& Gardner, D. (2008). Generational differences in work values, outcomes and person-organisation values fit. *Journal of Managerial Psychology, 23*(8), 891–906. Retrieved from ABI/INFORM Global. (Document ID: 1591442681)

28 U.S. Department of Labor, Bureau of Labor Statistics (2007, November). *Employment and Earnings, 2008 Annual Averages and the Monthly Labor Review*. Retrieved from http://www.dol.gov/wb/stats/main.htm

29 Wood, J. T. (1994). *Gendered lives: Communication, gender, and culture* (p. 141). Belmont, CA: Wadsworth.

30 Wood, *Gendered lives*, p. 140.

31 Kearney, P., & Plax, T. G. (2006). *Public speaking in a diverse society* (3rd ed.). Belmont, CA: Thomson Wadsworth.

32 Kadue, D. (2001). Preventing sexual harassment: A fact sheet for employees. Retrieved from http://www.dotcr.ost.dot.gov/Documents/complaint/Preventing_Sexual_Harassment.htm

33 Parks, M. (2006). 2006 workplace romances: Poll findings. *A study by the Society of Human Resource Management and Career Journal.com*. Retrieved from http://www.lrgllc.com/rpubs/7.pdf

34 Horan, S., & Chory, R. (2009). When work and love mix: Perceptions of peers in workplace romances. *Western Journal of Communication, 73*, 349–369. See also Brown, T. J., & Allgeier, E. R. (1996). The impact of participant characteristics, perceived motives, and job behaviors on co-workers' evaluations of workplace romances. *Journal of Applied Social Psychology, 26*, 577–595.

35 Fatal attractions: The (mis)management of workplace romance. (2007, July 1). *International Journal of Business Management*. Retrieved from http://goliath.ecnext.com/coms2/gi_0198-475353/Fatal-attractions-the-mis-management.html

36 Sias, P. M. (2009). *Organizing relationships: Traditional and emerging perspectives on workplace relationships*. Thousand Oaks, CA: Sage.

37 Clark, S. C. (2000). Work/family border theory: A new theory of work/family balance. *Human Relations, 53*, 747–770. Retrieved from ABI/INFORM Global. (Document ID: 54990585)

38 Parks, M., 2006 workplace romances.

39 Parks, M., 2006 workplace romances, p. 9.

40 Working Mother 100 best companies 2009. *Working Mother*. Retrieved from http://www.workingmother.com/BestCompanies/node/1671/list

41 Rivera, C. T. (2001, January 1). Working wars: Are new family-values workplaces valuing all workers? *Office Solutions*. Retrieved from http://www.highbeam.com/doc/1P3-244506841.html

42 Burkett, E. (2000). *The baby boon: How family-friendly American cheats the childless*. New York: Free Press.

43 BNET. (2010). Implementing a cafeteria-style benefits plan [editorial]. Retrieved from http://www.bnet.com/2410-13059_23-64280.html

44 Hamilton, K. (2002). Race matters—in the workplace. *Black Issues in Higher Education, 18 (24)*, 42+.

45 Clark, M. A. (2001). Perceived relational diversity: A fit conceptualization. Ph.D. dissertation, Arizona State University. Retrieved from ABI/INFORM Global. (Publication No. AAT 3031447).

46 Glaman, J. M., Jones, A. P., & Rozelle, R. M. (1996). The effects of co-worker similarity on the emergence of affect in work teams. *Group & Organization Management, 21*(2), 192. Retrieved from ABI/INFORM Global. (Document ID: 9698548)

47 DeFleur et al., *Fundamentals*.

48 Piccolo, C. M. (2009). *Your coworkers, your health*. Medhunters.com Retrieved from http://www.medhunters.com/articles/yourCoworkersYourHealth.html

49 Wulfhorst, E. (2008, July 10). Desk rage spoils workplace for many Americans. Reuters. Retrieved from http://www.reuters.com/article/idUSN0947145320080710

50 Bin, J. O. C. (2007, August–September). Keeping difficult customers happy. *Entrepreneur*. Retrieved from http://www.entrepreneur.com/tradejournals/article/167431709.html

51 Bin, Keeping difficult customers happy.

52 Brewda, E. (2008, August 1). Diffusing challenging customer situations. *Bulletin* (Northwest Public Power Association). Retrieved from http://www.allbusiness.com/marketing-advertising/marketing-advertising-measures/11493262-1.html

53 Traut, T. R. (n.d.). Handling challenging situations with a customer-focused mindset. Retrieved from http://www.themanager.org/strategy/Challenging_Situations.htm

54 Brewda, Diffusing.

55 Many employees would fire their boss (2007, October 11). *Gallup Management Journal*. Retrieved from http://gmj.gallup.com/content/28867/many-employees-would-fire-their-boss.aspx

56 Rath, T. (2006, August 10). Can employees be friends with the boss? *Gallup Management Journal*. Retrieved from http://gmj.gallup.com/content/23893/can-employees-be-friends-with-the-boss.aspx

57 Torres, D. (2007, September 11). Some bad boss statistics. Management Issues. Retrieved from http://www.management-issues.com/2007/9/11/blog/some-bad-boss-statistics.asp

58 Dotinga, R. (2009, November 6). Can a bad boss make you sick? *U.S. News and World Report*. Retrieved from http://www.usnews.com/health/family-health/heart/articles/2009/11/06/can-a-bad-boss-make-you-sick.html

59 Rath, Can employees be friends.

60 Heathfield, S. M. (n.d.). How to get along with your boss. About.com: Human Resources. Retrieved from http://humanresources.about.com/od/workrelationships/a/boss_relations.htm; New job can depend on boss approval. (2004, September 26). *Los Angeles Times*, p. 5 G/R.

Chapter 6

1 Palfrey, J., & Gasser, U. (2008). *Born digital: Understanding the first generation of digital natives*. New York: Basic Books.

2 *Millennials, a portrait of Generation Next: Confident, connected, open to change*. (2010, February). Washington, DC: Pew Research Center. Retrieved from http://pewsocialtrends.org/assets/pdf/millennials-confident-connected-open-to-change.pdf

3 *Millennials*.

4 Wardrip-Fruin, N., & Montfort, N. (2003). *The new media reader*. Boston, MA: MIT.

5 *Is social media the new addiction?* (2010, March 19). Retrieved from http://www.marketingprofs.com/charts/2010/3486/is-social-media-the-new-addiction

6 *Social media consumers more likely to buy, recommend*. (2010, March 25). Retrieved from http://www.marketingprofs.com/charts/2010/3501/social-media-consumers-more-likely-to-buy-recommend

7 Geisler, J. (2006, February 12). *Email misunderstandings*. Retrieved from http://www.poynter.org/column.asp?id=34&aid=96359

8 Ashley, J. (2003, December). Synchronous and asynchronous communication tools. Retrieved from http://www.asaecenter.com/PublicationsResources/article-detail.cfm?ItemNumber=13572

9 Trevino, L. K., Daft, R. L., & Lengel, R. H. (1990). Understanding managers' media choices: A symbolic interactionist perspective. In J. Fulk & C. Steinfield (Eds.), *Organizations and communication technology* (pp. 71–94). Thousand Oaks, CA: Sage.

10 Fulk, J., Steinfield, C. W., Schmitz, J., & Power, J. G. (1987). A social information processing model of media use in organizations. *Communication Research, 14*, 529–552.

11 Daft, R. L., & Lengel, R. H. (1986). Organizational information requirements, media richness and structural determinants. *Management Science, 32*, 554–571.

12 Ahonen, T. T., & Moore, A. (2009, March 6). 3 billion use SMS: What does that mean? Retrieved from http://communities-dominate.blogs.com/brands/2009/03/3-billion-use-sms-what-does-that-mean.html

13 Emily Post Institute. *Video conference etiquette tips*. Retrieved from http://www.emilypost.com/business/video_conference.htm

14 Weinberg, T. (2008, December 10). *The ultimate social media etiquette handbook*. Retrieved from http://www.techipedia.com/2008/social-media-etiquette-handbook/

Chapter 7

1 Shaw, G. G. Planning and communicating using stories. In M. Schultz, M. J. Hatch, & M. H. Larsen, *The expressive organization: Linking identity, reputation, and the corporate brand* (pp. 182–195). New York: Oxford.

2 Sunwolf. (2004). *Practical jury dynamics: From one juror's trial perceptions to the group's decision-making process*. New York, NY: LexisNexus.

3 See Witte, K. (1994). Fear control and danger control: A test of the extended parallel process model. *Communication Monographs, 61*, 113–145.

4 Shaw, Planning and communicating, p. 185.

5 Lindstrom, R. L., (1998, October). Presentation intelligence: The evolution of presentations in the new enterprise. *Presentations, 12*, 1–22.

6 Sproull, L., & Kiesler, S. (1991). *Connections: New ways of working in the networked organization*. Cambridge, MA: MIT.

7 Fisher, W. R. (1987). *Human communication as narration: Toward a philosophy of reason, value, and action*. Columbia: University of South Carolina.

8 Kearney, P., & Plax, T. G. (2006). *Public speaking in a diverse society* (3rd ed.). Belmont, CA: Thomson Wadsworth.

9   McCroskey, J. C., & Mehrley, R. S. (1969). The effects of disorganization and nonfluency on attitude change and source credibility. *Speech Monographs, 36,* 13–21; Sharp, H., Jr., & McClung, T. (1966). Effects of organizations on the speaker's ethos. *Speech Monographs, 33,* 182.

10 Smith, G. R. (1951). Effects of speech organization upon attitudes of college students. *Speech Monographs, 18,* 292–301.

11 Darnell, D. K. (1963). The relation between sentence order and comprehension. *Speech Monographs, 30,* 97–100; Thompson, E. (1967). Some effects of message structure on listening comprehension. *Speech Monographs, 34,* 51–57.

12 LeRoux, P., & Corwin, P. (2007). *Visual selling: Capture the eye and the customer will follow.* Hoboken, NJ: Wiley.

13 Kaplan, R. B. (1966). Cultural thought patterns revisited. In U. Connor & R. B. Kaplan (Eds.), *Writing across languages: Analysis of L₂ text* (pp. 9–21). Reading, MA: Addison-Wesley.

14 Kozhevnikov, M. (2007). *Cognitive styles in the context of modern psychology: Toward an integrated framework of cognitive style.* Psychological *Bulletin, 133,* 464–481.

15 Condon, J. C., & Yousef, F. (1975). *An introduction to intercultural communication* (pp. 240–245). New York: Macmillan; Hall, E. T., & Hall, M. R. (1987). *Hidden differences: Doing business with the Japanese.* New York: Doubleday; Lustig, M. W., & Koester, J. (1993). *Intercultural competence: Interpersonal communication across cultures.* New York: HarperCollins.

16 Adapted from Manjoo, F. (2011, April 6). Now you're talking! Google has developed speech-recognition technology that actually works. *Slate.com.* Retrieved from http://www.slate.com/id/2290516/

17 Treasure, J. (2009, July). *The four ways sound affects us.* Speech delivered at TEDGlobal 2009 Conference, Oxford, England. Retrieved from http://www.ted.com/talks/julian_treasure_the_4_ways_sound_affects_us.html

18 Lustig & Koester, *Intercultural competence.*

19 Carte, P., & Fox, C. (2004). *Bridging the culture gap: A practical guide to international business communication.* London: Kogan Page.

20 Mayer, R. E., & Moreno, R. (2003). Nine ways to reduce cognitive load in multimedia learning. *Educational Psychologist, 38,* 43–52.

21 Goffard, C. (2007, July 8). Nixon library's changes start with Watergate. *Los Angeles Times.* Retrieved from http://www.latimes.com/news/local/la-me-watergate-8jul08,1,6842346.story?ctrack=2&cset=true

22 Lustig & Koester, *Intercultural competence.*

23 Jamieson, K. H. (1998). *Eloquence in an electronic age: The transformation of political speechmaking.* New York: Oxford University Press.

24 Adapted from Bezos, M. (2011, March). A life lesson form a volunteer firefighter. TED Talks. Retrieved from http://www.ted.com/talks/mark_bezos_a_life_lesson_from_a_volunteer_firefighter.html

25 Adapted from Sandberg, S. (2010, December). Why we have too few women leaders. Speech delivered at TEDWomen. Retrieved from http://www.ted.com/talks/sheryl_sandberg_why_we_have_too_few_women_leaders.html

26 Cohen, D. (2010, April). Tough truths about Plastic pollution. Speech delivered at TED Talks. Retrieved from http://www.ted.com/talks/dianna_cohen_tough_truths_about_plastic_pollution.html

27 Connor, U., & McCagg, P. (1987). A contrastive study of English expository prose paraphrases. In U. Connor & R. B. Kaplan (Eds.), *Writing across languages: Analysis of L₂ text* (pp. 73–86). Reading, MA: Addison-Wesley.

28 Atkinson, C. (2005). *Beyond bullet points: Using Microsoft PowerPoint to create presentations that inform, motivate, and inspire.* Redmond, WA: Microsoft Press.

29 Cyphert, D. (2007). Presentation technology in the age of electronic eloquence: From visual aid to visual rhetoric. *Communication Education, 56,* 168–192. Jamieson, K. H. (1998). *Eloquence in an electronic age: The transformation of political speechmaking.* New York: Oxford University Press.

Chapter 8

1   Kearney, P., & Plax, T. G. (2006). *Public speaking in a diverse society* (3rd ed.). Belmont, CA: Thomson Wadsworth.

2   Kline, J. A. (Spring, 2007). How to give winning briefings. *Armed Forces Comptroller.* Retrieved from http://www.klinespeak.com/pdf/Give Winning Briefings—Kline.pdf

3   Sandberg, S. (2010, December). *Why we have too few women leaders.* Speech delivered at TEDWomen. http://www.ted.com/talks/sheryl_sandberg_why_we_have_too_few_women_leaders.html

4   Moore, M. (n.d.). How to use humorous one-liners in your speeches. SelfGrowth.com. Retrieved from http://www.selfgrowth.com/articles/Moore39.html

5   Funny Business Quotes. (n.d.). Retrieved from http://www.dennydavis.net/poemfiles/busnss2q.htm

6   Work Quotes. (n.d.). Retrieved from http://www.woopidoo.com/business_quotes/work-quotes.htm

7   Funny Business Quotes.

8   Work Quotes.

9   Work Quotes.

10 Carol Moseley Braun quotes. (n.d.). Brainy Quote. Retrieved from http://www.brainyquote.com/quotes/authors/c/carol_moseley_braun_2.html

11 Filek, J. (2001, August). Some startling statistics for anyone in sales. *Impact Communications.* Retrieved from http://www.impactcommunicationsinc.com/pdf/nwsltr_2001/ICINwsltrpr0108.pdf; Little known facts. (n.d.). Queens University Belfast, UNITE. Retrieved from http://www.qub.ac.uk/assoc/msf/little_known_facts.htm; Some little known facts. (n.d.). PageTutor.com. Retrieved from http://www.pagetutor.com/jokebreak/091.html; Jackson, R. (2003). Some startling statistics. *Erma Bombeck's Writer Workshop.* Retrieved from http://www.humorwriters.org/startlingstats.html; Ocean facts. (n.d.). Marine Bio.org. Retrieved from http://marinebio.org/MarineBio/Facts/

12 For an overview of the research findings pertinent to these and other strategies, see Woolfolk, A. (2009). *Educational psychology* (11th ed.). Upper Saddle River, NJ: Merrill; Cooper, P.J., & Simonds, C. (2010). *Communication for the classroom teacher* (9th ed). Boston, MA: Pearson Allyn & Bacon. See also Kearney & Plax, *Public speaking in a diverse society.*

Chapter 9

1   Kearney, P., & Plax, T. G. (2006). *Public speaking in a diverse society* (3rd ed.). Belmont, CA: Thomson Wadsworth.

2   Adapted from Marsh, N. (2010, May). *How to make work-life balance work.* Speech delivered at TEDxSydney. http://www.ted.com/talks/nigel_marsh_how_to_make_work_life_balance_work.html

3   Brehm, J. W. (1966). *A theory of psychological reactance.* New York, NY: Academic; Burroughs, N. F., Kearney, P., & Plax, T. G. (1989). Compliance-resistance in the college classroom. *Communication Education, 38,* 214–229. Kearney, P., Plax, T. G., & Burroughs, N. F. (1991). An attributional analysis of college students' resistance decisions. *Communication Education, 40,* 325–342; DeFleur, M. H., Kearney, P., Plax, T. G., & DeFleur, M. L. (2005). *Fundamentals of human communication* (3rd ed.). New York, NY: McGraw-Hill.

4   Redding, W. C. (1983). An informal history of communication at Purdue. Retrieved from http://www.cla.purdue.edu/Communication/About/documents_&_media/informalhistory.pdf

5   Lauder, G. (2010, February). *Gary Lauder's new traffic sign: Take turns.* Video and transcript of presentation to the annual conference of TED, Long Beach, CA. Retrieved from http://www.ted.com/talks/gary_lauder_s_new_traffic_sign_take_turns.html

6   All the proposed strategies are based on research. Reviews of relevant investigations underlying these and other strategies are available from a number of textbooks on persuasion and attitude change, including the following: Eagly, A. H., & Chaiken, S. (1993). *The psychology of attitudes.* Fort Worth, TX: Harcourt Brace Jovanovich; Frymier, A. B., & Nadler, M. K. (2010). *Persuasion: Investigating theory, research, and practice* (2nd ed.). Dubuque, IA: Kendall Hunt. See also Kearney & Plax, *Public speaking in a diverse society;* DeFleur, Kearney, Plax, & DeFleur, *Fundamentals.*

7   Texting while driving PSA. YouTube. Retrieved from http://www.youtube.com/watch?v=b707xc1-jSM

8   Bendapudi, N. (2009, September 3). Does fear in advertising work? How do I market myself? YouTube. Retrieved from http://www.youtube.com/watch?v=ILfLs7cKFel&feature=related

9   Cacioppo, J. T., & Petty, R. E. (1979). The effects of message repetition and position on cognitive response, recall, and persuasion. *Journal of Personality and Social Psychology, 37,* 97–109.

10 Moore, C. (2009, February). *Captain Charles Moore and the seas of plastic.* Video and transcript of presentation to the annual conference of TED, Long Beach, CA. Retrieved from http://www.ted.com/talks/capt_charles_moore_on_the_seas_of_plastic.html

11 Tulley, G. (2007, March). Gever Tulley on 5 dangerous things for kids. Video and transcript of presentation to the annual conference of TED, Long Beach, CA. Retrieved from http://www.ted.com/talks/gever_tulley_on_5_dangerous_things_for_kids.html

12 Pisani, E. (2010, February). *Elizabeth Pisani: Sex, drugs and HIV—Let's get rational.* Video and transcript of presentation to the annual conference of TED, Long Beach, CA. Retrieved from http://www.ted.com/talks/elizabeth_pisani_sex_drugs_and_hiv_let_s_get_rational_1.html

13 Used with permission.

Chapter 10

1   Clark, R. C., & C. Lyons. 2004. *Graphics for learning.* San Francisco: Pfeiffer.

2   Miller, S. (2009). The impact of trade show booth graphic elements. Trade-Show-Advisor.com. Retrieved from http://www.trade-show-advisor.com/trade-show-booth-graphic.html

3   LaBarre, P. (2007, December 19). Sophisticated sell. *Fast Company*. Retrieved from http://www.fastcompany.com/magazine/65/sophisticated.html

4   Schmitt, B. H. (1999). *Experiential marketing: How to get customers to sense, feel, think, act, relate*. New York, NY: Free Press.

5   Atkinson, C. (2009, March 4). An interview with Richard Mayer. *Indezine*. Retrieved from http://www.indezine.com/products/powerpoint/personality/richardmayer.html

6   Prensky, M. (2004). The emerging online life of the digital native: What they do differently because of technology and how they do it. Marc Prensky.com. Retrieved from http://www.marcprensky.com/writing/Prensky-The_Emerging_Online_Life_of_the_Digital_Native-03.pdf

7   Mayer, R. E. (2009). *Multimedia learning* (2nd ed). New York, NY: Cambridge University Press.

8   Kearney, P., & Plax, T. G. (1999). *Public speaking in a diverse society* (2nd ed.). Mountain View, CA: Mayfield.

9   Kearney & Plax, *Public speaking in a diverse society*.

10 Godin, S. (2007, January 29). Really bad PowerPoint. *Seth Godin's blog*. Retrieved from http://sethgodin.typepad.com/seths_blog/2007/01/really_bad_powe.html

11 Dangel, H. L., & Wang, C. X. (2008). Student response systems in higher education: Moving beyond linear teaching and surface learning. *Journal of Educational Technology Development and Exchange, 1*, 93–104.

12 MeetingsPodcastGuys. (2008, September 22). Six ways to utilize Twitter at your next conference. Grass Shack. Retrieved from http://grassshackroad.com/6-ways-to-utilize-twitter-at-your-next-conference

13 For a complete overview of Let's Focus, one example of digital visualization software developed for business and the professions, go to http://en.lets-focus.com

14 Atkinson, C. (2007). *Beyond bullet points*. Seattle, WA: Microsoft Press.

15 Godin, S. (2007, January 29). Really bad PowerPoint. *Seth Godin's blog*. Retrieved from http://sethgodin.typepad.com/seths_blog/2007/01/really_bad_powe.html

16 Reynolds, G. (2008, August 25). Learning slide design from an IKEA billboard. Retrieved from http://www.presentationzen.com/presentationzen/2008/08/learning-from-the-design-around-you-ikea.html

Chapter 11

1   Hartl, D. E. (2003). Different types of meetings and how to make them work. General Learning Climates, Inc. Retrieved from http://www.davidhartl.com/papers/show/Better+Meetings

2   Survey finds workers average only three productive days per week. (2005, March 15). Microsoft News Center. Retrieved from http://www.microsoft.com/presspass/press/2005/mar05/03-15threeproductivedayspr.mspx

3   InfoCom. (2010). *Meetings in America: A Verizon conferencing white paper*. Retrieved from https://e-meetings.verizonbusiness.com/global/en/meetingsinamerica/uswhitepaper.php#BACKGROUND

4   InfoCom, *Meetings in America*.

5   Strauss, D. (2002). *How to make collaboration work*. San Francisco, CA: Berrett-Koehler.

6   Luong, A., & Rogelberg, S. G. (2005). Meetings and more meetings: The relationship between meeting load and the daily well-being of employees. *Group Dynamics: Theory, Research, and Practice, 9*, 58.

7   Conducting effective meetings: Who should attend the meeting? (n.d.) *ASME Professional Practice Curriculum*. Retrieved from http://professionalpractice.asme.org/Communications/Meetings/Should_Attend_Meeting.cfm

8   Kerjulf, A. (2006, August 25). How to get people to arrive on time for meetings. *Happy at Work*. Retrieved from http://positivesharing.com/2006/08/how-to-get-people-to-arrive-on-time-for-meetings/

9   Baldoni, J. (2010, February 16). Learn how to ask better questions. *Harvard Business Review*. Retrieved from http://blogs.hbr.org/cs/2010/02/learn_to_ask_better_questions.html

10 Open and closed questions. (n.d.). Changing Minds.org. Retrieved from http://changingminds.org/techniques/questioning/open_closed_questions.htm

11 How to maintain momentum. (2008, December 2). The Success Professor. Retrieved from http://successprofessor.ca/2008/12/02/how-to-maintain-momentum/

12 How not to run a meeting. (2007, December 18). Retrieved from http://www.youtube.com/watch?v=kp6H8XMf5ec&feature=related

13 This checklist was adapted from Meeting evaluation checklist. (n.d.). Center for Student Involvement Resources, Dean of Students, Montclair State University. Retrieved from http://www.montclair.edu/csi/Meeting%20Evaluation%20Checklist.pdf

Chapter 12

1   Oldham, G. R., & Hackman, J. R. (2010). Not what it is and not what it will be: The future of job design research. *Journal of Organizational Behavior, 31*, 463–479.

2   Devine, D. J., Clayton, L. D., Philips, J. L., Dunford, B. B., & Melner, S. B. (1999). Teams in organizations: Prevalence, characteristics, and effectiveness. *Small Group Research, 30*, 678–711.

3   Kennedy, F., Loughry, M., Klammer, T., & Beyerlein, M. (2009). Effects of organizational support on potency in work teams: The mediating role of team processes. *Small Group Research, 40*, 72–93. doi:10.1177/1046496408326744

4   Locke, E., Tirnauer, D., Roberson, Q., Goldman, B., Latham, M., & Weldon, E. (2001). The importance of the individual in an age of groupism. In M. Turner (Ed.), *Groups at work: Theory and research* (pp. 501–528). Mahwah, NJ: Lawrence Erlbaum.

5   Hill, G. W. (1982). Group versus individual performance: Are N+1 heads better than one? *Psychological Bulletin, 91*, 517–539.

6   Hare, A. P. (2003). Roles, relationships, and groups in organizations: Some conclusions and recommendations. *Small Group Research, 34*, 132.

7   Hare. Roles relationships, and groups, 133.

8   Oldham & Hackman. Not what it is, 474.

9   Oldham & Hackman. Not what it is, 474.

10 Locke, E., Tirnauer, D., Roberson, Q., Goldman, B., Latham, M., & Weldon, E. (2001). The importance of the individual in an age of groupism. In M. Turner (Ed.), *Groups at work: Theory and research* (pp. 501–528). Mahwah, NJ: Erlbaum.

11 Hart, P. (1994). *Government: A study of small groups and policy failure*. Baltimore, MD: The Johns Hopkins University Press; Janis, I .L. (1972). *Victims of groupthink: A psychological study of foreign policy decisions and fiascoes*. Boston, MA: Houghton Mifflin; Janis, I. L. (1982). *Groupthink: A psychological study of policy decisions and fiascoes*. Boston, MA: Houghton Mifflin.

12 Jackson, J., & Harkins, S. (1985). Equity in effort: An explanation of the social loafing effect. *Journal of Personality and Social Psychology, 49*, 1199–1206. doi:10.1037/0022-3514.49.5.1199; Latane, B., Williams, K., & Harkins, S. (1979). Many hands make light the work: The causes and consequences of social loafing. *Journal of Personality and Social Psychology, 37*, 823–832.

13 DeFleur, M. H., Kearney, P., Plax, T. G., & DeFleur, M. L. (2005). *Fundamentals of human communication* (3rd ed.) (pp. 147–176). New York, NY: McGraw-Hill.

14 Cohen, S. G., & Bailey, D. E. (1997). What makes teams work: Group effectiveness research from the shop floor to the executive suite. *Journal of Management, 23*, 239–290.

15 Devine. Teams in organizations, 681.

16 Devine. Teams in organizations.

17 Oldham & Hackman. Not what it is.

18 Schweitzer, L., & Duxbury, L. (2010). Conceptualizing and measuring the virtuality of teams. *Information Systems Journal, 20*, 267–295. doi:10.1111/j.1365-2575.2009.00326.x

19 Kennedy. Effects of organizational support.

20 Kennedy. Effects of organizational support.

21 Lencioni, P. (2002). *The five dysfunctions of a team* (pp. 188–189). San Francisco, CA: Jossey-Bass.

22 Larson, C. E., & LaFasto, F. M. (1989). *Teamwork: What must go right/what can go wrong*. Newbury Park, CA: Sage.

23 Larson & LaFasto. *Teamwork*.

24 Larson & LaFasto. *Teamwork*, 73.

25 Eikenberry, K. (2008, July 16). Three types of team commitment. Retrieved from http://www.eyesonsales.com/content/article/the_three_types_of_team_commitment/

26 Kappleman, L.A., Mckeeman, R., & Zhang, L. (2006). Early warning signs of IT project failure: The dominant dozen. *Information Systems Management, 23*, 31–36.

27 Scott, K. D., & Townsend, A. (1994, August). Teams: Why some succeed and others fail. HRMagazine, 39(8), 62. Retrieved from ABI/INFORM Global (Document ID: 29908)

28 Turmel, D. (n.d.). 3 reasons why virtual teams fail and how to see it coming. A Greatwebmeetings.com white paper. Retrieved from http://www.greatwebmeetings.com/files/3reasonswhitepaperfinal.pdf

29 Tudor, T. G., Trumble, R. R., & Diaz, J. J. (1996). Work-teams: Why do they often fail? *SAM Advanced Management Journal, 61*(4), 31–39. Retrieved from Business Source Premier database (Document ID: 07497075)

30 Tudor, Trumble, & Diaz. Work-teams.

31 Turmel. 3 reasons.

32 Felps, W., Mitchell, T. R., & Byington, E. (2006). How, when, and why bad apples spoil the barrel: Negative group members and dysfunctional groups. *Research in Organizational Behavior, 27*, 175–222.

33 Wetlaufer, S. (1994). The team that wasn't. *Harvard Business Review, 72*, 22–38.

34 Andrews, L. W. (2004). Hard-core offenders. *HR Magazine, 49*, 45–55.

35 Felps, Mitchell, & Byington. How, when, and why, 207.

36 Felps, Mitchell, & Byington. How, when, and why, 209.

37 Lencioni. *The five dysfunctions*.

38 Hackman, M. Z., & Johnson, C. E. (2004). *Leadership: A communication perspective* (4th ed.). Long Grove, IL: Waveland; Friedrich, T. (2010). The history of leadership research. In M.D. Mumford (Ed.), *Leadership 101* (pp. 1–26). New York, NY: Springer. Retrieved from PsycINFO database; DuBrin, A. J. (2001). *Leadership: Research findings, practice, and skills* (3rd ed.). Boston, MA: Houghton Mifflin.

39 Bass, B. (1985). *Leadership and performance beyond expectations*. New York, NY: Free Press; Burns, J. M. (1978). *Leadership*. New York, NY: Harper & Row; Piccolo, R. F., & Colquitt, J. A. (2006). Transformational leadership and job behaviors: The mediating role of core job characteristics. *Academy of Management Journal, 49*, 327–340.

40 Judge, T. A., & Piccolo, R. F. (2004) Transformational and transactional leadership: A meta-analytic test of their relative validity. *Journal of Applied Psychology, 89*, 755–768.

41 Whitford, T., & Moss, S. A. (2009). Transformational leadership in distributed work groups: The moderating role of follower regulatory focus and goal orientation. *Communication Research, 36*, 810–837.

42 Hackman & Johnson. *Leadership*, 101.

43 Loughry, M., Ohland, M., & Moore, D. (2007). Development of a theory-based assessment of team member effectiveness. *Educational and Psychological Measurement, 67*(3), 505–524. Retrieved from ERIC database.

Chapter 13

1 Mathewson, J. (2010, July 4). A fourth of July lesson in the value of editors. *Writing for Digital* (blog). Retrieved from http://writingfordigital.com/2010/07/04/a-fourth-of-july-lesson-in-the-value-of-editors/

2 Nielsen, J. (2010, July 2). iPad and Kindle reading speeds. *Alertbox: Current Issues in Web Usability*. Retrieved from http://www.useit.com/alertbox/ipad-kindle-reading.html

3 Rzadkiewicz, C. (2009, October 13). Business communication and effective memos. Retrieved from http://factory-facilities-operations.suite101.com/article.cfm/business_communication_and_effective_memos

4 Wreden, N. (2006). Making your proposal come out on top. In *Written communications that inform and influence* (pp. 29–38). Boston, MA: Harvard Business School Press.

5 Ryan, C. W. (1974). *Writing: A practical guide for business and industry*. New York, NY: Wiley.

6 Wreden. Making your proposal, p. 30.

7 Wreden. Making your proposal.

8 Wreden. Making your proposal.

9 Pratt, M. K. (2005). How to write a progress report. Early Childhood Learning and Knowledge Center, U.S. Department of Health and Human Services. Retrieved from http://eclkc.ohs.acf.hhs.gov/hslc/Program%20Design%20and%20Management/Management%20and%20Administration/Communication/Reporting%20Systems/HowtoWriteaPr.htm

10 Kuiper, S., & Kohut, G. F. (1998). *Contemporary business report writing*. Boston, MA: South-Western.

11 Ryan. *Writing*.

12 Clayton, J. (2006). Writing an executive summary that means business. In *Written communications that inform and influence* (pp. 145–149). Boston, MA: Harvard Business School Press.

13 Blog. *WordNet: A lexical database for English*. Princeton University. http://wordnetweb.princeton.edu/perl/webwn?s=blog

14 Rowse, D. (2005, December 30). Ten tips for writing a better blog post. Problogger. Retrieved from http://www.problogger.net/archives/2005/12/30/tens-tips-for-writing-a-blog-post/

15 Brusaw, C. T., Alred, G. J., & Oliu, W. E. (1987). *The business writer's handbook* (3rd ed.). New York, NY: St. Martin's.

16 Ringwood, J. (1999). *Hints on technical report writing*. Retrieved from http://odtl.dcu.ie/wp/1999/odtl-1999-03.html

17 Blake, G., & Bly, R. W. (1992). *The elements of business writing: A guide to writing clear, concise letters, memos, reports, proposals, and other business documents*. Upper Saddle River, NJ: AB/Longman.

18 Haugtvedt, C. P., & Wegener, D. T. (1994). Message order effects in persuasion: An attitude strength perspective. *Journal of Consumer Research, 21*, 205–218.

19 Miller, G. A. (1956). The magical number seven, plus or minus two: Some limits on our capacity for processing information. *Psychological Review, 63*, 81–97.

20 Brusaw, Alred, & Oliu. *Business writer's handbook*.

Chapter 14

1 Plax, T. G., Kearney, P., Ross, T. J., & Jolly, J. C. (2008). Assessing the link between environmental concerns and consumers' decisions to use clean-air vehicles. *Communication Education, 57*, 417–422.

2 Plax, T. G., Kearney, P., Jolly, J. C., & Ross.Campbell, Inc. (2006, December). California consumer and fleet manager reactions to clean vehicle technologies: Results from statewide focus groups and surveys. California Air Resources Board. Retrieved from http://www.arb.ca.gov/msprog/zevprog/fg/cleantechfg.pdf

3 DeWine, S.(2001). *The consultant's craft: Improving organizational communication* (2nd ed.). Boston, MA: Bedford/St. Martin's.

4 Lewin, K. (1951). *Field theory in social science: Selected theoretical papers*. New York, NY: Harper & Row, 169.

5 Plax, T. G. (2006). Raising the question #2: How much are we worth? Estimating fee for services. *Communication Education, 55*, 242–246.

6 Jerusalem, M., & Schwarzer, R. (1993). The general self-efficacy scale. Retrieved from http://userpage.fu-berlin.de/~health/engscal.htm. See also Jerusalem, M., & Schwarzer, R. (1992). Self-efficacy as a resource factor in stress appraisal processes. In R. Schwarzer (Ed.), *Self-efficacy: Thought control of action* (pp. 195–213). Washington, DC: Hemisphere.

7 Plax, T. G., Kearney, P., Allen, T. H., & Ross, T. (2006). Using focus groups to design a nationwide debt-management educational program. In L. R. Frey (Ed.), *Facilitating group communication in context: Innovations and applications with natural groups* (Vol. 2, pp. 89–107). Cresskill, NJ: Hampton Press.

8 Beebe, S. A. (2007). What do communication trainers do? *Communication Education, 56*, 249–254.

9 Lucier, K. H. (2008). A consultative training program: Collateral effect of a needs assessment. *Communication Education, 57*, 485.

10 North Dakota Department of Public Instruction. (n.d.). Needs assessments. Retrieved from http://www.dpi.state.nd.us/grants/needs.pdf

11 Beebe, S. A. (2007). What do communication trainers do? *Communication Education, 56*, 249–254.

12 Trochim, W. M. K. (2006). Research methods knowledge base: Introduction to evaluation. Web Center for Social Research Methods. Retrieved from http://www.socialresearchmethods.net/kb/intreval.htm

Chapter 15

1 Dollars spent on employee training in the United States. Retrieved from http://maamodt.asp.radford.edu/HR Statistics/dollars_spent_on_training.htm

2 Corporate trainer certification and certificate programs. Retrieved from http://education-portal.com/corporate_trainer_certification.html

3 Salary wizard. Retrieved from http://salary.com/

4 DeWine, S.(2001). *The consultant's craft: Improving organizational communication* (2nd ed.). Boston, MA: Bedford/St. Martin's.

5 Beebe, S. A., Mottet, T. P., & Roach, K. D. (2004). *Training and development: Enhancing communication and leadership skills* (pp. 15–16). Boston, MA: Pearson.

6 Knowles, M. (1970). *The modern practice of adult education: Andragogy verus pedagogy*. Oxford, England: Association Press; Knowles, M. (1978). *The adult learner: A neglected species* (2nd ed). Oxford,.England: Gulf.

7 Adult learning principles. (2009, December 14). A KanNag Production. Retrieved from http://www.youtube.com/watch?v=Cu_PpkqWJGA&feature=related

8 White, T. (2008, August 17). Adult training techniques: How to deal with disruptive learners. Retrieved from http://www.youtube.com/watch?v=_9K_RCOzx9o&feature=related

9 Waters, N. (2004). Checklist for hiring a trainer. Retrieved from: http://www.nancywatters.com/virtuesconsulting/hiringchecklist.html

10 Plax, T. G. (2006). Raising the question #2: How much are we worth? Estimating fee for services. *Communication Education, 55*, 242–246.

11 Beebe, Mottet, & Roach. (2004)., *Training and development*, pp. 70–76; Mager, R. F. (1975). Preparing instructional objectives (2nd ed.). Belmont, CA: Fearon.

12 Dewer, D. B. How to delegate tasks at work. Retrieved from http://www.ehow.com/how_5624372_delegate-tasks-work.html

13 Beebe, Mottet, & Roach. *Training and development*, pp. 70–76.

14 Beebe, Mottet, & Roach. *Training and development*, p. 100.

15 Heathfield, S. M. (n.d.). The five of anything icebreaker. About.com: Human Resources. Retrieved from http://humanresources.about.com/od/icebreakers/a/icebreaker_five.htm; Heathfield, S. M. (n.d.). Meet and greet meeting ice breakers. About.com: Human Resources. Retrieved from http://humanresources.about.com/od/icebreakers/a/icebreaker_dev.htm

16 Four easy steps for folding sheets. *Better Homes and Gardens*. Retrieved from http://www.bhg.com/homekeeping/cleaning-and-care/linens-and-laundry/4-easy-steps-for-folding-sheets/

17 Beebe, Mottet, & Roach. *Training and development*, pp. 132–133.

18 Smith, M. (2007, October 12). Negotiation skills—Communication training—Speak first. Retrieved from http://www.youtube.com/watch?v=yK5fi8qQC6g

19 Trochim, W. M. K. (2006). Research methods knowledge base: Introduction to evaluation. Web Center for Social Research Methods. Retrieved from http://www.socialresearchmethods.net/kb/intreval.htm

20 Hochberger, J. (2008, February 26). Presentation skills and communication training. Retrieved from http://www.youtube.com/watch?v=JUwhB3lZvGE&feature=related